I0879998

VALOR AND COURAGE

MARITIME CURRENTS: HISTORY AND ARCHAEOLOGY

VALOR AND COURAGE

The Story of the USS *Block Island* Escort Carriers in World War II

Benjamin J. Hruska

THE UNIVERSITY OF ALABAMA PRESS
Tuscaloosa

The University of Alabama Press
Tuscaloosa, Alabama 35487-0380
uapress.ua.edu

Hardcover edition published 2021.
Paperback edition published 2022.
eBook edition published 2021.

Typeface: Adobe Garamond Pro, Bembo

Cover image: The USS *Block Island*, CVE 21, with Wildcats and Avengers; courtesy of the Naval History and Heritage Command
Cover design: David Nees

Paperback ISBN: 978-0-8173-6069-6

A previous edition of this book has been cataloged by the Library of Congress.
ISBN: 978-0-8173-2099-7 (cloth)
E-ISBN: 978-0-8173-9366-3

To all the servicemen of both Fighting Block Islands

CONTENTS

FIGURES

ACKNOWLEDGMENTS

My interest in the story of the two escort carriers that constitutes this narrative commenced over fifteen years ago. The first person I would like to thank is Dr. Jay Price of Wichita State University (WSU). Dr. Price, besides guiding me in the completion of my MA in public history at WSU, also encouraged me to locate a summer internship at a local history museum, not in Kansas but on the small island of Block Island, Rhode Island. It is here at the Block Island Historical Society (BIHS) where I first learned of the two USS *Block Islands* (CVE 21 and CVE 106). The series of events that followed included a summer exhibition on the vessels, the dedication of a permanent exhibition titled *Valor & Courage* housed at the American Legion Post 36 on the island, and attendance at annual reunions of the USS Block Island Association in Branson, Missouri, and San Antonio, Texas.

The board members and staff of the BIHS were beyond supportive for this project, and I wish to thank Pam Littlefield Gasner, Geoffrey Lawrence, Dr. Gerry Abbott, Douglas Gasner, Amy Jaffe, Nancy Ziomek, and Martha Ball. An oral history grant from the Stuart Higley Foundation of New Canaan, Connecticut, allowed for the completion of oral histories with veterans in the New England area linked to this story. Keith Lewis of Block Island assisted greatly with a preview of a biography of his father, Capt. John Robinson Lewis, who, from the deck of his merchant vessel during World War II, saw the escort carrier USS *Block Island*, CVE 21, named after his island home.

In May of 2007, the BIHS partnered with the American Legion Post 36 on Block Island in hosting members of the USS Block Island Association for a day visit to the island. Held on May 31, 2007, the visit allowed over 150 veterans and family members connected to the story of both escort carriers that shared a name with our island community to visit Block Island, Rhode Island. With regard to this event, I can honestly say that not one individual person or organization on Block Island said no to helping with the event.

At the American Legion Post 36, I wish to individually thank Cdr. Daniel Millea, Bill McKernan, Charlie Weber, and Charlie LaCoste. Interstate Navigation donated the ferry transportation for all guests to and from Block Island on the high-speed ferry. I also wish to thank the Block Island Tourism Council and the efforts of Director Jessica Willi. In addition, Fraser and Betty Lang of the *Block Island Times*, an award-winning weekly newspaper, provided continuous support for this visit. I wish to acknowledge island resident John Cullen for the design and production of the reunion hats marking the visit that all attendees received and greatly appreciated. Lastly, I wish to thank longtime family friend and Block Island resident Carrie Todd for providing housing and friendship while I researched and wrote about this topic while on Block Island, Rhode Island.

At Arizona State University (ASU), this topic served as the basis for my PhD in public history. I would first like to thank Dr. Noel Stowe, a founding father in the field of public history. My time working with Dr. Stowe was short, as he passed away during my first semester in the program. However, even in his weakened state, all of us were challenged in his last Introduction to Public History class. His course included hands-on learning that never lacked for intellectual vigor and caused us to rethink our preconceived notions of the use of history in the public sphere.

Dr. Victoria Thompson at ASU repeatedly encouraged me to ask bigger questions, especially in regard to memory and commemoration of World War II. I also wish to thank the late Dr. Jannelle Warren-Findley and Dr. Kyle Longley for their continuous feedback as members on this project. The recognized scholar of local history Joseph A. Amato also gave thoughtful suggestions on considering the role of place and space for naval veterans thinking back on their past service. My friend Roger Mehle of Washington, DC, graduate of the Naval Academy class of 1963, provided invaluable assistance in not only naval terminology and life on board ship but also in granting access to the extensive library at The Army & Navy Club located just two blocks north of the White House.

Over the years numerous pairs of eyes have perused my work as it evolved. I wish to thank Assistant Professor of History Dr. William S. Kiser of Texas A&M of San Antonio for his numerous suggestions. Mitchell Koffman, historian of commercial aviation, also provided valuable support and editorial suggestions. Michael Hurst, MBE, of the Taiwan POW Camps Memorial Society, not only commented on portions of the text but also gave me a personal tour of Taipei and the Kinkaseki POW Camp connected to the narrative of CVE 106. Both Geoffrey Lawrence and Daniel Millea commented on early portions of my work written during three winters spent on Block Island, Rhode Island. Peter Voskamp of the *Block Island Times* gave invaluable advice in developing an active writing style in publishing newspaper articles about both vessels. Judy and Bill MacInnes, longtime editors of the USS Block Island Association's newsletter *Chips Off the Old Block*, also commented on multiple drafts. They also provided a wealth of support and valuable assistance in research and gathering photographs. Co-teachers who specialize in the instruction of English, David Douglas, Stephan Howard, and Danielle Longworth, provided me with valuable edits and information on the fundamentals of writing clearly and concisely. Finally, I wish to thank my mother, Paula Hruska, for being a tireless editor in the entirety of this project.

Veterans and their family members of the USS Block Island Association welcomed me in with open arms from the start, when I attended my first annual reunion in 2005 in Branson, Missouri. While numerous oral histories with both veterans and their family members are used throughout this work, I specifically wish to thank Hector Vernetti. I first met Hector at his home in Scottsdale, Arizona, while a graduate student at ASU. His early years in a trilingual household in Globe, Arizona, provided colorful tales of growing up in Depression era Arizona.

I wish to thank my family for their support throughout this journey. My parents, Richard and Paula, encouraged my love of history since early childhood. My younger sisters, Katie and Megan, not only gave loving support but also both spent summers manning the front desk at the BIHS when I directed the nonprofit. All assisted in 2007 with the USS Block Island Association's visit to Block Island. I also wish to thank my sister Katie and her husband, Andres Castellanos, for letting me reside with them in beautiful New Smyrna Beach, Florida, for three months as I completed this manuscript. With regard to my time in Florida, I would also like to thank my cousin-in-law Dustin Brown for taking me on his boat for saltwater fishing therapy on the majestic Mosquito Lagoon with NASA on the southern horizon.

Lastly, I wish to thank my editor Claire Lewis Evans of the University of Alabama Press for her persistent and patient belief in this project. I also wish to express my thanks to the anonymous peer reviewers of earlier editions of the manuscript for their thoughtful advice in both suggested research questions and archival resources. And, finally, my copy editor, Lisa Williams, did an amazing job in bringing clarity to the final draft. Any mistakes in the manuscript are mine and mine alone.

ABBREVIATIONS

AVG aircraft tender, general purpose

BB battleship

CV aircraft carrier

CVE aircraft carrier, escort

CVL aircraft carrier, small

DD destroyer

DE destroyer escort

TBF Avenger torpedo bomber (manufactured by Grumman)

TBM Avenger torpedo bomber (manufactured by Eastern Aircraft)

USN United States Navy

USNR United States Navy Reserve

VALOR AND COURAGE

INTRODUCTION

On the early evening of May 29, 1944, Electrician Second Class Joe Booi was standing next to a noisy coffeemaker in the interior communications (IC) room on his aircraft carrier. Booi and other sailors gathered around the brewing of the black caffeinated beverage to fuel them all for another long night shift on board their escort carrier hunting U-boats in the Atlantic. Their vessel, USS *Block Island*, CVE 21, had resupplied six days earlier in the African port of Casablanca on the second half of a hunter-killer mission. On the flight deck above, members of the Navy Squadron VC-55 briskly finalized fighter aircraft for their upcoming missions.[2] At 2013, as the IC room cohort of sailors talked near the percolating coffee, a huge explosion rocked the 13,000-ton carrier.

One of Booi's fellow sailors inquisitively asked, "What we do, hit land?" Booi, a veteran sailor and survivor of the attack on Pearl Harbor, knew better. He quickly yelled, "We must be a thousand miles from the nearest land!"[3] General quarters (GQ) immediately followed Booi's statement. Two German torpedoes had struck the port side of the CVE nearly simultaneously. Booi later recalled the minutes that followed in the IC room as a blur. Those sealed in the IC compartment were blind to the events unfolding, but they still manned the vessel's dial-up telephone system on board. Booi would never forget one conversation on the phone that came from a fellow sailor on the hangar deck above the IC room. The sailor reported that a six-inch-wide vertical crack fractured the hangar deck wall, and, more disturbingly, the sailor could clearly see the ocean through this suddenly produced fracture. Now dead in the water, the back of the carrier was broken.

Ten tense minutes later, Booi was communicating with Electrician Second Class Henry Meyers, who was working on an electrical problem on the hangar deck when another torpedo struck the carrier. The subsequent explosion ripped a thirty-foot-square hole on the hangar deck, which killed Meyers and two other sailors. The explosion knocked out nearly all the vessel's remaining interior lighting and plunged those in the IC room into darkness. The emergency diesel generator in compartment A-406-AE, just one deck below Booi, continued to wail, but the blackness persisted.[4] Booi and the others remained at their general quarters station. While Booi knew at least a portion of the dialup telephone system still worked, no one was communicating on board via this system. The quiet proved almost as unsettling as the explosions, for all Booi and his fellow sailors could hear was the humming from the generator below. With a battle lantern, Booi and others peered around their compartment. Booi's mind registered a silent thought: "If we see water, we're going to get out of here!"[5] Then a voice came over the phone that Booi was still holding.

Booi heard, "Is there anyone on here?" Booi immediately replied, "Yeh, I'm here." The unknown voice asked, "Where are you at?" Booi replied, "In the IC room." The voice yelled, "We have been abandoning ship for twenty minutes!"[6] Booi immediately dropped the phone; however, with all his flurry of movement in the IC room over the previous chaotic minutes, his legs were entangled with the cord. Once freed, he was the last to exit the blackened IC room. Booi then remembered the humming one deck below. Were there more sailors who did not get the word?

Upon opening the hatch, Booi was enshrouded in the racket exiting from the generator room. He peered down into the blackness. A battle lantern shone up at him, and Booi motioned for the three sailors he could see to come up. With no response to his motioning and unable to yell above the noise, Booi climbed down the ladder. Once in the deafening environment, Booi quickly pulled one of the sailors to a corner with some sound protection from the diesel generator futilely attempting to breathe life into the electrical system of the broken ship. Once in the corner, the sailor removed his ear protection, and Booi yelled into his ear, "We are abandoning ship!!!" Booi later recalled, "They beat me up the stairs!"[7]

Exiting on the hangar deck, Booi witnessed the structural damage as a result of the torpedo strikes. Luckily, no sign of fire showed itself while smoke hung in the air. Most threatening, Booi saw the ever-growing vertical crack on the wall of the hangar as the ship's stern settled. As Booi could see the ocean and the setting sun through the fracture, he knew that salt water was rapidly seizing any remaining buoyancy on board. CVE 21, which would be the only American aircraft carrier lost in the Atlantic theater of World War II, was going down. The nearly one thousand sailors who abandoned the escort carrier were to experience an ordeal that one survivor described as being "baptized by salt water."[8]

Valor and Courage is a historical account of the wartime experiences of the crew members of two escort carriers named USS *Block Island*, CVE 21 and CVE 106. Their story encompasses a vast array of naval experiences. For CVE 21, in the Atlantic this included transporting Lend-Lease supplies, destroying U-boats in hunter-killer missions, and sustaining three torpedo hits that took the proud carrier to the ocean's bottom. For the first time in its history, the US Navy (USN) retained the surviving crew of a lost warship as a fighting entity, and on a second carrier of the same name, USS *Block Island*, CVE 106, they battled in the Pacific, braved typhoons, participated in the largest naval siege in military history, and, at the close of the war, evacuated hundreds of malnourished POWs interned by the Japanese. This story is unique in that looking at a single crew gives a window not only into two different classes of escort carriers but also into the differences (and similarities) between the naval wars of the Atlantic and the Pacific as viewed by the same crew. The tale of the *Block Islands* solicits a microhistory. With just one crew, a window is opened to examining sailors' views of two different enemies, oceans, theaters of operation, and classes of escort carrier.

Beyond the story of these two specific CVEs, this work proposes that escort carriers represented the best of American mass production. Using the experiences of CVE 21 and 106, I argue that escort carriers were far more than just tough little vessels in comparison with their better-armored, larger, and faster sister carriers (CVs and CVLs). Escort carriers derived directly from the American gift of industrial adaptation that is also clearly seen in a host of World War II weaponry. With regard to this study, the manning, training, and employment of an entirely new classification of aircraft carrier demonstrates the feat of entrepreneurial logistics on the part of the USN. Merging men and machines would not have been possible without US Navy officers who, in the interwar period, foresaw naval aviation as a central component to warfare in the middle portion of the twentieth century. The skippers who led these two CVEs during World War II represent the intersection of mass-produced aircraft carriers and USN personnel. A study of both naval aviator officers, Logan C. Ramsey and Francis "Massie" Hughes, demonstrates that interwar training of flight officers provided rich dividends once war returned. As one naval scholar wrote, "A military revolution involves much more than technology. It is a particular application of technology, through new or altered forms of organization, that radically changes the overall military situation."[9] An examination of this application of American mass production into quickly produced escort carriers provides a greater window into the rapid industrial and logistical transformation of the nation during World War II. Logan Ramsey and Massie Hughes, who captained these two vessels for the entire war excluding the final month, present an examination of contrasts and similarities.

The naval scholar W. J. R. Gardner, in writing about the Battle of the Atlantic, used the concept of "soft fields," these being naval intelligence, training, organization, and operational research.[10] Incorporating the backgrounds and leadership decisions of Ramsey and Hughes holds the potential for functioning as case studies in the application of these "soft fields" with a singular crew. Both these men captained CVE 21 in the Atlantic and grappled with the utilization of naval intelligence including, but not limited to, scientific innovations such as high-frequency direction finding (HF-DF) and magnetic anomaly detection (MAD). Ramsey took command of USS *Block Island*, CVE 21, in March 1943 at the Todd Pacific Shipyards in Tacoma, Washington. Twenty-one months later, in the same shipyards, Hughes took command of USS *Block Island*, CVE 106, in December 1944.[11] As for organizational and operational concerns, in the ever-expanding Navy incorporating new vessels, tactics, and technologies, both Ramsey and Hughes faced command decisions in their stated missions. By examining these "soft fields," along with tactical and strategical choices of Ramsey and Hughes, this work attempts to shed light onto the commanding officers who were charged with delivering fully functioning escort carriers to the USN. In short, officers such as Ramsey and Hughes made escort carriers deliverable.

In the vein of "soft fields," this monograph incorporates an unpublished memoir discovered in a nursing home library in Connecticut. In a 300-page single-spaced manuscript, Russell Lewis traces his World War II career as a civilian scientist working within a consortium between Columbia University and the Underwater Sound Laboratory of New London, Connecticut. If a single word summed up Lewis's career, it would be "globetrotter." Lewis, in advancing marine audio detection, traveled the world during World War II, including such locations as Nova Scotia and the South Pacific islands off Antarctica, and on patrols in the central Atlantic aboard USN vessels. After assignments floating in blimps, running submerged in submarines, and riding out Atlantic storms, Lewis always returned to the Underwater Sound Laboratory in New London to debrief on what he learned and gather additional intelligence on the ongoing evolution of marine audio detection equipment that sought to find the Axis enemy.

Lewis's narrative provides nothing short of unparalleled access to technological contributions of Underwater Sound to the Allied war effort. With Lewis in the unique position of a civilian wearing an officer's uniform with no sign of rank, he had near-total access to the two escort carriers (USS *Block Island*, CVE 21, and USS *Card*, CVE 11) on which he was assigned in the Atlantic theater. Thus, his narrative grants a cross-sectional view of the CVEs that transcends differing divisions of sailors, such as aviation and engineering, and also crossing back and forth over the divide between the enlisted sailors and officers. Lewis, beyond documenting the pioneering use of sonobuoys in the detection of submerged U-boats, also records personal encounters with pilots in the ready room, the topics of conversation of enlisted sailors in the engine compartments, and frank conversations with both Ramsey and Hughes within their quarters. Lewis's freedom of movement on board, plus his natural curiosity, grants a compelling account of the sailors' daily lives, personal information on surviving the sinking of CVE 21, and technological details on the advancement of underwater sound detection systems. This previously unknown typed memoir, with a central focus on his two missions assigned to USS *Block Island*, CVE 21, is woven throughout the work that follows.

The third contribution of this work is the utilization of diverse resources produced, gathered, and preserved by the very participants themselves, the veterans of CVE 21 and CVE 106. While such resources are utilized in many naval histories, this work argues that these escort carrier veterans functioned as their own documentarians. Aware that the national understanding of "aircraft carrier" focused on the exploits of the large fleet carriers, CVE reunion groups organized and coalesced around the concept of telling and preserving their own stories. Such groups framed for themselves their own individual and collective memories. For the modern scholar, the actions of these volunteers spanning decades after the war yields a rich and vibrant collage of World War II experiences. With oral histories, individual memoirs, and gathering of material culture, such grassroots veteran groups began the steps of perpetuating their stories that faced erasure with the passing of individual veterans.

In seizing the mantle of memory with their own hands, these sailors and their loved ones developed their own means of remembrance. The historical record created by these grassroots organizations bestows on the modern-day historian many avenues for moving forward with future scholarship. Thus, this work argues that the output of World War II studies based on a military unit or naval vessel can continue in the twenty-first century thanks to the actions of self-preservation taken by such groups. Even as scholars confront the deaths of the vast majority of World War II participants, the production of World War II–based studies based on first-person accounts need not discontinue. More specifically for the tale of USS *Block Islands*, the veterans' collective efforts in the preservation produced a rich enough collection for the writing of the work that follows. Over the decades, the USS Block Island Association published a newsletter, hosted annual reunions, and in the 1990s launched a website, all of which contributed to carving out space for remembering both CVEs.

A history of both USS *Block Islands* produces a snapshot that includes war experiences in the Atlantic and Pacific, braving North Atlantic squalls and South China Sea typhoons, and encountering death on both. However, one singular powerful experience forged an exceptional bond. A central tenet of this work is the brotherhood evident among sailors who survived the sinking of CVE 21. These sailors huddled together on the Atlantic's surface, swam through fuel oil, and suffered underwater explosions erupting around them. For these sailors, this exceptional experience created a connection that transcended race, religion, and rank, and forged a survivors' bond. The resources to adequately produce a history on the human level of this sinking are not found only in such repositories as the National Archives or the Naval History and Heritage Command at the Naval Yard in Washington, DC. This statement means no disrespect to these stellar archives, as both repositories provided invaluable resources for this work. But the fact remains that the missions of these depositories is not to record a detailed history of every single vessel of the USN. For this task, the historian needs the assistance of the sailors who served aboard the vessels. The historical resources culminating from naval reunion groups functioning as their own historians invite scholars seeking to incorporate history as told through the eyes of the participants.

Therefore, the text that follows seeks to illustrate the poignant stories found in the smallest of footnotes within World War II. This specific footnote from the experience of the USN in World War II centers on the only American aircraft carrier lost in the Atlantic. One sailor started his interview noting the terror he felt, and at times still feels, from the experience of the sinking of CVE 21. Seated on his couch in Natick, Massachusetts, he said something that starkly contradicted notions of high adventure on the seas battling the Nazi U-boats. Looking down at his clenched, aged hands, he admitted, "Sometimes at nighttime I still remember what happened. You know, being torpedoed is no picnic."[12]

I
Carrier Interpretation

In the not-too-distant future, school field trips to military-themed museums will be for the great-great-grandchildren of World War II servicemen. Four generations removed from the largest conflict in human history, what will be their perspective of the American experience in World War II after visiting these museums? This conflict is so central to American identity in the twentieth century that it echoes in public history sites devoted to preserving history on the local, regional, and national levels. Museums oftentimes sprout from the labors of historic preservationists. In seeking to save buildings in danger of destruction, such as Victorian era mansions, train depots, and former military installations, preservationists adopt new roles for these old structures to serve as emissaries to the past. Via adaptive reuse, aspects of the built environment are saved for future generations and now function in chaperoning museum visitors into an array of avenues into America's past. Buildings originally constructed for commerce or lodging morph into sites for sharing the histories of cities, families, and ever-accumulating forms of outdated technology. While these institutions play a critical role in shaping public memory, their power increases in scope once the living memory of the period interpreted ceases to exist. As the living memory of World War II is currently in its twilight phase, this provokes critical questions. When the day comes when no one alive on earth experienced 1945, what will the following generations think is worthy of remembering of the largest war in human history? As the twentieth century recedes further into the past, what aspects of World War II will be preserved in public memory and passed on to the generations that follow? Textbooks in history classrooms provide clues. In recalling the American Revolution, which grand battles, bold generals, and amazingly individual feats of bravery are memorized in schools? As time advances, the omission surrounding historical events increasingly intensifies.

Throughout military history and public memory, the battles, weapons, leaders, and campaigns in the margins are the first to be pitched aside, in part because of the never-ending problem of producing a single volume of an American history textbook. With regard to the aircraft carrier, the dominant naval weapon for the past seventy-five years, two deciding factors are actively shaping the remembrance of the American aircraft carrier battling from 1941 to 1945.

Decommissioned-carrier-based museums and Hollywood movies have crafted, and are still shaping, the public memory of the role of the aircraft carrier. These two factors are forging how and what the American public remembers when considering naval warfare in World War II. This tremendous power includes making the ever-important selections of which aspects are embraced and celebrated and, in doing so, which are marginalized and forgotten.

Of the five museums in the United States based on aircraft carriers, all five come from the World War II era. These five vessels function as floating ambassadors of the past. All are of the fast fleet designation class known as CV. Of these museums today, the organization accomplishing the most diverse tasks in the preservation and display of history is the *Intrepid* Air & Space Museum.[1] Docked at Pier 86 on the Hudson on the west side of Manhattan, the decommissioned USS *Intrepid*, CV 11, interprets not only World War II but also the other operations the vessel participated in as an active war vessel from 1943 to 1974. With an ecumenical approach to the preservation of air and spacecraft, the flight and hangar decks hold aircraft well outside the scope of the USN, such as the US Air Force's SR-71 Blackbird, a North Vietnamese MiG-17, and the Space Shuttle Orbiter *Enterprise*. Over a million visitors a year walk on board, experience the exhibitions, and participate in the public programs.[2] While exhibitions rotate and organizational missions change over time, *Intrepid* as an artifact retains a unique power in overcoming decades of time. Walking onto this artifact, visitors transcend both space and time, witnessing firsthand what sailors experienced on a daily basis. Fully restored sleeping quarters and galleys all point to the individual histories of the thousands of sailors who served on these carriers.

Naval history by definition is a story of movement, and the high seas lack the permanence of land. Terrestrial moments of importance, after the fact, can ground historical memory. The very soil can function as the foundation of a statue or public marker. While many naval engagements in World War II took place near small atolls or islands, these naval battles do not naturally bequeath a terrestrial location for the placement of a permanent marker that land engagements inherently inherit. Whether nation, navy, or individual sailor, those wishing to memorialize naval engagements require more innovative thinking in comparison with their terrestrial counterparts. Furthermore, there exists a fundamental difficulty in understanding the history of any particular vessel. One writer addressing the very nature of ships wrote that vessels are "quite independent of place."[3] This short phrase underlies the challenge in understanding a large man-made object that by its very nature is kinetic and never stationary except for periodic stops in faraway ports. The curators of these World War II era carriers transformed into museums confront a range of interpretive challenges, nearly all of which center on what is embraced for public exhibition and what is marginalized.

For the five CVs lucky enough to achieve a life beyond combat, a price is paid. Mobility is sacrificed for a stationary existence. While they are not under power and lack a full complement of sailors, similarities between past and present remain. Mirroring the days of a commissioned war vessel, these refashioned hulls still complete a range of functions simultaneously. The cooking of meals, housing of thousands of sailors, and capturing of aircraft on the flight deck are replaced with the display of exhibitions, presentation of public programs, and education of school groups. One could argue that their greatest role, however, has yet to be fulfilled. When no living memory of World War II exists, these CV hulls will provide the last tangible links to carrier aviation from the war. When the tides of time glide forward to the point of erasing all living memory of the naval feats of World War II, these ships will then truly transform into time capsules. These CVs have outlasted their designers and shipbuilders. These steel hulls represent all that is left of the carrier force of the USN during World War II, and these buoyant museums will continue on as historic artifacts floating into the future to function as testaments to crews, campaigns, and conflicts.

❋

The films of Hollywood starting in World War II commenced in manufacturing a national understanding of aircraft carriers. Movie scriptwriters, in addressing carrier aviation during the war, gravitated toward the fleet aircraft carriers (CV) and marginalized the existence of other classifications of carriers. The year 1944 alone witnessed the release of *Thirty Seconds over Tokyo*, *Wing and a Prayer*, and *The Fighting Lady*, all of which utilize the decks of CVs in setting the stage for conflict. This national understanding of carriers functioned during the war in highlighting the CVs that were designed, constructed, and utilized for the single purpose of waging war. This attention stemmed in part from the fact that the fleet aircraft carriers were visually impressive in both newspapers and motion pictures. Staccato images invited press coverage, and later commemoration after the war, for these vessels of a thousand feet in length that could cruise at thirty knots into a headwind and launch dozens of aircraft. With this as the measuring stick for directors, the escort carriers of roughly half the length cruising at just eighteen knots lacked the luster to play the protagonist.

This leading role of CVs in movies devoted to naval aviation continued after the war, as witnessed in the last seventy years of war films. Gary Cooper in 1949 starred in *Task Force*, a film showing the power of CVs not only during the recently concluded war but also in the beginnings of the Cold War. Fleet carriers and the Korean conflict were the stage for the film *The Bridges of Toko-Ri* in 1954. That decade of American self-examination, the 1970s, produced two major motion pictures on the CVs in World War II: *Tora! Tora! Tora!* in 1970 and *Midway* in 1976. In 1991 the actors Danny Glover and Willem Dafoe in *Flight of the Intruder* brought the Vietnam conflict and naval aviation to life. The author Tom Clancy first gained notoriety with his book *The Hunt for Red October*, released as a film in 1990. Whereas the advanced submarines on both sides of the Cold War dominate the storyline, the USN fleet carrier USS *Enterprise*, CVN 65, makes a number of appearances and supports the theory that carriers equate to surface dominance. Tom Cruise in *Top Gun* (1986) presents the modern-day impact of carrier aviation, where *The Final Countdown* (1980) includes the science fiction/alternative history plotline of the nuclear-powered carrier USS *Nimitz*, CVN 68, surviving a massive typhoon in the Pacific. Upon exiting the storm and approaching Pearl Harbor, she has been transported back in time to the hours before the Japanese attack on December 7, 1941. The movie-producing machine known as Marvel has also gotten into the action with both the Avenger and X-Men series of movies. In fighting for good, the fictional defense agency SHIELD utilizes the fictional Hellicarrier in carrying out and sustaining operations. Youth around the world today see Captain America and Iron Man on the signature capital ship of SHIELD, a flying aircraft carrier that can stay aloft indefinitely. This is the most recent take of Hollywood on modern fleet carriers of the USN. With much of public understanding and memory shaped by films, American audiences' mental recollections of an "aircraft carrier" have no room for the escort carriers and their auxiliary roles of World War II

Beyond the visually impressive component of the fleet aircraft carriers, the epic engagements these vessels fought in proved fertile ground for movies, cartoons, and books. With a single battle or ship, one could easily manufacture a thematic script of the struggle between the United States and the Empire of Japan. The fleet aircraft carriers presented the mythmakers of Hollywood with a prefabricated battle stage to demonstrate America's triumph over the Japanese naval force that humiliated the nation at Pearl Harbor. This same stage would come to dominate almost all celebrations of the achievements of carriers and naval aviation. However, for every specific act of bravery highlighted in these products of popular culture, countless omissions took place involving vessels, types of aircraft, and major command decisions. While many aspects of the USN in World War II experienced marginalization to some degree, such as vessel types, squadrons, and average sailors, one would be hard-pressed to find a classification more excluded from the national understanding than the CVEs. The term "aircraft carrier" is ubiquitous today. It is a weapons system seventy-five years after World War II that remains a dominant force of the seas. However, in a war that consumed at least sixty million lives, offensive weapons were ubiquitous. As the war receded into the past, just a handful of weapons systems became synonymous with the conflict. From the perspective of the twenty-first century, the vast majority of weapons from all participating nations are completely unknown except to a handful of military historians and readers of detailed military monographs. The aircraft carrier, however, is an anomaly, because it not only is understood today as critical to winning the Pacific theater for the USN in World War II but remains a dominant measuring stick in how nation-states gauge and project their power.

While escort carriers aided throughout the war in conducting antisubmarine patrols, training pilots, and providing ground support in the Pacific island-hopping campaigns, these smaller hulls with around twenty aircraft were regarded as a B actor at best by producers of films, books, and war documentaries. In the films commemorating World War II aircraft carriers and naval aviation, Hollywood placed Errol Flynn and Charlton Heston fighting and flying from the platform of the CV, not a Bogue classification of escort carrier converted from a prefabricated merchant hull originally designed to transport cargo such as crude oil, grain, or bananas.

2
"Combustible, Vulnerable, and Expendable"

Seaman First Class Walter Cyr hailed from Walpole, Massachusetts, just a short train ride from Boston Harbor, where, in early 1942, vessels pulling out into the Atlantic entered the U-boat-controlled waters. After completing boot camp, Cyr received orders to report to the Todd Shipyards Corporation in Tacoma, Washington. During the war this shipyard resembled a beehive of activity in building, converting, and outfitting thousands of vessels that included Liberty ships tankers, destroyers, and landing craft. However, arguably Todd's largest contribution was the production of fifty-six escort carriers.[1] While these ships did not exist before the war, the concept had already germinated. Within the USN during the interwar period, a small cohort of forward-thinking officers lobbied for the construction of small aircraft carriers. In 1927 Lt. Cmdr. Bruce G. Leighton wrote a report for the Navy Department titled "Light Aircraft Carriers, A Study of Their Possible Uses in So-Called 'Cruiser Operations'." Leighton's report theorized a host of possible duties for these proposed vessels in a range of operations, including attacks on enemy shore emplacements and antisubmarine activities.[2] While this report proved useful later, Leighton's concept rested under the proverbial coffeepot in the Navy Department files before his report resurfaced over a decade later.

In 1939 Capt. John S. McCain expanded on Leighton's work, proposing the construction of eight "pocket-size" carriers rated at cruiser speed. The next year the USN's Bureau of Construction and Repair initiated the drawing of plans for these ships to be constructed from converted passenger vessels. Soon this proposal caught the eye of the best sponsor one could hope for—former assistant secretary of the Navy and current president, Franklin D. Roosevelt.[3] Like his distant cousin Theodore Roosevelt before him, FDR had served as the assistant secretary of the Navy and retained throughout his life a love affair with the Navy. In addition, like Theodore, as president he also enjoyed theorizing on naval strategy. The renowned naval historian Samuel Eliot Morison wrote that in private conversations with FDR, he used the term "my Navy."[4]

In 1940 Roosevelt first proposed that autogyros operate from vessels converted from merchant vessels to combat German U-boats. Autogyros, first flown in 1923, were aircraft with large helicopter-like blades above the fuselage that facilitated takeoffs and landings at much slower speeds than traditional biplanes. In January 1941, in just three months' time, the Navy converted the merchant ship SS *Mormacmail* into USS *Long Island*, AVG 1. This first experiment, to modern eyes, would appear like a small carrier deck missing an island that served as the vessels' bridge. While these vessels are known today as escort carriers (CVEs), this represents the final wartime designation. As first-of-a-kind warship, *Long Island* held a crew of nine hundred and a complement of sixteen planes, and boasted a flight deck of over 350 feet. Just two of these Long Island classifications were constructed, the beforementioned *Long Island* and *Archer*, which served in the Royal Navy.[5]

The Avenger classification of escort carrier constructed in the United States built upon the *Long Island* design The four vessels of the Avenger class were also diesel powered and converted from a C3 cargo hull. The major difference in comparison to USS *Long Island* was being fitted with a small island. These two experiments in conversion (Long Island and Avenger classes) led to the first large-scale construction of the escort carriers, the Bogue classification. Forty-five of these carriers were built, of which thirty-four would serve in the Royal Navy. Of the eleven Bogue class of the CVEs to serve in the USN, all were constructed at the Todd Pacific Shipyards in Tacoma, Washington. The Bogue class addressed a number of the design problems found in the Long Island class. First the Bogue conversion would start with the upgraded C3-S-A1 merchant hull. Next the problematic diesel engines of the Long Island class were discarded and replaced with steam turbines, which not only increased speed but greatly increased reliability. The Bogue class also witnessed an expanded flight deck with dimensions of 442 feet in length and 111 feet in width. Two elevators, as opposed to the single one on the Long Island class, were on the deck, along with nine arresting wires and three crash barriers. Lastly, the Bogue class held a small island of just six feet across on the starboard side, which included a pilothouse, cabins for the captain and navigator, and a chart room. On top of the island, a mast provided housing for radar and other apparatus.[6]

When Seaman First Class Walter Cyr arrived in the Todd Pacific Shipyards, he witnessed ship workers swarming over at least ten Bogue CVEs. A strong movement toward mass production of aircraft carriers was the USN's purchase of nine of these C3-S-A1 merchant hulls on May 1, 1942. One of these was to be Cyr's vessel, USS *Block Island*, CVE 21, which was launched on June 6, 1942, and commissioned on March 8, 1943. After the eleven of Bogue classification were constructed at Todd Pacific Shipyards, other classifications of CVEs were constructed in shipyard companies across the United States. Previous to the Bogue class was the construction of two vessels of the Long Island class and four of the Avenger and Sangamon class (the latter built on tanker, rather than merchant, hulls.) Following the

Bogue class came fifty vessels of the Casablanca class, and finally the Commencement Bay class, of which seventeen were constructed and commissioned.[7] While individual states served as inspiration in naming battleships in the USN fleet, the CVEs were named for bodies of water or battlefields. In Cyr's ship's case, Block Island Sound, located off the southern coast of Rhode Island, provided CVE 21 with its more familiar name, USS *Block Island*.[8]

For the sailors such as Cyr, with orders to report to an escort carrier, the term "aircraft carrier" produced visions of the "big sisters." The term, with the assistance of Hollywood, conjured up mental notions of the beautiful lines of the large fleet carriers with aircraft by the dozens on the deck. However, the startled reaction of sailors seeing their first escort carrier included comments such as "this little tub," "unattractive old waddler," and a "stopgap ship."[9] Veteran sailors who had sailed on the "big sisters" before the war expressed the harshest criticism. The conversion of a merchant hull, lacking the armor of a warship built from the keel up, "seemed ludicrously small and dangerous."[10] Lacking the safe storage space for all torpedoes below decks, the Bogue class improvised with racking them up on the inside of the hangar deck. Furthermore, the short deck combined with slow cruising speed required that a catapult at times was needed just to get her aircraft aloft.[11] A British sailor displayed his lack of satisfaction: "We were not very proud of her at first."[12] The lines of the ship shocked him most, as he'd expected an impressive warship to aggressively take on the Axis enemy. He concluded his initial reaction thus: "For, indeed, she hardly looked like a ship at all."[13] Another British sailor wrote, "However, when I first saw the HMS *Nabob*, I was shocked and disappointed. None of the sleek lines of the fleet carriers I'd seen in photographs were present. As a matter of fact, she hardly looked like a warship at all, but rather like a newly built Woolworth freighter or maybe just a rectangular box with a flat lid."[14]

Cyr's orders called for him to wait for the completion of *Block Island*. The conversion process called for construction not only of a hangar deck to store the fighter aircraft but also facilities for daily life of over nine hundred sailors. With little to do while watching the laborers transform the cargo hull into an aircraft carrier, Cyr inquired about helping out. After some persuasion the workers agreed, but if Cyr journeyed below decks, he was required to wear a harness. These workers did not fear a fall, but rather feared Cyr becoming disoriented in the unlit, compartmentalized warship, resulting in getting lost.[15] As the future crew gathered in the final months of 1942, the men and women of Todd Shipyards, assisted by sailors such as Cyr, labored in the transformation of a merchant hull into a ship of war.

The engineers of the Bogue class of escort carriers wrestled with the naval concept of adaptive reuse. While this ancient naval technique goes back to the Phoenicians' dominating the Mediterranean, these practitioners of morphing hulls nearly three thousand years ago could never have imagined the colossal scale of this

Figure 1. CVE 21, morphed from a tanker hull, takes to the open waters for the first time as a reconfigured carrier on a sea trial outside Bremerton, Washington. On the bow men in civilian dress wave to the camera. Courtesy of the USS Block Island Association.

enterprise. The Bogue engineers meticulously devised detailed drawings in transforming a hull designed for commercial use into a floating airfield fashioned for warfare. Gone were the commercial spaces built for hauling items in the market economy. Engineers ameliorated this hull with flight and hangar decks, bunk space for nearly a thousand crew members, and other specifications for waging war at sea.

With short production times, these unglamorous unarmed hulls originally designed to move freight completed a range of missions outside the limelight of famous battles celebrated and embraced after the war. Through logistical support, aid of amphibious landings, and pursuit of enemy submarines, the CVEs earned the nickname "jeep carrier," a reference to the hardy jeep utilized by US land forces in a host of climates.[16] The scant wartime attention framed the smaller escort carriers as victims, most notably in the Battle of Samar on October 25, 1944, in the Philippine Sea, with the loss of two CVEs, one from naval gunfire and the other to kamikaze attack. Thus, the CVE was not a central character to be spotlighted in achieving victory by the producers of forms of national remembrance. After a number of the first series of CVEs exploded in an amazingly violent nature as the result of just one torpedo strike, other names emerged highlighting their vulnerability. CVE no longer stood for "escort carrier," but rather "Combustible, Vulnerable, and Expendable."[17] Beyond the charge of drabness, these vessels retained hazardous reputations.

The tragedy that brought into question escort carrier construction practices took place 125 miles west of Gibraltar on November 15, 1942, when HMS *Avenger*, D 14, took a single torpedo hit from a German U-boat. Converted by Sun Shipbuilding of Chester, Pennsylvania, this American Type C3 merchant hull transformed into an Avenger class escort carrier was given to the British Royal Navy under Lend-Lease. The unarmored hull of the escort carrier offered no resistance, and the detonating explosion set off the entire bomb-holding facility. The shattering explosion broke *Avenger* in half. She sank in minutes. More than five hundred crew members were lost, and only a dozen survived. The news of the horrific loss of an aircraft carrier, as the result of a single torpedo, caused American designers to work overtime to alleviate this vulnerability.[18] The story of this explosion not only affected the CVE designers and engineers but also rippled down the ranks to the men assigned to the escort carriers.

The year 1943 brought more unsettling news for the crews of the CVE, this time from one of the first models of the Kaiser Casablanca class. USS *Liscome Bay*, CVE 56, launched a month after *Block Island*, was struck by a Japanese torpedo just before dawn on November 24. A historian of the vessel wrote, "A split second later, a blast of almost unimaginable size followed as fragments from the torpedo ripped through the bulkheads shielding the carrier's bomb magazine and detonated its contents. A pillar of orange flame, speckled and dotted with burning pieces of white-hot metal, shot into the air a thousand feet."[19] The explosion was visible to those on the battleship USS *Pennsylvania*, BB 38, sixteen miles away. The battleship USS *New Mexico*, BB 40, cruised just under a mile away at the time of the impact. In his action report, Captain Zacharias wrote, "Oil particles and burning and extinguished fragments, deck splinters up to three feet in length, metal fragments in great numbers—mostly small but as large as one pound in weight—molten drops of metal, bits of clothing, dungarees, overshoes . . . and several pieces of human flesh" carpeted downward on the deck of his battleship.[20]

3
Triptych

Over the course of the war, the USN commissioned eighty-six escort carriers into service. Thirty-eight CVEs were constructed in American shipyards for the Royal Navy.[1] The escort carriers illustrate a triptych of American forces, which required merging of the USN thrust into the largest naval war in history. These three forces, that of freshly minted sailors, newly constructed aircraft carriers, and young commanding officers, are clearly encapsulated in the quick production and deployment of escort carriers. While this work argues that escort carriers epitomize mass production and demonstrate the best of American industrial mobilization, the notion that adaptation in the USN during World War II starts and ends with CVEs could not be further from the truth. This work seeks to build upon recent scholarship that the interwar USN, rather than being a hindrance to change, embraced permutations in thinking. Utilizing the career trajectories of both Logan Ramsey and Massie Hughes, I attempt to demonstrate that the interwar period served as a time of incubation for naval leadership that would be required in a vastly expanding USN during World War II.

The escort carrier, along with the hot dog, democracy, and the cowboy, is a concept that started someplace else and American innovation propelled to something new. The original inventors in Frankfurt (hot dog), Athens (democracy), and Spain (cowboys, or *vaqueros*) could never have fathomed how their early concepts would morph into strange and powerful forms in an unborn nation-state on the other side of the world. Likewise, not only the first escort carrier derived from overseas thinking but also the time-tested concept of naval adaptive reuse. The Royal Navy's HMS *Audacity*, launched in June 1941, had no hangar deck; so all aircraft were maintained and stored on the flight deck. Her hull was first launched in March 1939 in Germany as the cargo liner *Hannover*. Captured in the West Indies in the spring of 1940, after the crew unsuccessfully attempted to scuttle her, the 440-foot-long vessel transformed into the cargo ship *Sinbad*, registered in Jamaica. Six months later she morphed into *Empire Audacity* as an ocean boarding vessel meant to enforce naval blockades. Then the British admiralty proposed transforming this hull into the first escort carrier.[2]

It must be noted how few carriers existed before World War II. A worldwide survey in 1930 produced only thirteen carriers in commission, and in 1939, when the war started, just twenty carriers were in commission around the world. Of the year 1939, one historian wrote, "That year the world's navies stood on the precipice of a technological revolution."[3] In the next few years, naval aviation radically transformed. In 1939, some 82 percent of craft in the Royal Navy were biplanes, and these craft also represented more than half of all planes in the USN. In the six years of World War II, all aircraft carriers produced (by the USN, the British navy, and the Empire of Japan) represent a true miracle of production. As one author wrote, "The three carrier navies had acquired 204 flattops, which seven decades later still represents 80 percent of all conventional carriers ever produced."[4] At the close of the war, the USN had ninety-nine commissioned aircraft carriers, seventy-three of which were CVEs.

Moreover, this work proposes that naval officers who devoted their careers to naval aviation in the interwar period were critical in transforming newly commissioned escort carriers and green sailors into fighting entities. Examining the story of the USS *Block Islands* furnishes a window into two such officers, Logan Ramsey and Francis Massie Hughes. Both were born in the final years of the nineteenth century; both graduated from the US Naval Academy in Annapolis, Maryland (known hereafter as the Academy), and both became naval aviators. Their careers intertwined throughout their service, with Hughes serving under Ramsey at both Pearl Harbor and Midway. Americans in movie theaters in 1942 would see both Ramsey and Hughes appear side by side in John Ford's documentary film *The Battle of Midway*.

Differences in command styles between Ramsey and Hughes can be traced back to their extracurricular focuses at the Academy. While Ramsey worked on the yearbook, Hughes played football. Ramsey possessed a devout interest in the theorization of naval aviation. During the interwar period, he published nearly a dozen articles in *Proceedings*, the monthly magazine of the United States Naval Institute that started in 1874. Thus, Ramsey proved a perfect selection for the first commanding officer of CVE 21. In providing the scaffolding for the institutional framework, Ramsey transformed a newly morphed tanker hull turned carrier and an almost completely green crew into a fighting entity. Via methodical training, Ramsey crafted an aircraft carrier from the new assemblage of ship and sailors. In contrast, Hughes, one naval aviator recalled, reminded him of a football coach as he yelled obscenity-infused encouragement in his southern drawl.[5] This stemmed not only from Hughes's time playing as quarterback at the Academy but also from time as the coach of the football team on board the battleship USS *Pennsylvania*, BB 38. His aggressive and driven tactics in both training and war caused some to question his methods, and some sailors thought his actions reckless and blamed him for the loss of shipmates.[6] Nevertheless, Hughes's drive resulted in a first in the history of the USN when his crew lost their vessel but were retained as a fighting unit to serve on a second vessel of the same name.

Naval aviators in the interwar period in the USN, such as Logan Carlisle Ramsey and Francis Massie Hughes, grappled with the rapidly transforming field of naval aviation. Their years of toil on board ship, combined with their Academy education, allowed these men to play a key role in the challenge facing the US Navy. Turning theory into practice, molding together reserve officers and green sailors with a new classification of aircraft carrier, juggling the rapidly expanding methodologies in both weapons and detection, are evident in examining the naval careers of both Ramsey and Hughes and the story of the crew of the "Fighting *Block Island*."

❋

"The story of the escort carriers is like a story with a surprise ending," wrote Adm. Chester W. Nimitz at the conclusion of the war.[7] Designed as a stopgap measure originally purposed to bridge the gap in carrier strength resulting from interwar naval treaties, as the war progressed the escort carriers' mission and accomplishments evolved. Nimitz concluded, "It became a great deal more than its name implies. From a purely defensive measure, the escort carrier emerged as an offensive weapon."[8] As rapidly assembled adaptations and hastily manufactured quick fixes, the CVEs completed a range of duties including transporting aircraft, escorting convoys, training of pilots and flight deck personnel, and providing critical ground support.[9] This marginalization of the escort carriers results in near historic invisibility today. In short, in the decades after the war, the very existence of the CVEs and the sailors who manned them underwent a process of historical purging. At the war's conclusion, the main motivation for constructing also ended. As a result, the year 1945 witnessed the beginning of the physical purge with cancelation or outright scrappage of escort carriers under construction. Destinies of the already commissioned CVEs varied, including placement in the mothball fleet, conversion into other vessels, or delivery to the scrapyards. The postwar commemoration of the deeds of aircraft carriers followed a similar pattern. Movies, books, and other forms of popular culture were drawn to the fleet aircraft carriers. Such products in the decades following the war thus defined for the American public the look and feel of an "aircraft carrier."

For the sailors of the escort carriers, the legacy of CVEs is one of irony, as the CVEs represented the vast majority of the aircraft carriers within the USN fleet during World War II. When the Empire of Japan surrendered on September 2, 1945, the USN retained a total of ninety-nine commissioned aircraft carriers. Of these vessels, twenty-eight retained a top speed near that of a cruiser and included the two specific vessel types, "fleet aircraft carrier" (CVs) and "light aircraft carrier" (CVLs).[10] The other seventy-one carriers were classified as "escort carriers." Despite representing over 70 percent of the carriers in the entire USN fleet, in the years after the war the escort carriers were nearly completely forgotten in public memory.

❋

The historian and philosopher Lewis Mumford, in his classic work *Technics and Civilization*, explores humanity's long and evolving relationship with advancing technology. With a gift for clearly summarizing complex topics while simultaneously discovering the most-complex notions in our simplest innovations, Mumford, with this broad-based study, traces human inventions from the Paleolithic era to the 1930s, when he wrote his classic work. Like all sound researchers, he relied on a foundation built by earlier historians, including William Morris, a Victorian era historian and designer. Mumford wrote, "William Morris characterized the new steamships, with true insight, as the Cathedrals of the Industrial Age. He was right. They brought forth a fuller orchestration of the arts and sciences. . . . [A] miracle of compactness, speed, power, inter-relation, and esthetic unity."[11] In taking the long view of history, and examining what societies view as valuable in terms of the investment of human capital and resources, he demonstrates the true impact of the Industrial Revolution that transformed the world in the second half of the nineteenth century. The examinations of steamships of the 1880s, beyond maritime history, permits inquiry into social, material, and technological aspects of the societies that designed, constructed, and sailed said vessels. In viewing nineteenth-century steamships as an assemblage of various methods of technology, Mumford suggests that a more robust interpretation of vessels is possible outside the confines of ship enthusiasts.

Viewing vessels comprehensively, meaning the component alloys, methods of manufacturing, and even the elemental chemicals consisting of a sailor's navy-issued toiletries, all validate a nation's efforts in the production of a warship. The application of this school of thought to the escort carriers holds the potential for reshaping past interpretations. Mumford used the phrase "symphonies of steel."[12] While past narratives of the escort carriers viewed these as quick fixes to ameliorate a desperate shortage, using Mumford's reasoning allows for a reversal in logic. Why not ask what other nation had the capacity and know-how to develop such an answer as the CVE? Rather than give specs comparing CVEs to the Essex class, this work seeks to turn the comparison on its head. Why not consider the manpower, the mass production, and the marriage of federal power and private industry that allowed for the production of over 120 such escort carriers in just three and a half years? In short, this work proposes that the escort carriers, in their manufacture, manning, and mobilization, represented the best of American mass production. As one author recently wrote, "Among the miracles of production in the Second

World War was America's escort carrier program. For scale and efficiency, few industrial achievements could match it."[13]

Escort carriers, like all weapons systems, were made up of materials from differing portions of the world. From mining communities like Bisbee, Arizona, located in the Mule Mountains, came the nation's largest supply of copper ore. Once they'd formed it into electrical wiring, ship workers strung out thin miles of copper to breathe life into the electrical systems of the carrier. Iron ore, and the coal to smelt it into steel, coming from the Appalachian range, formed not only the hull but also interior compartments, galley equipment, and miles of piping. The flight deck made up of thousands of individual wooden blocks came from teak harvested from Caribbean hardwood forests. Precise amounts of sulfur, charcoal, and potassium nitrate rested in a spectrum of brass casings holding the explosive force of the ammunition ranging from .50-caliber to five-inch shells. Ironically, the dangers of one of the most deadly components of the vessel were unknown at the time of construction. Pulled from the earth in six forms, hundreds of pounds of asbestos insulated boilers, piping, and engine areas, and even formed fire-resistant suits worn by the flight deck crew. Resting in tanks, an assemblage of fuels snorted life into her hull and machines. The list is perplexing once you consider such things as lightbulbs, pencils, dentist's tools, plateware, fire hoses, shoes, barber's chairs, and

Figure 2. USS *Block Island*, CVE 21, as a fully commissioned war vessel at anchor. After completing two missions in shuttling Lend-Lease supplies to Europe, she would acquire an air group and track down and destroy German U-boats in hunter-killer missions. Courtesy of the USS Block Island Association.

towels. Resembling a gravitational pull exponentially accelerating, this steel hull of the CVE pulled in a vast array of alloys, oils, and materials foreign and domestic in forming a platform of war before the full crew ever materialized.

Weapons, like most human inventions, are a series of experiments. Weaponry undergoing modifications produces classifications different from the original design. The first series of the CVEs, the Bogue class, converted from C3 cargo hulls, equaled about half the size of their "big sister" Essex class (CVs) aircraft carriers. Despite the obvious disparity in size, a main difference between the Essex and the Bogue classifications was not size but speed. Where the CVs' hulls, based on those of cruisers, sliced through the water at speeds in excess of thirty knots, the hulls of the unarmored Bogue class, designed for transporting massive amounts of cargo, plowed through the ocean at a more sedate eighteen knots. The Bogue class refitted with a wooden flight deck of just over 450 feet long carried an air wing of only twenty-eight aircraft. The disparity in size earned these ships the nickname "baby flattops." Over time, however, the name "jeep carrier" arose and stuck, conveying the varied and flexible roles the CVEs played in both theaters of the conflict. In addition, escort carriers' streamlined construction required far less time, and the escort carriers presented a smaller risk to the Navy, compared to losing an Essex class carrier. While the CVs served in the dangerous role of seeking out the enemy surface fleet, the CVEs participated in a host of tasks, each with a unique threat to the vessel and crew.[14]

If anything, these morphed hulls defined multifaceted operations in naval warfare. Whether ferrying fighter aircraft to forward operating areas, shuttling Lend-Lease supplies, or protecting susceptible North Atlantic convoys, these small carriers performed a vast array of naval duties. However, these baby carriers' most indelible successes came in the Battle of the Atlantic in leading task forces in seeking, attacking, and annihilating U-boats.

4
Pearl

On the morning of December 7, 1941, Cdr. Logan Ramsey received a shock as the chief of staff and lieutenant commander Patrol Wing Two for the Hawaiian Islands. At his home on Ford Island with his family, Ramsey ran when his phone rang early on a Sunday morning. Ramsey later wrote to a friend, "I received word at about 7:30 that one of our patrol planes had sunk a submerged submarine one mile off the entrance to Pearl Harbor. I made a dash for the Command Center clad in an aloha shirt and a gaudy pair of slacks and drew up a search plan for all our patrol planes and turned it over to the coding officer for coding before sending it out to our planes already in the air. By this time it was 7:55 A.M., and the first dive bomber came over. He made his pass at the seaplane ramp on the south end of Ford Island and his bomb simply blasted the squadrons we had there lined up on the beach, ready for take-off, to smithereens."[1] Ramsey ran into the headquarters' radio room and ordered a statement read in plain English and on all frequencies: "Air raid, Pearl Harbor. This is no drill."[2]

❋

In August 1937 Logan Ramsey published an article titled "Aerial Attacks on Fleets at Anchor" in *Proceedings*, the monthly publication founded in 1874 by the United States Naval Institute. He pointed out the manifold dangers now faced by the anchored fleet with the accelerated advances in naval aviation. Ever more powerful engines allowed planes to fly higher; thus, pilots incrementally scouted more and more ocean. Conversely, the ever-higher spotting aircraft became smaller and smaller to those lookouts on the surface. While never specifically naming Pearl Harbor, the piece published four full years before the Japanese surprise attack provides clear warning to fleets at anchor with the aid of 20/20 hindsight. Ramsey proclaimed that naval commanders needed to shake off the centuries-long notion of being safe while anchored in a sheltered harbor. He wrote, "From time immemorial, coming to anchor has had the connotation of a certain surcease from the rigors of the seafaring life. Rest, recreation, and shore leave have always been the watchwords on anchoring."[3] Ramsey painted a picture of a future where the fleet's danger increased, not decreased, while at anchor. He foresaw expanded antiaircraft batteries not only on board vessels but also hidden on and near shore installations. On the tactical side, he argued that anchored ships of the fleet were "deprived of their tactical mobility."[4] While a detailed thinker and skillful writer, Ramsey had a gift of using a football analogy that would cut through elaborate theories and convey his message with one sentence. He wrote, "The only sure defense is to tackle the ball carrier before he crosses the line of scrimmage—in other words, to stop the aerial attack before the planes are launched."[5] His gift of wordcraft is seen in a sentence on the peril of ships at anchor in this new world of naval aviation. He wrote, "The defenses of the naval base, then, must extend considerably beyond the immediate vicinity of the fleet anchorage; and the range must be further expanded with each new aeronautical development which permits any material increase in the operating radius of ship-based aircraft."[6] Ramsey's insights into the theoretical writings of the danger posed to fleets at anchor would become evident in November 1940 with the decisive victory of the British navy over the Italian fleet anchored at Taranto.

❋

When the first Japanese bomb dropped on Pearl Harbor, naval officer Massie Hughes was in his residence in Navy Quarters P on Ford Island. His son was just five years old at the time and within one city block of the battleship USS *Arizona*, BB 39. Not wasting time to remove his pajama bottoms, Hughes tossed on his Navy uniform and ran to his jeep.[7] He raced to wing headquarters, parked, and, brightly colored pajama bottoms visible and flapping with his speed, ran inside. After receiving the search sector drawn up earlier by Ramsey in response to the reported Japanese submarine, Hughes, again in his jeep, sped toward the squadron's PBY Catalina seaplanes. Here he spotted Capt. James Ogden, who had just arrived. Hughes bellowed, "Come on Jimmy, I've got his search sector, so we'll go out and look for them. Pick yourself a crew."[8]

The ad hoc crew tossed aside preflight procedures such as engine warm-up, recording wind directions, and radioing for permission to commence channel takeoff. Once the beach gear was clear and the PBY afloat, engines were at full throttle. Ogden performed the takeoff. A biographical sketch of Hughes's career summed up the amazing feat of Ogden in this narrow channel at Pearl with the war waging around, above, and under them. "As his Catalina careened up the channel, getting underway in the midst of the chaotic battle, a Jap two-man submarine breached the surface just ahead and was taken under fire by a nearby ship. Just as the Squadron Commander's plane passed the scene, still trying to get up take-off speed, a destroyer came up and unloaded its depth charges on the midget sub. At only 55 knots, Lt. Comdr. Hughes found his plane airborne, thrown off the water by the force of the explosions. It staggered away, skimmed over canefields brushing the tops of the stalks, with Zeros overhead, and was off on a 1500 mile patrol flight that lasted well into the night."[9]

This transpired at 0830, and, while not the first aircraft in the skies, this PBY was the first up and on a path to serve as the eyes for a completely surprised US military on that December morning.

Ramsey designed a hairpin-shaped search pattern taking twelve hours. Striking out to the northwest, the flight took them out along the southern side of the Hawaiian island of Kauai and returned along the northern side. Ogden recalled years later that most of the flight consisted of Hughes using his well-honed skills in swearing. He wrote, "The thing I remember most is that his running remarks throughout, of rather an obscene nature, were applied more to U.S. congressmen than they were to the Japanese."[10] One sighting, however, did spark excitement, a carrier and escorting vessels spotted through the haze below, which turned out to be USS *Enterprise*, CV 6. The real danger awaited their return in attempting a nighttime landing back at Pearl in the wake of the attack. Ogden remembered the sky was as "black as the inside of a cow."[11] The only light seen from the sky emanated from the still-burning wreckage of *Arizona*, which gave the crew of the PBY a reference point for the location of Ford Island. Two challenges threatened their lives. First was incoming antiaircraft fire from friendly forces. Second was the very real possibility of the PBY striking unseen floating debris during landing on the harbor's surface.

In countering the first possibility, the crew turned on all navigation lighting on the PBY, seeking "to act as friendly as possible."[12] The second factor of striking debris from the attack was the matter of calculating which, if any, of the landing channels had been cleared for their landing. With no response to their transmissions via radio, both Hughes and Ogden thought the Pearl City channel was the safest bet. However, in preparing for final approach, a number of fighters from *Enterprise* entered the airspace near them. This caused the antiaircraft batteries at Pearl to light up the sky, including targeting their fully illuminated PBY. Ogden recalled, "We were only seeing one round in five, but the tracers lit up the sky like crazy, and the shrapnel was falling around like it was rain."[13] After successfully avoiding the incoming fire, the pilots edged their PBY ever closer to the unknown where, in the blackness ahead somewhere, sky met water. Luckily, the Pearl City channel had been cleared, and the landing was successful. However, once on the land, they realized selecting the other landing channel would have proved fatal, as they would have violently merged with the mast of the battleship USS *Nevada*, BB 36, beached by the captain in an effort to save his vessel from sinking.[14]

As dawn broke on Monday, December 8, the full extent of the damage came into focus. For both Hughes and Ramsey, this attack was personal. Not only was the USN attacked, but both had children living on Ford Island at the time of the attack.[15] Adjacent to both their residences on Ford Island was "battleship row," where eight of the nine battleships in the Pacific fleet lay destroyed or damaged. Other injured naval vessels included three destroyers and three light cruisers. Seventy-five percent of the aircraft based at Pearl Harbor, including some 164 planes, also lay destroyed. Fortunately for the USN, the three large fleet aircraft carriers (CVs) in the Pacific fleet were out to sea during the attack.[16] Fortunately indeed, for at the time of Franklin Delano Roosevelt's radio address to sixty million Americans on this Monday in December, these three vessels represented nearly half of America's entire carrier strength. On both oceans the Navy had only seven large fleet carriers.[17]

This attack revealed that aircraft carriers, not the battleships, were the true capital ships of the USN. A naval scholar of the USN in the interwar period wrote, "The demise of the battleship at Pearl Harbor was the occasion not for a revolutionary but rather evolutionary change in attitude."[18] USS *Yorktown*, CV 5, exemplified these massive capital vessels, with her displacement of over nineteen thousand tons, a crew of almost nineteen hundred sailors, and the capability to store and launch ninety-six aircraft. *Yorktown*, charged with bringing lethal USN airpower to the enemy, cruised at over thirty knots, as fast as any ship in the fleet. These sleek hulls sliced through the ocean creating their own flying weather. Even in perfectly calm weather, the powerful vessels produced enough forward speed to create the required lift for aircraft to become airborne.[19] Like a heavyweight boxer, these CVs were not constructed for aiding in auxiliary roles. Her designers sought to destroy the enemy in the open ocean in what was termed "blue-water fighting."[20] However, *Yorktown* and her six sister ships had required many years, manhours, and dollars to construct, resources that America did not immediately possess as black smoke billowed into the crisp Pacific air above Hawaii.

Throughout the days after December 7, Americans, glued to their radios, learned the full details surrounding the nearly simultaneous Japanese attacks on the Philippines, Hong Kong, and Wake Island. Three days after December 7, Germany and Italy declared war on the United States.[21] The USN faced three Axis enemies on two oceans with just seven carriers. A solution to this desperate problem required a weapon barely off the drawing boards in December 1941—the escort carrier. These yet-unborn vessels required not only manufacturing but also the crews needed to breathe a fighting spirit into steel. The USN would tap from a generation of naval aviators who came of age in the 1920s and 1930s to transform these newly constructed warships into fighting vessels. Capt. Logan Ramsey would receive orders in molding one of these new escort carriers and a group of newly minted young American sailors, many of whom had never been to sea before, into a cohesive fighting unit.

The story of USS *Block Island*, CVE 21, is of particular interest in bearing witness to the first portion of the conflict in the Atlantic Ocean against the feared German U-boats.[22] The exploits of USS *Block Island* demonstrate a nation moving rapidly away from strong isolationism in the interwar period to one fully engulfed in warfare. She first served as a platform to shuttle fighter aircraft to Great Britain. From there Ramsey led the crew in hunter-killer missions searching for the German U-boats that threatened the lifeline of the convoy routes from the United States to the European theater. Finally, the ship itself became a victim of one of these U-boats and thus represented the only US aircraft carrier lost in the Atlantic during World War II. The escort carrier exemplifies American mass production in quickly designing, developing, and creating an invention to address a wartime deficiency. Examining USS *Block Island*, CVE 21, and her crew presents a microhistory of the USN's venture into correcting its dangerous shortage of aircraft carriers, the nature of the Lend-Lease operations, and the use and implementation of new combinations of systems of weapons and detection equipment in directly confronting the U-boats that threatened Allied war and merchant vessels.

The aforementioned USS *Long Island* provided an important experiment for the USN in the days following Pearl Harbor. Within three weeks of America's entry into the war, the secretary of the Navy approved the conversion of twenty-four C3 cargo tanker hulls into escort carriers. The Navy foresaw the dangers in the Atlantic due to the U-boat menace that quickly materialized in the wake of the German declaration of war against the United States. U-boats off the east coast of the United States decimated the unprepared USN and merchant ships, sending four hundred vessels, over two million tons of shipping, to the Atlantic floor during the first six months after Pearl Harbor. From Boston to Miami, German U-boat captains quickly racked up sinkings of merchant vessels. The historian for the USN called this loss "[as] much a national disaster as if saboteurs had destroyed half a dozen of our biggest war plants."[23] The amazing successes of Operation Drumbeat, the German designation for the operation off the American seaboard, stemmed not so much from advanced submarine tactics but from unpreparedness by the USN. In the wake of Pearl Harbor, the entire 1,500 miles of coast from Florida to Maine was almost completely exposed to the German enemy. One author summed up the USN's situation as "a sea and air force so antiquated, so unprepared, so untrained, and so deficient in craft and weaponry that it stunned the Germans and British when they saw it go to war."[24]

The simple execution of a blackout order along the East Coast would have prevented much of this damage close to shore. However, protests from Florida to New

Jersey loudly claimed that the "tourist season would be ruined."[25] Allied intelligence reported after the war that the American east coast was for the Germans "the greenest pastures the war was ever to offer."[26] With engines at idle and looking west onto the horizon blazing with lights from such forms of entertainment as Ferris wheels along the eastern seaboard, U-boat captains simply waited for targets to present themselves in the forms of silhouettes. In the summer nights of 1942, tourists looked east and watched the war with ships ablaze in the distance. In fact, the most dangerous shipping lane in the world for a time was from Jacksonville, Florida, to Galveston, Texas. One seasoned merchant sailor commented, "The only safe run is from St. Louis to Cincinnati."[27] Long-standing shipping companies could no longer get merchant vessels insured for ocean travel.[28] One historian wrote, "The Pacific Pearl Harbor lasted two hours and ten minutes on a Sunday morning. The Atlantic Pearl Harbor lasted six months."[29]

While the shipping lanes off America's east and southern coasts provided valuable targets for the Germans, the USN worked on an ad hoc basis in developing weapons and strategies to address the problem of protecting the Allied convoys of merchant vessels providing Europe with a link to American production As for the escort carrier, it did not yet exist outside of the blueprints and the single experiment of USS *Long Island*, CVE 1. Twenty-four hours a day, ship workers climbed over C3 cargo hulls, practicing an ancient tactic of naval warfare, adaptability. Hulls designed to carry commerce underwent transformation and conversion into a new weapon to take back the Atlantic waters.

5
Amalgamation

In 1942 the Navy needed a range of vessels to prosecute this war, and the sailors to operate and fight from these yet-unbuilt vessels. Under the guidance of the Navy, private companies constructed ships while the Navy recruited and trained the sailors to man them. At the time of Pearl Harbor, the Navy was a remarkably small organization in terms of personnel, compared to the massive organization it morphed into by the close of the war. Future sailors started their journey by undergoing boot camp, where they were simply known as "boots." Four of these boot camps existed at the beginning of the war in San Diego, California; Bainbridge, Maryland; Newport, Rhode Island; and Great Lakes, Illinois. Here young civilians morphed into the world of the sailor, which included its own clothing, signs of status, method of keeping time with a twenty-four-hour clock, and language.

Mirroring the segregated America of the early 1940s, the USN also divided its sailors into the spheres of "white" and "black." African American sailors assigned to CVE 21 did so only in the capacity of serving as stewards for the officers. As a small number of stewards, never exceeding twenty in number, worked and resided in "officers' country," the nine hundred enlisted sailors had almost no contact with them. One sailor recalled that the only time he ever saw a steward on board was during the rationing of freshwater when the African American stewards would shower with salt water in the head of the enlisted sailors. The sailor recalled that segregation within the USN persisted in this unusual event, as a specific enlisted sailor's head was cleared of all "white" personnel, and then all the stewards showered en masse as one cohort.[1] Due to the very small number of these stewards ever assigned to CVE 21 or CVE 106, I was unable to make contact and interview any of these African American stewards who served on either escort carrier. However, a glimpse into their experience is seen in the long naval career of Cook Third Class Espiridion Escumbise. Born on the island of Cebu in the Philippines in 1896, Escumbise migrated to the island of Hawaii seeking employment on the island's sugar plantations. In 1918 he joined the USN and was relegated to the only position allowed for Filipinos and other people of color at the time, the role of cook. At the conclusion of World War I, Escumbise stayed on with the Navy and retired in 1940 after twenty-two years. With the attack on Pearl Harbor, Escumbise, nearing fifty years of age, reenlisted with the USN and would serve on board CVE 21 with African Americans in "officers' country."[2]

❋

For those young men growing up in 1930s America, travel was a novelty. Outside of the migrations of those families fleeing the Dust Bowl for California in the hopes of work and food, many young boys had not traveled more than a day's distance from home. Samuel Hynes, in his excellent memoir *Flights of Passage*, wrote that boot camp was a series of firsts, including "first time away from home, the first time out of the home state, the first time in a Pullman car."[3] Walking into induction centers, these men stood out not only with their civilian clothes but also with their own individually selected hairstyles, both of which changed immediately. Sailors, seeing these young men, heckled them from afar with chants of "Fresh meat! Fresh meat!"[4] After handing over their civilian clothes, and with freshly shorn heads, the individual nature of self began to evaporate. As one sailor recalled, "When your hair hit the deck, you were a first class boot. It was the best way I could think of to break a man into the hard job he had to do. Everyone even looked alike."[5] Navy tutelage centered on putting ship and shipmates before the individual.

Their ability or inability to swim demonstrated the diversity of these young men's experiences growing up. Chester Wentworth was raised in the rural areas outside Boston and thus grew up swimming in local ponds. In boot camp, he recalled, "I did not have much problem swimming because of we had ponds around here. But I was with fellows from New Jersey, and they could not swim a stroke because they were from the big cities."[6] Nearly all Navy training, including swimming from an abandoned ship, centered on operating as a team on a vessel at sea, whether a relatively small PT boat or a battleship. Marching together, eating together, showering and sleeping together crystallized a singular unit working together to reach an objective. Whether running an obstacle course or cleaning a head, sailors fused into a cohesive unit in weeks of intensive training. All learned one major skill set, firefighting. It is an irony that one of the biggest dangers to a ship of war at sea is fire. An out-of-control fire, either caused on board accidently or the result of enemy action, mixed with stored fuel and weapons, could spell a ship's demise in a matter of minutes. Think of all USN vessels, but especially carriers, as a combination of a floating gas refinery and fireworks factory. No matter the tonnage of the vessel, each contained, proportional to its size, massive amounts of combustible fuels and explosives. An uncontrolled fire on board meant the destruction of the ship and thus sailors' homes on an unforgiving ocean. As one scholar wrote, "What marksmanship training was to the Army, firefighting and damage-control drill became to the Navy."[7]

A close second to firefighting was the art of cleaning. Whether in their person, uniform, or bunk space, the Navy demanded flawless cleanliness of its sailors. One veteran recalled, "Cleanliness was not next to godliness in the United States Navy; it was godliness."[8] Cleanliness also included the continuous battle with rust, waged by chipping away old paint and applying new coats of grey protection.[9] An additional test in boot camp was the proper use of the Navy seabag, with all issued items needing to fit therein. Life in the Navy was not stationary; it revolved around movement, whether on board ship or on assignments on land. Newly minted sailors learned this skill of efficient packing, which was no easy task. One veteran quipped, "Packing everything into that seabag was like trying to put a ten-pound kitty in a two-pound box."[10]

Despite the segregation against African Americans and the outright banning of Japanese Americans, the spectrum of births, backgrounds, and boyhoods found in boot camps still showcased the diversity found in the term "white." The first clue of the latitude of the human experience occurred with the calling out of the roster. Surnames hinted at the layers of migrations that had occurred over the centuries to the Americas. While English and French names highlighted the experience of European empires on the continent of North America, Chinese, Slavic, and Italian last names illuminated later migrations. Diversity also extended to religion, education, and demographic influences. Many of these societal barriers soon melted away. Weeks and weeks of not only training, but also eating, sleeping, and showering collectively, quickly produced nicknames, inside jokes, and friendships. Many sailors who had never traveled outside their home state found themselves with shipmates from across the nation, which negated not only geographic differences but also other divisions within 1940s America. One sailor recalled boot camp as a series of events in a row, including "physicals, haircuts, inoculations, dental examinations, uniform issues."[11] A range of new experiences included health education warnings such as "She May Look Clean—But" and new foods, like shrimp.[12] They learned the meanings of markings on uniforms, which one sailor recalled as "(a)n entire symbology of hierarchy and skill."[13] In the terminology of this new world, dinner was called "supper," bathroom was the "head," and hammocks were termed "fart sacks."[14] This world was run by officers who were recalled as "strange and distant creatures."[15] Most boots trained for individual vessels that did not physically exist when America entered the war. Once out of boot camp, these sailors turned their training into reality when assigned to their first vessel.

❋

Just as randomness assembled young recruits to boot camp for training, chance spread graduated sailors to their first assignments across the Navy, including air squadrons, submarines, and carriers. Six hundred sixty sailors opened paper orders to report to Bremerton, Washington, and the carrier USS *Block Island*. Three forces would be amalgamating on Puget Sound: newly produced sailors, a mass-produced carrier, and the leadership of a naval officer who devoted his career to naval aviation in the interwar years. The first skipper of CVE 21, Capt. Logan Ramsey, exemplifies those naval officers who embraced naval aviation in the wake of World War I. When the next war commenced, the USN would rely on young skippers such as Ramsey in the amalgamation of mass-produced carriers and droves of "green" sailors.

Logan C. Ramsey personally witnessed the evolution of naval aviation through the lens of the ever-transforming aircraft cockpits in which he sat. In 1924 the USN retained just three hundred qualified naval aviators; one of these was Logan Ramsey, who in 1921 earned his wings from Pensacola.[16] The open cockpits of biplanes at the start of Ramsey's flying career gave way to faster aircraft incorporating a single wing and enclosed cockpit. Corresponding with ever-evolving aircraft was the commissioning of the first aircraft carrier in the fleet of the USN. The Naval Appropriations Act of 1920 called for the conversion of the new collier (a bulk merchant vessel designed to haul coal) *Jupiter* into America's first carrier, USS *Langley*, CV 1. Six years later this first experiment in carrier operations commenced.[17] Over these years the ever more capable aircraft included a reciprocal increase in weight. More powerful radial engines, variable pitch propellers, and cowl flaps (engine cooling) allowed the monoplane to replace the biplane. For pilots this meant ever-increasing range of operations and speeds of both sea-based and carrier-based aircraft.[18] Adaptation for naval aviators in the interwar period was not only an asset but a requirement. Beyond changing aircraft, pilots also conducted operations from more and more vessels, including aircraft carriers, battleships, and cruisers. In short, by the time of the attack on Pearl Harbor, Ramsey and Francis Massie Hughes had a combined thirty years of service in the continuously evolving field of naval aviation. Where Hughes had one decade as a naval aviator at the time of the attack on Pearl Harbor, Ramsey had two. The career trajectories of adaptation by both men placed them in a position to later command the untried and unproven escort carriers.

Participating in the Fleet Problems proved a critical factor for those naval aviators of the interwar period who would go on to command in World War II. These naval exercises from 1923 to 1940 granted young officers practical real-world experiences after digesting lofty theoretical strategy in the classrooms of Annapolis and Newport. Marked with Roman numerals, the 1935 exercises named Fleet Problem XVI witnessed for the first time the inclusion of USS *Ranger*, CV 4 (with Massie Hughes on board). Not a single exercise in 1935, but rather five separate naval exercises, all these operations took place over a vast swath of the Pacific including the Aleutian Islands, Midway, and Hawaii. Other military branches that participated included the US Army and the Coast Guard.[19] A thirty-seven-year-old Logan Ramsey, a lieutenant commander and the commander of Scouting Plane Squadron Ten, participated as an officer on the cruiser USS *Chicago*, CA 29. He served in the White Fleet during these games. His squadron's objective was to gather intelligence on the unknown strength of the enemy defenses and infantry on Midway. The Operation Order he wrote for Squadron Ten stated, "This force will reconnoiter and report on defenses of MIDWAY, deliver dive bombing attacks on SAND ISLAND defenses, and then observe gunfire from parent vessels in order to assist in the seizure and consolidation of MIDWAY by the WESTERN FORCE, WHITE FLEET."[20] Beyond gaining experience in coordinating with officers of the western forces that included USS *Chester*, CA 27, USS *Portland*, CA 33, and USS *Lexington*, CV 2, Ramsey garnered the actual experience of being the aggressor in attempting to seize Midway. This command experience of leading a squadron over Midway boded well for him seven years later as the Japanese attempted their invasion.

For those naval aviators who first came of age in the era of the biplanes of the 1920s and '30s, such as Ramsey and Hughes, these Fleet Problems provided valuable experience in leading men and transforming thinking into action. One scholar wrote, "Naval officers experienced the problems of coordinating three dimensions of naval warfare in an operational setting. Concepts such as dive bombing, independent submarine operations, anti-submarine warfare, and amphibious operations were explored in a medium that stressed not only machines and people but also the thinking of naval officers as to how best to employ them."[21] Ramsey not only participated in these Fleet Problems but also thought and wrote about the rapid advances in naval aviation. A decade and a month before Pearl Harbor, he received a letter from the skipper of USS *Lexington*, CV 2, the sixty-two-year-old Capt. Ernest J. King. King, who during the war would go on to serve as commander in chief, United States Fleet (COMINCH) and chief of naval operations (CNO), wrote in November 1931, "I have just read your article in the November 'Proceedings' on 'Bombing vs Torpedo Planes' and wish to congratulate you on your thorough and clear presentation of the case. I wish also to say that I am quite in agreement with your article, so far as I have experience and observation to date."[22]

As Ramsey worked his way up the Navy hierarchy, he would encounter even more challenging requirements in caring for both machines and men. In 1935 on the *Chicago*, he coordinated communication with the other senior aviators of the scouting squadrons on *Chester* and *Portland*. Ramsey and his pilots dealt with the ever-erratic wildcat of military history, the weather, which in naval aviation required factoring in both visibility and wind when navigating to, and back from,

Midway. Of the Fleet Problems and the officers participating in them, one historian wrote, "Through simulation they developed a good, though incomplete, understanding of the new tools of naval warfare and a reasonable strategic scheme for applying them."[23] While minuscule in operational complexity in comparison to later World War II operations, these Fleet Problems starting in 1923 granted officers critical hands-on experience with both planning and implementation. One scholar succinctly wrote, "Aviators learned that they had to crawl before they could walk and walk before they could run."[24]

Alfred Thayer Mahan wrote his long-remembered naval strategy in the era of Ramsey's and Hughes's births, before the advent of aviation.[25] Ramsey's keen mind digested these experiences and shaped his further writings. Building upon Mahan's thinking, Ramsey published the article "The Influence of Aircraft on the Exercise of Sea Command," which was published in *Proceedings* in 1938. He eloquently traces the history of the notion of territorial waters starting with the negotiation of the Dutch in 1610 with English king James I through the Russo-Japanese War of 1904–1905. In considering the use of aircraft in future blockading operations, Ramsey foresaw that aviation would not present a blinding single strike carrying the day; rather, he prophesied a long-drawn-out engagement. While naval aviation presented unparalleled chances for offensive operations, it also yielded the possibility that future blockading operations would become of primary importance rather than relegated to second-rate vessels and officers. Ramsey wrote: "All of these requirements will necessitate great activity on the part of any future blockading force. No longer will it be possible to assign antiquated hulks to accomplish this mission. Only the most efficient service, under arduous conditions for both parent vessels and their aircraft, can even begin to deny the use of the sea to the enemy. The 'exercise' in the phrase 'the exercise of sea command' will be no dreary gazing around the horizon while steaming at moderate speeds, but will be 'exercise' in every sense of the word—as wearying as a long workout on a rowing machine, and as endless as dish washing."[26]

6
"Well Done, Massie Hughes"

Throughout the war Hollywood director John Ford served as an officer in the USN making documentaries, where he witnessed firsthand the battle of Midway and the D-Day landing in Normandy. In September of 1942, Ford released the film *The Battle of Midway*. Just eighteen minutes long, the documentary included live-action shots of the battle filmed only three months earlier by Ford and his crew on the small island halfway between Japan and California. Ford pushed the boundaries in presenting the war on the silver screen to Americans. First, he shot the film in color, which at the time was considered better suited for musicals and fantasies such as *The Wizard of Oz*, as opposed to the more realistic-looking black and white. This was only the second time Ford had shot in color, the first being the film *Drums along the Mohawk*. Second, he used live-action shots from the battle, not recycled stock footage of aircraft and ships utilized in most newsreel updates about the war. Realistic footage included the blurriness resulting from the impact of Japanese bombs rattling the 16 mm camera in his hands. Jolting scenes, orange fireballs resulting from Japanese aircraft striking out of a crisp blue Pacific sky, brought the war to the American public in a way never seen before.[1] It is all too easy to think of John Ford's working career as sitting in a director's chair on a sunny afternoon in Monument Valley discussing a scene with John Wayne for a western. On Midway he was filming real life in a war zone. In fact, during the attack on Midway, Ford was knocked unconscious and received shrapnel to his arm.

Once back in Hollywood, Ford was terrified of losing control of the footage he and his crew shot on the small Pacific atoll. Ford showed the footage to Field Photo recruit Robert Parrish, who before the war had worked with him in editing one of his major motion pictures. Ford gave the film to Parrish and ordered him to leave town. He said, "And don't bother to change your clothes. Just pick up the film and get out to the airport. The navy censor will be around here looking for our film. I want to be able to tell him I don't have any film."[2] His biggest fear was the interservice squabbling complicating completion of the project. He told Parrish, "The four services will start bickering over it and the goddamn thing will get so bogged down in red tape that we'll never get it released."[3]

Working at a brisk pace, Ford used almost all of the footage shot on Midway. In editing the film he decided to use the voices of four narrators, including Henry

Fonda and Jane Darwell. At eighteen minutes the film was short enough to be shown before the regularly scheduled feature film. Distributed by Twentieth Century Fox, it is estimated that three out of four movie screens in the United States showed the film, and it was selected as one of the winners for the 1942 Academy Award for Best Documentary. In showing a reality of war unknown to the American public, it is credited today as one of the most important war documentaries from the twentieth century.[4]

Pertaining to this study, something extraordinary takes place toward the end of the film. After witnessing battle scenes shot from the sea, ground, and air, the audience is introduced to two officers, the first two individuals who are specifically named and shown in the film. Fourteen minutes into the film, billowing black smoke is seen arising from the airfield, and the narrator informs the audience that downed aircrews from American carriers are still missing at sea. For days PBYs flew over the ocean searching for any sign of downed pilots and aircrew. Eleven days after the battle, PBYs still located and rescued men who had gone days without food and water. The film shows an empty stretcher being carefully inserted into a PBY to assist a rescued airman. The next shot cuts to a silver-haired officer in sunglasses, standing alone, patiently waiting alongside a PBY. As this medium-built man in his forties looks at the camera the narrator says, "Well done, Massie Hughes."[5] This was John Ford's way of tipping his hat to Hughes, who led the thirteen-day effort to locate and save forty-three pilots and aircrew downed during the battle. In this period, just a day short of a fortnight, his patrol aircraft averaged 110 hours of flight time, a tribute not only to the aircrews but also to the maintenance personnel of the PBYs.[6] Just seconds later a stocky officer with an unfastened battle helmet on his head is seen talking with Massie Hughes. In this shot the narrator states, "And, Logan Ramsey."[7] Both Hughes and Ramsey worked with John Ford on Midway, and Ford respected their leadership enough to individually show and name them for the American audience. Both officers would go on to command USS *Block Island*, CVE 21. While very different in terms of background and demeanor, a biographical investigation of Ramsey and Hughes demonstrates naval officers who, in the 1920s, saw that the future of naval warfare was directly linked to the future of aviation. The USN recognized both these officers' flying and leadership experience during the interwar years when it commissioned a wave of new escort carriers during the war.

❋

The contrasts are stark when comparing Ramsey and Hughes, two men born within a year of each other. While at the Academy, Hughes played all four years on the football team at the position of quarterback, while Ramsey played only his first year, making the Plebe team. Ironically, the larger Ramsey left the football team and gravitated more toward intellectual pursuits, such as the choir, glee club, and as a staff member of the annual yearbook, *Lucky Bag*. The historian, in researching cadets who graduated one hundred years ago, is granted a much bigger window of examination when his subject writes as opposed to throws footballs. Ramsey's senior-year biography summed up his literary pursuits. It reads, "To be poetically brief, he is a wordmonger."[8]

Logan C. Ramsey was a large man but slow moving. Upon first meeting him, some mistakenly interpreted his physical manner as corresponding to his mental powers. However, watching him defeat an opponent in bridge while simultaneously completing navigation problems quickly dispelled this notion.[9] Born in Jackson, Mississippi, on February 26, 1898, Ramsey was born just six months before the USN flexed its muscles, courtesy of Commodore George Dewey, against the Spanish navy at the Battle of Manila in the Spanish-American War. He received an appointment to the US Naval Academy in 1914. He formally graduated in 1919 as a result of joining the war effort and accepting the commission of ensign on board the battleship USS *Texas* (BB 35), in 1918. In 1921 he left the *Texas* for flight training at the Naval Air Station in Pensacola, becoming a naval aviator on December 21 of that same year. Over the next four years, he served with the Aircraft Squadron, Atlantic Fleet, and at the Naval Air Station at Hampton Roads, Virginia.

Ramsey demonstrated early in his working career an organizational ability in conceptualizing forward-thinking aspects in naval aviation. In 1925 he worked for the Navy Department in Washington, DC, taking a leading role in the Aerial Navigation Section within the Hydrographic Office. In developing navigational techniques for pilots flying aircraft with ever-increasing speeds and range, Ramsey was assigned as a navigator on the first aircraft carrier of the USN, USS *Langley*, CV 1. He later became the first group commander of the first USS *Yorktown*, CV 5, and also flew off of the carriers USS *Lexington*, CV 2, and USS *Saratoga*, CV 3.[10] He commenced publishing articles in *Proceedings* that demonstrated his intellectual curiosity on the implementation of such ever-evolving aspects of technology on the future of naval aviation. Ramsey's career trajectory in the 1920s demonstrates the innovation that took place during the interwar period. Rather than a time of tactical and strategic stagnation, advanced by historians in the immediate wake of World War I, the interwar period was a time of advancement in naval aviation. Considering Ramsey's biography in the 1920s and 1930s, and his writings during this time, demonstrates the specific location where theory meets practice in the field. One group of historians wrote, "For innovation to occur, a military force must have a set of organizational relationships and a process which examine critically and fairly all new concepts with the potential for exploitation."[11]

Ramsey's analytical mind in evaluating the pros and cons of individual components of aviation is clearly evident in his first publication in *Proceedings* in 1927, writing about the operational usefulness of cameras mounted on aircraft in surveying. Just sampling one sentence from his piece "Hydrographic Surveying with Aircraft" presents a window into his fondness for the myriad small details that composed the evolving inventions of naval aviation in the 1920s. He wrote, "Assuming a shutter with .5 inch wide slit giving an exposure of .01 second on an 18 by 24 centimeter plate, the travel will be approximately seven inches so that the time elapsing between the exposure of the first edge and the last edge will be about .14 seconds."[12] With a highly technical writing style, Ramsey concluded his article by presenting six sound methods of consideration in improving this developing field of naval aviation.[13] It is this developing multitiered problem-solving skill, combined with mental tenacity, that Ramsey applied in developing and writing about the application of developing technological innovations to the rapidly advancing field of naval aviation. The *New York Herald* in 1930 published an editorial on Ramsey's writings in *Proceedings*. It stated, "Such observations as those of Lt. Ramsey may well make us grateful that our modest five-year aircraft programs are being, on the whole, satisfactorily carried out. They may also incline us to hope that the United States will not be allowed to fall behind in its development of this vitally important arm."[14]

Ramsey's leadership and flying skills in seaplanes earned him the assignment of senior aviator on the battleship USS *New York*, BB 34. In 1934 he was promoted to wing commander, heavy cruisers, and command of the unit Scouting Squadron 10 on board USS *Chicago*, CA 29. The following year he was a student in the 1935–1936 class of the Naval War College in Newport, Rhode Island.[15] Theorized war-gaming was one of the central components of the coursework at Newport, starting in the 1880s. One particular war-gaming scenario at the Naval War College was a theoretical Japanese attack on Midway, which seven years later would grant Ramsey familiarity with Midway when the Japanese did attack, in June of 1942.[16] Upon graduation, he worked within the Navy Department's Bureau of Aeronautics and was placed in charge of Industrial War Plans. At the same time, he also served as a member of a working committee on the Aeronautical Board on the Commodity Committees of the Army and Navy Munitions Board.[17] This last position granted him particular experience in interservice operations between the Army and the Navy, which again was a skill required of his commands at both Pearl Harbor and Midway.

In 1966 Ramsey was interviewed about Midway. He recalled being ordered to headquarters in Pearl Harbor by Commander in Chief Chester W. Nimitz and his staff officers in the final week of May 1942, for a briefing about the situation on and near Midway. Nimitz was considering selecting Ramsey to become operations officer on the island of Midway for the expected Japanese attack. For Nimitz, two aspects of Ramsey's distinguished career stood out for this role. First was his command as chief of staff to Rear Admiral Patrick Bellinger, commander of Patrol Wing Two on Ford Island, during the attack on Pearl Harbor. Second was Ramsey's familiarity with Midway resulting from his experience at the Naval War College in the war-gaming exercises involving a theorized Japanese attack on the island.[18] While only simulations, these experiences granted participating officers detailed knowledge of specifications related to Midway, including the capacity of the airfield, carrying out search patterns, and coordination of interservice operations. During the detailed briefing with Ramsey, Nimitz did not shy away from the possibility of defeat. Thus, he ordered Ramsey, "If the island should be in danger of falling, be sure to bring out the heavy stuff, the PBYs and B-17s." After completing the presentations, Nimitz asked Ramsey, "Have you any requests?"

"Yes I do," Ramsey replied. "If this turns out all right, will you bring me back from Midway?" Nimitz replied with an affirmative.[19] Thus, on May 29, 1942, just six days before the battle, Logan Ramsey flew out of Ford Island in a PBY so heavy with a torpedo it had difficulty clearing the water. A grouping of twelve PBYs made the trip to Midway, which after landing were quickly refueled and took off in completing search patterns looking for signs of the Japanese enemy.[20]

The path to Midway for Francis Massie Hughes commenced in the Deep South. The 1923 volume of *Lucky Bag*, the yearbook of the Academy, lists his hometown as Selma, Alabama, and the second sentence of his yearbook description notes that four years at the Academy did not in any way impact his southern accent or dialect. He lettered on both the wrestling and football teams, and for the latter played the position of quarterback.[21] After his graduation from the Academy in 1923, the first portion of his career centered on the surface fleet, serving on the battleship USS *Texas*, BB 35, and then transferring to USS *Pennsylvania*, BB 38. His football career did not end upon leaving the Academy. He coached and played on the fleet team of *Pennsylvania*, which participated but lost in the fleet championship. While stationed on BB 38, Hughes was the control officer on the five-inch battery. In 1928 Hughes was assigned as the coach and a player on the All Navy team, which was composed of all personnel from the service, rather than midshipmen from the Academy.[22] Starting in 1924, under President Calvin Coolidge, the top Army and Navy teams battled in Washington's Griffith Stadium for the President's Cup. The following year the Marine Corps was allowed to field its own team, and the Leathernecks from Quantico dominated by winning the cup 20–0 in 1925, 26–7 in 1926, and 14–0 in 1927.[23] With Hughes's central focus on running, he handed off the ball repeatedly to fullback "Navy Tom" Hamilton and led the team to a 12–0 win over the Marines. Hughes as a coach, and a player, received the President's Cups from Calvin Coolidge.[24] His leadership as a football coach would directly impact his leadership style as a skipper.

In 1931 he transferred to naval aviation and at Pensacola earned his wings.[25] At the time of the Battle of Midway, Hughes commanded the Sand Island Seaplane Base, which was the largest island on the Midway Atoll.[26] This consisted of six Catalina flying boats and six US Army Air Corps B-17 bombers that patrolled the approaches toward Midway.[27] It is in this position where the paths of John Ford and Massie Hughes crossed and left an indelible impression on the Hollywood director.

In 1943 John Ford did an interview about his reflections on the battle. He recalled the day before the battle, Commander Hughes asked him to join a search mission he was flying on a PBY. Ford remembered Hughes's southern accent saying, "Well, it looks like there is going to be a little trouble out there."[28] He paused and then restated, "Well it might be some trouble tomorrow, you and I are too damned old for this war anyway, so we better take the easy dog leg."[29] They took a segment of the aerial patrol route to the northeast. This day in early June proved very cloudy as Ford with his camera in hand looked down toward the Pacific somewhere below. However, a radar plot radioed to Hughes the nearby coordinates of aircraft believed to be friendly. Ford remembered being about sixty miles from Midway when a break in the clouds suddenly appeared, and they found two aircraft headed their way. They soon realized these were Japanese aircraft launched from a nearby cruiser. Hughes quickly ducked back into the cloudbank. Murphy's Law then struck, and the cloudbank protecting them gave way, and then Hughes took the PBY at full speed down toward the surface of the Pacific. Ford recalled, "We got down to about three feet from the water and really got some speed out of that old PBY."[30]

Of all aspects of the American victory at Midway, Ramsey was most proud of the aviation components of multiple service branches working seamlessly. In a letter to a close personal friend, Ramsey wrote, "When the battle of Midway came off we were fairly well organized and, for the first time in our history, aviation units of our Army, Navy and Marine Corps fought under a unified command."[31] In this same letter about his experience on Midway, he opened up to both the humor and the horror of the engagement. He wrote after the battle, "Radio Tokio 'sic' gave us some laughs. On June 4 the Japanese propaganda announced that they had captured Midway and freed the natives. On June 5 an additional statement stated while 10,000 men landed that the barbarous U.S. Marines came out of the woods and massacred them all." In his letter Ramsey remarked, "The only Jap I saw while on the Island was a dead aviator who crashed about 50 yards from our command center."[32] To his friend, he continued that returning to Pearl after the battle, "I received a pleasant surprise as Admiral Nimitz showed me a dispatch recommending my immediate promotion to Captain for my part in the battle. Two days later I put on my four stripes and pinned on the eagles and have been rather giddy ever since."[33]

Holding a dispatch written by his superior and naval aviation pioneer Patrick L. Bellinger that included a glowing endorsement, Ramsey read: "I consider that Commander Ramsey is largely responsible for the success of the air operations at Midway, that he is a thoroughly capable hard working, zealous all around officer fully qualified for promotion and I recommend most earnestly that in recognition of his excellent performance of duty at Naval Air Station, Midway, he be immediately promoted to the rank of captain, U.S. Navy."[34]

7
"Luminous Metallic Underworld"

The shipbuilders of Todd Shipyards in Tacoma, Washington, transformed a C3 merchant hull into USS *Block Island*, CVE 21. Welders, via a combination and ignition of explosive gases, produced searing heat, bending metal to their will. Viewed from afar, the shipyard welders labored in individual clouds of vapor, which were in fact fine particles of metallic oxides, fluorides, and silicates. In the interior of the vessel, workers could be heard yelling instructions to one another as they strung miles of electrical wiring, fitted hundreds of electrical fixtures, and installed vast amounts of piping for pressurized steam and water. Conversion witnessed the seamless blending of both analytical and practical vigor. Hatched by engineers in drawing rooms, the transformation was completed by male and female ship workers' brawn. As Logan Ramsey arrived at Todd Shipyards in late 1942 to oversee the conversion, he was thinking of the upcoming operations in the Pacific against the true enemy of the USN, the Empire of Japan. Shock came just days into 1943 when orders informed Ramsey of his upcoming mission in the Atlantic theater, not the Pacific. Ramsey, from Tacoma, wrote a personal friend in the upper levels of the Navy hierarchy, a Capt. Tom P. Jeter in the Navy Department in Washington on the staff to the commander in chief of the US fleet.

> Dear Tom:
>
> With respect to the fleet assignment of my ship (U.S.S. BLOCK ISLAND) I have been working all along on the premise that we were going to the Pacific.
>
> Now, under a date of January 2, 1943, we have received a 13th District diagram indicating that U.S.S. BLOCK ISLAND (delivery date March 12) is to be assigned to Carriers, Atlantic, and that U.S.S. BENTON (delivery date March 26) is going to Airpac, Pacific.
>
> Is there any way in which the BLOCK ISLAND could be shifted to the Pacific Fleet?
>
> If this can be done I would greatly appreciate it as I am very anxious to get another crack at the Japs. If the Atlantic assignment is going to stick I would appreciate that information,

> as I will have to cancel a lot of things that have been done already, such as requisitions for equipment, material, etc. and re-requisition gear for Atlantic service.
>
> Sincerely yours,
> Logan C. Ramsey"[1]

Ramsey's proposal fell upon deaf ears. *Block Island* was bound for the Atlantic.

On March 8, 1943, with construction completed, the Navy commissioned USS *Block Island*, CVE 21. The 465-foot vessel, with no aircraft or flight crew personnel, sailed out of Puget Sound with a skeleton crew. For the majority of the sailors, as the engines came to life they sailed the open ocean for the first time.[2] Seasickness and vomiting soon descended as the vessel left the sheltered waters. However, most of the men grew accustomed to the movement and earned their "sea legs."[3] One sailor recalled his first experience on an escort carrier as one of a "luminous metallic underworld."[4] This world below decks consisted of metal pipes, compartments, and glowing lightbulbs that when combined functioned as a small town, producing meals, providing laundry and showering facilities, and publishing a daily newspaper.

The men also experienced the noises at sea, the humming of pumps, the creaking of pipes as steam pressure ebbed and flowed, and the motions of the hull interacting with the Pacific.[5] Smells encountered included tobacco burning, cooks breaking in new galleys, and that of new paint. Sailors learned of the compartmentalized nature of war vessels. The interiors of the ships consisted of a series of compartments with watertight doors, called hatches, which sailors during drills quickly closed and dogged down. This prevented the spreading of water beyond the compartments compromised if the thin merchant hull ruptured and salt water poured into the exposed area. Navigating these barriers between the compartments produced bruised and bloody shins in the first days. Stairways to other levels of the vessel, called in the Navy "ladders," also produced injuries called "ladder chancres."[6] The sailors became acquainted with their new surroundings, learning the location of daily life, and the men around them. For the men on their first mission at sea, this first cruise seemed like a massive amount of movement and activity. Young sailors and a newly minted CVE morphed into an active aircraft carrier. Ramsey and the athletic officer stressed the playing of team sports on board, while in port and at sea, including volleyball, badminton, and basketball. Of these early days Ramsey is quoted as saying, "Teamwork was stressed."[7] Mistakes surfaced, of course, in these very early operations, including funny ones. One of Captain Ramsey's first orderlies hailed from South Philadelphia. Working late into the night, Ramsey slept in till 1000. When he arose he asked the orderly of any important messages that arrived while he was asleep. With a thick Philly accent, the orderly reported that at 0800 a messenger from the officer of the deck requested information as to whether the course should be changed or not. The orderly, thinking that the request was of little importance, told the messenger to go ahead and change course. Ramsey later said, "I immediately got a new orderly."[8]

In early 1943 women and men labored on assembly lines producing the weapons to win the war, but not the personnel to operate these machines. As the nation fought a war on two fronts simultaneously, the young sailors, soldiers, and airmen were hurriedly trained. For escort carriers, this training required breaking in new wooden flight decks for naval aviation with the first series of landings and takeoffs. The small size of the escort carrier greatly added to the difficultly of flight operations. As one pilot explained, "Looking down on a CV, you had the feeling you were going to land on a shingle. Looking down on a baby flat-top, you had the feeling you were going to land on a playing card—and it was probably a joker, at that."[9] Pilot Denny Moller, when in fleet operations, occasionally landed on an Essex-class carrier, which, after his experience operating on an escort carrier, appeared massive. After he was granted clearance to land on the fleet aircraft carrier, he would ask over the radio, "Which runway?"[10]

Planting a multi-ton aircraft moving forward at 150 knots on the very aft portion of a flight deck, which cruised into the wind at eighteen knots, and subject to the whims of the ocean, even for a seasoned pilot and deck crew was no easy feat. It proved stressful on seen and unseen parts of both machine and man. The controlled collision placed torque and strain on countless rivets, wires, and molded pieces of aircraft aluminum. Newton's third law states that one body exerting force on another simultaneously pushes back with the same amount of energy.[11] Hence, the flight deck crew paid constant surveillance to themselves and fellow sailors so that they did not became a part of this equation, as near-certain death awaited anyone hit by a landing plane or severed arresting cable. If all went as planned, the wooden flight deck composed of teak, the minute metal fastenings holding these wooden blocks together, and arresting cables absorbed the impacting energy. Rubber tires, specially designed landing gear, steel wires, tail hooks, engineering principles, and the bravado of young pilots molded together into an amazingly fast transfer of energy of a multi-ton aircraft, full of an assortment of fuel, weapons, and humans all in motion into a relatively stationary object in a matter of seconds. Movement still occurred as the CVE flight deck cruised forward at eighteen knots into whatever sea breeze that existed.

Simply watching carrier landings produced stress, as the famed war correspondent Ernie Pyle experienced firsthand. Pyle gained attention for reporting the story of enlisted men, not the generals and admirals making the major strategic decisions. Attracted to the stories of the enlisted men outside the newspaper headlines, Pyle was assigned to a light carrier (CVL), an expedient classification of carrier built on a Cleveland-class cruiser hull that was slightly longer than the escort carriers. Pyle wrote, "The smaller carriers have had very little credit and almost no glory, and I've always had a sort of yen for poor little ships that have been neglected."[12] Pyle visited and gathered the tales of those on board. Walking the passageways of the carrier, Pyle found two libraries, a daily newspaper, two dentists, and a chaplain. However, the activity outside on the flight deck captivated the seasoned war correspondent. On watching the landings, he wrote that "first time you see a plane land on a carrier you almost die."[13] The excitement mingled with nervousness of witnessing the ordeal affected not only his imagination but his body. Tensing up watching the controlled crashes left his muscles sore. His awe for the action of placing a plane safely on the deck knew no limit. His tribute to the operations on the carrier included writing, "For landing on a deck of a small carrier in a rough sea is just about like landing on half a block of Main Street while a combination hurricane and earthquake is going on."[14] While Pyle watched planes land on a "Main Street" of over 550 feet, the "Main Street" on *Block Island* was just over 450.[15]

While the flight deck held the activity of major excitement, many other happenings took place around the clock below decks. Men stripped and repaired aircraft engines, endlessly scrapped and painted portions of the vessel, and labored in the engine compartments, activities that all required energy for the sailors. The amount of human energy required grants a view into the scale of this floating operation. The 1944 edition of *The Cookbook of the U.S. Navy* includes a recipe for Knickerbocker Bean Soup. Served as the first course of one meal on board USN vessels, 1,000 eight-ounce servings required for this escort carrier included sixty-three pounds of dried navy beans, six pounds of cubed salt pork, forty-nine pounds of potatoes, and fifty-seven pounds of tomatoes.[16] This single soup course gives another measure for a vessel that produced over three thousand meals daily. Energy on board included not only a host of carbon-based fuels but the four million calories required daily for the crew at sea conducting such diverse activities as landing airplanes, washing dishes, and packing parachutes.

Escort carriers exemplify the massive growth of the USN during America's forty-five months in World War II. At the time of the attack on Pearl Harbor, the Navy retained only 383,000 personnel and just 790 vessels afloat.[17] The CVEs illustrated the massive growth not only of the numbers of ships but also of the number of sailors who breathed the fighting spirit into metal. Growth and change, by nature, are painful; likewise, the Navy experienced growing pains in its ballooning in the days after Pearl Harbor. For the first commanding officers of these new CVEs, like Ramsey, these pains were twofold. First, their orders called for turning a new class of vessel into a fighting ship. Second, in the case of *Block Island*, the crew was mostly composed of "green" personnel, which included the vast majority of the officers coming from the US Naval Reserve. From the officers down to the enlisted sailor, the Navy required a nearly ninefold increase in the number of fighting men. In managing this expansion, the Navy fell back onto men who possessed the most valuable tool of the USN, an education from its beloved Academy.

As Capt. Logan Ramsey took command of CVE 21 in March 1943, on his left hand was one of the few "nuggets" on board, a ring from the Academy exhibiting his membership in the 1919 class. His organizational skill, first crafted at the Academy, transformed this newly converted merchant hull, and the men under his command, into a cohesive fighting entity. The diversity of officers selected to be under Ramsey reflected the vast America of 150 million citizens. Reserve officers reporting to CVE 21 included an attorney from Philadelphia, a stockbroker from Wall Street, an accountant, and even a geologist.[18] Ramsey very quickly placed incredible amounts of trust onto these reserve officers, for he was human and needed to sleep. In Ramsey's handwriting on the inside cover of the Night Order Book are his standing night orders. Number three states, "ACT. Inform me of all events before action is necessary, if possible, *BUT*, if time does not permit, ACT FIRST and then inform me. This includes the opening of fire."[19] Standing night order #8 demonstrated the level of authority Ramsey placed with these officers. It reads, "If in action or contact with the enemy use any device on board without reference to me."[20]

The expansion of the enlisted sailors proved even more troublesome. One of the sailors of the newly commissioned CVE 21 exemplified the Navy's ever-expanding bureaucratic maze. Harold Shortridge hailed from Cottonwood, Arizona, where the most water he had ever seen flowed in the Verde River, where one could easily skip a rock completely across with little effort. Reporting to the USN for enlistment, Shortridge disclosed a skill set that caused a delay to his shipment to boot camp. He was a rarity of his generation in that he could type. Gobbled up by the induction office staff, he speedily produced the bureaucratic lifeblood of large organizations, more paperwork. After weeks of typing paperwork for new recruits, Shortridge received orders to report to CVE 21, without completing the training of boot camp, which included introduction to basic daily naval life, firefighting training, and receiving a medical examination. Once on board Shortridge explained his predicament; however, orders were orders in this expanding Navy. Thus, Shortridge read all he could get his hands on about Navy protocol, which paid off, since during general quarters, he was on the bridge next to Captain Ramsey.[21]

Reporting to Ramsey in Bremerton were fifty men for the radio department who were not "green." This cohort of radiomen, veterans of USS *Lexington*, CV 2, lost their vessel at the Battle of Coral Sea in May 1942, the first sea battle in history in which the enemy fleets never laid eyes on each other. Men such as these, who possessed critical experience in functioning on a fighting vessel, also held valuable knowledge on an aspect of technology just in its infancy at the time of Ramsey's birth. Near-instantaneous communication over hundreds of miles between multiple craft, including airplanes, ships at sea, and stations on land, was outside the conceptual framework of the American public during the administration of President William McKinley. These veteran radiomen retained nicknames, a symbol of their time served in the Navy. Men of the *Lexington* reporting to CVE 21 included a Sammy, Swivel Hips, Slick, and Snake.[22]

As CVE 21 cruised south off the coasts of Oregon and California, men labored in their new duties and working environments. Alarms screamed out GQ drills.[23] Once these sounded, the men had two minutes to reach their battle stations, requiring intimate knowledge of the layout of all portions of the ship. Every ladder, hatch, and doorway provided a chance to injure yourself. After two minutes, one observer noted, "every hatch and scuttle is bolted down, and every door is dogged tight, in order to confine fire, flooding, or other damage to the smallest possible area."[24] Repetitive drills ingrained in the men the knowledge of how to react without even thinking. Even in a dead sleep, muscle memory would automatically answer alarms and other orders. As one sailor wrote, "By the time shakedown is over, your subconscious hears the battle station alarm—your reflexes are automatic—when you wake up—there you are at your battle station—all dressed with lifebelt on."[25] However, Ramsey's task was to produce a crew not just for a warship but for a floating airfield. Docking in San Diego, CVE 21 moved into the next phase of Ramsey's lesson plan.

❋

The environs of the flight deck are savage. One veteran summed up, "No actuary on earth could list all the ways that you can get killed or maimed on a flight deck."[26] In speaking of a fleet aircraft carrier deck, he wrote, "Tolerances on a live flight deck are always small."[27] However, the crews of escort carriers operated on a compressed flight deck nearly half the size of that of the large CVs. All the dangers, the whirling propellers, bombs, machine-guns, and aviation fuel, were restricted to this 450-foot-long wooden deck of CVE 21. Tolerances were a fraction above nil.

Reporting to Captain Ramsey in San Diego was the commanding officer of VC-6 (originally designated VC-25), John L. Counihan, an Annapolis 1932 graduate, and his orders called for the training of his squadron to track, locate, and destroy submarines from the deck of CVE 21. On April 10, 1943, this freshly assembled squadron sailed into the blue Pacific on their first shipboard assignment. With their FM-1 Wildcats and TBF Avengers dogged down by chains in the hangar deck, the men prepared for operations from these smallest of floating airfields. As the first aircraft lifted off, these men flew over the Pacific and looked back at a virgin carrier deck. The first days of landings on the carrier proved dangerous not only for the pilots and the aircrews in the planes but for the men working on the flight deck as well. Of these opening operations one officer wrote that they "were catastrophic to materiel and harrowing to the fliers as well as the ship's company."[28]

Ramsey realized his men had a long way to go, and much to learn, before ship and air group were ready to take on the Axis enemy. However, after six weeks of training and drilling off the California coast, which of course included damaged aircraft as the result of accidents, all were deemed ready for war. For even in accidents knowledge was gained. Personnel quickly removed damaged aircraft from the flight deck, mechanics learned the skills of repairing mangled planes, and the crew below decks gained experience in their multitude of other tasks. Ever mindful of his responsibly of crafting a virgin carrier and a green crew into a vessel worthy of war, Ramsey still remained a father to his two children. During this period Ramsey sent his daughter Mary Ann a short note on USS *Block Island* stationery along with a collection of black-and-white images that included photographs of him and Massie Hughes together. He wrote, "Comdr. John Ford just sent me these blow ups of snaps he took at Midway. The damaged people you see are the chaps we rescued from rubber boats after the battle. Lots of love, Daddy."[29]

With VC-6 still aboard, after a month and a half of training operations, CVE 21 plowed south away from the California coast for the Atlantic. Ramsey had in fact invited John Ford on this trip. He wrote, "While Security will not permit me to go into details, you might check up on my prospective employment and consider making what I expect would be about a two-week trip with me. You could use my cabin as at sea I always sleep in the sea cabin. It probably wouldn't be as exciting as the last time we were together, but, on the other hand, you might get some good stuff."[30] Leaving on May 22, 1943, and escorted by USS *McCook*, DD 496, the two ships cruised in predetermined zigzag patterns toward Panama. Operational training, however, continued, and on May 30 planes of VC-6 launched a surprise Sunday morning attack on the defenses of the Panama Canal. Ramsey's training paid off: the weeks of consistent operations transformed this "green" crew into a streamlined fighting unit. Returning safely to the deck, the men climbed out of their cockpits and congratulated one another.[31] One witness remembered that "the jubilant young pilots declared [the attack] would have knocked that artery of shipping out of commission for years."[32]

One unique individual, a civilian artist, witnessed the return of VC-6 from its practice attack. Roy Crane, a successful cartoonist, was developing a Sunday cartoon strip about a carrier pilot. The Navy, never bashful in self-promotion of its service and vessels, retained a long tradition of boosting its image through the use of media in the forms of print and film. While movie stars like Errol Flynn showcased the Navy on the big screen, an additional form of promotion included a possible weekly cartoon strip. Stationed on CVE 21 during its cruise to the

Atlantic, Crane gathered material for his artistic creation. He witnessed flight operations, spoke with members of the crew, and even submitted a cartoon for the *Block Island* newspaper. As the vessel's paper reported, Crane's goal was to obtain a "genuine flavor of the Navy, the actual color of ship-board life are the objectives of the illustrator."[33]

However, once Crane's artistic imagination produced a strip for national newspapers, his character did not fly off the deck of an escort carrier. Crane's character, *Buz Sawyer*, seen by the American public on a weekly basis, flew off and fought from the large CV. His promotion of aircraft carriers centered on the large carriers taking the war directly to the enemy in pitched battles against Japanese naval forces. The cartoons that show Sawyer's vessel include the massive flight deck and tall super-structure of a CV.[34] Crane neglected the escort carriers in his cartoon strips. In portraying naval aviation during the war, Crane shunned not only the escort carriers but also the main mission of the VC-6 pilots he witnessed in training, that of pilots and aircrew hunting U-boats in the Atlantic. Crane selected the excitement of depicting an individual pilot in the air war against Japanese Zeros, rather than the often less-conclusive results of naval aviation in the Battle of the Atlantic.

For most of the young men of CVE 21, passing through the Panama Canal granted them their first views of the tropics. Outside of those from the Deep South, most had never seen anything like this ecosystem, and the sights and sounds of the jungle, which unfolded as their ship traversed a continent. Gone were the cold spring days of Bremerton and the cool open sea during training operations off California, replaced by the warm, humid air of May in Central America, which also altered the living conditions inside the ship, with men requiring only a sheet at night. Gunner's Mate Third Class Irv Biron served as the captain's messenger and thus spent many hours on the bridge. Captain Ramsey was well respected by the young sailors. Biron remembered him and Captain Ramsey both looking with binoculars at the unique landscape around them as the escort carrier passed though the canal. He recalled, "He and I went through the canal side by side looking at all the gun installations. He would say, 'Look, Biron, over there, two o'clock.'" Biron said, "It was a big honor for me, because he was a father to us kids, and we were just kids, believe me."[35]

In the Gulf of Mexico, air operations commenced once again. The dangers of the flight deck soon surfaced. A particularly violent landing destroyed a plane, but luckily no human costs transpired, with the pilot walking away from the crash. The plane, beyond repair, was to be pushed overboard. As the crew gathered around the plane, like ants working together in moving an obstacle, near disaster struck. Radioman First Class Jeb Turner, pushing with the others near the end of the wing, realized just before the plane went over the side that his sleeve was entangled with the tip of the wing. Pulled by his arm to the edge of the flight deck by the wing tip, Turner's quick mind devised his only recourse, to jump parallel to and away from the fuselage of the aircraft. This athletic step worked, freeing him from the plane as gravity pulled both Turner and the mangled machine toward the Caribbean waters. Splashing into the sea several feet from the aircraft, Turner swam away safely. Luckily, the DD escort *McCook*, following CVE 21, witnessed Turner's plight and quickly plucked him from the seas.

Later in the day, a breeches buoy, a canvas sack, and a system of ropes that allowed for the transfer of men and supplies between ships while still in motion, brought Turner back home to CVE 21. Very quickly a chorus of boos, curses, and shaking fists erupted from the men of *McCook*. Normally, the screening escorting vessel rescued a pilot from the waters after his aircraft crashed in the act of landing or taking off. Thus, the individual saved would in all likelihood be an officer; however, there were enlisted pilots during the war. Under normal conditions, with the naval aviator safely delivered to his carrier, the thankful crew paid tribute to the escort by inserting several gallons of ice cream into the empty returning canvas sack. Receiving no ice cream tribute on this particular rescue, the men of *McCook* vocally rebelled. Turner later recalled, "It was at that time that I became aware that the life of an enlisted man was worth less than a canister of ice cream."[36]

One week after passing through the Panama Canal, CVE 21 cruised north up along the American eastern seaboard and pulled into her new home at Pier 7, Norfolk Naval Base, Virginia. Once docked, the remaining air group personnel of VC-6 were transferred off, fully trained to take on the German U-boat menace.[37] At this point in the war in April 1943, the escort carrier USS *Bogue*, CVE 9, was pioneering operations known as hunter-killer missions, taking the war to the enemy. Based out of naval facilities in Newfoundland and Iceland, Capt. Giles E. Short led the first hunter-killer mission, which, at this early stage, still followed either an east- or westbound Allied convoy. March and April provided no results; however, in the month of May, *Bogue*'s Composite Squadron VC-9 gathered some success and hinted at the possibilities of the effectiveness of the hunter-killer task force. On the early evening of May 21, Lt. Cdr. William M. Drane, CO of VC-9, located a surfaced U-boat. Drane, from the cockpit of his Avenger, dropped four depth bombs on the conning tower of U-231. While not sinking the vessel, the attack forced the U-boat back to France for repairs.[38] Captain Ramsey wished for his men and ship to prove themselves in these newly formed hunter-killer missions; however, the logistical magicians of the USN had other plans.

The stoppage allowed the men to explore Norfolk, with its very strong connection to the USN. Situated at the entrance of Chesapeake Bay, Norfolk was the largest naval base on the entire eastern seaboard, thus home for many of the USN's vessels battling in the Atlantic. Not only were the docks massive in number to hold a range of vessels, but also the city itself represented the largest town most of the sailors had ever seen. One sailor recalled in his memoirs not only the impression of the scale of Norfolk but also an important factor for young men at sea for weeks: beer. He wrote, "Beer gardens in Norfolk were easier to find than a traffic light."[39]

In these beer joints, the "green" crew mingled with seasoned sailors with years at sea. Older arms held bottles of beer and displayed the symbols of Navy life, not ones issued by the Navy but personal tattoos acquired in ports both foreign and domestic. They included X-rated images of women, and naval themes such as anchors and mermaids. One young sailor recalled, "The very best tattoos were on those who had served in the Asiatic fleet where the Michelangelo's of the tattoo artist plied their trade."[40] Beyond the beer joints and seeing the sheer scale of the Navy's presence in Norfolk, an additional factor also loomed for those sailors never before below the Mason-Dixon Line. For many, this was their first time visiting not only a city in the East but one in the South. For white sailors who lived their entire short lives north of the Mason-Dixon Line, venturing off ship included experiencing segregated America. Water fountains, sections of public buses and trains, and neighborhoods retained clear delineations based on white and black.[41] However, the experience of these new environs was short-lived, as the first war mission awaited *Block Island*.

8
"Better Part of Six Years"

Renowned naval historian Samuel Eliot Morison described the Battle of the Atlantic as "second to none in its influence on the outcome of the war."[1] In his *History of the United States Naval Operations in World War II*, volume 1, *The Battle of the Atlantic, September 1939–1943*, he wrote about the complexity of the operations that made it "exceedingly difficult to relate in an acceptable literary form."[2] Of the battle another scholar wrote, "It was a huge affair, involving hundreds of U boats, thousands of ships, aircraft and people and it lasted for the better part of six years."[3] For over two thousand days the Battle of the Atlantic mirrored a chessboard, with surface vessels plying the oceans, enemy submarines cruising both on and under the seas, and airplanes scouting and hunting from the skies. Over the course of the war, the Allies attacked U-boats with an array of weapons, including depth charges, torpedoes, and later rockets. The location and tracking of U-boats included the use of radio, sonar, and magnetic detection. Development in detection and weapons made the Battle of the Atlantic primarily a technological struggle. Transcending technology, the unpredictable and harsh weather patterns in the North Atlantic produced boisterous seas that impacted all operations.[4] The battle was the longest and most complex naval operation in human history—as attested by thousands of wreckages that serve as tombs for sailors resting on the Atlantic's bottom.[5]

The very month *Block Island* entered offensive operations in the Battle of the Atlantic, Captain Ramsey in *Proceedings* published an essay entitled, "The Aero-Amphibious Phase of the Present War." Descriptively and colorfully he addressed that innovation in warfare was nothing new. He wrote, "With each new step in the development of transportation came the inevitable adaptation of the new vehicles to the grim business of war. The Egyptian chariot, the elephant of the Carthaginians, and even the cavalry of Genghis Khan, were the direct, if remote, ancestors of modern mechanized warfare."[6] He went on to argue that the simultaneous inventions of the internal combustion engine and the airplane produced "a metamorphosis in terrestrial warfare to a point where an understanding of the strategy and tactics of the vehicle became of equal importance to a similar knowledge of the old rules concerning land warfare."[7] Ramsey theorized that after 1914 theorists broke down modern warfare into seven forms of fighting, these being "terrestrial, aero-terrestrial, naval, aero-naval, aerial, amphibious, and aero-amphibious."[8] He suggested that for commanders, whether on land or sea, to continue with this antiquated conclusion was risking their understanding to suffer from compartmentalization, and the warfare seen in the current conflict waging was much too fluid and nimble to fit into this rigid categorization. He argued, "Instead, there is only one species of war, even though it may be characterized by fighting on land, sea, and in the air, with various types of vehicles carrying many kinds of weapons."[9] One can clearly see the impact of command at the Battle of Midway just two years previous to this publication with his oversight of all land-based aircraft (both USN and US Army Air Corps) on the islands.

Although Ramsey sought reassignment of CVE 21 to the Pacific theater, he strongly wrote about the difficulty of waging war against the German U-boats. This was going to be no cakewalk. As a student of history, Ramsey started his discussion with the last conflict and stated that before 1914 the only way for an enemy to successfully exercise command of the sea was via winning a decisive battle. He wrote, "In that year the appearance of the long range submarine provided a means by which the inferior naval power could, and did, attempt to deny its stronger adversary the advantages naturally accruing from his command of the sea."[10] President Woodrow Wilson during the Great War colorfully addressed the problem of the coalition of allies for the first time confronting the U-boat menace. Wilson stated, "We are hunting hornets all over the farm and letting the nest alone."[11] The complexity of naval warfare, and its costs, in this second go at the U-boats Ramsey foresaw as both time-consuming and deadly. While there might be more glory and immediate tangible satisfaction in assisting in the Pacific island-hopping campaigns by strafing enemy troops and shooting down Japanese Zeros, Ramsey did not see the Battle of the Atlantic as any less critical or complicated. As he wrote, "The combination of airplane and submarine has converted the previously simple problem of exercising command of the sea into one of extreme complexity and great difficulty. Eternal vigilance, ceaseless patrolling, and disheartening losses from hostile attrition efforts must be expected. The surmounting of German submarine activity alone is a truly stupendous problem, and one that requires a vast expenditure in patrol vessels, escorts, seamen, and aircraft."[12]

❋

When *Block Island* entered the fray in May 1943, the Battle of the Atlantic had reached a turning point. Two months earlier the Germans achieved what would be their peak of success in constricting supply routes to both Britain and Russia, with 108 merchant ships sunk with the loss of just fourteen U-boats. However, in

Figure 3. In convoy on her first mission in the Atlantic, P-47 Army Air Corps fighters destined for the skies of Europe were strapped down to the deck of CVE 21 bound for Belfast. On this mission her sailors received their first taste of the Atlantic in foul weather. Courtesy of the USS Block Island Association.

May the number of Allied ships lost was reduced to only fifty, and the German U-boat losses increased to forty.[13] The Battle of the Atlantic involved code breakers, shipbuilders, airmen, logisticians, and scientists; thus, any attempt to select a single reason for this shift in May 1943 is a fool's errand. As one historian wrote, "But there was no single panacea, no miracle weapon, device, or even intelligence breakthrough that would win the Atlantic campaign for the Allies."[14] One major step forward for the Allies was the near elimination of merchant ships sailing independently in the North Atlantic after 1942. Via grouping merchant ships in convoys, which were normally accompanied with Allied war vessels in various configurations of screening missions, the dangers from U-boat encounters reduced (at least statistically) for any given merchant vessel.[15] While Logan Ramsey was keen on taking USS *Block Island* with an air group into the Atlantic in active pursuit of enemy U-boats, his first two missions would be in the role of shuttling war materiel across on the North Atlantic as part of a convoy.

The Allies, by the spring of 1942, were up against Adm. Karl Dönitz's "tonnage war" strategy. In the U-boat commander's war diary, an entry dated April 15, 1942, reads as follows: "The enemy's shipping constitutes one single, great entity. It is therefore immaterial where a ship is sunk. Once it has been destroyed, it has to be replaced by a new ship; and that's that. In the long run the result of the war

Figure 4. A tug pulling CVE 21 into harbor at Belfast, loaded with weapons for the European theater. The capital of Northern Ireland would be the first foreign port visited for most of her newly minted sailors. Courtesy of the USS Block Island Association.

will depend on the result of the race between sinkings and new construction."[16] The Allies in confronting this strategy would employ a range of countermeasures, including new weapons, enemy detection, and operational tactics. One such countermeasure was the deployment of CVEs into the Battle of the Atlantic in seeking to destroy lurking U-boats. In the late spring and early summer of 1943, the escort carriers USS *Bogue*, CVE 9, and USS *Card*, CVE 11, began leading hunter-killer missions, which entailed operating with a contingent of other vessels and aircraft in the offensive action of tracking and destroying enemy U-boats. Prime hunting was found in the mid-air gap outside of the range of land-based bombers, where before the Germans had found little to no harassment. These CVE missions by the sister carriers of USS *Block Island*, CVE 21, decreased the overall effectiveness of the German U-boats and thus assisted in increasing the flow of American arms and military personnel to the European theater in order to take the war directly to Germany.[17]

❋

CVE 21 entered the Battle of the Atlantic not in leading hunter-killer missions but rather in running supplies as part of a convoy bound for Britain. As the escort carrier pushed off into New York Harbor, and her single screw clawed for the first time in the direction of the open ocean of the Atlantic, the carrier hauled an abnormally large number of aircraft. In this mission she acted not as a floating airfield in launching planes but in transporting aircraft for the US Army Air Corps. Stuffed on both the hangar and flight decks, P-47 fighters destined for the European air war were latched down. Engine spaces and cockpits were tightly shrouded against the Atlantic seas. Pushing off from Staten Island on July 17, 1943, CVE 21 was part of a convoy of other escorts, including troopships transporting American forces to the United Kingdom. The North Atlantic proved kind on this nine-day journey, and CVE 21 entered Holy Loch and moored in Northern Ireland at the Royal Air Force's Sydenham Airfield on the outskirts of Belfast. Soon after, cranes lifted the recently unshrouded fighters, and once on the ground mechanics prepared the P-47s for flight. Pilots climbed in and fired up these massive Pratt & Whitney R-2800 Double Wasp engines, taxied onto the short runway, and then took off over the Irish hills bound for bases in England.[18]

While these planes were offloaded, most sailors of CVE 21 experienced their first foreign nation. Walking the streets of Belfast, they witnessed cars driving on the opposite side of the road. Since joining the Navy, they heard accents from all over America, but the locals here could hardly be understood. Dining on Irish food and drink, the sailors talked with the locals, learning a taste of Irish humor. One *Block Island* sailor, on receiving a pint of room-temperature beer and his first foreign meal, complained to the barkeep. His mutton was cold and his pint of Guinness was warm. The barkeep, referring to Great Britain battling World War II since 1939 and the United States just entering the war, quipped back, "Well, myte, it's been a-settin' here waitin' fer you fer three years!"[19]

Departing Belfast on August 3, and joining a convoy off the coast of Scotland, CVE 21 headed back west for the one-week journey to New York.[20] Taking these men into battle soon enough, and as a lifelong member of the Navy, Ramsey understood the psychological need of these young men to blow off steam when the time presented itself on shore. Thus, Ramsey hosted a party at the Roosevelt Hotel on Forty-Fifth Street for the crew in midtown Manhattan, just a block away from Grand Central Station. To describe this place as iconic is an understatement. Opened in 1924, no other place in New York better symbolized the Roaring Twenties. Guy Lombardo and his orchestra started wowing the crowds in the ballroom in 1929, starting a tradition that lasted thirty years.[21] The young sailors of CVE 21 walked around ornate cloth-draped tables, saw the organizational skills of a maître d' in action, and experienced tuxedoed waiters seeking them out personally for a drink order. For those from rural areas, some of whom were southerners who never owned a pair of shoes until they enlisted, this was another world.

However, they knew of this place, and in a sense nearly all had experienced it in the past via radio. For years, in the Roosevelt Grill, radio broadcasts of New Year's

Eve took place. The first song after New Year's played by Guy Lombardo and the orchestra, which through the radio became a national tradition, was "Auld Lang Syne." The famed lyrics derive from the Scots-language poem of Robert Burns, written in 1788, and start with, "Should old acquaintance be forgot, and never thought upon."[22] As the drinks flowed that August night in 1943, the men of CVE 21 experienced a celebration long remembered. As one wrote decades later, "Few sailors of the *Block Island* will ever forget the huge party in the grand ballroom of the Hotel Roosevelt."[23]

The time in New York allowed the sailors to explore, see the tallest buildings in the world, and walk the streets that formed canyons. Subway outlets coughed out an unending stream of citizens headed about their daily routines. One sailor recalled riding the subway as "wilder that riding a mule with a sore back."[24] Central Park also attracted *Block Island* sailors in the hopes of meeting and chatting up the one thing completely banned from the ship, women. Parachute Rigger First Class Hector Vernetti, of Globe, Arizona, and another shipmate were successful in meeting two women. A short conversation turned into visiting a nearby bar for an afternoon cocktail. Vernetti, not a big drinker, was introduced to the Cuba Libre (rum and Coke). Before he knew it, he was beyond imbibed.

Vernetti awoke the next morning and, seeing no piping on the ceiling, was confused as to his location. Waking up in an unknown apartment, in the next room he found the two women sleeping. Thinking through the fog, Vernetti realized the last time they saw his shipmate, he was lying on the street. Vernetti needed two pieces of information: where he was and how to get back to his ship. One of the women tried to simply explain this by the streets and avenues of the city, which meant nothing to this young man from the White Mountains of eastern Arizona. He asked her to draw him a map—which worked—and as he ran on board he heard roll call taking place on the hangar deck. Luckily, Vernetti's last name did not start with a letter at the front of the alphabet. As the names were yelled out in ascending order, the sailor would yell back, "Here!" Just as the V's were reached, Vernetti was in position to shout "Here!"[25]

Vernetti's lack of experience in urban landscapes did not equate to lacking sophistication, for he had international experience without even realizing it, a statement that requires explanation. Born to Italian immigrants in the northern Mexican province of Sonora, Vernetti moved to Globe, Arizona, before entering school. This small adjustment in location did not feel much like immigration to his parents, for the locals in Globe also spoke a mixture of English and Spanish. In fact, this was hardly a transition at all in comparison to crossing the Atlantic fleeing Italy. In the summer months of his youth, Vernetti crossed the border between the United States and Mexico countless times on horseback as he pushed cattle with his uncle in the mountains of southern Arizona and northern Sonora. While this international border meant something to government bureaucrats in Washington, DC, and Mexico City, folks living on both sides of this imaginary line, which crosses the deserts and sky islands of this region of North America, traversed it without much thought. With American entry into the war, Vernetti migrated west by loading up his Model A Ford and driving a full day down and over the Superstition Mountains. The migratory pull factor was a well-paying job building aircraft canopies for PBY flying boats constructed by Goodyear Aircraft Corporation in a town outside of Phoenix called Goodyear, Arizona. In realizing he would be drafted, he signed up for the Navy rather than the Army, thinking, "I would rather swim than walk through mud."[26] Vernetti did not realize till later the irony of this prophecy, for his first assigned vessel was fated to sink in the Battle of the Atlantic.

❋

While some men explored New York, others on *Block Island* docked at Staten Island again chained down P-47s on board. Pushing off on August 21, CVE 21 this time cruised to the Atlantic not in a convoy of transports but with three World War I era destroyers. As the calendar pushed toward the final days of summer, CVE 21 did not experience the placid waters of the North Atlantic on her last run. On this mission the carrier maneuvered in thick fog, thus giving the officers and crew their first lesson in the value of a new technological innovation, radar.[27]

For this generation of young men, the concept of a detection system utilizing invisible waves resembled science-fiction storylines. For many sailors raised in homes without electricity, the concept of radar sounded like the realm of the comic strip. Buck Rogers, the most famous of futuristic heroes, made his first appearance in 1928 in a novel titled *Armageddon 2419 A.D.* He quickly spiraled into a comic strip entertaining American children with a storyline based on Rogers from the present crashing in a dirigible at the North Pole and waking up some five hundred years later to find the world under the control of a ruthless dictator.[28] Using a host of futuristic weapons and machines, Rogers battled for representative government and the notion of democracy five centuries in the future. For those raised on a steady diet of comics, hearing of radar seeing beyond the capabilities of the human eye blended fiction with fact. Many questions surrounded this new operating system, as it assisted CVE 21 maneuvering blindly through a thick fog bank with a number of navigational hazards. As one officer remembered, "it convinced the topside officers of the value of a 'gadget' they hitherto had viewed with considerable skepticism."[29] Radar data broke with centuries of tradition where a vessel's perception of its environs was relayed verbally, either by shouting or by radio. Now information came in the visual form of images on a screen.[30] However, thick fog was just one hazard encountered on the North Atlantic seas.

Samuel Eliot Morison considered the dangers of the North Atlantic seas just as deadly as the German U-boats. He wrote, "Winds of gale force, mountainous seas, biting cold, body-piercing fog and blinding snow squalls were the rule rather than the exception."[31] In the five months between November 1942 and March 1943, ninety-two merchant vessels sank due to weather alone.[32] As *Block Island* cruised to Belfast, the placid North Atlantic from their previous mission disappeared, replaced by driving rain, pockets of thick fog, and the largest waves this hull had yet encountered. On the last day of August 1943, the vessel found relief from the heaving seas by pulling into Belfast Harbor, and one more time moored at the RAF base on the outskirts of Belfast. After three days of intensive unloading of the P-47s, *Block Island* sailed back west.[33] During this mission the crew learned a very personal physics lesson related to displacement. One sailor recalled, "Going over was murder, and coming back was worse because we were empty."[34] In the voyage over to Northern Ireland, CVE 21 struggled with the rough sea packed with warplanes that added ballast. Going home empty, the same waves caused massive oscillation. Seasickness reigned and the galley was forced to close. Sailors held on and thought of anything stationary particularly the next piece of land they would step foot on. As a young sailor from Arizona, Hector Vernetti wished to see the force causing this attack on his ship. In the hangar deck, he carefully climbed a ladder to the catwalk, where a hatch opened and allowed him to see out. Peering out, the scene at first reminded him of his native White Mountains, as the vessel lay in a valley between two ranges, and then he realized that these mountains were massive waves that dwarfed their 10,000-ton aircraft carrier.

Riding these storms together, the crew members formed bonds. Lacking privacy on board, sailors quickly learned of the backgrounds of those around them. They came from small farming communities and large urban centers, western states and the commonwealths of the East, and the plains of the Midwest to the bayous of the South. One sailor described his ship as "a small, floating United Nations."[35] Among just the thirty-six men of the Radio Gang on CVE 21, names included DeVanna, Maslanka, Cousineau, Connolly, and Boudreaux.[36] The ethnic diversity included not only a range of surnames in the ship's manifest but also tangible evidence of the recent migrations. Many sailors grew up in bilingual households where languages such as German, Norwegian, and Italian were spoken at the dinner table.

Block Island plowed on, anchoring off Hampton Roads on September 10.[37] Ramsey was about to receive new orders for a new role. The crew earned its sea legs in two missions shuttling P-47s to the European theater. *Block Island* would now actively track down U-boats, as opposed to avoiding them.

9

"The Lord Looks Out for Drunks, Small Children, and CVEs"

Despite their relatively small appearance, the USN quickly found new uses for the small carriers, which commenced with the experimental conversion of a cargo hull into a carrier, USS *Long Island*, CVE 1. Her genealogy can be traced back to a 1935 Navy report on the possibility of converting merchant hulls into small carriers, "for quick action when the war emergency required the conversion of merchant type vessels into auxiliary aircraft carriers." Half a dozen years later, a "war emergency" occurred, and CVEs initially performed necessary auxiliary duties. CVE 1 materialized in the early months of 1941. Small and slow, she had no island on the starboard side of the flight deck and held just a handful of outdated aircraft. Whereas the CVs took years to construct, *Long Island* was hastily converted in just three months.[1] While no fleet carrier in terms of speed, armament, or appearance, she answered the question of carrier logistics in aircraft transport and providing aircraft cover in escorting convoys.

In May 1942, six months after Pearl Harbor, the *Washington Post* reported on the role of carrier aviation in an article titled "Aircraft Carrier Is Navy's New Queen of the Seas." It stated, "For it is now generally accepted naval doctrine that the carrier has supplanted the battleship as the chief 'punch' of the sea."[2] The article outlined the plan of constructing eighteen large fleet aircraft carriers. Added to the seven CVs already in the fleet, these proposed vessels would take the war to the Japanese Navy. It stated, "The bigger, faster craft, protected by cruisers and destroyers, will be in the forefront of the battle."[3] The piece also reported that as the USN was in such short supply of carriers, it was implementing an expedited measure. As reported, "Many [carriers] will be slower, smaller vessels, probably something like the U.S.S. Long Island, [a] former cargo ship."[4] The large fleet carriers represented the future, but with the construction costs and years required to build, smaller carriers refitted from cargo hulls would fill a desperate void with short construction times and at greatly reduced cost. In describing these vessels, the reporter wrote, "Such carriers, however, cannot go within range of enemy bombers or warships without running serious risk of being sunk."[5] The article also stated, "The slower, more vulnerable carriers . . . will remain a considerable distance from the scene of operations."[6]

Months later, the actions of a single escort carrier did receive some positive press. In 1943 the *Washington Post* reported on an unnamed CVE that completed a task well beyond its intended support role, as her aircraft struck Japanese ground forces on the Alaskan Aleutian Islands. While the piece noted the success of the mission and the expanded role of escort carriers, their secondary rank to the large fleet aircraft carriers was clearly explained to readers. Terms used in describing these vessels included "baby flat-tops," "pocket carriers," and "auxiliary carriers."[7] Whereas this particular vessel successfully took on the enemy, their overall status in the Navy hierarchy was made quite clear. These were not the majestic fleet carriers of the future. While this particular escort carrier proved itself, CVEs remained "auxiliary" in nature.

The American output of weapons after the strong isolationism in the interwar period was remarkable but did come with a high price for CVE sailors. In January 1942 the Kaiser Corporation won a government contract to produce fifty CVEs of the Casablanca class. One of these fifty was the aforementioned *Liscome Bay*, which in taking a single Japanese torpedo strike in November of 1943 exploded in amazing violence as the entire bomb magazine ignited and killed over six hundred sailors on board. The stories of this massive explosion from just one torpedo strike caused much fear and anxiety for the CVE crews, especially for those like the crew of *Block Island* charged with taking on the U-boat menace in the Atlantic. Rumors and nicknames about the CVEs passed quickly among new crew members. These included the CVE standing for "combustible-vulnerable-expendable," "Kaiser coffins," and "two-torpedo carriers." Of the latter, one reporter wrote, "One torpedo, the sailors reasoned derisively, would be the one that would sink it, and the second would simply pass over the sinking ship's flight deck."[8] These factors highlighted an irony of modern naval warfare; while one faced the danger of drowning in a vessel, a very real cause of death could be burning—either from explosions in the forms of enemy bombs and torpedoes or from the eruption of steam pipes on board. Burning to death in the bowels of the vessel was a very real fear and possibility.[9] One naval scholar described this aspect of modernity with "a special horror in the kind of instantaneous mass death that naval combat was capable of producing."[10] With these images in their minds, in the autumn of 1943 the crew of *Block Island* set out on their first hunter-killer mission armed with a composite fighter squadron to hunt U-boats.

Sailors going to battle confronted fears and the possibility of their young lives ending violently short. The Navy addressed these issues by assigning a chaplain to larger vessels. In the case of *Block Island*, this was reserve officer Lt. Gordon A. MacInnes. One of the biggest challenges for MacInnes, as an officer born in the last century and now in his forties, was breaking the ice in talking with the young enlisted men. MacInnes carried a pocketful of peanuts, and handing these out provided a means of starting a conversation with sailors. The enlisted men developed a nickname for him, "Peanut." As the only chaplain on board, his assignment called for a very ecumenical approach. Trained in the Presbyterian faith, he approached French Catholics and gave them rosaries and prayer books. He also sought out men of unique ethical philosophies in 1940s America. Seaman First Class Patrick Chan, a Chinese American, was raised on Confucian thought. Often these two men, from very different backgrounds, shared lunch and held lively discussions on the social and ethical comparisons of their upbringings.[11] With faith on many of the men's minds, *Block Island* changed roles from avoiding to seeking enemy contact.

❋

Growing up in Oakland, California, Irv Biron saw snow only once, in the distant mountains. Biron experienced more kinds of cold weather than he thought possible on the Atlantic seas in the winters of 1943 and 1944. In his battle station manning one of the 40 mm guns on the port side of the carrier, Biron wore three layers of clothing to survive the cold and snow.[12] The CVE-led hunter-killer groups cruised in the central Atlantic which, at this stage of the war, provided the best hunting grounds. More specifically, they searched an area called the "black pit," which was unreachable for Allied land-based aircraft.[13] While Allied land-based bombers and blimps suppressed U-boat activity by denying them the ability to remain surfaced for extended periods during the daylight hours, the "black pit" offered U-boats safety from shore-based aircraft. On this new mission, Biron watched *Block Island*'s fighter planes take off and hunt the elusive enemy lurking below the Atlantic waves. In concert with *Block Island*'s warplanes, World War I era destroyers worked in unison to locate and destroy the German menace.[14]

One military historian wrote of this tactic, "So the U boat skipper saw aircraft winging across the No-Man's-Land sky of mid-ocean where only Lindbergh and a few others had previously flown."[15] Previous to mid-1943, U-boat captains felt free to surface in the central Atlantic. The very first Allied naval aircraft aloft from the CVE decks of *Bogue* and *Card* above the "black pit" hinted at the future success of hunter-killer task forces. One author described this new threat with the analogy, "The CVE was quarterback of a team, a destroyer group devoted solely to the enterprise of sinking Nazi submarines."[16] The CVE coached the task force team by calling the plays for the fighter planes and destroyer escorts (DE) in locating and eliminating the U-boat threat. While not the first such "quarterback," *Block Island* played a critical role in probing this U-boat safe haven. This mission placed Captain Ramsey in a unique position in that he had almost total freedom in hunting the enemy. In most missions a new captain was just one part of a massive operation involving hundreds of ships. However, Ramsey experienced a freedom of command unique in modern warfare. One historian wrote, "These orders were a joy to the young escort carrier commanders, making them feel as free sounding as John Paul Jones or Lord Nelson."[17] In a speech to naval officers, Ramsey said, "Practically all of the *Block Island's* trips were independent missions. Just hunting for subs, you might say."[18]

While a carrier houses a city at sea below decks, the offensive punch is the air group she houses. The composite squadron VC-1, consisting of nine Wildcats (FM-1) and twelve Avengers (TBF-1-C), boarded CVE 21 in the middle of September. Intensive training off the Virginia coast allowed the thirty-two pilots of VC-1 to hone their skills in searching the seas.[19] In contrast to the battles against the Japanese, with large surface fleets and dogfighting between opposing aircraft, the experience of the pilots of VC-1 in the Atlantic resembled searching for a needle in a haystack. The needle could take the form of a sighted periscope or the silhouette of a surfaced U-boat at night. Adrenaline-filled hours of dogfighting in the Pacific were contrasted with dull hours of searching the Atlantic's surface. Eyes would strain looking for clues, such as droplets of oil spotted from above, pointing to a wounded U-boat lurking below. They searched for faint signs of the elusive enemy rarely seen.

For modern-day observers, it is easy to view World War II aircraft with a hint of nostalgia, or even as relatively simple propeller-powered inventions from a bygone era displayed at a museum devoted to aviation. But to do this misses the complexity and awe these weapons systems inspired in young sailors at the time. For a generation with a better understanding of a Model T Ford than the complexity of a radial engine, these craft represented some of the most advanced stages of American technological know-how. An insight into this perspective is seen in the memoir of Alvin Kernan, who in describing the Avenger wrote that it "looked like some spaceship bound for Mars."[20]

An Avenger, TBF-1, a massive aircraft, with a single Wright-constructed air-cooled radial engine, produced 1,700 hp. Large enough for a crew to include a pilot, bombardier, and gunner, the aircraft when empty and unarmed weighed over five tons. With wings folded out, the craft measured fifty-four feet wide, making for harrowing landings on a narrow escort carrier deck at 150 knots. When in the hangar below, with wings folded back, the Avenger presented a bizarre appearance. One sailor described it this way: "It looked, on the ground, like some barnyard fowl, and pilots called it the Pregnant Turkey."[21] Composite squadron VC-1 also included Wildcats, about half the mass of the TBF. The small stature in comparison to the Avenger produced a colorful saying among Grumman aircraft pilots: "Having an engine in his lap and a feather in his ass."[22] The craft had a wingspan of thirty-eight feet and a Pratt & Whitney engine that produced 1,350 hp, and it carried four .50 machine guns and payload for two 250-pound bombs.

Figure 5. Operations in the Atlantic quickly demonstrated the hazards of landing on a small escort carrier. Here, an Avenger torpedo bomber is lost in attempting to land and, in the process goes over the heads of a number of CVE 21 sailors on the flight deck. Courtesy of the USS Block Island Association.

At this very early stage of the hunter-killer operations, pilots of the Avengers dropped the standard weapon for hunting U-boats, depth charges, which sank to a predetermined depth and then exploded in the hopes of ripping a submarine apart. However, the crew's interest stirred as the result of an additional weapon, the Mark 24 mine. Know to the crew as "Fido," it was an air-dropped torpedo that once in the water "thought," for the weapon utilized acoustic sensing to home in on the engine noise of a submerged U-boat. Weighing just short of seven hundred pounds and measuring over seven feet in length, it housed a 5 hp electric motor in the rear and ninety-two pounds of high explosive at the front. It cruised at twelve knots and could inflict death at a range of four thousand yards, or about 2.5 miles.[23] While the concept of dropping an explosive device on your enemy was centuries old, the notion of a mechanical invention gathering and processing information in order to seek and destroy it was unique. One sailor recalled looking at these weapons up close. He wrote, "A torpedo . . . is sleek, shining, and alive. It gives the impression of having a remorseless brain of its own—as, of course, some torpedoes really have."[24]

In the first half of October 1943, after completing a round of training off Virginia, and ready for the first hunter-killer mission, CVE 21 cruised into Hampton Roads. Nearing her pier, Captain Ramsey noticed a destroyer starting to back away from her berth. Ramsey ordered a crossing signal issued to warn of his right-of-way and, more importantly, his vessel's ten thousand tons of forward momentum. Instead of stopping, the captain of USS *Black*, DD 666, panicked and increased speed, pulling away from the pier, placing her on a course to cross right into the path of CVE 21. Repeated signals were sent by Ramsey, and, seeing the incompetence of the commander of *Black*, he ordered full speed emergency back power and sounded collision quarters. As the engines surged to slow the inertia pushing her forward, the men braced themselves. The bow of the escort carrier slammed into the port quarter of the destroyer.[25]

The men of *Block Island* heard the alarm and then felt the jolt as the brand-new 2,000-ton destroyer and the 10,000-ton escort carrier violently merged. After the collision Hector Vernetti ran to the flight deck and headed for the bow. His nose indicated something very wrong; a strong smell of oil was in the air. Peering down into the water, he saw men from *Black* who were in the water, having been knocked off the ship by the collision.[26] *Black* was cut almost to its keel, while *Block Island* took a huge hole in her hull, luckily well above the waterline. Amazingly, no one outside of the destroyer captain's career was injured. After the investigation completely cleared Ramsey, and with the hole in the hull patched, CVE 21 made final preparations to steam eastward into the hunting grounds.[27]

In the fall of 1942, an intrepid reporter inquired of an old Navy acquaintance about these new contraptions called "escort carriers." His interest was stimulated after finding no prewar mention of these vessels. The old sea-salt friend succinctly explained this lack of knowledge with the statement "Born of the war."[28] He continued his definition with "Merchant hulls with flight decks hastily added." Escort carriers quickly retrofitted from merchant hulls illuminate the industrial know-how of the United States in developing a quick fix in overcoming the shortage of interwar funding due to isolationism and the limitations imposed by the Washington Naval Treaty. This intrepid reporter, sensing an overlooked aspect of the war, inquired about hitching a ride on a CVE to gather background information. He received an inquisitive look and heard, "Well, why not? No reason why you shouldn't, just because most reporters prefer to go on the big, glamorous carriers which see all the action."[29]

Additionally, the German Officer Corps also underestimated the escort carriers—both American and British—that were beginning to challenge their dominance in the middle portion of the Atlantic. The Germans snidely labeled the CVEs "tired crows," as these were not the Essex class of carriers cruising at thirty knots and launching eighty-plus aircraft.[30] However, one German, Adm. Karl

Dönitz, foresaw the deadly potential of the escort carriers. He urged U-boat captains that "the sinking of an aircraft carrier is of greatest importance. If a boat sights a carrier she should attack at all costs; the carrier is always the most important target."[31]

Dönitz realized that the success of the "black pit" stemmed from the fact that no Allied aircraft were in the skies above. Escort carrier aircraft transformed the overall equation. Allied aircraft could now attack located U-boats or radio nearby surface forces to continue the hunt. If this trend caused by the CVEs continued, the very potency of the U-boat strategy to win the Battle of the Atlantic was put into question. If future Allied convoys cruised with near impunity, and ever more supplies were consolidated in Britain, the German U-boats would find themselves on the losing end of a predetermined mathematical equation. If the CVEs transformed the hours the U-boats spent hunting to hours evading, the very nature of the Battle of the Atlantic would be radically called into question.[32] However, Dönitz's call for the destruction of the carrier "at all costs" set forth a chain of events for the sailors of USS *Block Island*, CVE 21.

10
"Quickening of Pulse"

In early October 1943, Merchant Marine captain John R. Lewis left his moored merchant vessel to attend a convoy conference held in an auditorium at the Norfolk Naval Base. Lewis grew up in a small community with as deep a maritime connection as any in the United States. Block Island, Rhode Island, located thirteen miles off Rhode Island's south shore and twenty miles east of the lighthouse on Montauk, New York (on the very eastern end of Long Island), had witnessed naval history off its shores since before King Philip's War. With English settlement in 1661, the sixteen founding families had scratched out a living either by fishing or by farming. However, on this island of just three by seven miles, the Atlantic was visible when looking in almost every direction. Lewis, on walking into the auditorium, was given a sheaf of documents related to the upcoming convoy his vessel was a part of that was prepping to cross the Atlantic. In scanning the documents, Lewis encountered a surprise. He remembered later, "Here's a list of escorts. I see the name USS *Block Island*. I didn't know there was such a vessel. I don't think anyone on the island knew. It was a baby flattop, a small aircraft carrier built for anti-submarine work."[1] During the meeting Captain Ramsey addressed the gathering of sea captains of the Merchant Marines and officers of the USN. Motoring out on a whaleboat to his merchant vessel at the conclusion of the meeting, Lewis saw the nearby silhouette of USS *Block Island*, CVE 21. Years later Lewis recalled, "Then later at anchorage, I saw this neat little escort carrier. Imagine the quickening of pulse and pride I felt."[2]

On October 15, 1943, convoy UGS-21 consisting of seventy merchant vessels and eleven escorts exited Hampton Roads. For the first two days of this patrol to North Africa, *Block Island* and her screening DDs followed the convoy. Lewis remembered after navigating through Chesapeake Bay, "*Block Island* approached from astern, overhauling us close aboard to take up her position in the middle of the convoy."[3] The next morning CVE 21 pulled away from the convoy for full-fledged offensive operations. In the late afternoon, CVE 21 and her escorting DDs for this first hunter-killer mission, returned to the convoy making their way back to the middle of the grouping of merchant ships for the night cruise. Lewis recalled, "Thus, we protected her as she protected us."[4] On October 17, CVE 21 and her escorting destroyers, all old enough to have battled against the Germans during World War I, broke off from Lewis's convoy for the final time to begin their hunter-killer mission.

A particularly attractive target for the Allies in the evolving Battle of the Atlantic was a German submarine with no offensive punch other than mounted AA guns. Only ten of the Type XIV U-boats were ever constructed. Labeled "clumsy" by Dönitz, what made these vessels so valuable was their ability to refuel and resupply U-boats already in position to harass the enemy.[5] These Type XIV (labeled by the Germans as "milch cow") could replenish empty fuel tanks of attacking U-boats and thus prolong loitering time and add weeks onto missions in finding and securing enemy targets.[6] Thus, these refueling U-boats were of particular interest to the hierarchy of the USN.

Ramsey's theoretical thinking on radical transformation of submarine warfare over the short course of America's entry into the war continued during this time as the skipper of CVE 21. The submarine represented technology that allowed a weaker nation-state to challenge a much stronger naval power clandestinely. Via stealth and surprise attacks, U-boats wreaked havoc on the much stronger surface fleets of the United States and Britain. Ramsey, in his thinking on the expanded role of naval aviation, saw more likenesses between the two platforms of war, these being the airplane and submarine, than differences. Just before America's entry into the war against the German menace, he wrote:

> The development of the airplane provided another instrumentality capable of use in identical fashion, and the combination of submarine and airplane has changed the formerly simple problem of exercising command of the sea into one of complexity and potentially great difficulty. Parenthetically it might be argued that the submarine and the airplane are more akin in many respects than any other two instrumentalities of war. Both can operate tactically to limited extent in a third dimension. Both are structurally weak but can destroy the most powerful surface vessels by essentially surprise attacks. Both attempt to evade the efforts of surface craft to destroy them; the submarine by concealment, and the airplane by speed. And finally, but most important of all, both may be used to interfere with the exercise of sea command.[7]

Ramsey's musing on the relationships between these rapidly developing pieces of naval technology aside, he currently retained the responsibility in leading task group 21.16 (TG 21.16) and all the lives on board this assemblage of USN vessels. It cruised the central Atlantic on a portion of the world's surface where only naval aviation launched from vessels could penetrate. However, at this early stage of the war, the vast majority of flights took place only during the daylight hours. Following the electronic scent of intercepted U-boat radio transmissions in the "black pit," TG 21.16 edged into the German refueling grounds north of the Azores Islands on the early evening of October 25. In comparison to later task groups, these early missions retained a number of offensive handicaps that stemmed directly from the DDs of the task group being older than the vast majority of her sailors. Launched in 1919, USS *Parrott*, DD 218, three days earlier had dropped a depth charge pattern and injured herself. As Ramsey wrote, the self-inflicted attack "weakened the repairs to an old leak and PARROTT had reported inability to drop a full scale pattern without hazard to her water-tight integrity. In fact, PARROTT had reported specifically the loss of 70% of her offensive striking power."[8] On this October evening a radio direction finder (RDF) bearing allowed *Parrott* to maneuver toward a radar fix on an unidentified craft ten thousand yards away. Cruising stealthily closer in the near moonless night, her lookouts scanned silently for an agonizing twenty-five minutes. Firing an illuminating star shell off of the deck of the twenty-four-year-old vessel cast a brilliant light, and with it a surfaced U-boat appeared just three hundred yards away. At 1904, as *Parrott* opened fire with her four-inch guns, lookouts on the port side of CVE 21 witnessed the illuminated firing in the distance. Ramsey was literally left in the dark as to what was transpiring until 1915, when the communications department on board CVE 21 received a coded message. It read, "Caught bastard on surface. Gave him a good pasting. Several hits observed."[9]

For the radio operators and aircrews, these sightings produced incredible amounts of excitement after cruising for days, even weeks, toward the horizon seeing nothing but the Atlantic and the other vessels of the task group. Each mission adopted a predetermined set of terms called the Voice Code and Call Signs. The purpose was explained as, "The code words in this annex are established to deny the enemy information on this task group or its movements even though our voice radio traffic may be intercepted."[10] Thus, TG 21.16 was "HORSE," and Captain Ramsey "YANK." For those listening, a convoy became "GRAVITY," and CVE 21 "DYNAMITE." Naval aviator terms transformed as well, with "true bearing" becoming "TILLIE," "1/3 speed" changing to "BOX," and "Adjust base course to" becoming "HOTFOOT." Despite the war, whoever devised these terms demonstrated a sense of humor. For "attacking, I am," pilots said "WHOOPEE." A definitive sighting of an enemy submarine was typed up as "TALLYHO." However, in examining the personal papers of Logan Ramsey at the Navy Yard in Washington, DC, I found that a red pencil crossed out "TALLYHO," and in red block letters is written the word "BASTARD."[11]

This particular "BASTARD," U 488, was a massive Type XIV 1,600-ton "milch cow" that the Allies desperately sought to destroy to stop the refueling of smaller attack submarines. In fact, it is believed a refueling operation between U-boats was interrupted, as lookouts on *Parrott* reported the strong odor of diesel oil when approaching her. Upon seeing the illuminated U-boat, the four-inch guns of *Parrott* exploded in launching shells, with at least one shell reportedly slamming into the conning tower of the exposed U-boat. U 488 quickly submerged; however, *Parrott* continued her attack in dropping a limited depth charge attack. While *Parrott* was engaged, *Block Island* and the other ships of the group moved closer to the scene. As the surface battle waged off her port quarter, lookouts spotted two red vertical lights off the escort carrier's starboard quarter. Ramsey, realizing his team had tracked and found a concentration of U-boats, vectored USS *Paul Jones*, DD 230, to attack. For two hours TG 21.16 played electronic cat-and-mouse with surfaced and submerged U-boats, which included attempting to locate these vessels with radar and sonar and then unleashing depth charges. Stress-filled hours on all the vessels of the task group produced a memorable wartime experience yet yielded only mysteries as to the true impact of these evasive actions and depth charge attacks. *Paul Jones* engaged in three separate attacks on one or more U-boats. Ramsey chalked up the mission with scoring one sub "definitely sunk" by *Parrott*, another "probably damaged," and a third "probably sunk" by *Paul Jones*. However, Ramsey openly admitted the mysterious nature of these complex operations with multiple enemies engaged simultaneously. Ramsey wrote, "Unfortunately, neither of the destroyers involved had a dead reckoning tracer and a complete analysis of the action is unobtainable."[12]

In reality, no submarines were sunk in this action. The captain of U 488 dropped his vessel to a depth of 235 meters. The crew felt and heard not only depth charges exploding above them but also the destroyers circling over the scene on the surface. At this extreme depth, the German submarine slowly left the area and continued on.[13] However, U 488 and *Block Island* would experience another rendezvous on the high seas. While in hindsight once the German records were opened, no U-boat was destroyed, CVE 21 was in the main event of the Battle of the Atlantic.

❋

The worlds of the Army and Navy differ. The former fights on land, and the latter on the water. However, both soldier and sailor fight and are just a small part of the greater organization around them. One of the major differences between the services was the diversity of assignments sailors could be assigned to while under fire. Traditionally, in the Army soldiers in combat carried firearms, which they physically held onto and fired back at the enemy, though they also manned artillery and provided logistical support. With this individual firearm in combat, they could also direct their fear, excitement, or anxiety in returning fire. This contrasted sharply from what Navy sailors experienced in combat. Sailors rarely possessed individual arms to function as coping mechanisms. If manning a large weapon such as antiaircraft batteries or a range of large-caliber cannons, you were part of a team trusting each other to operate the large offensive weapon firing at an enemy many miles away. Additionally, for each one manning a large gun in the Navy, many others were sealed below decks in compartmentalized spaces. Rather than clenching a rifle in the heat of battle, during GQ a sailor below decks watched gauges, manned firefighting equipment, and sealed hatches. Most sailors were completely blind to the conflict being waged outside and were left to only imagine the deadly occurrences deciding their fate. For those below the waterline, this must have been particularly agonizing. One sudden explosion could result in numerous ways to die, including burning in a fire, being poached by exploding steam piping, or drowning in seawater. The sailors of hunter-killer missions experienced such strain during GQ as these vessels probed the "black pit."

While the circumstances of combat differed greatly from those in infantry engagements, these events could produce just as intense psychological pressure. A CVE 21 veteran who could testify to this notion was Joe Booi, whose first combat experience transpired in near-total silence. On the morning of December 7, 1941, Booi was on board the docked cruiser USS *New Orleans*, CA 32, when the alarm of GQ was heard. Undergoing engine repair at the time in Pearl, the cruiser was taking electrical power from the nearby docking facilities. Thoughts of frustration and anger centered on the officer who dreamed up running a GQ exercise on a Sunday morning for these sailors like Booi who had GQ positions below the waterline. Silence reigned for these sailors sealed in the engineering spaces insulated from the chaos of battle. Sailors initially exchanged curious glances with one another at the unprecedented commentary coming over the loudspeakers describing the horror above them. This was new. Even at sea no GQ drills included descriptions of battle. Curious looks soon changed to worried glances as Booi and his fellow shipmates heard excited comments about the destruction of *Arizona*. In a sealed compartmentalized engineering space on the stationary ship, the only indication that war in fact was raging above them was the commentary over the loudspeakers. It was not until the near miss of a Japanese bomb that any of these sailors physically sensed the actual battle, as the shock wave then suddenly lifted up the 10,000-ton cruiser. Only many hours later, when the sailors climbed ladders to the deck, did they actually see the outcome of the battle they had survived.[14]

Block Island sailors were not unique in this experience, as sailors had for centuries lacked the daily interactions with foreign lands and tongues in comparison with their counterparts waging war on land. As witnessed in the writings of participants in the Napoleonic wars, those that fought on land continuously encountered interesting foods, landscapes, and languages, which they recorded in written diaries and letters home. While British sailors experienced the horrors and glory in 1805 at the Battle of Trafalgar, their daily lives were of monotonous boredom, resulting in a lack of documentation in life on board ship in comparison with those writing about terrestrial warfare. Some two centuries after Nelson's victory at Trafalgar, one escort carrier sailor summed up his war experience this way: "Sheer boredom followed by sheer panic."[15] This sailor, Clifford Shaw, served on the escort carrier USS *Kitkun Bay*, CVE 71, in the famed Battle of Samar, where six unarmored CVEs and their escorts known as Taffy 3 fought off the superior forces of the Japanese commander Vice Admiral Takeo Kurita. Shaw, as an electrician on board, was stationed in a very small cubicle manning a fuse box during GQ. During the battle armor-piercing rounds from the Japanese effortlessly punched through the side of the ship, passed through the hangar, and exited the other side of the CVE as if they were cutting cheesecloth. These armor-piercing rounds failed to detonate against the prefabricated merchant hull and left gaping holes on both sides of the hangar deck. As these unexploding rounds passed overhead, Shaw could hear the concussions from the incoming rounds. A fellow sailor told him the Japanese fleet was spotted on the horizon, and he would man Shaw's post if he wanted to run up and see the actual enemy. Shaw declined the offer, as during GQ you were never allowed to leave your post. In all his time in the Pacific, Shaw never saw a Japanese sailor or vessel. It was not until after retirement, four decades later, in reading histories of the Battle of Samar and Taffy 3, that he gleaned a true understanding of the battle. While he experienced one of the most famed battles of the war in a small cubicle wearing headphones waiting for instructions on changing fuses, in his entire war experience he rarely saw anything other than the ocean.[16] Shaw summed up his understanding of the battle situation at GQ with, "We had no clue."[17]

The Battle of the Atlantic demonstrates how naval warfare had evolved into a very impersonal business. One could argue that this impersonal nature of naval combat commenced in World War I, as clearly seen in the Battle of Jutland. However, now not only did both sides rarely see the enemy in the flesh but many times Allied surface ships now attacked blips on some advanced electronic device pointing to a possible U-boat either on or below the Atlantic. Adrenaline pumped in the bodies of sailors on both sides; however, in contrast to battle on land, only rarely did tangible, visual evidence point to a successfully destroyed enemy. At best, oil and debris floated on the surface as evidence of the violence inflicted and the extinguishing of enemy lives. Bafflement was central to the escort carrier operations in the Battle of the Atlantic. It was not until years after the war that the intelligence officer of CVE 21, Roy Swift, combed the archives of both the United States and the German navies and traced his ship's experiences using the parallel documentations from the archives of both navies. Detective work of the historian decades after the war produced some clarity in the blind man's game of three-dimensional warfare with Allied planes searching the air, ships cruising the surfaces, and U-boats stalking underwater. This was detached, impersonal killing at its highest level.

While instances of World War I era destroyers of TG 21.16 sighting and engaging the enemy occurred, a far more likely sighting of a U-boat was what happened just three days later, on October 28, when a pilot from VC-1 spotted two "bastards." Planes from CVE 21 flew missions in patterns designed to produce the most sea observation per gallon of fuel consumed. When drawn on paper, such patterns looked like abstract works of art.[18] However, such patterns yielded results. Fifty miles away from the carrier, Lt. Franklin M. Murray in his Avenger spotted two U-boats on the surface and immediately reported to CVE 21. However, while CVE 21 received the radio transmission, she was engulfed in nasty weather and unable to launch reinforcing aircraft Murray and his wingman, Ens. Gerald Handshuh in his Wildcat, commenced their attack on the closer of the two submarines. As the .50-caliber machine guns of the Avenger and Wildcat blanketed the conning tower, Murray opened the bomb bay doors of his Avenger. Formulating a series of cold calculations in his mind at attack speed, Murray released his depth charges on the first U-boat. As the pilots buzzed over their target, they realized that the second of the two U-boats, with extra time to react to the surprise attack, had commenced firing her antiaircraft guns at both Murray and Handshuh.[19]

Murray's aiming paid off as depth charges rained down around the first U-boat while she was in the act of submerging. The pair looked for signs of damage in the wake where she entered the Atlantic. As Murray recorded later, "about 80 or 90 seconds after the bombing, the stern of the bombed sub suddenly arose out of the water at an angle of at least 45 degrees, hung there a moment, and then slid under the water."[20] The second submarine refused to submerge and threw up heavy antiaircraft fire. Apart from .50-caliber machine guns, Murray retained one more weapon of use, the Fido torpedo, which could be deployed only against a submerged submarine. The pair of pilots of VC-1 circled at a safe distance, waiting for members of their squadron to arrive and slay the second submarine that remained on the surface. However, the storm that enveloped CVE 21 just fifty miles away also interfered with radio transmissions between the pair of aircraft and the escort carrier. Mistakenly thinking support would soon arrive, the pilots grew frustrated as they circled, waiting for reinforcements. Forty minutes after the first sighting, the U-boat submerged. Shortly thereafter Murray's Avenger cruised over the scene and dropped its Fido, hoping to reach its designated target, but no explosion was forthcoming.[21]

Unknown to VC-1, both submarines got away. U 220 was badly damaged by the attack but had successfully submerged. She radioed to headquarters that she had been attacked and was returning to base. However, she was never heard from again and was presumed by U-boat Command to be lost on October 31. U 220 finally succumbed to the damage inflicted by the pair of planes of VC-1, and fifty-six young lives and one U-boat were eliminated. VC-1 and CVE 21 were credited with their first kill in their hunter-killer operations. While the official location and time of the USN report differed in reality from the German records viewed after the war, the first kill was credited correctly.[22] The mysterious nature of many of the credited kills in the Battle of the Atlantic is seen in the final hours of U 220. While the score of the USN was correct, its destruction took place days later, and the exact location remains unknown. These U-boats, and their victims, disappeared, and it was up to the historians after the war to piece together, with information gleaned from archives from both sides of the Atlantic, the true nature of the battles waged. The Battle of the Atlantic contrasted sharply with the land battles, where destroyed war materiel rusted away in North Africa or the Ukraine offering relatively easy investigation for drafting military reports. Hunter-killer missions, led by escort carriers, were involved in some of the most complex and mysterious combat of World War II.

After three weeks at sea, and earning her first successful kill of the war, CVE 21 and her DDs headed to the North African port of Casablanca. As the ships sailed into the harbor, tangible signs of the war materialized. Rusting in the harbor and sticking out of the water lay the sunken Vichy French fleet, slain by the USN in November 1942. Casablanca provided a safe port for *Block Island* to resupply both machines and men. It also gave sailors a chance to enjoy some time on land. For the young Americans, this called for beer (which could not legally be consumed on board), hot dogs, and baseball games. Five days in Casablanca gave CVE 21 ample time to resupply. Sailors loaded weapons, fuel, food for thousands of meals, and tons of other supplies. This break also gave the crew time on another continent and with another culture. They explored the streets of this North African city. Before the war most Americans had not heard of Casablanca; however, the feature film with Humphrey Bogart, and FDR's Casablanca Conference with other Allied leaders, brought this location to the forefront of American imagination and understanding of the war. Sailors walking the city experienced layers of culture, heard Arabic spoken by the population, and saw buildings and street layout with discernible French patterns. While these sailors battled in World War II, compared to ground forces they saw very little physical evidence of the war outside of their ships and crew members. They fought, for the most part, an unseen enemy. Fighting from the sea, planes from CVE 21 sought out the elusive enemy submarines, but for the average sailors, they could claim no tangible piece of the war, just days on the high seas chasing phantoms feared but rarely, if ever, seen.

Figure 6. Capt. Logan Ramsey (center looking left) enjoying a bottle of beer with other *Block Island* sailors at a baseball diamond in Casablanca. Courtesy of the USS Block Island Association.

In this respect Casablanca offered a unique experience, for here tangible evidence of the war was marketed to USN sailors seeking physical corroboration of the war. Sailors bartered in the market spaces of Casablanca for war relics scavenged by locals from nearby battlefields. *Block Island* sailors, with the skill of western mule traders, let the USN provide the currency to exchange with the local population. As one sailor remembered, they used a number of high-demand items to sweeten the pot of bartering, including mattress covers, American cigarettes, sugar, coffee, and tea. Besides items from this foreign land, these sailors craved physical evidence of the ground war that provided the bountiful trinkets of battle they lacked fighting on the seas. German and Italian army-issue equipment rounded up by local traders included bayonets, firearms, and helmets harvested from still-seared battlefields. War rubble transformed into war souvenirs. As one sailor remembers, when these two commerce forces met, "A lot of trades were made."[23]

Casablanca included other temptations, such as gambling. The games varied, including cards and dice, yet the thrill of the win transcended culture and language. Young sailors combed the smoke-filled cafés looking to expand their naval income by hazarding and winning money from the locals. One USS *Block Island* sailor did very well. After he won a hefty amount, angry locals increased their bets in an effort to win back lost funds, which resulted in the sailor gathering more of their money. As their anger neared the boiling point, the sailor latched onto his money and ran down a back alley. An angry crowd of unlucky gamblers soon followed in pursuit. In coping with this disgruntled mob, the sailor dropped US dollar bills in small increments, which caused those at the very front of the pack to stop and retrieve them, thus creating a human dam to hold up this flood of human anger in the narrow alley. This strategy allowed the sailor to flee with the majority of his winnings.[24] Years later, a member of the ship's company summed up his crew's experience in Casablanca with one sentence: "All hands made the most of their opportunity, returning to duty with Moroccan headaches, evil-smelling leather goods, and heightened morale."[25]

While the crew explored the curious city, tons of provisions filled the hunter-killer group. Besides the weapons hauled on board to destroy U-boats, an additional weapon was also picked up in Casablanca: information. Captain Ramsey visited the office of Moroccan Sea Frontiers to share and receive tactical intelligence on U-boat operations.[26] While nowhere near as exciting as openly engaging the enemy on the sea, accurate intelligence on the enemy operations was just as important as bravery in the Battle of the Atlantic. Ramsey gained the current best guess at the location of German U-boats before beginning the second half of this first hunter-killer mission.

11
"Like Bananas in Bunches"

On November 10, 1943, CVE 21 and her Great War era DDs sailed out of the African port. For a short time, she escorted the northbound convoy designated GUS-220, with her planes providing cover in waters thought to hold U-boats. A few days into the mission, CVE 21 and her DDs broke off from GUS-220 in active pursuit of the enemy, hunting south of the Azores Islands. In winter months patrol flights north of the Azores encountered not only poor weather and visibility but also shortened days. Thus, the task group probed south. The experience of these long days of planes searching the ocean truly resembled the term "hunting." While "hunting" brings to mind pursuing and killing game, the vast majority of big-game hunting in the field is waiting and in the end seeing nothing. So was this hunting trip. As the task force searched in a westward direction away from the Azores, they saw nothing. Thus, Ramsey continued his patrol west and headed to Norfolk, arriving on November 25.[1] With *Block Island*'s first war patrol over, she had scored her first kill, and her crew had wet their feet in the hunter-killer game.

While resupply took place at Casablanca on the east side of the Atlantic, the homeport on the western side of the ocean was Norfolk. While this was American soil, and the men enjoyed their time away from ship, they encountered far less glamorous aspects of the home front, including long-forgotten tension between sailors and the civilian population that existed during the war. Front lawns of Norfolk neighborhoods displayed signs warning: "Sailors and dogs—keep off the grass."[2] Sailors returning after weeks of stress, fueled with alcohol from the local beer joints, urinated on and vandalized signs via numerous methods.[3]

Many World War II studies focus with a myopic intensity on the battles, tactics, and machines, and the average enlisted man can be easily overlooked. In the decades after the war, with movies exploring the individual bravery of Navy sailors with middle-aged, well-established actors, it is especially easy to overlook the fact that teenagers made up the crew of these ships. Many officers and some noncommissioned officers had more years in the Navy than the average enlisted man had in years of life. However, it must be noted that wartime service, in a very short time, quickly transformed these kids into battle-hardened veteran sailors. This is exemplified by CVE 21 crew member Richard Brown, who before joining the vessel had survived two sinkings, the battleship *West Virginia* BB 48 at Pearl Harbor, and later at the Battle of Coral Sea, USS *Lexington*, CV 2.[4] Nevertheless, the average sailors pushing an aircraft, pulling on a line, or making ice cream, were teenagers. During periods of calm, these teenagers did what teenagers do. They picked on each other, snapped each other with wet towels while showering, and orchestrated practical jokes on one another, all the things that make up the complex system of interactions that transpire during male bonding. Adding to this situation were the regional, ethnic, and religious differences that influenced the nicknames and practical jokes transpiring on ship. One must also wonder if beyond male bonding these ribbings and jokes gave those involved a slight, however brief, break from the mental strain of worry.

One standby practical joke was called "hot foot." When a group of sailors discovered an unsuspecting friend sleeping, they inserted a match in his shoe's seam along the sole and then lit it. They suppressed their snickers and giggles, waiting for the reaction when the match burned down and into their mate's shoe. Many of these events seemed to transpire in the "head." One classic event involved someone in the act of defecating. While the ship had individual stalls, all items placed into the toilet fell into a single metal trough, which had seawater pushing all waste to the far end and into the ship's internal plumbing and out to sea. The prankster would sit in one of the first seating areas. When his victim sat in one of the seats downwater from him, he ignited a balled-up piece of paper and dropped it into the trough.[5] While the reactions varied, flames licking at one's exposed bottom guaranteed acknowledgment.

Another form of mischief was stealing. One sailor wrote of the mind-set during the war, "In a world where everything belonged to the government, nothing belonged to anybody."[6] This attitude on CVE 21 formed a legend: the "jeep" carrier with its own "jeep." While docked in port, the crew, using the ship's crane, lifted and loaded supplies onto the flight deck. During one loading procedure, a green Army jeep pulled up on the dock, and its driver ran off with a dispatch of orders. The sailors on the ground crew, spying the unattended jeep and using hand signals, motioned the crane operator toward it. These sailors, to use a Soviet term, "liberated" this jeep from the Army and quickly hoisted it onto the flight deck of CVE 21. Here the crew lowered their new jeep onto the hangar deck, and another group of sailors briskly replaced the jeep's army green paint with a coat of navy gray. The crew used the jeep in shuttling material on both the flight and hangar decks. Captain Ramsey soon witnessed a teenage sailor driving around in a rather reckless manner. As one historian wrote, "Captain Ramsey finally traded the jeep because he was afraid his crew would kill each other driving it around the flight deck."[7]

The antics practiced on board also included group rebellion, one example being communal fighting against the Navy's tight standards. After three weeks at sea, days without relaxation, seeing land, or other previously minor joys of civilian life, the crew "raised a beard." Collectively, members of the crew stopped shaving, challenging Navy regulations. Captain Ramsey employed an extremely effective tactic in addressing this minor act of mutiny. Weeks at sea drained not only the morale of the crew but the supplies of the ship, requiring replenishment. Due to enter the sights and sounds of port, and with sailors excitedly thinking of shore leave, Ramsey read a brief announcement over the loudspeakers: "All crew not meeting hygiene standards will not be granted shore leave. That is all."[8] Long lines quickly formed at the ship's barbershop.

For the average sailor on CVE 21, weeks at sea soon turned monotonous. As enlisted sailors ate the same meals, ran together when klaxons sounded alarms, and went to bed in shifts, each day mirrored the one preceding it. Nothing but ocean around them, no unique cultures encountered, the same duties performed on a daily basis. One sailor recorded in a diary his belief that the CVE simply cruised in circles. He wrote, "Undoubtedly, there is some reason for doing this, but I can't figure it out."[9] He confessed that "this sea duty gets monotonous."[10] He summed up the average daily experience, once the novelty of the vessel wore off, with the following: "Our ninth day at sea and still nowhere and it doesn't seem as if we're going anywhere."[11] Outside of actual combat that produced searing memories, boredom summed up the vast majority of sea duty. Boredom highlighted by high moments of tension was not just relegated to life on CVEs. As one historian wrote, "We also must remember that 90 percent of the deeds done in World War II were themselves far from glamorous in nature."[12] On CVE 21, for every hour spent flying from the carrier deck in search of the enemy, hundreds of other crew hours were spent maintaining, cooking and cleaning. The only break from this pattern was liberty in port. For a set number of days, the men got free rein in Norfolk, Belfast, or Casablanca. Weeks' worth of excitement and activities, crammed into these few hours, resulted in some of the most colorful and memorable tales of the war. Decades after the war, this pattern reemerged with ships' reunions, allowing veterans and family members a chance to gather together again and explore a new host city.

❋

In the last month of 1943, CVE 21 was a beehive of activity when docked at Norfolk with the transfer off of VC-1 and replacement with VC-58. This squadron group brought on board a state-of-the-art weapon. Escort carriers functioned as platforms for the incubation of weapons systems. The brightest minds of the American sciences developed weapons and systems of detection, and USS *Block Island*, CVE 21, was in the vanguard of testing advanced innovation in both rocket design and underwater sound detection. While these new gadgets could be hidden from the bulk of the crew, the sailors who handled the rockets and strapped these to aircraft later sired wild rumors. One sailor recalled, "I remember the puzzled looks when we first saw the equipment on the planes. Someone referred to it as curtain rods."[13] Another sailor was "surprised at the innocence of their appearance, which is more like a big silver pencil than anything else. I know they're murderous, but they don't look it."[14] Termed HVAR, for high velocity aircraft rockets, these were the latest weapons devised for taking on U-boats. As described by one officer on board, "It was a simple two-inch projectile with a solid case-hardened steel head, with laboratory-rated capacity for passing clean through the pressure hull of a submarine if struck when submerged not more that 20 or 30 feet."[15]

Loaded and provisioned, CVE 21 and the same group of DDs sailed on December 15 and brought HVAR to bear. As an officer wrote decades later, this mission ushered in "the era of rocket warfare for the U.S. Armed Forces."[16] While these rockets seemed otherworldly to the crew of CVE 21 at the time, these weapons had in fact already been used against German U-boats. The British led the way in the Allied use of rockets, successfully sinking a U-boat in May 1943. A British Swordfish, a biplane operating from the escort carrier HMS *Archer*, D78, located the surfaced U 752 and made history in damaging her to the point where the crew scuttled her to avoid capture.[17]

Again, pushing away from the Atlantic seaboard into the war, TG 21.16 headed by CVE 21 provided air cover for a convoy transporting supplies to Britain. After four days, however, Ramsey broke off and headed into the "black pit." North of the Azores, German admiral Dönitz packed groupings of U-boats in the hopes of slowing down the American war materiel concentrating in England. CVE 21's second hunter-killer mission was about to commence. As the task force neared the Azores, Christmas Eve arrived and brought in an intelligence report of a group of U-boats at roughly 41–38 N, 33–42 E.[18] As the crew members' anxiety about battle increased, dreadful news arrived and was read to the crew via the intercom. A sister CVE, USS *Card*, CVE 11, leading a task force in the vicinity, experienced a quick role reversal between hunter and prey. A destroyer of the group, USS *Leary*, DD 158, under two hundred miles away, in tracking a cornered U-boat, fell victim to three German torpedoes, which produced gaping holes in her hull. The ship sank in just thirty minutes, and ninety-seven of the crew were lost in the cold Atlantic waters, including the commanding officer, Cdr. James E. Kyes, who, in an act of self-sacrifice, gave a mess attendant his life jacket. The mess attendant survived to tell of Kyes's heroism.[19]

Even at sea, in the middle of the Battle of the Atlantic, the crew's thoughts drifted toward Christmas at home. In communal areas the men decorated small Christmas trees. The galleys smelled of turkeys roasting in ovens for the holiday meal. Captain Ramsey, thinking of his men, and always mindful of morale, prior to shipping out purchased a lighter for each crew member to mark the holiday. At the holiday meal, at each place setting a lighter rested for every sailor, each engraved with "USS Block Island, Xmas at Sea, 1943."[20] On Christ's birthday the flight operations ran all day, but hours of flying search patterns found nothing. Despite the lack of offensive operations, dangers still existed on the flight deck.

Ramsey's report summarizing the second mission of TG 21.16 Annex F was titled "Resume of Crashes." While each crash is meticulously detailed as to cause and effect on personnel and aircraft, the list is amazingly short, with only nineteen crashes for over a thousand landings. The most destructive occurred on December 26, in the darkening skies at 1611, on what was the 831st landing of the mission. A Wildcat's rough landing on the deck resulted in a solid bounce, and the aircraft's tailhook missed all the arrester wires. Ramsey wrote, "With right wing still down, plane crashed into island, starboard wing hitting first and spinning plane to left. Plane was a complete washout. Pilot uninjured."[21] Those working on the deck, besides arming and fueling aircraft, also became skilled at clearing the deck after crashes, as seen in this crash, with the deck cleared for additional landings within fifteen minutes.[22] Over the course of this patrol, the catapult launchings averaged just 65 seconds each in good weather and 120 seconds during heavy weather. The most dangerous landings took place after 1600, as this was the slated time for sunset. Clocks required constant changing to counteract traversing thousands of miles on the Atlantic. Ramsey wrote, "During the entire cruise, ships clocks were reset so as to put sunrise at approximately 0700 (plus or minus 7.5 minutes) each day. With this schedule, sunset was approximately 1600."[23] Dangers, however, lurked outside of landings after sunset, as the vessel possessed a range of combustible fuels and weapons, which now included rockets. A mishap with the new rockets soon occurred. As reported: "Accidental firing while testing firing circuit of plane on flight deck. The wings of the TBF were folded, and rocket gouged a small hole in the wood planking of the flight deck."[24] Luckily, no other damage occurred in the incident, which surely garnered the attention of those handling the new "curtain rods."

Adding to the anxiety of the officers on watch on both CVE 21 and the DDs of the task force were the numbers of the enemy believed to be in close proximity. On the night orders for December 26–27, Ramsey wrote, "About 12 submarines in the immediate vicinity." At noon on December 27, however, an intelligence report informed Ramsey of a unique target. Some 240 miles north of his current location, a German ship of war, *Alsterufer*, disguised as a merchant vessel, was seeking to reconnoiter with some German warships and safely return to the continent. Her captain attempted to avoid detection, returning from a clandestine visit to the Orient via the Indian Ocean, and loaded with supplies. Ramsey immediately ordered four Avengers, already airborne and seeking a submarine contact, to be vectored north to prey on this blockade-runner. But danger loomed on the horizon

Figure 7. This image of Avengers parked on the deck of CVE 21 gives the viewer a window into the difficulty of landing such a large aircraft on the small deck of the escort carrier. All pilots required incredible skill in safely landing their aircraft on the deck of CVE 21 in a range of weather conditions found in the Atlantic. Naval History and Heritage Command.

for these pilots, as these December afternoons provided a quite limited amount of daylight.[25] Unknown to the Avengers under full power, *Alsterufer* had already been under attack. First, British-manned Sunderlands, a four-engine aircraft, attacked with minimal success. Second, American-built B-24 Liberators, manned by exiled Czech crews based in the Azores Islands, sought revenge for their homeland. Despite the ship throwing up waves of flak and launching balloon-suspending cables in the hopes of deterring a low-level attack, the Czechs powered in low and dropped bombs, fired rockets, and unloaded machine guns.[26]

By the time the bomb-loaded Avengers arrived, the Czechs had completed their revenge for their occupied Bohemia. With the ship ablaze and the surviving crew abandoning ship, the four Avengers left the smoke-billowing scene and headed back. Unlike the scenes portraying naval aviation in many war movies, once the fighting stopped, pilots and crew were still in danger, for they floated above a featureless expanse and needed to locate the carrier they called home. With the sun setting, Ramsey issued an order that may have seemed counterproductive;

he wanted the pilots to expend their weapons and slow down in order to conserve fuel. As a pilot himself, he was well aware that unchecked nerves could cause pilots to accelerate and, in the process, vastly increase fuel consumption. As a result pilots, instead of landing on the deck at dusk, would run out of fuel before the flight deck ever materialized on the horizon. All the pilots heeded Ramsey except the flight leader, who, disregarding the instructions, pulled away in his Avenger in the fast-fading Atlantic evening. Ramsey harshly wrote, "The flight leader . . . apparently lost his head completely and, despite positive orders to keep his group assembled, voluntarily left this group and became lost."[27] Of the three other Avengers following his orders he wrote, "The remainder of the group located the carrier well after dark and, with considerable difficulty, were landed on board with almost empty fuel tanks."[28]

The dismissal of military orders oftentimes results in the loss of lives. The Avenger pilot's actions affected not only him but the two other crew members. One half hour after sunset, at 1635, the pilot radioed he had just thirty-five gallons of gasoline remaining and was going to "pancake."[29] In the dark December night, Captain Ramsey pondered his responsibilities to the USN, the nearly one thousand crew members of CVE 21, and the three missing aircrew, possibly floating somewhere over the horizon. An intelligence officer wrote, "During the night Ramsey resolved that despite his utter indignation with the addled flight leader who had flubbed his mission, he would have to conduct flight searches in the morning to try and locate him."[30] As dawn broke, and intelligence reports rolled in on possible locations of U-boat positions, a number of CVE 21 aircraft conducted search patterns in the believed location of the ditched Avenger. With no results over the course of this short December day, any hopes of finding the crew died with the sun's setting.

The next dawn, on December 29, the aircraft were back in the business of hunting. Intelligence reported a disabled submarine just eighty-five miles from the vessel. In the cold crisp air of the Atlantic, eight aircraft lifted off from CVE 21. Breaking off in their intricate search patterns, the pilots strained their eyes and concentration in the hopes of seeing signs of a wounded U-boat struggling on the surface. One team of two aircraft, led by an Avenger piloted by Lt. Leonard McFord, circled above the waves just fifty-eight miles from CVE 21. An object was sighted, resulting in a great deal of excitement; it was not the gray hull of an enemy submarine but a small yellow life raft. Inside were the three lost crew of the pancaked Avenger, who had crash-landed some forty hours earlier. Ramsey, upon hearing about the sighted life raft, ordered McFord to drop a sonobuoy, a listening detection system that also secreted dye. Later, Ramsey wrote that he issued the order "to mark the spot, and to keep the raft in sight. Previous experience has demonstrated the extreme difficulty of keeping a life raft in sight unless the utmost precautions are used."[31] Then, McFord gunned his Avenger up to fourteen thousand feet, thus granting him the ability to serve as a homing beacon for the task force's destroyer USS *Barker*, DD 213, to rescue the frantically waving crew. One officer recalled these three were "well, uninjured, and without even a head cold!"[32]

While quick relief spread throughout the ship on word of the rescued airmen, the task force still patrolled a war zone, which became abundantly clear within minutes. The group's USS *Parrott* obtained a submerged sound contact and moved in for the attack. Ramsey, hoping for a kill, ordered USS *Bulmer*, DD 222, to detach and join the attacking *Parrott*. This was the opening salvo of a stress-filled situation that spilled into the dark hours of the night, compounded with deteriorating weather, and thus no night flights to aid in the hunting. As Captain Ramsey reported, "This was the start of a somewhat hectic evening—which resulted in contacts with a total of 8 or 9 submarines."[33] In seeking the best intelligence of the complex situation, Ramsey left the time-tested location for the captain of a man-of-war, the bridge. During the Age of Sail, captains manned the bridge and scanned the seas. These captains, mirroring master chess players, calculated wind speed, location of the enemy, and other evolving factors to ascertain the best position in destroying the enemy.

Ramsey, in deviating from this centuries-long methodology, made his decisions from the radar plot. As a man born in the last century, where men were more comfortable driving a horse-drawn wagon than a motorcar, Ramsey knew technological innovations moved fast. In his twenty years as a naval aviator, he witnessed the adoption of such technological advances as air-cooled radial engines, arrester hooks, and brakes on landing gear.[34] He fully embraced the invention of radar and found that the best place to formulate decisions was next to the radar operator. Looking into the green screen, which interpreted the electronic scent of this new contraption working above them, Ramsey calculated the best decisions of not only CVE 21 but also the task force's DDs. In these anxiety-filled hours, the operator and Ramsey juggled multiple contacts, visually recorded on a screen, some signifying DDs of the task group, and others surfaced U-boats. In the green-tinted light, Ramsey witnessed one particular blip, just a thousand yards off, slowly gaining on CVE 21. Though it was designated earlier as one of the friendly DDs in position protecting the escort carrier, Ramsey noticed this particular blip's action of closing the distance between the two vessels as he stood behind the radar operator. He wrote afterward, "I accordingly ordered and executed a change of course to the northeastward in order to clear this submarine."[35]

The green "blip" registering on the screen was in fact U 270, under the command of Capt. Paul-Friedrich Otto.[36] A veteran of the Atlantic, during the preceding September, her seasoned crew was the first to launch and score a hit with the new T5 acoustic homing torpedo. Known to the Allies under the acronym GNAT

(German naval acoustic torpedo), this weapon gave German U-boat commanders the ability to fire a torpedo that tracked the enemy by following noise signatures from the targeted vessel. In the early hours of September 20, 1943, Captain Otto first fired GNAT toward a British frigate among a westbound convoy, ON202. The new weapon indeed proved formidable as it exploded against the hull of HMS *Lagan*, K 259, producing massive damage that forced her to be scrapped once towed to shore.[37] Now, Otto and U 270 were inching toward CVE 21 attempting to make military history once again, in doing the unprecedented: sinking an American carrier in the Atlantic.

Ramsey realized at this moment that the registration on the screen approaching the carrier was in fact an unidentified U-boat. He quickly grabbed the phone linking him with the bridge and ordered an emergency turn. In the final procedures of lining up a firing position, Captain Otto of U 270 watched from his periscope as his prey steered away out of danger.[38] The rest of the night was a melee of DDs tracking sound contacts and launching depth charges, as the task group's radar group tracked the gang of submerging and resurfacing U-boats. Despite the stress of impersonal combat on the ships' captains and crews, all members of the task force and the German wolfpack survived the night. Reporting after the engagement, Ramsey provided advice for future operations. He wrote, "As submarines in concentrations come, like bananas in bunches, it is considered advisable to

Figure 8. Visits to Casablanca consisted of bursts of activity such as shopping, sightseeing, and drinking. Here, enlisted sailors and officers from CVE 21 enjoy beer and watch a baseball game in Casablanca. Courtesy of the USS Block Island Association.

maneuver the remainder of the formation about the scene of the original contact at about seven or eight miles to detect and attack."[39]

For the crew of CVE 21, while 1943 started relatively calmly, the year exited with plenty of excitement. With depleting supplies of aviation fuel oil, and provisions running low, the task force readied for Casablanca and resupply. Exiting the "black pit," the group of vessels spotted TG 21.14, led by their sister carrier USS *Core*, CVE 13, also constructed in Tacoma, entering the hunting grounds. Both carriers exchanged updated intelligence as they passed each other. Pulling into the North African harbor on January 4, 1944, the men of Ramsey's task group were granted an additional visit to the port city.[40] The vessel's *War Diary* noted a rather unique event that took place while moored in the Moroccan harbor.

It recorded, "On 5 January a 40 man working party of Italian prisoners of war were brought on board under the supervision of Chief Police Petty Officer and Police Petty Officers of NOB Casablanca. They were occupied in moving stores from 0905 until 1500."[41] These Italian prisoners of war captured by Allied forces in North Africa came on board via whaleboats in the form of work parties. These POWs, among other duties, hauled the cases of beer stored within the escort carrier to smaller craft, which then transported the beverages to a nearby baseball diamond. Left field was delineated by a large chain-link fence behind which resided the Italian POWs. These POWs, seeking a reprieve from captivity, gathered along the fence for the American game. This ever-rotating crop of baseball players also presented American sailors of Italian heritage the opportunity to converse with them in both simple and detailed conversations.[42]

Such fraternization also took place on board CVE 21, as the POWs collected cases of beer. During this process, Hector Vernetti, while in the hangar, struck up a conversation with an Italian who happened to know his dialect from northern Italy. The conversation turned into a chance to swap items, in which Vernetti bartered a cap from the Italian. In the course of the conversation, another *Block Island* sailor from New York City overheard their chatting. Recognizing the regional dialect, he asked this Italian if he knew of a particular man from Italy. The Italian confirmed that he knew the gentleman in question and, in fact, pointed him out among the work party on board. This young sailor from New York walked over and introduced himself to this middle-aged prisoner, his aged uncle. Here on *Block Island*, this young American sailor met his mother's brother for the first time.[43]

12
"Rocket Business"

After resupply in Casablanca, CVE 21 and her task force cruised north. She escorted a Britain-bound convoy through the same dangerous waters where she had battled the German wolfpack in the last week of 1943. Once safely past, she departed and joined a southbound convoy and again successfully provided air cover for the movement of men and war materiel.[1] While not cut loose from the convoy to seek out the enemy, in a war won in part by logistical know-how, these escort carrier missions again aided in the ever-constricting noose around the German war machine. Protecting convoys, however, still proved dangerous. Whether the pilots flew missions attacking submarines, or in escorting convoys, threats still lingered for any operations leaving the flight deck.

On January 11, 1944, CVE 21 experienced her first loss of a man. On a cold morning, Ens. T. P. Ridley boarded his FM Wildcat. With the carrier headed into the winter Atlantic air, over the teak deck Ridley opened up the Pratt & Whitney fourteen-cylinder radial engine. As his propeller gripped the air, and his aircraft cleared the flight deck, Ridley failed to maintain airspeed, and his plane stalled and plunged into the Atlantic, throwing up a wall of seawater. The crew of the flight deck watched in amazement as the fully loaded four-ton aircraft sank into the deep within seconds. Ridley, unable to escape the Wildcat, sank into the deep as CVE 21 cruised over the spot of impact where the plane transformed from an aircraft to an 8,000-pound sinking stone. Ramsey solemnly wrote, "Although this crash was the result of a simple piloting error, it was nevertheless the first instance of a pilot being lost while operating from BLOCK ISLAND."[2]

However disturbing the loss of Ridley, the war continued, and CVE 21 on this day was scheduled to make history. Fear—not wonder—centered on the handling of the newly arrived rockets. After the loss of Ridley, the *War Diary* reported, "Rocket from TBF was accidentally discharged. It buried itself almost to the fins in the flight deck."[3] Two other Avengers, piloted by Lieutenant McFord and Lt. Willis Seeley, lifted off the flight deck armed with the new rockets and soon after spotted a surfaced U-boat. Using clouds as cover, the pair of pilots nosed their aircraft forward and attacked, helping usher the US military into the rocket age. Wing cameras mounted on the Avengers captured thin trails of exhaust smoke exiting behind accelerating rockets plunging toward the surprised U-boat. Of the six fired, two swung away wildly off target. The four others followed the designed plan of the engineers who imagined this weapon and eerily mirrored the pages of prewar sci-fi comic books. The four rockets struck the water just short of the exposed U-boat hull, violently tossing up billows of seawater.

McFord and Seeley, undeterred by the rocket misses, circled around toward the surprised submarine to drop a pattern of depth charges. Germans quickly poured onto the deck to defend their ship. Manning the antiaircraft guns, they threw up shells in the hopes of causing the attacking Avengers to retreat. McFord recalled about this second approach, "I could see the tracers coming by me and forming a cone around the plane."[4] Seeley, on his second pass, was unable to open his bomb bay doors; however, he had a perfect view of McFord's attack. Seeley remembered, "He scored a perfect straddle."[5] One weapon exploded directly next to the submarine's hull, causing her to slow to a halt. With the U-boat slowing, the pair of flyers circled around for a third attack. McFord led this attack again using the only weapon remaining, his .50-caliber machine guns. "I could see my bullets hitting, making white marks on the conning tower," he said.[6] On this pass Seeley successfully cleared his bomb bay doors and delivered a depth charge attack on the wounded U-boat, which was in the act of submerging. As the charges exploded, the U-boat inverted its position, with the bow reaching an angle of 50 degrees out of the Atlantic. Dead in the water, the U-boat bobbed up and down on the surface. Soon after, a large puff of yellowish-green smoke erupted from the submarine, and she sank stern first. Of the attack Ramsey wrote, "two Avengers from BLOCK ISLAND sighted a submarine . . . and sank it promptly with a beautifully coordinated attack involving for the first time, I believe, the triple-threat attack of rockets, depth bombs, and the Mark 24 mine."[7]

Five full months after this attack, in the July 1944 issue of *All Hands* under a feature called "True Story Adventures," was a picture of Lt. (jg) L. McFord and his crew. The article featured an image of McFord, who is seen smiling and flanked by Charles H. Geetsch, ARM3c, and William H. Ryder, AMM2c. All three stand in front of his Avenger *Len Sharon*. While the Navy officially discouraged the naming and painting of personal markings on aircraft, this image demonstrates that it did in fact occur. The article begins with, "Rockets made their debut in the air war on submarines when two Navy bombers recently used the new weapons against a U boat."[8] While the specifics of the mission were not mentioned, such as the location of the hunter-killer group or CVE 21, the author described it as a "Buck Rogers attack."[9] The rocket weapons systems used throughout the postwar USN could trace their genealogy to the deck of USS *Block Island*. By the time sailors throughout the Navy read the article in July 1944, *Block Island* was already lost and resting on the Atlantic floor.

The industrial might of nation-states in World War II produced a range of weapons to kill the enemy, high-altitude aircraft rained down bombs from miles above, German rockets targeted population centers in England, and, in the New Mexican desert, physicists were developing a weapon that existed only in theoretical formulas scribbled on chalkboards. One side effect for service members fighting was the reduction in the likelihood of seeing in human form the enemy you were attempting to kill. Modern warfare was wiping away the face of the enemy from the experience of warfare.[10]

The crew of *Block Island*, on their second hunter-killer mission, never laid eyes on the enemy. Only a handful of pilots and aircrew had actually seen a U-boat. Modern technology blurred the concept of the enemy as human. With no enemy in the flesh, moral codes of war altered. Rockets, bullets, and depth charges were employed in the destruction of U-boats, not of young Germans serving their country. With advances in submarine technology since the Great War, "seeing" the enemy was reduced to the electronic scent of sonar and radar registrations, either over earphones or as blips on green screens. One scholar termed naval warfare in World War II "a cold, long-distance business."[11] He concluded, "Naval warfare became thoroughly depersonalized."[12] For the crews of the U-boats, sensory insulation proved so complete it obscured not only the enemy but the very natural world. For men confined inside the metal man-made world during almost the entirety of a war patrol, only the inner workings of their ears provided sensations of movement such as surfacing and diving.[13] Electric lights, foul air, and near nonexistent personal space defined these German sailors' time on board. One commander wrote that "the very food tasted of U boat, that is, diesel oil, with a flavor of mold. . . . The bulkheads sweated, every thing turned moldy. Leather outfits and shoes went green in a fortnight if we didn't use them."[14]

Allied and German vessels rarely knew the full circumstances of the battles in which they took part. In some ways they very much resembled the postwar version of the board game Battleship. For Allied forces interested in the bean counting of which specific U-boat sank in what particular location, their tools could only be described as a slightly improved crystal ball. It would take historians in the decades after the war to piece together action reports from all sides to gain a clear understanding of who attacked whom at what time and place. Even then, some U-boats and Allied ships still sank as a result of enemy attacks that historians were never able to credit to a specific vessel. The theater of war *Block Island* engaged in was enigmatic.

For CVE 21, this shadow war took place with the detection of enemy submarines, DDs and aircraft attacking, and then waiting. Hints of success ranged from the surfacing of oil and U-boat debris to a massive underwater disturbance as a submarine imploded. For the pilots and aircrew of VC-58, days such as these stood in stark contrast with those of their fellow naval aviators in the Pacific. If the excitement of dogfighting with Japanese Zeros in aerial combat had a complete opposite, it was the hunter-killer mission. Pilots and crews preformed a mental and physical marathon with tedious hours of searching the seas for U-boats. Staying sharp proved a challenge. On repeated missions they saw nothing. Many flights consisted of chasing electrical registrations from a range of detection devices. Endless searching of empty seas could rust rehearsed training and threaten a successful attack when the time actually presented itself: "Atrophied skills and the excitement of the chase often combined to cause a bungled contact or attack."[15] The sighting of a periscope on the Atlantic's surface produced a rush because of the rarity of the event. In this new war, at times the enemy was heard and not seen. Sonar operators of TG 21.16 heard enemy torpedoes launched from a phantom U-boat. An example of this phenomenon was reported by Ramsey: "At 1217 on this date, PARROTT again heard a torpedo propeller in her sound gear, and again the torpedo passed clear of the formation without a wake being visible."[16] In modern naval combat in this theater, specter submarines at times invisibly fired torpedoes at the passing task force.

Dehumanization of the enemy stemmed not only from rarely seeing him in the flesh but also from the increasingly sophisticated methods of locating the vessels he operated from. By mid-1943 ship-based radar allowed for the registering of surfaced U-boats at over four miles, whereas at the beginning phase of the war, it was just over 1.5 miles.[17] Detection underwater was complicated by a range of factors, including natural forces, such as animal life and variations in ocean temperatures, and distinguishing not only the direction and range of a man-made noise but whether it was friendly or hostile. Throughout the war a submerged U-boat could be detected at best with sonar at two thousand yards, or just over a mile. A less successful method of underwater detection aimed not at recording sound but at measuring disturbances caused in the earth's magnetic field as the result of a large metal object, such as a U-boat, cruising under the ocean's surface. Called magnetic anomaly detection (MAD), this system never expanded detection past one thousand feet. Thus, at best it could be used in refining the position of a known U-boat, rather than in locating one individually on the open ocean.[18]

Additional detection equipment centered on U-boats sending radio transmissions, which at the time could take place only while surfaced. The British program known as Ultra cracked the transmitted coded messages, thus cultivating detailed information on enemy movements and strategy, such as pinpointing the location of future concentrations of German U-boats. However, the information garnered from intercepted messages took time to digest; thus, valuable information hours old was like the road in a rearview mirror in terms of tactical application to the battlefield. Although knowing exactly what detailed instructions the enemy is communicating can be invaluable, just detecting the radio transmission delivered usefulness on the tactical level. Any radio transmission produced an atmospheric anomaly, which if triangulated could yield a location of a surfaced vessel. A transmission just seconds long was thus a possible game changer. High-frequency direction finding (HF/DF), using detection stations ringing the Atlantic on land and on board Allied vessels, produced coordinates with devastating results for the U-boat sending the message.[19] "Like somebody giving away their location in the dark by coughing, the U boats revealed themselves to HF/DF."[20]

The official historian for the USN during the war, Samuel Eliot Morison, using a colorful analogy, wrote that HF/DF was "highly sensitive and elongated cat's whiskers."[21] Many times inventions take on the personality traits of their inventors, and this notion is illustrated by the consortium of individuals giving birth to both Ultra and HF/DF. Ultra, designed by chess players, linguists, and mathematicians, was highly convoluted and, when fully functioning, produced rich detail. However, this conglomerate of complexity could take place only on land. HF/DF, devised by engineers and scientists, produced no information on what the transmissions contained and did not attempt to. HF/DF's singular focus was to assert in real time the location of the radio communication. Eventually HF/DF technology was compressed, which made it seaworthy. While nowhere near as specific as the fully deciphered Ultra intelligence (which could take days to fully process), HF/DF provided information for immediate tactical use. These three detection methodologies—radar, sonar, and HF/DF—when combined with newly developed weapons and tactics, yielded a winning formula for the Allies in the Battle of the Atlantic. Innovation, adaptation, and at times, improvisation by CVE captains such as Logan Ramsey were used in this theater where sailors rarely saw one another when engaged in battle.[22]

Ramsey had HF/DF not only on CVE 21 but also on three of the task group's escorts, greatly increasing the capacity of the vessels in detecting and tracking the elusive enemy.[23] In the Night Order Book for the night of January 13–14, Ramsey wrote, "We are in the exact middle of the submarine concentration. Keep a particularly keen look out down moon from us."[24] On January 14, as Lieutenant Pattison flew his Avenger, and as he and his crew scanned the ocean northeast of the Azores Islands, they detected the unexpected. They spotted debris floating on the ocean, including a number of life rafts full of men. Again, mystery surrounded the discovery. Who were these men? Where did they come from? Which side were they on? Captain Ramsey ordered two of the task force's DDs to investigate. Just forty-one miles from CVE 21, these eleven life rafts full of men had, up until recently, manned a U-boat. Ramsey wrote, "Forty-three survivors of a German submarine, sunk on the night before by an unidentified aircraft, were recovered and made prisoners."[25]

During the war the average enlisted sailor and soldier knew surprisingly little of the actual battle in which they were engaged. Daily newspapers, full of basic information on the campaigns and general strategy of the war effort, were unavailable. One World War II veteran's memoir looked back on how little he understood of the overall scene of the war. He wrote that he was "woefully ignorant of the strategy and geopolitics of the war. The folks back home actually had a clearer view than we on the scene."[26] He concluded, "I knew war in a way no civilian could, but I had no synoptic view of it such as I might have gained from reading the daily papers."[27] Confusion about the war amplified with the Battle of the Atlantic as tracking sonar/radar contacts, attacking "blips" on green screens, and the stress of thinking of the loss of one's vessel all made for a perplexing situation. However, as the CVE neared the DDs, her sailors would see the German enemy in human form for the first time.

A breeches buoy device, utilizing a series of ropes and canvas sacks, permitted the transfer of personnel between ships on the open sea without stopping. One *Block Island* officer remembered the "topside and hangar deck were festooned by curious sailors to watch the bedraggled Germans come swinging over in the canvas sacks."[28] For the crew, this was an opportunity to see the enemy that Americans had heard about for years inflicting damage to Allied shipping. Like many in the US military, a number of the sailors of CVE 21 descended from recent European migrations to North America. Not far removed from European heritage, these sailors grew up in multilingual households with mixtures of European tongues spoken, with the older members speaking the language of the old country and the next generation conversing in that particular language and English. Kitchens also contained links to the old country. Sailors came from homes where family meals consisted of communal gatherings, where Norwegians ate lutefisk, Czechs ate kolaches, and Greeks ate moussaka.

One of the sailors struggling for a view of these German POWs was Hector Vernetti, who grew up in a trilingual household in Globe, Arizona. Italian and English were spoken at home, and at the family's service station in 1930s Arizona, transactions with customers consisted of English and Spanish. Jammed next to other sailors hoping for a glimpse, he was surprised by the sight of the enemy in the flesh. He recalled, "Down in the hangar deck when they brought them in, they had it all roped off. Guys were hanging from all over just trying to get a look and see what them people looked like." These German supermen, who, according to Nazi propaganda, were superior in all ways physically and intellectually, looked eerily familiar. "They were just like us. Blond and blue eyes, just kids."[29]

Once on the ship, they were placed in T-shirts with "P W" in large black letters on the front, designating them as prisoners of war. For Irv Biron, these Germans proved a curiosity. Biron's parents came from Italy, and these prisoners did not seem that much different from himself. Biron took pictures of them and enjoyed hearing their perspective on the war. One German had studied at a university in the United States, another asked of reported damage done to American cities on the eastern seaboard by German forces, and a third wished to go to America. The prisoners would be removed from the ship during the next resupply visit to Casablanca or Norfolk. Biron remembered one German not wanting to leave when Casablanca was reached. He recollected, "One we almost had to put in chains to get him off the ship. He wanted to go to the United States."[30]

The vessel's *War Diary* noted on January 19, "At request of Kapitanleutnant (Capt.) Wolfgang Wenzel, Chaplin G. A. MacInnes, USNR, held divine services for the German prisoners so that they could commemorate their lost shipmates. Three separate services were held for officers, petty officers and non-rated men, to prevent intercourse between the three groups."[31] Most of the German officers spoke English at an intermediate, and some at a higher, level. One of the first requests of the commanding officer of U 231, Capt. Wolfgang Wenzel, was to remember his lost crew. During interrogation he asked in English, "I wonder if it would be possible for us to have a memorial service for our departed comrades."[32] USS *Block Island* chaplain Lt. G. A. MacInnes held services that included "a short opening prayer, a portion of the usual verses from the Bible, which are read at funerals, and longer, final prayer."[33] MacInnes spoke in English, and a junior grade officer on CVE 21 translated the statements into German. With no bodies of their former comrades to mourn over, this was the nearest form of closure for the Germans saying goodbye to their dead shipmates and U 231. However, the Germans also improvised, developing other methods of memorializing their doomed vessel and lost crew members.

Hector Vernetti served as a parachute rigger on board CVE 21. His position included the packing and repairing of parachutes, including working with cloth, silk, thread, and sewing equipment. While at work one day, someone showed up with orders to gather supplies—colored pencils, material, and needle and thread—to be given to the POWs held on board. With spare time on their hands, these prisoners hand-made memorials. Using these donated materials, they made overseas caps, among other items, all of which were constructed as memorials to their lost ship and crew members. A likeness of U 231 appeared on some of these memorials, while others included the names of lost comrades or the swastika. Beyond acts of closure, these also served as currency in bartering with *Block Island* sailors, who traded cartons of American cigarettes for these handmade memorials. For American sailors, hungry for tangible pieces from the Battle of the Atlantic, these items proved very popular.[34] For the Germans, these provided a means for acquiring American tobacco, as well as a way to commemorate their lost shipmates.

Obviously, Captain Wenzel of U 231 garnered the most interest. After interrogation he complained of a sore throat and saw the ship's flight surgeon, Cdr. Jasper L. Custer. Examining his opened mouth, Custer found what appeared to be burns and a puncture wound in the back of his throat. Using the X-ray machine on board, Custer found to his amazement a .32-caliber bullet lodged in the back of Wenzel's throat. Upon questioning, Captain Wenzel confessed that once in the water after abandoning ship, and with his U-boat lost, he placed a pistol in his mouth and fired. The weapon discharged and produced only a weakened dud, likely due to seawater entering the pistol. The captain later recalled, "It was a 'sore throat,' and he had a bullet in it! We had the bullet removed, and the doctor kept it for a souvenir."[35] The story published in the *New York Times* granted readers a new perspective on the fearless German U-boat commanders.[36]

In fulfilling their assigned duties to the USN, some CVE 21 sailors experienced guilt. Raised in the Judeo-Christian philosophy that killing another human is immoral, warriors for centuries have wrestled with juggling duties of protecting their society on one hand and morality (as they understood it) on the other. After a CVE 21 plane successfully destroyed one particular U-boat, the gunner from this aircraft, after the attack, learned that a number of survivors had been plucked out of the Atlantic waters and transferred to *Block Island*. One of the survivors wounded during the attack, lay recovering in the medical ward. This American gunner decided to visit this wounded sailor from the enemy's navy and speak with him. He told him simply, "Sorry—it was my duty."[37] While for those sitting in the comfort of their American homes it was simple to say the enemy must be destroyed, for those witnessing the results of their actions firsthand the moral reality was not so clear-cut.

13
Denver Omelet Sandwiches

While the German POWs provided a unique break from the hunter-killer missions, the crew members also invented their own forms of entertainment in line with a long tradition of the USN: gambling. At a USO show, a female performer once asked Bob Hope, "I meant to ask you, Bob. . . . Are there any sharks around San Diego?" Hope replied, "Did you ever meet a Marine with a pair of dice?"[1] All good jokes are based in some resemblance to fact; Hope's quip is no exception. Military life included gambling in all services, especially so for the USN. Lt. Richard Nixon on a naval base in the Solomon Islands played poker. As president decades later, Nixon said, "In the intense loneliness and boredom of the South Pacific our poker games were more than idle pastimes."[2] Nixon was a natural. A wartime friend recalled of Nixon, "I once saw him bluff a lieutenant commander out of $1,500 with a pair of deuces."[3] By the end of the war, Nixon had accumulated $8,000, which bankrolled his first congressional campaign in 1946.

Block Island sailor Hector Vernetti was not a gambler himself, but he partook in the illegal communal activities on board. These events, which took place in their sleeping quarters, relied on Vernetti's connections with other crew members. From a cook Vernetti received fresh eggs and vegetables. As alcohol could not be legally consumed on board without prescription from the medical ward, Vernetti acquired some from a pharmacist's mate and mixed it with bottles of Coke. A box covered in cloth made a gambling table, which was accompanied by an extension light hanging from the ceiling in a darkened compartment. Using an illegal hot plate, Vernetti made Denver omelet sandwiches. As the card games continued, Vernetti played host in producing sandwiches for the players and providing rum and Cokes. Bathroom breaks provided the only point of danger of exposing their makeshift gambling joint, as all members needed to make the appearance of sobriety as they walked to the head in a range of sea conditions.[4]

While not all sailors were as resourceful as Vernetti, other methods existed on board to obtain illegal alcohol. Torpedoes required fuel, of the high-octane variety, to propel hundreds of pounds, and this energy could also be transformed, with the proper knowledge, into improvised alcoholic drinks allowing sailors to get "tight." Drinking granted some relief from the two emotional extremes of Navy life, extreme boredom and extreme stress. On some vessels this became such a problem that junior officers were ordered to keep a watchful eye on the levels of fuel inside torpedoes. Besides the danger of drunken crew members in a crisis, there also existed the risk of torpedoes launched at the enemy and simply running out of propellant on the way to the intended target.[5] As for many things in the Navy, nicknames for the illicit drink abounded, including "torpedo juice," "torp," and "Condition Red."[6] Bombsights served as an additional source of alcohol, which one seasoned petty officer mixed with coffee to produce "moosemilk."[7]

While drinking on board required clandestine skills, sailors off ship encountered copious opportunities to drink. Vernetti and other *Block Island* sailors, when hitting the bars stateside, had a little way of having fun. While not fighters themselves, they knew how to start a fight easily enough. They would scan the room, and if they noticed a mixing of the services, with members of the Army or Marines in the bar as well, they launched their plan. One of them would yell, "The US Navy is winning this war!!" This would get the soldiers and Marines fired up, and they loudly asserted that in fact their particular branch of the service was winning this war. Vernetti and his pals simply stood back and watched the fights erupt in the crowded saloons. After the brawl died down, they moved on to the next bar to continue the agitation.[8]

❋

Hunter-killer missions patrolling the open ocean of the central Atlantic chipped away at the German safe haven. The air patrols and task force groups broke up packs of U-boats. As a result, locating the U-boats became more difficult. One historian noted, "So the U.S. Navy's new CVE-DD(DE) teams had to beat the bushes for game. And beat the bushes they did, driving deep into the U boats' mid-Atlantic territory."[9] Or, as another historian wrote, "The success of the jeep carrier was proven every time a convoy arrived intact at its destination."[10] Also, the German tactic of sending out the large "milch cow" U-boats to refuel and resupply smaller attack U-boats was compromised. One author wrote, "No longer could the 'tanker submarines' browse around the Azores in bucolic peace."[11]

Thanks in part to the air attacks from the very first CVE-based aircraft, German commander-in-chief Dönitz recalled that in the middle of 1943, the U-boats added antiaircraft weaponry to the vessels. However, the serious shock to the morale of the U-boat high command as a result of these setbacks could not be as easily augmented as the weapons of the submarines. In April of 1943, Dönitz reported to Hitler, "I fear that the submarine war will be a failure if we do not sink more ships than the enemy is able to build."[12] Such air attacks from hunter-killer missions forced a radical transformation in U-boat tactics. It caused the breaking up the famed U-boat packs to work solo in carrying on the war. The threat of air attack also caused U-boats to remain submerged during the day and to surface only at night. This caused the CVE composite squadrons to train and launch night-flight operations in search of the vulnerable surfaced U-boats. This scouting, combined with HF/DF information passed to the task force running night operations, further compressed the "black pit."[13]

For the old World War I era DDs, fuel consumption was high in tracking and attacking the believed locations of U-boats for the two weeks in the heavy winter seas of the Atlantic. Ramsey, aware that his ships were pressing the limits on fuel levels, ordered the force to the vicinity of the Azores Islands. Here the fuel lines from CVE 21 transferred thousands of gallons of energy to the decades-old DDs. The distribution of fuel, especially in rough seas, could be just as deadly as engaging submarines. As Ramsey wrote, "I was able to refuel the destroyers only with extreme difficulty in occasional lulls between strong gales. Fuel hoses parted three times during these operations."[14] Ramsey, ever mindful of the morale of all the men of the task group, had these fuel transfers include special fuel for the sailors as well. He wrote, "I made it a matter of routine to furnish each destroyer with 400 pounds of bread, 15 gallons of ice cream, and cake or pie at each refueling."[15] As the group was critically short of depth charges, *Parrott* and *Bulmer* received orders from Ramsey to the island of Horta in the Azores to load these loaned weapons from the British.[16]

Continuing the hunt, the task force witnessed the full fury of the Atlantic in winter. Monstrous seas and gales canceled all flight operations.[17] While the men of CVE 21 bucked the heaving seas in their 10,000-ton vessel, thoughts of the smaller DDs in the same seas kept fears in check. Ramsey, knowing the Atlantic was more the enemy now than the Germans, ordered his ships to slow down as they plowed to the west. Even as he slept, he still wanted to know the situation. He ordered on night watch, "Inform me as to barometer and wind velocity every 2 hours or whenever a significant change occurs." While this certainly delayed their reaching Norfolk, the reduction in speed lessened the impact, and thus the force, of these heaving seas on CVE 21 and the World War I era destroyers. As the group neared Cape Henry, the southern entrance into Chesapeake Bay, the crews breathed a sigh of relief. The horn of CVE 21 blew a salute to the DDs, which pulled to the north, bound for Boston Harbor and on to their next assignment. These escorts, except for three days in port at Casablanca, had been under way for forty-nine days and steamed over 16,000 engine miles.[18] USS *Block Island*'s missions in the Atlantic would continue, however, with new teammates.

On February 3, 1944, CVE 21 docked at Norfolk, delayed by the winter seas. In Norfolk orders awaited Ramsey on his upcoming mission. Captain Ramsey's continued lobbying with the upper levels of Navy command finally bore fruit. First, the replacement squadron soon to come on board, VC-6, included nine new model FM Wildcats. This Wildcat not only was faster but included a strengthened landing gear for rough landings, and most importantly the increased operational range allowed for longer flights, thus increasing the chances of locating enemy submarines. In addition, the next mission included a modern state-of-the-art destroyer. USS *Corry*, DD 463, which in comparison to the World War 1 era DDs, not only granted Ramsey improved screening ability and expanded search radii as the result of *Corry*'s increased speed but also greatly amplified the offensive measures and lethality of the task force. However, arguably the greatest asset on board *Corry* came not in the form of a weapons system but a complex network of machines and men that allowed for the processing of the amazing amount of data available in this electronic war, granted by an ever-expanding realm of detection systems. Known as Combat Information Center (CIC), this system seemed tailor-made for the nuances of modern naval warfare. A leading scholar of CIC wrote "With six possible sources of information—own-ship's radar, lines of bearing from direction finders, own-ship's sonar, radio reports from patrol aircraft or other vessels, Ultra intelligence, and old-fashioned visual sighting—the CIC was a natural fit for the Battle of the Atlantic."[19] For Ramsey and other naval commanders, the days of sail, with Nelson analyzing the entire command situation with a look through the eyeglass, were gone. The very nature of what one historian called the "cognitive experience of command" had radically transformed in just a matter of decades.[20] In terms of command experience, World War II was light-years away from the Japanese victory over the Imperial Russian Navy in 1905 at the Battle of Tsushima. For Ramsey and other skippers, the amount of information pouring in necessitated placing an astonishing amount of trust in a system composed of three parts: manual, automated, and semi-automated.[21] Spotting a submarine visually, a sonar registration, and a blip on a radar screen were all juggled with the other incoming data in computing a clear command picture for Ramsey and TG 21.15. One historian wrote that the new CIC system functioned as a "metaphorical second brain."[22] Ramsey fully welcomed this new form of technology on board, as clearly witnessed in a night order issued during an upcoming mission. He wrote, "In case of contacts take immediate action. Inform me as soon as possible and I will proceed to CIC from sea cabin."[23]

TG 21.16 would also include an entirely new class of warship. Gone were the old and slow World War I era DDs, and with them their high fuel use and slow speed. Ramsey's wish list to improve the offensive prowess of future hunter-killer missions was encapsulated in two words—"destroyer escorts." The DEs, similar to the escort carriers, were labeled "small" in comparison with their larger sister classification of vessels. Considering all physical objects, however, size is relative. Few places in the United States outside of the major cities can claim a building as tall as a DE was long, which was over the length of a football field. She displaced 1,600 tons and was powered by four General Motors diesel engines yielding 4,000-shaft hp, giving her a top speed of twenty-one knots. While a number of classifications were constructed, the Cannon class of DE included one 40 mm and eight 20 mm antiaircraft guns. For engaging surface vessels, she retained one three-inch gun. However, her real offensive punch came from her ability to launch torpedoes, drop depth charges, and lob forward-launching Hedgehog antisubmarine mortars.[24] These weapons, combined with the much greater speed and range of the DEs, represented a huge leap forward from the previous World War I era destroyers.

One World War II newspaper reporter who strove to tell the military stories outside the limelight of admirals' and generals' stars was Ernie Pyle. During the war he sought out where the rubber met the road in terms of combat. Throughout the war he rejected dinner with officers to dine in mess tents with the enlisted men. Pyle understood the war well, for he slept in foxholes. When it came to the Navy, Pyle sought what other reporters ignored, and he was drawn to stories found on such vessels as the destroyer escorts. Of the vessels he wrote, "It is a wartime product, and it has done very valiantly. They are rough and tumble little ships."[25] Having spent time with the grunts to understand the land war, Pyle resided on board a DE with her crew to understand their conditions. Of the ship itself, he reported, "They buck and they twist. They shudder and they fall through space." Compared to large warships making the headlines, these DEs were small and thus much more susceptible to the ocean's whims and wishes. Pyle learned by the time-tested method of listening. After talking with the crews of DEs, Pyle wrote, "Their sailors say they should have flight pay and sub pay both—they're in the air half the time, under water the other half. Their men are accustomed to being wet and think nothing of it."[26]

If offensive punch was divided by the displacement, pound for pound DEs were tough vessels. With a combination of high reserve buoyancy and first-rate compartmentalization, the DEs, despite their relatively small size, were well suited for the Atlantic. Congress, in particular, loved the fact that DEs fetched just over half of what a new Benson-class destroyer cost the Treasury Department. However, these, like the escort carriers, lacked one major component, an armored hull.[27] As with CVE 21, a Bogue classification of the escort carriers, the hulls were only a quarter inch of steel. While sailors on the battleships knew their hull was armored and could deflect some of the explosive force from enemy shells and torpedoes, the DEs had only a quarter inch of brittle metal separating them from the waters of the Atlantic. Like the men of CVE 21, the DEs' sailors were well aware of what one enemy torpedo could inflict on their thin hull.

Joining TG 21.16 was Lt. Sheldon Kinney, the first commander of USS *Bronstein*, DE 189, who accepted his commission at the age of twenty-five. While extremely young by today's standards, Kinney had proved his ability to overcome adversity throughout his young life. Dropping out of high school at the age of sixteen, two years later he joined the 1937 plebe class of the US Naval Academy. After Annapolis, he served on the destroyer USS *Sturtevant*, DD 240. When a pair of downed aviators needed assistance, Kinney dove off the destroyer to aid in their rescue. When *Sturtevant* sank in April 1942 as the result of striking a mine, Kinney survived by holding on to a bag of floating coffee beans.[28]

Similar to the escort carriers, DEs encapsulated many of the same qualities of their larger classification of sister ships at a fraction of the cost and construction time. Four of the newest DEs joined TG 21.16. Whereas the old DDs retained only the limited ability to fire four-inch guns and drop depth charges, the new DEs were armed with the forward-tossing Mark 10 Hedgehog. Designed as a multiple-charge system, the Hedgehog lobbed forward twenty-four smaller projectiles, in comparison to a depth charge. Each projectile, weighing sixty-five pounds, was tossed forward and landed in a circular pattern up to two hundred yards in front of the vessel firing this system. Unlike the depth charge, this Hedgehog system exploded only if it made contact with a submerged enemy. While smaller in explosive punch, the Hedgehog system overcame the guesswork of determining the depth of the enemy, and thus if these weapons did make contact, the effect was deadly.[29] These DEs armed with Hedgehogs, working as a team with the longer-ranged Wildcats of VC-6, all directed with the CIC system on board *Corry*, greatly increased the lethality of TG 21.16, which was demonstrated in a textbook manner in short order.

"Green" crews manning these DEs rushed into the war with men new not only to the Navy but also to the sea. USS *Paine*, DE 578, exemplified these vessels, with 95 percent of all the officers and enlisted sailors going to sea for the first time on the vessel's shakedown cruise. Pulling out of Boston Harbor on a training mission to Bermuda, they learned their duties on the fly. They tracked an American submarine, fired their guns, and watched in awe the explosive bursts erupting from the sea caused by their own depth charges. However, in practicing firing a side-launched torpedo armed with a dummy warhead, excitement ensued for the wrong reason. One crew member recalled, "The darn thing turned around and headed right back at us. Thank goodness it was set to run at a depth deeper than our keel!"[30]

All these lessons, crammed into one short shakedown cruise, granted these DE sailors all the experience the Navy required for entering the Battle of the Atlantic. Four of these new hulls joining TG 21.16 included USS *Bronstein*, DE 189, USS *Bostwick*, DE 103, USS *Breeman*, DE 104, and USS *Thomas*, DE 102, and in short order all proved themselves deadly players. Ramsey, leading his third hunter-killer mission, would prove that America's industrial mass production and the leadership of CVE skippers could help wrest complete control of the Atlantic away from the German U-boats.

For the crews of TG 21.16, the "black pit" awaited.

14
"Long Haired Scientists"

While *Block Island* served as a platform of war, she also functioned as a platform of science and experimentation in weaponry. In the straitlaced environment of the military, any civilian scientists on board a Navy vessel were an anomaly and thus referred to as "long haired scientists."[1] The U-boat menace in the Battle of the Atlantic in particular necessitated cooperation of the USN with the American scientific community. One historian wrote, "American scientists provided an analytical framework and produced a variety of new weapons that greatly expanded the range of possibilities for counterstrike."[2] One such scientist aboard CVE 21 was Paul Dimock, who specialized in magnetic anomaly detection (MAD) and worked for a consortium called Airborne Instruments Laboratory. Advances in MAD detection devices greatly reduced the size of these devices; thus, scientists such as Dimock could load these into Avengers and go aloft.[3] This system of detection sought to register the small irregularities created in the earth's magnetic field caused by a large submerged metal object like a submarine. However, with an average effective range of 1,000 feet the MAD system had limited effectiveness.[4] Crammed within the already tight confines of an Avenger, Dimock and his MAD equipment lifted off the flight deck in the hopes of probing the sea for U-boats below with the use of the earth's magnetic field.[5]

An unpublished memoir of a civilian named Russell Lewis not only provides a window into the development of a form of underwater detection but also holds rich details of life on board CVEs, from his missions assigned to hunter-killer groups. Throughout World War II, Lewis traveled the world working for the Navy Underwater Sound Laboratory, which was under the larger bureaucratic umbrella of the National Defense Research Committee (NDRC).[6] In addition to missions based from escort carriers *Block Island* and *Card*, Lewis led short periods of intensive training of Allied personnel in Nova Scotia, Hawaii, and Seymour Island off the Antarctic Peninsula. All of Lewis's missions centered on the detection of enemy submarines, and mission locations varied, so a package of fudge mailed to him by his sister took over a year to reach him. When the worn package arrived, it contained a collage of stamps from fleet post offices and even the Royal Canadian Air Force. When not in the labs at Underwater Sound located in New London, Connecticut, learning about the newest updates on underwater detection, Lewis served clandestinely on board Allied submarines, blimps, and aircraft launched from the decks of escort carriers. More than once when leaving an assignment, he heard, "You were never here."[7]

Lewis served his country as a civilian/scientist on two hunter-killer missions aboard *Block Island* and brought with him a secret detection system. Again the story of CVE 21 demonstrates the greater effort of the American science community assisting in the war effort of the escort carriers taking on the German U-boats.[8] Lewis, in his memoir, termed sonobuoys "the most up-to-date radio test equipment then in existence."[9] His initial briefing to the aircrews was in the pilots' ready room. On board aircraft carriers this room was generally located one deck below the flight deck. Here pilots found their own personal space, a portion of which mirrored a classroom with chairs and chalkboards for outlining future missions. Standing in front of these pilots for the first time, Lewis sounded like a proponent of science fiction. Holding a case roughly the size of a golf bag in his hands, he described how this would be dropped from an Avenger into the ocean below. After surviving the downward impact of 45 mph, this container made of saltwater-resistant paper commenced its mission. Colored dye in hues of purple, red, yellow, blue, and green was secreted into the ocean, visible to aircraft above but still beyond detection by the periscope of an enemy submarine. The battery-powered device then lowered a listening probe downward, away from the waves of the ocean's surface. Before the invention of the transistor, a glass vacuum tube secured inside the floating case facilitated the current to flow within the buoy and the lowered microphone. The recorded noise was transmitted via radio signal from a sonobuoy to the specially outfitted Avenger circling above, which contained a high-quality sound FM receiver. With space and weight a concern on the Avenger, the electronic engineers at Underwater Sound had reduced this FM receiver to the size of just two lunch boxes, a mass of twenty-four pounds.

Deployed in groupings of five, the sonobuoys floated many miles apart in an X pattern similar to that symbolizing the number five on the side of a die. The operator above could listen to each buoy separately, and with the five colors clearly delineating the area under audio surveillance, triangulate any detected submarine noise for further investigation by members of the task group. In favorable conditions an individual aircraft could receive the signal from an individual buoy up to thirty miles away. Once the battery life ended within the buoy, the container still floated on the surface; however, a chemical engineer at Underwater Sound devised a method for its self-destruction. While the chemically treated paper container resisted seawater, a small plug on the bottom, over time, would dissolve. Salt water rushing in sank the device. As Lewis noted in his memoir, "That was done to deny the enemy, who might otherwise find one, the knowledge of what the buoys were and how they were made."[10] Over the course of the war six thousand sonobuoys were produced, along with five hundred receivers.[11]

In the 1940s eavesdropping in the ocean was an early science, and a host of problems were encountered in detecting noises, for much more lurked under the surface of the Atlantic than just U-boats. One historian noted early problems that included "snapping shrimps on the ocean bottoms [that] made a curious crackling noise that disturbed sound listeners."[12] In addition to researching, Lewis sought to train the aircrew of *Block Island* to operate these new scientific devices without his assistance. Sonobuoys, when combined with the tracking abilities of the task group, allowed for an ocean search of almost three thousand square miles in a single hour.[13] The Allied combination of scientific know-how and improvisation in designing and building CVEs and DEs penetrated deep into the Germans' safe haven of the central Atlantic. As one historian wrote, "Scientists often built the first lot of gear by hand and worked with fighting units to install the equipment in aircraft or ships, which immediately began combat operations with it."[14]

In the first week of February 1944, Lewis arrived in Norfolk and reported to the duty officer on the quarter-deck of CVE 21. Later he wrote, "The officer was a bit puzzled because I had Navy Orders (from the US Navy Bureau of Ships), and I was a civilian. Further, my orders stated that I was to report directly to the ship's Commanding Officer—Capt. Logan Ramsey."[15] On board ship Lewis would wear an officer's uniform with no sign of rank. His berthing assignment was officers' state room 418, along with five pilots. After his personal gear was squared away, Lewis was escorted within the escort carrier to report to the captain. Lewis wrote, "He was a pleasant person, and, after saying that he was glad to have me aboard, he spoke of how important our mission was and explained that it would likely tax all of us to the limit."[16]

On February 16, 1944, a cold winter day, TG 21.16 pushed off from the Norfolk docks. Russell Lewis met the squadron commander and began giving lectures in the pilots' ready room on the concept of the sonobuoy and the overall use of the new detection systems. Lewis privately noted in his journal that while he had done these lectures before, they were always in lecture rooms situated on solid earth. Far removed from the laboratories of Underwater Sound in New London, Lewis interpreted technical jargon for the aircrew. As *Block Island* sailed toward the enemy's operating area, the theory of the classroom melted away, replaced by the realization that Lewis was headed to a war zone. As he made clear in his journal, just one torpedo strike would radically alter the fate of the crew. This was made abundantly clear when the squadron commander informed Lewis of his battle station once the carrier entered the operating area. Lewis wrote, "In hazardous areas muster occurred just before daybreak because, since the ship silhouetted against the early light made an ideal target for submarine attack, it was a time of maximum danger."[17] Once the group was 350 miles northwest of the Azores Islands, Lewis heard the boatswain read an announcement. Lewis remembered that it stated "all hands were cautioned to remain alert and ready for action."[18] As this was read, Lewis was privy to an additional piece of information unknown to the crew: a radio-direction-finder fix placed a German submarine within twenty-five miles of their location. Lewis wrote, "I noted that after the announcement was made voices that had been loud and animated became noticeably quieter."[19] On this last day of February, this being a leap year, *Block Island* and the hunter-killer vessels stalked within the "black pit" north of the Azores. As the final hours of the month clicked down, radar and sonar returned no contacts. Ramsey wrote, "We are in the midst of a sub concentration."[20]

The DEs continued their radar and sonar searches, and night pilots flew off CVE 21 and searched from the skies for visual evidence of the enemy. Nothing materialized. With dusk setting in, however, a *Block Island* Avenger and a Wildcat spotted a periscope producing a wake across the Atlantic's surface below them. The Avenger dropped sonobuoys seeking to track a lurking U-boat. As the pair of aircraft returned to *Block Island*, USS *Corry*, DD 463, with its 50,000 shaft hp, poured on the coal and, making thirty knots, quickly closed the fifteen miles distance toward the pattern of Lewis's sonobuoys floating on the Atlantic's surface.

On the dark bridge of *Corry*, as the ship neared the location of the dropped sonobuoys, the radar room picked up not one but two "blips" some eight thousand yards off. *Corry* closed the distance. Ten tense minutes later, sailors from *Corry* launched a star shell, which stretched into the darkened night and then burst with an explosion of illuminating light, clearly revealing a U-boat on the surface. The sailors manning *Corry*'s 20 mm guns poured rounds into the exposed submarine. Sailors on the *Block Island*, within miles of the scene of battle, watched the fireworks display on the horizon. Unknown, however, to Ramsey was that while *Corry* had cornered the U-boat, at least two other U-boats were also on the scene just below the cruising task group.[21]

At the time, in the ready room of *Block Island*, Lewis exited with a pilot and quickly climbed a ladder to get to the flight deck. Any theoretical doubts Lewis might have held that he was not in a war zone evaporated as he looked toward the blackened horizon. He wrote, "In the distance we could see star-shells being fired by the *Corry* and soon thereafter tracers and gun fire."[22] After the attack, returning to the ready room, Lewis nervously commenced a conversation with the pilot. Soon after, the pilot gave nonverbal cues to stop speaking. Lewis recorded, "Every once in a while he would hold up his finger for silence, and finally, I asked him why he did that. 'Can't you feel the depth charges?' he said."[23] After a few minutes, Lewis too learned to detect the subtle sensation of shockwaves from exploding depth charges echoing away from a battle royal waging miles away. The final hours of February and the beginning hours of March were ones of total chaos in this small pocket of the Atlantic. Ramsey's task force gained sound contacts that soon disappeared, only to reappear minutes later. The total number of U-boats involved in this concentration was unknown. *Thomas*, in gaining a sound contact, delivered a pattern of charges. Captain Ramsey, learning of this, ordered *Bostwick* to assist *Thomas* in the attack. Minutes later CVE 21's radar registered an enemy U-boat headed toward the attacking *Thomas* and *Bostwick*. Ramsey quickly countered by ordering Kinney and his *Bronstein* toward this contact to protect his pair of attacking DEs.

Within three minutes *Bronstein* gained radar contact on the U-boat attempting to line up an attack on *Thomas* and *Bostwick*. Kinney, sensing a kill with the distracted U-boat, had *Bronstein* close the distance within two miles; he then ordered the firing of a star shell. Its billowing light revealed a fully surfaced 700-ton U-boat in the act of stalking. *Bronstein*'s three-inch guns and 40 mm weapons exploded to life on the surprised U-boat, which immediately crash-dived to evade the surprise attack. Kinney quickly followed with a Hedgehog attack, which proved ineffective. However, Kinney's sonar operators tracked the submerged U-boat, which continued in the direction of *Thomas* and *Bostwick*.

Meanwhile, *Thomas* and *Bostwick* continued the cat-and-mouse game with their own sonar contact, dropped depth charges, and lobbed Hedgehogs, which exploded and produced ever-expanding illuminated bubbles erupting from the seawater in the dark night. As quickly as this battle started, it ended. Sonar contacts ceased, explosions stopped, guns were silenced; however, the anxiety of all the crews remained, including the Germans beneath the waves. Clocks ticked past midnight, and March began with still no detection of the wolfpack. *Block Island*, protected and screened by all four DEs and the DD *Corry* cruised, all of them seeking to detect the U-boats previously engaged. Two hours after midnight, the action they all sensed would erupt at any moment did. *Bronstein*, off the port bow of *Block Island*, gained a sonar contact just 450 yards away. Kinney speeded toward the contact with his primary mission in mind, protection of the carrier. Ramsey's action report stated, "At any rate the submarine was between BLOCK ISLAND and the screen. BLOCK ISLAND made a sharp turn to the left away from the escorts and illuminated the radar contact but nothing was seen."[24] Kinney, from *Bronstein*, dropped an embracing pattern of charges to stop the U-boat from firing torpedoes on CVE 21. Ramsey wrote, "The sole purpose of this barrage was to thwart any submarine attempt to fire torpedoes at the carrier. Range at last contact was 175 yards."[25]

At 0222 on March 1, *Bronstein*'s sonar operators immediately yelled out another contact under a mile away. Kinney, wanting a kill, stealthily glided his vessel near the submerged contact; once within range he ordered a massive drop of eighteen depth charges onto the contact. Tense seconds seemed an eternity, and then the surface belched up bubbles resulting from underwater explosions, hinting at the violence occurring below the surface. Ramsey wrote, "Six seconds following the explosion of the last depth charge, an underwater explosion occurred which was louder in intensity than any of the previous depth charge explosions. A large phosphorescence around the ship was observed extending about 200 yards ahead. This had not occurred as a result of depth charges. The vibration in the ship caused by the explosion threw out the port engine. Radar was also knocked out. Personnel on the fantail noted astern shortly thereafter a considerable boiling, a great deal more than had been caused by the depth charges. All repair parties had the hell scared out of them, etc. Very violent explosion. (0231)."[26] The officer Roy Swift, who witnessed the explosion, wrote, "Shaken and awe-struck, the crew watched the huge phosphorescent turbulence astern where U 603, with 54 Germans aboard, had been destroyed."[27]

While much in naval warfare involved patiently waiting, or even boredom, these first hours of March proved the opposite. Ramsey, and the 1,500 men under his command, in these stress-filled days at the conclusion of one month and the beginning of another, attacked a handful of U-boats and destroyed one if not two submarines. In his after-action report, Ramsey estimated that five to seven submarines were involved in the complicated chess match on the seas. The men other than those of *Corry*, with her armored hull, fought in the deepest portion of the "black pit" with just a quarter inch of steel between them and the Atlantic.[28] In fact, after the war, research showed Ramsey and his task group had encountered a portion of Admiral Dönitz's group code-named Preussen, composed of more than twenty submarines. Dönitz's orders had these U-boats fanned out in a crescent-shaped pattern one hundred miles long, like a net, in the hopes of encountering Allied convoys. CVE 21 and her task force struck the middle of this crescent, placing her within approximately twenty-five miles of at least fifteen German U-boats.[29]

After a wild start to this hunter-killer mission, Ramsey received coordinates from naval intelligence for a new operating area some 350 miles north. While this order placed the group within a greater chance of encountering the dangerous German enemy, it also put them on a course with a different enemy. While the calendar read March and hinted at spring, winter storms still shrouded the central Atlantic. Cruising north, veteran sailors soon discerned a transition of the sea. The boatswain whistle over the intercom was followed by, "Secure all gear for heavy rolling."[30] The civilian/scientist Russell Lewis remembered a first lieutenant telling him to latch down all "tax-payer owned equipment entrusted to the navy."[31] He quickly sought out the expertise of sailors to assist him in securing all his specialized gear and boxed sonobuoys on the hangar deck. While Lewis thought the storm was about to peak, he realized later the heaving seas and rolling of the vessel were just a taste of this storm's strength. Following the advice of a veteran sailor, Lewis learned the value of sleeping on his stomach as the lengthy storm continued to wail.

As dawn broke, the waves reached twenty feet and were still building. As thirty-foot waves gathered, Ramsey weighed his options. Slowing down, they would reach the gathered intelligence point later, thus reducing its potential of success. However, the overall welfare of the vessels of the task force took precedence, as the sea, more than Germany, was the enemy now. The order to slow to six knots was given. Lewis, exiting from the pilots' ready room, ventured out on the catwalk and was greeted with towering, nearly fifty-foot waves and gale-force winds. He wrote, "The wind appeared to tear the tops off the waves and tons of water would come crashing down on the decks with a force that would destroy any exposed object."[32] In fact, Lewis's words were truer than he realized, as later the impact of a massive wave bent a steel beam upward under the forward portion of the flight deck. Of his brief time on the catwalk, Lewis years later wrote, "It was a fascinating beautiful sight, but I could not long endure the exposure required to see it."[33] As soon as he returned to the safety of the ready room he heard over the PA system, "Make turn for four knots."[34] At minimum speed, the task force gained one hundred miles only every twenty-four hours toward the new operating position. In fact, Ramsey's decision greatly increased the chances of the entire task force surviving the gale with minimal damage. Despite the order to slow down, besides the noted and repairable damage to the flight deck, a rogue wave severely damaged a forward three-inch gun on one of the DEs.

Coming out of the storm, flight operations commenced searching for U-boats. In the very first flight, the gunner of an Avenger claimed he saw a German periscope. However, doubt surrounded his sighting of such a small object in so rough a sea. Captain Ramsey ordered the gunner to the bridge to visit with him. Russell Lewis witnessed the conversation, and he wrote that the conversation seemed like a "friendly chat" and that the sailor appeared comfortable and reiterated his claim. Ramsey then thanked the sailor and dismissed him. As soon as he closed the door behind him, he turned to Lewis and said, "That man saw a periscope!"[35] Ramsey then asked Lewis to report on the progress of the squadron using the sonobuoys. Lewis explained that his training of the aircrew was nearing completion, and, while the sonobuoys had been deployed, he had not personally participated in these operations and, more importantly, listened to the FM receiver from the circling Avenger. Given his experience in listening to and deciphering sounds underwater, this skill set could improve the sonobuoys' effectiveness. Ramsey immediately replied, "Are you willing to fly?"[36]

The next day was a Sunday, and as Lewis prepared for his first flight, the PA system announced the Sunday service about to commence. It concluded with, "Maintain quiet about the decks."[37] Attendance of worshippers increased, compared to the service of Chaplin MacInnes just a week before. Lewis wrote, "Apparently the events of the previous week had made many, of the less reverent, think more about possible limits to their mortality."[38] After the service Lewis reported to the Avenger preloaded with his equipment, including sonobuoys cradled in the radio operator's compartment. Lewis would ride in the gunner's position, in the turret on the topside of the Avenger directly behind the pilot. Of the three crew members, the others being the pilot and the radio-radar operator, this position offered the best visibility in scanning the ocean below. After a brief tutorial in operating the gun and having been issued a Mae West life jacket, Lewis climbed into the Avenger on a flight deck still rolling from the storm. After taxiing just a few feet, Lewis waited for takeoff. He wrote, "Suddenly my forehead pressed against the supporting pad with enormous pressure. Just as suddenly the pressure ceased and I saw the flight deck two or three hundred yards behind us."[39]

Within minutes Lewis's skill set was put to work. After detecting an oil slick from a suspected submerged U-boat, the Avenger pilot lowered his craft and slowed for the deployment of a pattern of five sonobuoys. As these were individually dropped, Lewis listened with his high-fidelity-type headphones to the hydrophone as the sonobuoys exited the bomb bay. He heard the wind whistling in the drop, impact of the water and, once floating, the unwinding of the cable lowering the hydrophone away from the ocean's surface. Soon after, Lewis heard a faint noise. He wrote, "We heard the sh . . . sh . . . sh . . . noise generated by the propeller of a German submarine at low speed on battery power."[40] The transmission was relayed to the pilot, and even without Lewis's specialized headphones, he could make out the noise. He radioed the coordinates back to *Block Island*.

The Avenger remained in a circling pattern as a DE approached the area. Green dye continued to secrete from the buoy closest to the contact and allowed the crew to stay in position on the featureless ocean. As the DE neared the coordinates, the noise over the headset changed. Lewis recalled, "A short time later . . . their WHARCH!, WHARCH! propeller sounds drowned out every other sound, and, in my mind's eye, I saw the submarine captain issuing orders for evasive maneuvers."[41] As the DE neared the probable location of the U-boat, she fired forward-throwing Hedgehogs. No explosions followed, as these weapons exploded only as the result of striking a submerged object. Soon after, due to fuel consumption, Lewis's Avenger turned back toward *Block Island*. Lewis described the landing as a succession of events where "four things happened at once."[42] They included the flight deck coming into view from the gunner's position, slamming onto the deck, the engine throttling down, and the forward momentum ceasing. Exiting the craft, Lewis experienced his first debriefing as a member of the flight crew in the ready room, after which a discussion ensued on the best tactics in adapting the new detection system into the operations of the squadron aircraft.[43] This last point demonstrates the underappreciated contribution of American scientists to the war effort. Not only did they help forge new weapons, but they also provided unbiased analysis of the effectiveness of both weapons systems and deployment.[44]

Over the ensuing five days, around the clock, the task force search operations continued with multiple forms of detection, including visual, radar, sonobuoy, and sonar. Four detections occurred, resulting in the deployment of the DEs and the destroyer *Corry* to investigate and deploy Hedgehog and depth charges. Evidence from underwater detection gear and oil slicks classified two of these events as "probable," meaning the probable destruction of two U-boats.[45] However, German records do not support such a claim. Nevertheless, over these 120 straight hours, all U-boats in this portion of the Atlantic were at best busy fleeing detection, and at worst sustaining physical damage. And during this period, said German U-boats could not harass Allied shipping lanes. The escort carriers, leading task forces with updated vessel and weapons systems, were beginning to impose the Allied will over the Nazi enemy in the "black pit." On this cruise Ramsey demonstrated the application of innovation resulting from the marriage of naval leadership with the American skill of improvisation in designing and building advanced weapons systems. However, as Ramsey led his depleted task group out of the "black pit" and toward Casablanca, the Navy planned his replacement. Riding along on the first half of this mission as an observer was the next skipper of *Block Island*.

15
Massie

Docking in Casablanca, Russell Lewis disembarked from the vessel and toured the city with a group of officers. The sights of life on land, after three weeks at sea, took on new meaning. Plant life in particular stood out to this civilian after weeks at sea. In his journal he remarked on walking palm-lined streets and traffic islands full of decorative flowers and shrubs. Casablanca was a tale of two cities, and the officers in the USN (and Lewis dressed as one) had access to the top of the Navy hierarchy. As they walked the streets, their uniforms attracted the poor and destitute of Casablanca. Nearing the Ambassador Hotel, which housed the Navy Officers' Club, a group of youngsters encircled them. Lewis wrote in his journal, "We were immediately met by Arab boys who did somersaults, and then held out their hands in expectation of a reward." They dined on a lunch of goat meat prepared by a French chef and later viewed original works of art by French Impressionists at a nearby art gallery.[1] Lewis's memoir gives a glimpse into the experiences of officers on shore, which contrasted sharply with those of the enlisted men touring the ancient markets of Casablanca. Here sailors entered the busy environment phalanx style. Armed guards on the edges of the phalanx, with service revolvers drawn, got the sailors into the market area.

In the port of Casablanca, tons of provisions were unloaded onto the vessels of the task force. On CVE 21 a transfer of command from Logan Ramsey to Massie Hughes, who had been along on this entire mission as an observer, took place. Resting in the Logan C. Ramsey Papers at the Naval History and Heritage Command at the Navy Yard in Washington, DC, is the final handwritten statement Ramsey read over the PA system to the crew, on March 10, 1944:

> This is the last time you will hear me say "This is the Captain speaking." A whole lot of water has passed under our keel since we were commissioned one year and two days ago. We have seen action with the enemy more than once. Our employment has been hard duty and has called for our utmost efforts and our full loyalty. I will consider myself fortunate anytime in the future when I find a former *Block Island* shipmate again under my command. My regret at leaving you would be far greater were it not for the knowledge that your new commanding officer is a man who can and

> will lead you to continued success and greater achievements if you give him, and I am sure you will, the same loyalty and support I am proud to say you have tendered me. Goodbye—good luck—God bless you.[2]

The official change-of-command ceremony took place on the moored escort carrier. Centuries old, this formal event, with the entire crew standing at attention, marked the official transfer of authority of the vessel from Capt. Logan Ramsey to Capt. Francis Massie Hughes. Both officers had survived the battles of Pearl Harbor and Midway. The contrasts between the men traced back to Annapolis. While Ramsey worked on editing the annual yearbook, Hughes as a cadet played on the football team as quarterback.[3] His feisty spirit easily transitioned onto CVE 21. Pilot John Carr recalled the tenacity of Hughes. Carr wrote, "Most carrier skippers with whom I served were rather austere, Olympian figures whom you would only glimpse on the bridge."[4] Hughes, however, was more "like a football coach."[5] Daily he stomped down to the pilots' ready room and shouted advice and encouragement to this small band of fighters, such as "Flush the Hun" and "Hit the square head."[6] While Carr and his peers certainly respected Hughes's career, Carr admitted years later, "We considered him somewhat mad."[7]

Hughes accepted his authority over the vessel in an ecumenical space on board the vessel. Like most American towns containing a central gathering point for joyous celebrations or somber memorials, such as a courthouse or public park, CVE 21 utilized the flight and hangar decks for a range of functions. Besides the designed function of storing, repairing, and maintaining aircraft, the hangar was utilized for a host of social functions, chiefly for the viewing of films from Hollywood. One scholar wrote, "One of the few genuinely popular diversions available to most servicemen was movies. No matter how badly mutilated from repeated screenings, films enjoyed a universal popularity. For many men they were a link—however tenuous and fanciful—with the richer, happier, world back home."[8] Besides films, this space also provided a place of worship with Chaplain MacInnes, known to the crew as "Peanuts."

Walking through the ship one day, Chaplain MacInnes heard music coming from the electrical shop. Stepping in to investigate, he found a gathering of sailors playing a banjo, mandolin, fiddle, and slap bass. This homegrown assemblage materializing outside the formal regulations of the USN on board an escort carrier contrasted sharply with the large fast-fleet carriers. USS *Enterprise*, for example, had not one organized band but three groupings of musicians. One played for dances, another for military ceremonies, and a third for concerts.[9] Chaplain MacInnes invited the group to play during the service on Sunday.

Holding a religious service on a craft designed for war certainly held some irony. One World War II sailor recalled his chaplain making do the best he could in transforming a space on the hangar deck into a place of worship, which included a small organ, a small altar with a cross and two candles, and metal benches lined up like pews. He wrote, "These were the only trappings of religion. Everything else in the compartment was an implement of war."[10] The organist sat on a bomb crate, and a nearby sign read, "Notice! No smoking while explosives are stored here."[11] However, MacInnes and the other chaplains in the Navy service provided immeasurable comfort to those experiencing the stress and traumas of modern naval warfare. The impromptu band from the electric shop may have brought a few more souls in, who certainly could use any comfort available to them in the stresses of battle. These services introduced the ship to their "band," and this group played on sunny afternoons when outside of hunter-killer missions. One natural stage for the crew to perform on within the hangar was the sunken flight elevator, where two crowds gathered, one inside the hangar and the other up on the flight deck looking down. Listening from above, sailors found a little piece of home echoing up, and this offered a brief escape from the war.[12]

Stress and anxiety manifest themselves in many forms. Prolonged strain in wartime produces a range of psychological difficulties. The stress of tracking submarines on these hunter-killer missions, while knowing full well that roles of hunter and prey could quickly be reversed, tried the sailors' nerves. The Atlantic was an ocean that had swallowed many a vessel since man first dared to sail. The biggest fear was not death in battle but the loss of one's ship, of being thrust from the vessel protecting you and devoured by the sea. Of this fear, one sailor wrote, "The thought of being lost at sea became a new nightmare, the worst form of dying."[13] Hidden fears and stresses manifested in unique ways, including dreams, as one sailor discovered as he slept in his bunk. In a powerful dream, he was on CVE 21 at sea. An explosion rocked the escort carrier, her thin hull ripped open, letting in copious amounts of salt water, and she sank quickly by the stern. The dreamer reacted by running up the ascending bow in a futile attempt to avoid the inevitable. Once on the bow, he held on to the railing as the ship's forward section went near vertical in the air. As the Atlantic imbibed the fast-sinking *Block Island*, and the sailor on the bow descended toward the boiling waters swallowing his home, he awoke. Finding himself in a cold sweat in his bunk, and on board the motionless *Block Island*, he told his bunkmate, who was awake, "We're going out and getting sunk this time, you'll see."[14]

❋

All ships over time develop a personality. Occurrences transpired both on the seas and when the crew was in port that crystallized the group into a cohesive unit. Certain events, such as surviving a North Atlantic gale or sinking an enemy submarine,

Figure 9. The nickname Fighting Block Island, or FBI, is seen here on the jerseys of the USS *Block Island* basketball team posing for a team photograph on the deck of the carrier. Courtesy of the USS Block Island Association.

added to the collective identity and history of the vessel.[15] This lore of a vessel often yields a name. For CVE 21, this produced the nickname the "FBI," or "Fighting *Block Island*."[16] This name developed in the taking of the fight to the U-boats not only in the daylight hours but pioneering night operations, where planes from the FBI searched from the dark skies. These operations took men to fly them. Men such as Norman Dowty, who grew up in Alexander, Louisiana, and attended college at Northwestern State University where he was dismissed for being bold enough to drive a car with an unchaperoned female student. During the Depression, Dowty spent a year riding the rails with hobos. In 1941 he returned to college and then joined the Navy.[17] In the dark predawn hours of March 19, 1944, Dowty prepared his Avenger for takeoff on a night patrol. Once in the air, he received the location of an HF/DF bearing. Teamed with USS *Corry*, they converged on the coordinates.

While HF/DF equipment resided on board ship, the large size of the required antenna prevented the detection apparatus from being placed on an aircraft during the war.[18] Avengers were armed with radar detection that had an effective range of about five miles, and on his approach Dowty focused on the radar screen in his Avenger. Aviation Radioman First Class Edgar Burton spotted the surfaced submarine less than a mile away, in the act of submerging. Knowing the sub's location, they circled the night sky hoping for another sighting. An hour later, spotting the wake of a forward-moving periscope, Dowty unsuccessfully dropped a Fido torpedo onto this location, but the hoped-for subsequent explosion was not forthcoming. At the same time, *Corry* knocked down radar decoy balloons sent aloft by U 801 to distract her pursuers. With the dawn came the visible dark oil trail in the blue waters below, indicating an injured U-boat. Running low on fuel, Dowty returned to *Block Island* but was relieved by pilot Lt. Theodore Elefter, who continued to circle the area. With the U-boat wounded, USS *Bronstein*, DE 189, joined forces with USS *Corry*. After several hours of tracking the oil trail, *Corry* gained a sound contact. Homing in, *Corry* dropped a deep ten depth-charge pattern. Sustaining further damage to his vessel, the German commander decided to surface. With torpedo tubes loaded as the U-boat neared the surface, the commander hoped for a shot at her attackers *Corry* and *Bronstein*.

Block Island and her screening ships, USS *Thomas*, DE 102, and USS *Breeman*, DE 104, watched this battle from a distance of seven miles. With almost no control of the damaged U-boat on the surface, the German vessel was fully exposed to the three- and five-inch guns of *Corry* and *Bronstein*. The German commander issued the order to abandon ship, and the first man on the bridge was killed immediately. As the remaining German sailors abandoned ship, the beating of their vessel continued. For the men of *Block Island*, this represented a rare instance where they saw the battle actually raging before their eyes in a war they had been involved with for over a year. Captain Hughes recalled in a later interview, "It was a running fight with all hands aboard the deck of the carrier cheering him [sailors of *Corry* and *Bronstein*] on."[19] A memoir recalled the shock on the faces of the FBI sailors in seeing the enemy in battle for the first time: "Suddenly PEOPLE poured out of the hatches of the submarine and flung themselves into the sea. Up until this time nobody thought about people being involved."[20] Forty-two of these Germans survived the ordeal and, after being picked up by the task force's DE, were transferred to CVE 21. The captain of the doomed sub was twenty-four years old; the crew consisted of boys as young as fourteen.[21]

❋

The hunter-killer group's detection capabilities improved greatly from the "night owl" missions. The concept of adaptation was central to these missions, as the weapons systems of an Avenger were removed and the empty bomb bay area filled with extra fuel tankage. In addition, flame dampeners fitted over the exhaust ports concealed the aircraft from any lurking submarines below. With expanded flight time from extra fuel, these "night owl" pilots hunted in the blackened Atlantic nights for up to fourteen hours. Flying in coordinated, mathematically devised search patterns, these night owl pilots scanned for unsuspecting surfaced U-boats.[22] Missions commenced with pilots taking off at 1930 in the evening and returning at 0830 the next day. Of these pilots Captain Hughes boasted, "Launching and retrieving of aircraft we always do at night on a darkened ship and various conditions of weather which naturally brings out the training features of our pilots. There's no question that they're the best trained pilots in the world."[23] Periodically, these searching night owl aircrews flew over the location of the cruising CVE 21. Crew members on board CVE 21 heard these hunting aircraft as they flew over *Block Island* searching round the clock.[24]

While operations at night added another layer of complexity, operations during the daylight hours also proved dangerous. Landings on an escort carrier even in the best conditions sometimes proved lethal. An Avenger piloted by Lt. John Pearce lined up his approach for the CVE 21 flight deck, during which the landing signal officer (LSO) waved him off. Pearce banked left away from the flight deck and then lost control, and the five-ton Avenger slammed into the Atlantic. The force of the impact slammed Pearce's face into the control panel, which caused serious bleeding and nearly knocked him out at a time when seconds counted. Luckily, Aviation Radioman Third Class Charles Wilson Foster, alert and ready for any situation during the attempted landing, climbed out onto the wing of the Avenger. Sailors on the flight deck rushed to the port side. As one eyewitness recalled, "I remember seeing Charlie on the wing and releasing the safety belt of John and inflating his yellow 'Mae West' life jacket."[25] A nearby DE rescued the pair as they were exiting from the sinking aircraft and safely returned them to CVE 21. Pearce, badly wounded in the face, made a full recovery after a few weeks' time.

At dawn on March 19, the ever-aggressive Captain Hughes launched six pairs of Wildcats and Avengers to cruise out in a radius of 150 miles. One pair, led by Lt. Norman T. Dowty in an Avenger and Lt. William H. "Tex" Cole in a Wildcat, soon encountered scattered cloud cover. Flying at eight thousand feet and scanning the ocean below, Cole was the first to spot a surfaced U-boat. The pair attacked with the sun at their backs, with Cole in his Wildcat in the lead, and completely surprised U 1059, a new Type VIIF 1,100-ton transport model, dead in the water with a third of her crew swimming around the vessel. Those in the water included the skipper, Oberleutnant Gunter Leopold. Some of the naked swimmers spotted Cole pressing his attack as they swam and tried to climb aboard their vessel. Cole's machine guns produced parallel lines of billowing seawater as .50-caliber bullets slammed into the water around the submarine and into the vessel's hull. After Cole's initial pass, the Germans quickly manned their antiaircraft weapons and fired at the pair of planes. They concentrated their fire at Dowty as, in his larger Avenger, he lined up a depth charge attack. Dowty's aim was perfect as the two dropped charges straddled the submarine. The subsequent explosions penetrated the U-boat hull deep enough to cause the U-boat's magazine to explode. The deafening explosion broke the vessel in two.

By now Cole had circled for his second attack, but he found no useful target. The two portions of the hull were settling in the water, and flames and smoke reigned where the newly commissioned U-boat floated a minute before. Dowty's Avenger, however, sustained hits from the German fire, and in banking he lost control and sharply turned. In an instant his wing tip touched the water. The three crew members inside experienced the violent stoppage of forward momentum as their craft quickly spun into the water. Dowty and the radioman Edgar Burton sank with the Avenger into the deep. However, the third man of the crew, Ens. Mark Fitzgerald, managed to escape and also secured a life raft in the process. Once it was inflated, Fitzgerald found himself alone on the sea, with Cole circling overhead. Cole radioed back to CVE 21 that a lone crew member of the Avenger survived the crash. Hughes ordered *Corry*, some seventy miles away, to the location. Cole also reported he saw roughly fifteen Germans still swimming in the water and holding on to debris from the destroyed U-boat. Fitzgerald, recovering from the crash and the loss of two crew members, bobbed in his yellow life raft on the ocean half a mile from this scene.

Gathering himself after the plane crash, he searched the horizon for signs of rescue. Roughly an hour after the crash, he spotted a naked man swimming to him from out of nowhere. Badly wounded, this German without a life belt figured his best chance at rescue was to swim toward where the Avenger crashed. Fitzgerald yelled to the naked man, asking if he spoke English, The German replied in poor English, "Ja, a little." Fitzgerald's next question was "Did you shoot at me?" The German responded with a question, "Are you mad?" Fitzgerald said, "No, I'm not mad, but I want to know if you shot at me." The German then said, "Ja, I shot you down." Then these men floating alone on a vast ocean shook hands, and the German said, "You, good fellow!"[26] Cole, who was still circling above waiting for *Corry*, saw this second man and assumed he was one of the other crew members of the downed Avenger. He flew over and dropped a second life raft. Fitzgerald, cautious of the German, made him retrieve the second raft and bring it back. He then helped the German inflate it and got him situated inside the rubber raft. Fitzgerald tended to the German's ghastly wound with medical supplies attached to the life raft. A few minutes later, a second young German swam up; this time it was Capt. Gunter Leopold, with his scalp badly torn and part of one knee shot away. Fitzgerald this time pulled the young captain into his life raft and treated his wounds. He also gave both men sedatives while they waited for rescue.

Two hours after the attack, *Corry* reached the scene. After picking up Fitzgerald and the two Germans, the vessel returned to the site of the sinking and found six more Germans. Saving the Germans, *Corry* headed back toward the task force. While the hunter-killer group claimed another kill, it came at the high cost of losing both Norman Dowty and Edgar Burton. Flight operations continued over the next several days, with CVE 21 launching aircraft to run searches and the DEs following sound contacts. Finally, a week later, on March 26, operations slowed down enough for a memorial service. The crew gathered on the sun-drenched flight deck as Captain Hughes and Chaplain MacInnes led the memorial service for Dowty and Burton. Remembering the deceased when the human remains are present is a difficult enough experience; however, a challenge is presented in obtaining both meaning and closure for dead shipmates lost at sea. For centuries both empires and widows have devised their own forms of mourning. Here on CVE 21, the brave pair of flyers lost the previous week in successfully destroying a German U-boat were remembered.

Ramsey's continued interest in the CVE 21 is seen in his putting forth the nomination of Dowty for the Congressional Medal of Honor. In a signed typed statement attached to the proposed citation, he included a personal memory of Dowty when he was skipper on the first half of this very mission. A fellow pilot had spotted a German U-boat but in dropping his depth charges missed by the proverbial mile. Ramsey recalled the pilots later discussing the strike. Dowty made his intentions quite clear. In his thick Louisiana accent, he said, "Well, if my plane gets a chance like that I am going to do my durndest to lay those depth bombs right down the sub skipper's throat, no matter what happens."[27] Ramsey noted that Dowty answered Massie Hughes's call in the ready room for volunteers for a night flight in bad weather. He also thought flying through antiaircraft fire and sacrificing his life in the clear destruction of a surfaced German U-boat constituted the awarding of the Medal of Honor. While Ramsey's efforts were unsuccessful, in October 1944 Lt. Jr. Norman Taylor Dowty was posthumously awarded the Navy Cross.[28]

Once leaving the hunting area, the task force had half an ocean to cross to return to Norfolk. The enlisted men's main nighttime activity consisted of watching movies seated in chairs lined up in rows on the hangar deck. In the ready room the pilots gathered and played bridge and chess. The most interesting and challenging game in the opinion of the civilian Russell Lewis took place at night on the fantail. With the luminescence of the wake behind them, the pilots' competitive nature turned celestial navigation into a competition with the identification of stars and the use of a sextant in measuring the angle of stars in relation to the horizon. As a gathering of type-A personalities, this contest steadily increased in toughness as participants compared their skills not only with one another but also to the best navigators of all time. The Polynesians, using only their eyesight, navigated at night and explored the intricate chains of islands of the central Pacific centuries ago. It was said these ancient mariners could gauge the exact position of a star with less than a two-degree error. The best eyeshot measurement that these pilots produced on the back of the moving escort carrier was within five degrees.[29] Activities such as this allowed for much-needed decompression time before disembarking stateside. The sight of a USN blimp overhead escorting the task force on the westbound journey hinted that the American coast was fast approaching.

Modern war consists of not only killing the enemy but also gathering information and, along this vein, keeping information from the enemy. Thus, the success of the FBI was to be kept secret. Toward home Captain Hughes mustered the crew on the hangar deck and spoke of the seriousness of not discussing with anyone stateside the nature of their operations and, most importantly, not making mention of U-boats destroyed on their latest mission. One witness wrote "CAPT Hughes cautioned all hands against saying anything to anyone about what had been accomplished on our cruise."[30] While Hughes could control those on his vessel, he could not control their reception. Docking at Pier Seven in Norfolk Naval Base, the crew of *Block Island* was greeted with a huge banner reading "Welcome Home, Champ!"[31] On the dock stood a greeting committee and a Navy band loudly playing, and very publicly, congratulating the crew on their accomplishments against the enemy. Lewis wrote, "Our accomplishments had been well published at the navy base and preparations had been made for a very elaborate reception."[32] By April 1944 *Block Island* ranked number two in escort carrier hunter-killer missions, with six credited U-boat kills.[33]

However, the noise of the band echoing into the vessel almost caused a tragic event, which was checked only by the quick work of an officer on board. Lewis wrote, "The German submarine commander, upon hearing the band playing, assumed that he would be executed publicly and he tried to commit suicide by slashing his wrists. The ship's medical officer saved his life—and convinced him that Americans didn't do things like that."[34]

16
"Stand by to Repel Boarders!"

Block *Island* returned to sea on her fourth combat patrol on April 29, 1944, this time armed with the VC-55 air group and four new destroyer escorts. These new DEs contained "black oil" electric turbines rated at twenty-four knots and included USS *Ahrens*, DE 575, USS *Barr*, DE 576, USS *Buckley*, DE 51, and USS *Eugene E. Elmore*, DE 686. These combined vessels made up task group 21.11. The new orders included relieving USS *Croatan*, CVE 25, and task group 21.15, which was hunting west of the Cape Verde Islands. First *Croatan* and then *Block Island* sought to intercept U-boats hoping to rendezvous with a refueler. This area proved active early on, with *Block Island* planes locating a surfaced enemy around midnight on May 1. Before lining up an attack run, the U-boat managed to successfully submerge. A team of aircraft then deployed a system of sonobuoys and tracked her on the southerly course. During this process, the Avenger dropped a Fido torpedo, which proved unsuccessful. This deadly game of hide-and-seek continued with the U-boat surfacing a few hours later and the team of aircraft dropping a depth charge attack. Due to the darkness of this May night, the success of the attack was unknown. Those operating the sonobuoys from the circling Avenger continued to listen to the U-boat into the next day. However, the DEs sent to the area were unable to gain a sound contact.[1]

On board CVE 21 for his second mission was Russell Lewis. After a hurried trip to New London, Connecticut, to report back and gather the latest technical developments at the Underwater Sound Laboratory, he oversaw the loading of six hundred sonobuoys onto CVE 21. Once he was within the operation area near the Cape Verde Islands, his days were full of assisting and training the crews of the Avengers. Back in the hunting grounds, *Block Island* had a memorable encounter with a German submarine that got within a mile of the carrier undetected. Just after dark one evening, Lewis was sitting in the ready room when general quarters sounded. "Man your battle stations!" bellowed twice throughout the ship. Immediately thereafter, Lewis was jolted by the two five-inch guns firing off the fantail just aft of his position. From the ready room, Lewis and another officer could hear over the PA system operational communications, and thus they were aware that a German U-boat had surfaced just a mile astern of the escort carrier. As two of the screening destroyer escorts immediately initiated an attack on the submarine, the *Block Island* went into evasive maneuvers. The U-boat dove from the scene.

After a few minutes of tension, Lewis attempted to relieve the stress of the sudden encounter. Lewis wrote, "I slapped the Athletics Officer on the back and said, with a chuckle, 'Those Germans have got it all wrong. They seem to think they're hunting us. They don't seem to know that we are hunting them.'" The officer just froze and stared at him. Lewis wrote he then "turned pale and started shaking."[2] Even though the officer recovered after a few minutes, this event demonstrates the physical manifestations produced by psychological stress and anxiety for the crew of escort carriers. Mental strain stemmed from knowing you were on what was considered a "target ship," this being the largest prize of the task force.[3] Sailors suppressed thoughts of one sudden explosion on board.

For some CVE 21 sailors, surviving a sinking and recalling the numerous ways one could die was not an abstraction. The Radio Department in particular was composed of survivors of USS *Lexington*, CV 2, lost earlier in the war at the Battle of Coral Sea. The loss of such a large vessel produced veteran sailors with a range of skill sets with no ship to fight from; thus, newly minted vessels such as CVE 21 inherited a nucleus of seasoned sailors to build a crew around. One such sailor was Bill "Slick" Connolly from the "Lady Lex," who for green sailors functioned as a daily reminder that carriers did in fact sink. Before the order to abandon *Lexington* was given, he and others manned their battle stations for hours in the hot sun. While they were without water and struggling with thirst, someone handed out gallons of ice cream to eat. This brief hiatus from reality was broken by the order to abandon ship. Thinking it would be easier to guide themselves down the knotted line without their shoes, Slick and his fellow sailors took these off. Even in this period of crisis, the regimented nature of Navy life persisted, as sailors placed these pairs in a neat row on the deck of the sinking carrier.[4]

Once in the Pacific, Slick and his fellow sailors got in a life raft; however, they encountered the problem of being unable to get their rafts away from the nearby fast-burning carrier. A destroyer on the scene witnessed their plight and shot a line in their direction to pull them out of harm's way. In the process of waiting for the line, a huge explosion rocked the forward section of *Lex*, tossing a towering wall of flame upward. Slick found the sight so terrifyingly he fainted. After an undetermined amount of time he awoke alone, floating in the life raft. Further explosions caused sections of the wooden flight deck and portions of aircraft to rain around his raft. In an interview he recalled, "I can't swim much, but I swam a lot when the ship started blowing up." He described his half-mile swim away from the site of the sinking and to sanctuary on USS *New Orleans*, CA 32, as "going like a motorboat."[5] After his survivor's leave back in the US, orders arrived to report to CVE 21. He was pleased, as he mistakenly thought operating on a carrier in the Atlantic was safer than in the Pacific.

❋

In the waters west of the Cape Verde Islands lurked U 66. In just three years her veteran crew of ten patrols racked up sinkings of over thirty vessels, equating to over 200,000 gross register tonnage (GRT) of Allied shipping. On this cruise she was under the command of Kapitänleutnant Gerhard Seehausen, a thirty-three-year-old with two Iron Crosses. So far, the fusion of Seehausen's leadership and U 66 had claimed four vessels in just twenty-three days.[6] While many histories of the Battle of the Atlantic incorporate the command decisions of U-boat commanders, many overlook the crew. Not all crew members volunteered or were rabid members of the Nazi Party. In fact, some received their assignment as a form of punishment. One such unfortunate was Wolf Loch, who at the beginning of the war trained as a pharmacist's mate and served the first portion of the war in the Netherlands, where he could pick up British broadcasts on the radio. As this was an illegal act, upon discovery his commander sentenced him to "stand a test at the front."[7] In early 1943 this could mean two things: terrestrial combat in fighting the Soviet army in the east or Atlantic submarine service. At this late stage of the war, either punishment was a near death sentence. So, Wolf, with no training at all in U-boat service, stepped onto a submarine for the first time. His commanding officer, Seehausen, welcomed him on board U 66 by pulling out his pistol and pointing it at Wolf's head, making crystal clear the punishment for insubordination.[8] U 66, with nearly sixty souls, with varying degrees of allegiance to the cause, sought to survive yet another war patrol.[9] In these very waters, task force 21.11, led by CVE 21, was seeking contact.

Even in these stress-filled weeks, humorous events took place within the task force. One particular sonobuoy, deployed by the task force, detected the propeller noise of a U-boat growing in intensity. Two Avenger pilots in the skies above the scene dropped two Fido torpedoes in the hopes of a kill. What occurred next was a comedy of errors when the two torpedoes chased each other as opposed to the German submarine. As an officer reported on the scene of the torpedoes, "not purposefully moving toward the submarine—but broaching like porpoises and chasing each other in playful circles!"[10]

For ten days the task force, led by *Block Island*, made daily contact tracking a U-boat, which was in fact U 66. This standard 750-ton Type IX-C U-boat had encountered CVEs before with successfully dodging a Fido torpedo dropped from the aircraft off the CVE *Card* the year before. On this patrol U 66 had already sunk the 5,000-ton British merchantmen vessel SS *John Holt* in her approach to the Gulf of Lagos just sixty miles off the African coast where the Opobo River empties into the sea. During this attack, the vessel picked up two English survivors, who, for two months, resided on U 66. Nearing the end of the patrol, the bearded crew suffered from a vitamin-deficient diet, and the vessel was low on both torpedoes and fuel. She sought to rendezvous with a "milch cow" that happened to be in the area where *Block Island* was operating.[11]

The Allied HF-DF tracking stations picked up a signal registering back from an unidentified vessel, and the coordinates were relayed to TG 21.11. The ever-aggressive Hughes ordered CVE 21 to within sixty miles of the reported position and launched aircraft in the hopes of sighting a surfaced U-boat. In the dark hours of May 6, just before midnight, *Block Island*'s own radar picked up a strong surface blip just five thousand yards off the starboard quarter. This was Commander Seehausen and U 66 lining up an attack on CVE 21. Hughes ordered an emergency turn at flank speed to take CVE 21 out of danger. He then ordered Capt. Brent M. Abel and his USS *Buckley*, DE 51, to investigate the contact.[12]

At this time, Hughes had aloft a number of night owl Avengers. Stripped of weapons and filled with extra fuel tanks, these craft stayed airborne throughout the night. Lt. Jimmie J. Sellars, who hailed from Oklahoma, and whom the others called "Geronimo," used his radar as a guide and spotted the surfaced U 66 on this moon-filled night and radioed back to *Buckley* her location. U 66 remained surfaced and fired her antiaircraft guns at Sellars if he ventured too close. Thus, at a distance, Sellars continued to fly overhead. Frustrated that he had a surfaced U-boat in his sights but was unarmed, Sellars dove on U 66 and emptied his Colt .45 sidearm at the conning tower.[13] Meanwhile, back on *Block Island*, word spread among the squadron that Sellars had made visual confirmation. Pilots quickly gathered around the ready-room radio to hear the exchange of "Geronimo" guiding *Buckley* to the location of the surfaced U-boat. Sellars described back over the airwaves to those on *Block Island* the battle royal between the DE and the U-boat. Russell Lewis wrote, "What we heard was almost like a sports event broadcast without the theatrics."[14] Those gathered in the ready room were not alone in hearing of the battle, as Captain Hughes passed along over the vessel's speaker circuit a running account of the battle for the entire crew.[15]

Captain Abel cruised *Buckley* at flank speed toward the scene. Taking forty-five minutes to reach the location, Abel cruised up a path toward the U-boat with the setting moon ahead of him, further concealing *Buckley*. Abel hoped that the German crew lookouts, who were expecting a rendezvous with a milch cow, would confuse the DE with a German refueling submarine. For *Buckley*, the deck crew silently manning their battle stations, the approach caused palpable tension as they steamed closer to the U-boat without engaging. As the battle report read, "It was also decided to withhold fire until the last possible minute on the chance that the sub might think *Buckley* was the other sub due at the rendezvous."[16] Three red flares shot up from U 66, believed to be a recognition signal to a fellow U-boat. Again, the DE crew held their breath and fire. *Buckley* closed within four thousand yards of U 66, which was fully silhouetted against a sinking moon. Then, suddenly, German machine-gun fire interrupted the blackness of this May night. Still closing the distance in this moonlit night, Abel ordered his three-inch guns to commence firing when some two thousand yards from the submarine. Training and patience paid off, as the first shots scored a direct hit on the conning tower.

Abel then ordered *Buckley* on a near-parallel, but still slightly intersecting, course with U 66, and then the two ships cruised side by side and fully engaged each other. At a range of 1,500 yards, 20 mm, 40 mm, and three-inch fire poured off the DE deck, producing explosive bursts of light as both craft cruised on an intersecting path. This gunfight continued until both vessels cruised just 200 yards apart.[17] Sellars, still in the skies above the scene, radioed back to *Block Island*, "*Buckley* is cutting the hell out of the conning tower!!"[18]

During this time, other planes armed with weapons that had taken off from *Block Island* arrived at the scene but could not engage for fear of hitting *Buckley*. After about four minutes of cruising side by side within two hundred yards of each other, Captain Abel ordered, "Hard right rudder!" Abel decided to ram U 66. *Buckley*'s bow slammed into the foredeck, producing a metallic scream. The searing impact raised the bow of the DE as she rode over the top of U 66. Commander Seehausen ordered his men to abandon ship. Many of the Germans coming out of the conning tower jumped into the water in an attempt to get away from the scene of destruction. Others, however, jumped onto *Buckley*. It had been more than a century since an American naval officer had to issue the order "Stand by to repel boarders!"[19]

The men on *Buckley*, armed with light machine guns, started firing at the Germans attempting to board. Unarmed sailors tossed down nearby items, including coffee cups and empty three-inch gun casings, at the invaders, while others simply used their fists in punching Germans seeking to come aboard. The men of the DE had the best of this fight in killing a number of Germans and successfully pushing the others back onto the deck of U 66. After two minutes of battle, Captain Abel then ordered to stop all engines, and this allowed his DE to slip off the deck of the submarine. The damaged U 66 still had full engine power and plowed forward at eighteen knots. German sailors continued to funnel out of the conning tower and jump into the Atlantic waters. While some Germans were wishing to surrender or abandon the submarine, others continued to man the antiaircraft guns and fight. "A man on the deck of the sub attempted to man a gun [was] disintegrated when hit by four 40 mm shells."[20] *Buckley* drew near U 66 in the water once again. One sailor wrote after the fact that "the submarine, either out of control or intentionally, veered and struck *Buckley* a glancing blow; its bow rode under *Buckley*'s forward engine room and the U boat rolled over toward the DE in a 60 degree angle."[21] At this point a *Buckley* sailor lobbed a hand grenade into the hatch of U 66 that exploded inside the hull.

With a fire blazing from the conning tower, this veteran raider of the Atlantic began to slip under the ocean's surface. She sank at 0436, a little over an hour after Sellars in his night owl first spotted her. Three minutes after she sank, a deep underwater explosion occurred, followed by smaller concussions, all of which spelled the death of U 66. For the next several hours, *Buckley*, with her newly bent bow, cruised over the scene picking up survivors. In total, some thirty-six German officers and enlisted men were plucked out of the Atlantic waters. At a slower speed, due to her damaged bow, *Buckley* cruised back for a rendezvous with *Block Island*. Of the casualties on board the *Buckley*, Captain Hughes stated, "her only casualty was one Chief Petty Officer with a badly bruised fist, which had been obtained from knocking one of the enemy over the side."[22] *Buckley*, tossing up an irregular wake as she plowed forward, pulled alongside CVE 21. The FBI crew, aware of their DE's feat of bravery, raced to the flight deck bearing gifts for the victorious warriors. As the breeches buoy transferred individual German POWs to *Block Island*, the FBI sailors tossed down candy bars to the sailors of *Buckley* in an act of tribute. Hughes recalled "all hands topside on the flight deck—a rousing reception."[23] This shower of candy was accompanied with cheers from the FBI crew as the defeated POWs traversed across the gap between the vessels. Unable to make full speed, but otherwise structurally sound, *Buckley* broke away from the hunter-killer group and journeyed stateside for repairs.

Seeing these prisoners of U 66 up close produced stunned disbelief at the condition of the Germans. With little to no fresh air, and weeks on a vitamin-deficient diet, the pale and weakened Germans suffered from skin eruptions. The most alarming symptom of their underwater existence was the dead white and loosened fingernails. The battle report summed up their overall condition, that they "look[ed] like the very antithesis of the rugged, virile "superman" with which one is given to understand Germany is now populated."[24] From the questioning of the Germans, it was learned that the two British prisoners, taken on board after the sinking of their vessel by the U-boat weeks before, died in the hail of gunfire exiting the submarine. However, even in interrogations the human capacity for humor surfaced. One German POW was asked about the "milch cow," the Allied term for a larger scale of German submarine that served as a refueler. After questioning, the term struck him funny. One sailor recalled years later, "It tickled his fancy so much after its connotations sank in that he lay in his bed chuckling and murmuring the word over and over appreciatively."[25]

While the naval aviator captured much of the national attention as the most important individual on board a carrier, these flights required the skill of the landing signal officer (LSO) for pilots to have a life span of more than one mission. In the summer of 1943, the LSO finally received some national attention by gracing the cover of the *Saturday Evening Post*. During the war the periodical contained not only narratives about the conflict but also works of art adorning its cover summarizing such themes as individual sacrifice, bravery, and overcoming adversity. On the cover of the June 12, 1943, issue, Mead Schaeffer's painting titled *Aircraft Carrier Signal Lieutenant* clearly shows the dedicated LSO perched on his platform, eyes forward, bundled up in warm clothes protecting him from the North Atlantic weather, attempting to safely land planes on the pitching deck. The brilliant red and yellow of his paddles highlights his responsibility in directing the unseen approaching aircraft safely to providence.

One pilot named Denny Moller, on board CVE 21 in the spring of 1944, had recently arrived with VC-55, and he knew full well the details of flying and landing in the North Atlantic depicted by Schaeffer. Before reporting to CVE 21, VC-55 completed two hunter-killer missions on USS *Card*, CVE 11. Landing on the oscillating deck of a Bogue-class escort carrier was a question of timing. In rough seas the approaching pilot witnessed the severity of the pitching deck, which ranged from her single screw coming out of the water on one extreme to the bow pointing to the sky on the opposite end of the swing. The LSO sought for the approaching plane and the deck to merge in the middle of this wide swing.

With *Buckley* returning stateside, the remaining ships of the TG 21.11 sought out the German prey. Hughes pushed the LSOs and pilots to their physical and mental extremes during the month of May. One officer described this drive as "doggedly hunting, to the outer limits of his capabilities."[26] Captain Hughes proudly boasted that one pilot landed after a thirteen-hour mission with just a quart of fuel remaining. He ran out of gas on the flight deck and needed to be pushed to the elevator.[27] Denny Moller, who piloted an Avenger, recalled Hughes interacting with the pilots in the ready room after their missions. Most of the time, the only thing Moller and the other pilots looked down and saw was a great deal of water, and when they told this to Hughes, he replied, "Yeah, son, but you only saw the top of it!"[28] In an interview Hughes said, "Our motto was whenever we got a contact with a sub—stay with him, regardless of how long—wear him down—do anything, but get him."[29] Victories were not displayed on aircraft or anywhere on board CVE 21. When Captain Hughes was asked about pilots being allowed to individually mark their aircraft with personalized artwork, he replied with a negative. "No, no decorations were done at all save decorations for depth charges."[30] These messages, chalked onto the depth charges, included, "Take this and see how you like it!"[31] During these long missions, the flight surgeon kept a watchful eye on pilots for signs of fatigue, and if he suspected concealed sleeplessness, he ordered the pilot to sleep for ten hours. In these hard hunting days after successfully destroying U 66, no contacts were made; however, Hughes pressed on pushing himself and the deck officers around him to the limits. He stated, "If you try to do it all yourself, it's going to be a one-man brass band. You can't do it. They've got to be able to take over the ship just like the Captain." He continued, "You've got to get rest, or you don't get it at all and start making funny decisions—you go goofy. I started sleeping in the daytime."[32]

17
Buoyant Battlefield

Relief for the injured *Buckley* arrived on May 15 with USS *R. I. Paine*, DE 578, joining the task force. Three days later, after twenty-six days of constant operations, *Block Island* and her group moored in Casablanca's harbor. The POWs from U 66 transferred off, and resupply hastily transpired. Hughes, in a personal letter to Capt. Logan Ramsey, now serving as chief of staff of Air Fleet in Norfolk, summed up his appraisal of the operation so far. He wrote, "We feel like we had a very successful cruise, bringing in thirty-six knuckleheads with us from the sub that the BUCKLEY sank and feeling very certain of another (hope it was a refueler) on which we got three hedgehog hits." Hughes openly admitted how hard he had pushed both pilots and aircraft. "The only gas we had left was what was in five planes. This, of course, was the result of round-the-clock operations for a period of twelve days and it extended everybody almost to the elastic limit." He also pointed to the "fruit" such operations produced in intelligence gathered from the thirty-six POWs Hughes colorfully labeled as "knuckleheads" saved off U-66. He wrote, "Prisoner of war information indicates that this was the sub we were over for four days and due to our hold-down tactics made it necessary for them to come up and run." In closing his letter, Hughes eagerly looked forward to further success on the upcoming mission that would end when CVE 21 entered the harbor at Norfolk. His last line was, "Best of luck and will see you in June."[1] Just a week later, when this letter signed "Massie" on May 22, 1944, reached Ramsey in Virginia, fate would intervene regarding CVE 21 ever seeing an American port again.

With a quick turnaround, the group pulled out of Casablanca on May 23, 1944, with orders of operations off the west coast of North Africa between the Madeira and Canary Islands. Flight operations commenced on May 27 at dawn. The next day, a few minutes after midnight on the twenty-eighth, an Avenger picked up a radar contact just four miles away. This vessel, a 750-ton IX-C U-boat, was U 549, sailing on her first war patrol out of the U-boat base from Lorient, France, and under the command of Kapitänleutnant Detlev Krankenhagen. Shortly after detection however, the pursuing Avenger experienced radar problems and sought to regain the signal. Hughes pushed his ships and planes to regain contact, to no avail. However, Hughes understood a submerged U-boat was cornered. At 2045 on May 28, Hughes launched planes to conduct night operations in the hopes of regaining contact.[2]

During the night Lt. Joseph R. Rees, in his unarmed "night owl," acquired a strong signal. Rees kept the U-boat on his scope as an armed Avenger vectored out to join him. Once the pair of Avengers teamed up, Rees dropped a 750,000-candle power flare, which illuminated the watery environs underneath. The pilot in the armed Avenger, after two minutes, witnessed the white wake of a U-boat on the black surface of the ocean. He maneuvered his Avenger to just 150 feet off the ocean's surface and, with his bomb bay doors open, strained his eyes looking for the U-boat producing the wake. As he continued on his course, the flare burned out and U 549 got away. Rees lost the radar contact and dropped an additional flare. This revealed only black Atlantic waters. This missed opportunity of engaging U 549 would have fateful consequences for TG 21.11.

With the cornered U-boat at the front of Hughes's mind, throughout the day of May 29, he ordered the saturation of the area with planes and DEs. At 1703 Hughes ordered six fighter planes off the deck to continue searches into the final hours of daylight. Air plot reported to Hughes, stationed at the bridge at 1925, that CVE 21, on a course of 215, was at the projected location of the enemy U-boat. Hughes ordered two night owl Avengers readied on the flight deck to launch and continue the hunting into the nighttime hours. Little did those technicians know the accuracy of their projected location. U 549 was exactly at these coordinates. The Germans, submerged in their U-boat, heard the propellers of the hunter-killer group as it cruised over them. Looking through his periscope, Krankenhagen saw an entire task force. Knowing he was cornered, he ordered an attack and selected the biggest target.[3]

❋

Henry Jones was twenty-seven years old when bombs fell on Pearl Harbor on a Sunday in December. Jones, like thousands of other men, visited a Navy recruiting office the very next day. On May 29, 1944, he was serving on the bridge of the destroyer escort USS *Elmore*, DE 686, part of task force 21.11. The DEs' primary mission was the safety of the escort carrier leading the hunter-killer group, which Jones described thus: "The DE would be in different positions to protect the *Block Island* at all times." While an enemy submarine contact miles away could require one or two DEs leaving the task force to investigate, two DEs would normally remain in protection of the carrier.[4] In the warfare raging in the Atlantic, carriers were designed to be a platform many miles away from battle. The carrier's offensive measures centered on the deadly planes launched to strike the enemy. After the war one captain wrote a colorful phrase of the predicament *Block Island* found herself in. He wrote, "A carrier right smack at the scene of a sound contact is like an old lady in a barroom brawl. She has no business there, and can do nothing but get out of the way."[5]

Jones and the crew of *Elmore* viewed *Block Island* as "Big Mom."[6] When "Big Mom" pinpointed locations for U-boats, she issued orders for the DEs. The mother escort carrier refueled her DE "kids" not only with oil but also with food for the sailors. Without request, provisions passed over to *Elmore* included such treats as ice cream. *Block Island* truly represented the heart of the task group. On May 29 Jones was on the bridge of *Elmore*, then just two thousand yards from *Block Island*, when the first loud explosion occurred. Jones recalled, "Everybody ran topside, because out at sea you don't hear much of anything."[7] *Elmore* immediately went into GQ and attempted to gain a contact on the hidden U-boat that had lashed out at "Big Mom." While the sailors of the DEs instantly moved to search for the U-boat, the men of *Block Island* experienced firsthand what their enemy had inflicted on Allied ships for years in the Battle of the Atlantic.

Bill "Slick" Connolly was serving as supervisor of the radio room on *Block Island*. Connolly had firsthand knowledge of surviving a sinking after abandoning USS *Lexington*, CV 2, lost in the Battle of the Coral Sea. When the first two torpedoes struck *Block Island*, sailors and equipment in the radio room were thrown around violently. Connolly stated, "There were message forms flying through the air. Typewriters bounding off the deck." With all the papers scattered around, Connolly stated, the radio room "looked like a snowstorm."[8]

For the 957 sailors on board, the two German torpedoes with 660 pounds of explosives slamming into *Block Island* caught them in a range of activities including showering, cooking meals, and doing laundry. Captain Hughes reported the two explosives hit three seconds apart. Immediately heading for the bridge, Hughes witnessed visible damage: "En route I noticed the port side of the flight deck curled back about ten feet and the forward part of the flight deck covered with oily water."[9] Sailors on the flight deck at the time of the explosions remember that after they collected themselves, the first thing they noticed was the visible damage to the bow. One said, "The forward end of the flight deck was rolled up like a newspaper."[10] A group of sailors soon gathered on the bow around a wounded sailor who was serving as a lookout when the torpedo struck. Besides being badly injured, his legs were trapped in the mangled catwalk as a result of the explosion.

The first torpedo struck the bow at 2015, creating a 20 x 26 foot hole that penetrated both the port and starboard sides of the ship and killed two lookouts. The second torpedo hit, which occurred within seconds of the first, struck in the more dangerous position into the aftermost oil tank on board. Luckily, this was empty and no secondary explosions or fire resulted from either torpedo.[11] However, for Hughes and the men on *Block Island*, the very real threat of another torpedo hit lingered, due to the thousands of gallons of fuel and weapons aboard the recently resupplied carrier. Damage sustained included the engine room taking on water, a jammed rudder, and the "ship settl[ing] nine feet by the stern."[12] After coming to a stop in the water, Hughes later wrote, "I felt certain that we were going to get hit again any minute. The word was passed for all hands that did not have particular jobs to go topside."[13] Central to Hughes's thinking was the bomb magazine, with its 142 depth charges and sixty-five thousand gallons of aviation fuel aboard. Dead in the water, his men faced the very real danger of one torpedo blowing the ship in half, similar to the damage inflicted on *Liscome Bay*. Once on the deck, Hughes issued orders to prepare to abandon ship. Hughes's order for the men to move topside proved wise in the minutes ahead.

As parachute rigger Hector Vernetti rushed to his battle station, he witnessed the chaos inside the hangar deck. Large portions of the vessel lost all electrical power, and thus all lighting. Vernetti recalled, "When I got there, everything was in disarray. The kid that was on duty with the earphones, he was walking around in a daze. It was disconnected and it was trailing him."[14] Officers seeking to regain control of the crew relayed messages using megaphones. With radio communication out, Captain Hughes was reduced to communicating with his screening DEs using Morse code imparted by flashlights.

With CVE 21 dead in the water, U 549 fired another acoustic type torpedo. Because Big Mom's propeller created no vibrations, the German torpedo homed in on the propeller noise from the screening DE *Barr*. A massive explosion rocked the aft portion of *Barr*. Electrician's Mate First Class Marvin A Johnson, his battle station at the bow of the DE, recalled, "When I turned around I saw one of our shipmates, named Barrett, and two depth charges about 50 feet in the air. The explosion blew all of our depth charges overboard and since we lost our rudder and propellers, we were dead in the water."[15]

Electrician's Mate Third Class Daniel DiBono, also on *Barr*, recalled a deafening explosion tossing him and others into the sea. Gathering themselves, they quickly reboarded the wounded DE. Depth charges on her wounded aft end rolled into the sea, sank, and then exploded underneath the stationary *Barr*, inflicting further damage. For those *Barr* sailors recovering from the blast, thoughts first went to friends whose battle stations were in the aft portion of the ship. Torpedoman's Mate Second Class Harold MacNeill remembered thinking of men stationed aft. He recalled, "A good friend, Brady, who was a gunner's mate was stationed on the aft gun. The impact of the torpedo bent the screws and fantail over on top of him, and he was buried in the debris. My friend, Tom Ellis, was missing in action."[16]

All the men gathered on the deck of CVE 21 threw up a celebratory cheer at the time of the torpedo strike on *Barr*, for they mistakenly interpreted the explosion as a successful depth charge attack by *Barr* on the submerged U-boat. However, when the men on the carrier witnessed the damage inflicted on *Barr*, they quickly realized their mistaken celebration. Many of those killed on *Barr* were simply atomized as the joint simultaneous explosions of the torpedo and the exposed depth charges proved so massive that they simply vanished into the ocean. These men were listed later as "missing in action." In total, seventeen *Barr* men were killed. However, for the moment, the men of *Barr* fought to save their battle-damaged vessel.[17] Back on *Block Island*, her sailors prepared to abandon ship.

Machinist Mate First Class Rex Coen enlisted in the Navy in 1942 at the age of sixteen. The first thing that stood out about the Navy for him was the haircuts, as these were free and did not require the normal thirty-five cents. He worked in the engineering room on CVE 21, converting seawater into drinkable water for consumption and for freshwater showers. Coming out of the shower when the first torpedo struck, Coen wore nothing but a towel. With the sound of general quarters, wearing only his Navy-issue towel, Coen ran to the battle station topside on an antiaircraft battery. Once topside, he recalled, "Someone told me to forget the antiaircraft, that we were fighting submarines."[18] Suddenly realizing he was without a life jacket he headed below decks. Here he located a pair of pants and a leather bomber jacket. As he was seeking a life preserver, the third torpedo slammed into the hull of CVE 21. Coen remembered years later, "It blew me up into the torpedo compartment and when I came down, I thought 'Well, I've got something broke.'"[19] This torpedo struck midship on the port side approximately ten minutes after the first two torpedo strikes. The force of the violent explosion caused near-instantaneous warping of inner compartments and hatchways. Coen, after gathering himself from the force, noticed the mutation in both deck and doorway. He recalled, "I looked up and saw the door to the locker-room was open about six inches and I hoped to heaven that it wasn't jammed. I pushed the door and heard a squeak."[20] When he forced the door open, he remembered, "It was the sweetest sound I've ever heard in my life."[21]

The third torpedo explosion ripped a thirty-five-foot hole up and into the hangar deck. This explosion tested the recent escort carrier's modifications resulting from the violent explosions that destroyed HMS *Avenger* and USS *Liscome Bay*. The reports after the sinking attested, "Recently authorized alterations to protect the bomb stowage had been accomplished and there was no bomb magazine explosion."[22] While modifications protected the CVE crew from prompt annihilation from the ignition of the entire bomb magazine, this third torpedo strike still proved deadly for the crew.

Irv Biron was traversing the flight deck when the third torpedo struck, knocking him down, as the blast was directly beneath him. He remembered with emotion, "When I picked myself up, there was a crack about a foot or a foot and a half along the flight deck, and I could look down and see water. That scared the hell out of me."[23] With the ship already dead in the water, this explosion literally and metaphorically broke the back of the escort carrier. A subsequent report and investigation of the attack stated, "A third torpedo hit in a most unfavorable location brought about the loss of the vessel."[24] The explosion caused the immediate deaths of two men, and another crew member was mortally wounded. However, Hughes's order of nonessential personnel topside greatly reduced the number killed in this third explosion. This torpedo also knocked out any little remaining electrical power, thus eliminating nearly all remaining interior lighting and reducing communication to sailors yelling into megaphones. Hughes gave the order, "All hands topside."[25] By now, the ship was rapidly settling by the stern.

Actually hearing the order to abandon ship produced varying degrees of disbelief and fear. One recalled, "This was a shock to hear. Nothing before this meant as much as hearing this. My visions of disasters at sea now became a reality."[26] Avoiding the growing gap stretching horizontally across the flight deck, the men gathered and climbed down ropes into almost a foot of oil secreting from the wounded *Block Island.* With the sun setting, only forty-five minutes of daylight remained, and Hughes continued to issue orders to the DEs by a sailor signaling Morse Code via flashlight.[27]

Bill "Slick" Connolly, a veteran of the sinking of USS *Lexington*, CV-2, remembered abandoning *Block Island* on the starboard side just forward of the superstructure. For the second time, Connolly climbed down a knotted line, abandoning his carrier lost to the enemy. His time in the water would be vastly different from the sinking of the "Lady Lex" in the Pacific. At the Battle of the Coral Sea, before the order to abandon ship was given, *Lexington* cruised for a number of hours as the crew battled to save her. As "Lady Lex" powered forward, all leaking fuels from the wounded vessel were dispersed in the trailing wake. This contrasted sharply with the waters around the stalled CVE 21, with close to a foot of oil and aviation fuel on the surface of the ocean. Sailors struggled not only to escape the sinking vessel but also to keep their heads well above the nauseating fuels. As the sailors swam away in groups, oil was kicked up and ingested, which led to sailors throwing up while continuing to depart the dangerous scene of their bleeding vessel. Thoughts of one spark from the fast-sinking carrier igniting the oil around them drove weakened arms and legs.[28]

By 2100 almost all 950 sailors had abandoned ship. Captain Hughes and a small group of officers remained on board as the ship was checked one more time for survivors. A small party still remained gathered at the bow of the vessel. Here, James O'Neil Franks, on duty as a lookout when the first torpedo exploded below him, lay trapped. The force of the blast ripped the metal below his feet upward and enclosed it around his leg. For an hour after the first blast, a team of men led by Flight Surgeon Cdr. Jasper Custer worked in an attempt to free Franks from the twisted catwalk with the use of an acetylene torch. When this proved impossible due to the time constraints of the sinking ship, Custer amputated the leg. However, blood loss claimed Franks's life. In a last act of honoring Franks, the crew placed his covered body on a stretcher on the flight deck. He would be buried with the ship that was fast sinking.[29]

The *Loss of Action Report* noted that most of the men abandoned ship within seventeen minutes after the third torpedo hit.[30] Seaman First Class Walter Cyr, taking a shower when the first torpedo struck, climbed down sixty feet of knotted rope into the oily water. Cyr and others swam away in the oily water wearing life jackets. Other sailors also held on to and used a variety of lifeboats and held on to floating nets. From Cyr's vantage point of bobbing in the ocean swells, it looked as if the DEs were leaving the scene.[31] However, in searching for the enemy U-boat, they had disappeared over the horizon. The cornered submarine posed a grave danger to the remaining DEs. Before stopping to pick up *Block Island* crew members, the DEs needed to successfully destroy the U-boat.

The range of emotions felt by the crew members floating in the waters was as diverse as their backgrounds. Some prayed and made peace with their maker, others called out to fellow sailors, some yelled at the Nazis for sinking their ship. Swimming in the ocean, sailor Joe Booi focused his emotions on a happy notion: "Hallelujah, I'm gonna get 30 days survivor's leave!"[32] However, no matter what their emotions were on the surface, from their training all the men realized the transformation in their relationship with *Block Island*. She had served as their home and safe platform on a range of missions. Now the ship posed a grave danger, as massive holes from the torpedo strikes sucked in water. The men's training told them to flee from their former vessel. So the men continued swimming away from their stricken ship, as she still housed a diverse collection of explosives and weapons, and a range of combustible fuels.[33]

In the rush to get off *Block Island*, a group of sailors climbed down ropes on the windward side, thus pushing them toward the sinking vessel once in the water. A circling whaleboat from the carrier witnessed their distress and tossed a line, pulling them to safety. Upon finding himself drifting back toward the sinking carrier, Hector Vernetti took off swimming in the rough seas. With adrenaline fueling his arms, he quickly found himself completely alone. Bobbing in a life jacket in the rough Atlantic waters, one's horizon nearly ends at one's nose. Just under an hour before, Vernetti was one of a crew of a thousand members; now in the fast-fading light, he floated by himself on a vast ocean. Then he heard some talking. He immediately yelled, "Hey, you guys, wait for me!" A thankful reply came back from an unseen source. "Is that you, Vernetti?"[34]

Figure 10. Hector Vernetti saved the shoes he wore during the sinking and transformed them into a memorial to the experience and the lost CVE 21. He placed plaster inside the shoes and then painted them gold. After the war the shoes served as a testament to the lost *Block Island* in his home in Scottsdale, Arizona. Photo by Benjamin J. Hruska.

The men swimming in a mixture of oil and salt water soon encountered an exotic and painful resident of the central Atlantic. The very sight of these organisms caused fear. The Portuguese man-of-war is, in fact, not one organism but what in biology is termed a "colonial organism." Mirroring the function of the escort carriers, these were in fact a series of organisms working in compartmentalized fashion to achieve the goal of survival. Under the surface, venom-filled tentacles, up to fifty feet in length, paralyzed fish for consumption. But what looked alien to these oil-soaked sailors were the clear bladders full of air on the surface, which keep the man o' war afloat and also act as a sail harnessing the ocean winds. This last characteristic accounts for its name, after the centuries-old naval term for a particular class of warship.[35] When the men encountered these foreign-looking creatures, advice came from an experienced seaman. As the young sailors struggled physically and emotionally in fighting for survival, a chief warrant officer known as "Old Ironsides" swam by nonchalantly with his cap still in place. He yelled, "Swim on your backs, men."[36] This position protected them from any possible underwater explosions. The confident orders from a familiar source overcame the shock of seeing the concentration of Portuguese men-of-war around them; however, sting injuries still

Figure 11. A view from a nearby destroyer escort of the task force of the USS *Block Island* wounded and her stern settling. Naval History and Heritage Command.

occurred. One sailor wrote, "Anyone who was foolish enough to remove their shirt and/or pants was in for a very painful surprise."[37] As the men navigated through the group of Mother Nature's men-of-war, over the horizon the DEs of the task force continued to search for U 549.

Meanwhile, on *Block Island*, just a core group of enlisted men and officers remained on board. The remaining enlisted were lookouts and assisted in communicating with the DEs via flashlight. One such sailor was Gunner's Mate Third Class Bill Tokarz, who recalled the shattered state of CVE 21. The first spread of two torpedoes caused holes in the port side of the hull in both the bow and stern. However, the third torpedo inflicted major damage. Tokarz recalled, "The third torpedo hit dead center and split the ship in half. We had about an eighteen-inch gap in the flight deck, and you could look right down into the hangar deck."[38] These lookouts were some of the last of the enlisted men to enter the black waters surrounding CVE 21 and swim away. Tokarz, speaking decades later, said, "Even at eighteen years old, you get scared. I got out of there as fast as I could. In fact, I passed some of the boys who left fifteen minutes earlier."[39]

At 2140 Hughes ordered the remaining party of officers off the stricken carrier. All, including Captain Hughes, stepped off the starboard sponson onto a small launch floating in waters that slowly swallowed the escort carrier. Then Hughes and the last of the officers slowly motored away from USS *Block Island*, CVE 21.

With *Block Island* abandoned and the men of *Barr* fighting to save their wounded vessel, the remaining three unharmed DEs sought desperately to gain a sonar contact on the cornered U-boat. With the fast-fading light, one wounded DE, and nearly a thousand sailors floating in the Atlantic, Hughes had to reconsider his options with regard to having all three DEs actively engaged in seeking the enemy. Roughly an hour after the first torpedo strikes, Hughes ordered *Paine* and *Ahrens* to prepare to pick up the survivors from the escort carrier while *Elmore* continued in pursuit of the German submarine. However, the *Ahrens* sonar department continued to search and, in the process, discovered a contact, which was quickly radioed to the patrolling *Elmore*. As *Elmore* closed in, she established a sonar contact. U 549 fired a torpedo at the pursuing *Elmore*, which she successfully dodged with a hard right turn. Three minutes later *Elmore* launched a Hedgehog salvo, and a massive explosion in front of the DE signaled a scored hit. Four minutes after the launch, the soundman on *Elmore* "heard the crackly, tearing noises and harsh rumble that mean a submarine is breaking up like a crushed bushel basket."[40] Henry Jones on the bridge of *Elmore* recalled, "After a short while debris and oil came up. We had sunk it."[41] An hour and a half after the first torpedoes hit CVE 21, the U 549 was successfully destroyed, killing all fifty-seven crew members.[42]

For the hundreds of CVE 21 crew members floating in the water, witnessing the approaching *Ahrens* coming to their rescue caused elation. Unexpectedly, underwater explosions erupted, and the subsequent shock waves hit the men. One sailor likened the sudden change in pressure around them to receiving an enema from a utility pole. These explosions for the sailors floating near *Ahrens* produced fears that she, too, was struck. However, these explosions erupted around the wounded *Block Island*. With her stern sinking, the men saw in the waning light her flight deck reaching a 60-degree angle. Hughes reported, "She went down fighting, just like she fought on the surface. She stood right on the stern for about five minutes, the bow standing straight up in the air in a silhouette. You could see the hole completely through the bow."[43] The planes on the deck, loaded with armed depth charges, slipped into the water. Roughly two minutes later, the charges in these swiftly sinking aircraft exploded underneath the mortally wounded carrier. Captain Hughes wrote that these charges, "were the coup de grace for the *Block Island* for the bow remained completely vertical for a few moments and then slowly disappeared from sight at 2155."[44]

While the sinking obviously had the greatest impact on the crew of CVE 21, it is easy to overlook the psychological impact for those crew members of the destroyer escorts. The vessel they protected sank in front of their eyes. The sailors of the FBI had a reduced horizon of their ship due to being in the water; however, the DE sailors, standing on their bridges, had the best view of the CVE 21 going vertical as she was sinking beneath the waves. Looking at the empty space she had occupied minutes earlier in her wounded condition produced a range of challenging emotions. *Elmore* sailor Henry Jones recalled, "I remember it was such a void without her."[45] A short poem he penned of the experience ended with, "Oh what a big ocean, it seemed even bigger without the *Block Island* there."[46]

While Captain Hughes was the last to step off the dying CVE 21, pulling away in a whaleboat to a DE, one would think that with his superior position he retained the most sea experience. This was not the case. The oldest sailor floated amid the oil with the entire ship's company in a collection of lifeboats and floating nets. While Captain Hughes was born in 1899, Cook Third Class Espiridion Escumbise was not only older than Hughes but had come out of retirement for his second enlistment.[47] Now the nearly fifty-year-old Escumbise floated in fuel oil with other sailors, some of whom were thirty-five years younger. Like the oil covering up identities of hair and skin color, the stressful experience of abandoning ship in the high seas proved very democratic. As a naval battle still waged, as attested by the underwater explosions going off in the distance, these men looked to the ever-listing carrier. With her bow high in the water, they witnessed the setting sun casting orange light on the American flag still flying from the ship's mast. Then, as gravity forced the last amounts of air out of the vessel, she quickly disappeared below the waves. The ship that had been everything to them, their platform for war and their metal cocoon against the inhospitable sea, was gone. The rising currents recirculating on the surface signified the multiple voids her obliteration promised.

In addressing the difference between the battle sites of land versus the sea, one scholar wrote, "When a ship sinks, the battlefield goes away."[48] While in the water watching CVE 21, surviving Radioman Third Class John "Joe" Browne recalled floating in the oily water and looking where the ship had slipped under the waves. He wrote, "Finally everything was smooth again and where there had been a 10,000 ton carrier just a short time ago there was now nothing."[49] As darkness fell, all that remained in giving a visible clue that the vessel existed were the men in the water and debris floating around them. However, as CVE 21 sank into the deep, she still posed a threat to the men. Eight minutes after she sank, Captain Hughes and his staff in their whaleboat were just four hundred yards from where the carrier succumbed to the Atlantic. At this point, as CVE 21 descended into the abyss, a series of massive explosions transpired. Hughes recalled, "These explosions were so terrific that all hands aboard the rescue ships were certain they were attacked again. They were the most violent explosions that I ever witnessed."[50] At just a quarter-mile away, Hughes told an interviewer, "We thought it would blow the bottom out of the boat. It was so violent that I didn't think we were going to get aboard the DE."[51]

Although the sinking erased the barrier of race, as nearly all were equally covered in black fuel oil, one barrier did not vanish. More than one sailor, when interviewed about the sinking, spoke of the enduring division between officers and the enlisted sailors. Racial divisions evaporated in all seeking not to die on this May evening in the Atlantic. As sailors fought for their lives and swam in oily seas amidst underwater explosions, whaleboats carried officers safely away from the sinking. Veterans recalled that these whaleboats, like the one Hughes rode in, carried the "big shots."[52] Others outright blamed Hughes for the loss of CVE 21. In comparing Ramsey and Hughes, one veteran referred to Hughes as "Oh, the one that got us sunk."[53]

18
Crucible

As for the men who had not been pulled from the water, they either remembered their training or were reminded by experienced older sailors nearby and lay on their backs in the water to reduce the concussions from the weapons. Under them CVE 21 sank ever downward into fifteen thousand feet of seawater, toward the Gambia Abyssal Plain on the Atlantic's bottom. The sailors' training paid off, for a number of horrific explosions took place, as submerging weapons within CVE 21 detonated in unison. Most of the crew members by this time were at least 1.5 miles south of the location of the sinking, assisted in part by a breeze from the north. One sailor recalled that the last explosion proved so powerful that "it knocked out both engine rooms of the approaching DE some three miles now from the carrier."[1] This particular explosion created an upward wave of pressure so violent it forced crew members upward and completely out of the water.

With U 549 destroyed, the unharmed DEs stopped in the water and began the long task of plucking the survivors out of the oily sea. Brown estimated that his cohort of men struggled in the water for two hours and fifteen minutes.[2] Beyond exhausted, DE sailors reached down and dragged ever more drained sailors aboard. Legs and arms refused to work due to fatigue. Unable to walk, sailors lay down on the decks. Saturated in oil and cold salt water, sailors smoked cigarettes and consumed medical brandy. Walter Cyr was so tired he could not move his arms to adjust his cigarette, thus burning his lips.[3] Even in this time of trauma, lighter moments surfaced. Some sailors arrived on the DEs completely naked, because they were showering when the first torpedoes struck. Requests for clothing on board the DEs came over the loudspeakers. One humorously called, "Will you please bring an assortment of clothing to the deck? We have a sailor here wearing nothing but a smile."[4] Another sailor remembered decades later with a laugh an inner DE compartment so filthy that oil covered the entire deck and all the wall space. Looking up he noticed the oil smudges from a sailor placing the oil-soaked soles of his shoes on the ceiling. A messman who had proved quite successful gambling on board CVE 21 ran below decks during the initial attack and stuffed his winnings, some $6,000, in his pockets. In reaching a DE, he was penniless and was able to recover only $137 in the waters adjacent to the vessel granting him deliverance.[5]

Hector Vernetti was one of the last sailors pulled from the water. After sunset the remaining survivors hung on to one another in a collection of floating nets, life rafts, or individual life jackets. Over two hours after entering the oily waters, their adrenaline glands were spent, and the coldness began to set in. Those in lifeboats stamped their feet. Sailors scanned the now-blackened horizon for the DEs, which were darkened in case of a U-boat attack. Vernetti remembered, "All you could see was the little red light on the mast."[6] As the DE *Ahrens* neared their position, her engines stopped, and she bobbed like a cork in the Atlantic swells. As the men approached the nets hanging off the sides and saw the fluctuations in elevations of the deck above them, they feared being crushed. However, as they waited their turn to get on board, a voice yelled from the darkness. The *Ahrens* was overloaded; the sailors would have to await rescue. After finally getting on the deck of *Paine*, the true coldness struck. Vernetti recalled, "I was shaking like the devil."[7] Offered hot coffee or brandy, Hector Vernetti drank a hearty portion of the latter. Warming up inside the vessel's engine room, the men discarded their oil-soaked clothing. In the lighted compartments, they witnessed the extent of the oil and aviation fuel they had swum in. The very thought of how one spark could have radically altered their fate produced a shudder. Vernetti remembered thinking of this after seeing a familiar face with a completely different hue. He said, "He was a blond, blue-eyed guy, and he was black from here down [pointing to the top of his head]."[8] Replacement clothing from DE sailors was handed out to *Block Island* survivors.

For the next several dark hours, the DEs circled the site of the sinking, sailing through floating debris, waiting for daylight to continue the search for survivors. The morning light revealed the remains of the battlefield. On this Memorial Day 1944, one sailor recalled, "The sea for miles around was just covered with life rafts and other debris."[9] With the final check for survivors completed, the DEs that constituted all that remained of TG 21.11 left the site with the wounded *Barr* in tow. As these overloaded DEs pulled away to the north, for most this represented the final goodbye to the location of their defining wartime experience. As one scholar describes the site of battle on the ocean: "On the sea there is no place to anchor a memorial flagpole or a headstone. It is a vanishing graveyard."[10]

The vessels cruised at a slow five knots as *Elmore* towed the wounded *Barr*, where her sailors were busily recovering the dead and securing the lower compartments from seawater. This was Tuesday, May 30, 1944. It was also Memorial Day, as the holiday at the time was still celebrated on the thirtieth. As the group slowly cruised northeast toward Casablanca, in cities across the United States, local citizens and aging veterans gathered at events remembering the nation's honored dead. So too on the overloaded *Elmore*, the sailors gathered on her deck for a funeral with full military honors. That morning Capt. G. L. Conkey announced over the PA system that one of the badly wounded *Barr* sailors had died in the early morning hours. On the deck of *Elmore*, sailors stood at attention while this sailor was laid to rest in the ancient form of sea burial, respectfully placed in the ocean that he had recently fought from. Henry Jones remembered, "The captain came down from his quarters with a Navy manual and read the service."[11] He then gave the command, "Bury the dead." Jones said, "He slid out from under the American flag, and splash. I see that every Memorial Day."[12] The ceremony also functioned as a method of remembrance for those sailors, on both *Barr* and *Block Island*, whose bodies were not recovered, and who were now at peace in the Atlantic.

Even though the crew of *Block Island* experienced cramped quarters, after the emotional stress of the sinking, the minor inconveniences of riding on an overloaded DE seemed like welcome aspects of just being alive. USS *Ahrens* and USS *Paine* crews normally consisted of roughly 150 men; now *Paine* added 277 and *Ahrens* an additional 674 survivors.[13] Cooks in small DE galleys labored overtime in brewing coffee and making sandwiches for the suddenly expanded crew. *Ahrens*, so overloaded its captain was worried about capsizing, issued orders over the loudspeakers for the CVE 21 sailors not to move around. A system was implemented of dividing the survivors into groups of thirds, which rotated in shifts, sleeping on the deck, standing, and sitting on tables and chairs. Every two hours the groups switched. The hundreds of oil-drenched FBI survivors quickly transformed vessels into an oily mess. Galleys quickly introduced rationing as pantries designed to last for weeks dwindled.[14] One sailor recalled standing in a long line only to be handed a piece of white bread. Another remembered, "We ate everything they had on that ship."[15] Motion sickness also occurred for these CVE sailors used to the motions of a 10,000-ton carrier, and not the small DEs.[16] However, emotional stress of surviving the sinking soon manifested.

For civilian Russell Lewis, resting on a DE, the first sign of mental stress surfaced after an unexpected noise. While taking his turn on the deck sleeping, using his oil-covered life jacket as a pillow, he suddenly awoke. A loud crash occurred from an undisclosed source. He recalled, "As a result of the noise I started shaking violently and uncontrollably."[17] Witnessing his stress, a crew member told him, "Easy buddy, you've got yourself a case of shellshock."[18] His thoughts immediately returned to his boyhood home in Indiana and a World War I veteran who still shook decades after his experience in the trenches. The next day a similar incident occurred. Years later Lewis wrote, "I resolved to get myself under control and become the person I was before the first torpedo struck the *Block Island*."[19]

As they cruised at a sluggish five knots, the threat of a German U-boat finding these easy targets was very real. To counter this threat, rotating PBY Catalina flying boats circled overhead, vectored out from Casablanca. After a rendezvous with a tug vessel sent from Casablanca to tow the wounded *Barr*, the three remaining DEs made flank speed.[20] After a four-day ordeal, a first step toward normalcy took

Figure 12. Fighting *Block Island* sailors on dry land after departing the DEs on June 1, 1944. Here in Casablanca they would lose their clothing from the sinking and be issued surplus clothing from the US Army. Courtesy of the USS Block Island Association.

place when the men disembarked from the DEs and felt solid earth underfoot. Here in Casablanca the Navy conducted a headcount. Most survivors then walked into a chapel, formerly a camel barn, where an Episcopalian chaplain led a service offering thanks for their deliverance and prayers for those lost crew members. During the service, the "Navy Hymn" was sung.[21] The sailors' reaction to the song gave new meaning to their ordeal, especially the lines: "*Oh hear us when we cry to Thee / For those in peril on the sea.*"[22]

From the chapel the oil-covered crew lined up in the front of a nearby warehouse. Inside, Army personnel stood behind tables stacked with survival kits. These included "towels, wash cloths, soap, razors, shaving cream, cigarettes, khaki underwear, and uniforms intended for army privates."[23] The men's appearance was very un-Navy-like. After a shower and a shave, they dressed in their Army-issued clothes. Men passed the time playing baseball, drinking cases of beer, and sleeping in Army cots. Sailor Rex Coen, after being issued his Army clothing, also received a Red Cross package. It included something of no use to Coen, American cigarettes. However, this resourceful sailor walking the docks found some Portuguese sailors interested in his recently acquired supply of American tobacco. Trading the smokes for some Scotch, Coen shared his trade with fellow FBI sailors and they celebrated surviving the sinking together. Word spread quickly and his chief

Figure 13. Fighting *Block Island* sailors, seen here wearing an assortment of oil-soaked clothing, checking in upon arrival in Casablanca. Naval History and Heritage Command.

approached him with a warning. He told him, "I'll have you arrested . . . unless you bring me some."[24]

While the men awaited further orders, the news of the Allied landings in France on June 6, 1944, overshadowed any detailed accounts of the sinking of the lonely carrier. One recalled, "With the invasion absorbing major attention, scant newspaper space was given a brief release two days later, announcing the loss of the *Block Island* 'the first American carrier lost in the Atlantic,' with only the word that 'casualties were light.'"[25] Other news for families stateside included telegrams from the Navy reporting their loved one "missing in action." From Casablanca, the Navy allowed some sailors to cable home from a number of very short predrafted statements. Walter Cyr cabled two messages, one to his parents and the other to his girlfriend, that simply read, "Well and safe."[26] A return trip across the Atlantic awaited them.

❋

While only six sailors died on board CVE 21 and eighteen were wounded as a result of the three torpedo strikes, sadly four other deaths did result well away from the lost carrier. When the attack commenced, *Block Island* had six aircraft aloft. The CIC officer, Lt. I. H. Houston, radioed these aircraft miles away from CVE 21. Unable to land on the carrier, Houston vectored out the nearest land location: he radioed, "Tenerife Island, Canaries, bearing 117 T, distance 290 miles."[27] Houston and his team, after alerting the airborne pilots of the situation, destroyed anything of value to the enemy. This included emptying a pistol into the radio and destroying massive piles of intelligence paperwork in the communications area.[28] The Wildcats, already airborne over three hours, could barely stay aloft for more than six. The pilots debated over the airways on what to do, both options requiring returning to the site of the wounded *Block Island*. From there they could attempt to pancake their craft in the water and, if successful, be picked up by a DE. Or, once back and knowing their exact coordinates, make way for Las Palmas.

Arriving at the site of the stricken carrier, they looked down at the chaos below. With the sun nearing the horizon, the six aircraft opted to fly for the nearest land. They flew in formation and nervously watched their fuel gauges as the minutes passed by. As evening came on and the darkness swallowed them up, the pilots strained their eyes below them for any sign of the island. Before long, the moonlight pouring from above revealed an island. Instead of bailing out of the aircraft in the skies and risking a parachute landing into an unknown location at night, the group decided to form "a line perpendicular to their flight path and then headed out into the moon's path in order to see the water as they touched down."[29] As their Wildcats slammed into the water, the men attempted to quickly unharness themselves and escape their fast-sinking aircraft. Only two of the pilots, Lt. Jim McDaniel and Lt. John Carr, managed this maneuver and survived. However, even as they landed relatively close to one another, the similarities of their experiences ended there.

McDaniel managed to extract the inflatable rubber raft from his plane. After inflating the raft, McDaniel waited in the boat for dawn as he floated off the island's coast. During the daylight hours, a search plane spotted him and dropped a larger raft that included provisions. Once in the larger raft, McDaniel, mistakenly thinking the provisions an anchor, tossed these into the water. The search plane radioed a nearby DE, which later picked up the lone pilot, transporting him back to Casablanca.[30]

Carr's story was far more adventurous; after exiting his plane, he inflated his Mae West and floated completely alone. As he bobbed in the ocean's swell during the night, the waves pushed him ashore. Once there at dawn, Carr confronted enclosed sea cliffs. He spent a number of morning hours attempting to scale these cliffs before giving up. Later in the day, he spotted two men in a rowboat. They picked him up and turned him over to local authorities. Shipped to Cadiz, and

Figure 14. Captain Hughes and officers of CVE 21 can smile once safely arrived in Casablanca thanks to the DEs of the task force. Naval History and Heritage Command.

then driven to Gibraltar, Carr was turned over to a US Naval attaché. He then flew on a transport to Casablanca However, by this time the rescued crew of *Block Island* and VC-55 had already shipped out for the United States. So, Carr took another flight to the United States and reached home before the men of VC-55. He stood on the pier in Norfolk when the men of his air group disembarked.

What happened to the four other pilots remains a mystery. Either during the attempted landing or sometime after, they simply vanished. Lt. Robert P. Buell, Lt. Julian L. Pitts, Lt. Robert W. Wyatt, and Ensign Robert E. Innis represent the last four deaths from the sinking.[31]

Of all those who survived the sinking, one of the first to arrive back in the United States was the only civilian on board. On the morning of D-Day, June 6, 1944, Russell Lewis and a small group of *Block Island* officers rode a bus bound for an airfield south of Casablanca. Here they boarded a four-engine DC-4 aircraft and took off on their first leg of the journey home, which was a 1,200-mile flight to the Azores. After a quick stop in Stevensville, Newfoundland, their aircraft landed at National Airport in Washington, DC. As the military personnel filed off the plane, Lewis had to walk in a different direction upon exiting the plane. He recalled, "Being a civilian, I was required to clear through Customs, and the

Customs Agent wanted to know where my luggage was." Lewis's only possessions were inside the survivor's kit handed to him in Casablanca, consisting of a razor, spare socks, and an extra pair of underwear. He explained his experience without naming specific vessels or dates; the agent understood. Lewis wrote, "He wished me well and passed me through."[32]

19
"Seeing Ghosts"

The FBI survivors, like those of all sinkings in the USN, were due to receive thirty days survivor's leave once stateside. The Navy designated three CVEs, including USS *Mission Bay*, CVE 59; USS *Kasaan Bay*, CVE 69; and USS *Tulagi*, CVE 72, to return the survivors home to Norfolk. For the men who had just survived a sinking, the thought of returning to the Atlantic was worrisome. Moreover, these three CVEs, manufactured by the Kaiser Corporation, which built the doomed *Liscome Bay*, were infamous for the entire bomb magazine exploding as the result of a single torpedo strike. Thus, the entire classification earned the nickname "Kaiser coffins."[1] About boarding these vessels, Joe Booi remembered, "None of us were too crazy about being on board one of the Kaiser's coffins."[2] The sail across the middle portion of the ocean proved uneventful. Men passed the time by gambling in the hangar. Wooden crates, full of engines that needed overhauling, served as card tables. However, the psychological weight of the sinking persisted. Nearing the end of their journey and with the American coast coming into view, Booi remembered seeing fifty card games in progress. Then an unexpected lurch took place, similar to a torpedo hit. Booi recalled, "Fifty decks of cards went flying into the air and everybody ran up onto the flight deck. When I looked out a short way, there was a tugboat with the biggest anchor I ever saw on a small boat. I commented about it and one sailor there said, 'Hell that's our anchor hanging on the side of the tug, our anchor chain broke.'"[3] Booi's escort carrier slamming into a tugboat, and their anchor breaking off and falling onto the deck of the tug, shook emotionally raw nerves. Sailor Irv Biron remembered a similar incident on his escort carrier. Biron recalled, "They fired those five-inch guns without telling us, and every one of us was up on the flight deck with our life jackets."[4] While funny in hindsight after they realized their collective overreaction, events such as these demonstrated that even as the conscious portions of the sailors' minds could be distracted with talking and card games, the more persistent unconscious sections of their minds still grappled with the sinking.

Docking in Norfolk, the men were processed and received their thirty-day survivor's leave. Crew members said goodbye to one another. Historically, the surviving crews of lost USN vessels were broken up. Survivor Bill "Slick" Connolly received his second survivor's leave. His first was for surviving a sinking at the Battle of Coral Sea; now he could chalk up an Atlantic sinking.[5] Life in the Navy consisted of rotation, with the ebb and flow of crews, men, air groups, and commanding officers. Sinkings only added to this cycle, producing experienced sailors lacking a vessel. Rotation became a way of life. One sailor summed up his experience as feeling part of a game of chess. He wrote that an unknown force "decides one day to pick you up between finger and thumb like a pawn on a chess-board and move you to a different square."[6]

Walking out of the Norfolk naval station, the survivors felt a diverse range of emotions that affected the ways they spent their first hours back in America. Most sent a telegram or called home, and relieved parents thanked their God not only for their son's life but that he was coming home. Others, however, found relief in the company of other crew members and enjoying the beer joints. One particular group of FBI sailors had some unfinished business. Before their last mission, at one of the numerous waterholes of Norfolk, these sailors got involved in an altercation with a group of other drinkers. A feisty barmaid, seeking to grab the FBI sailors' attention, yelled that she hoped their ship would be sunk on her next mission. Now whatever remained of CVE 21 rested on the bottom of the Atlantic, and these sailors certainly remembered her remarks. As one historian wrote, "When they got back to Norfolk, they made it a point to tear the bar apart."[7]

❋

With USN history starting in 1775, at times the service would rechristen a new vessel for one lost in combat. Due to the length of construction, this policy did not include retaining the original crew. As the FBI sailors exited the Navy Yard of Norfolk, they had no idea about their future duties. While the men began their leave, a force lobbied for the unprecedented in the history of the USN, the retention of a crew to serve on a replacement vessel lost in combat. This force was Massie Hughes and Logan Ramsey. Stressing the importance of keeping the crew of the Fighting *Block Island* together, Hughes (with the assistance of Ramsey), once back within the Norfolk hierarchy, pushed for this goal.[8] His drive is seen in an interview with Lt. A. Wright of the Aviation Section of the Navy's Department of Public Relations. Wright confirmed that he had previously interviewed Captain Ramsey, and he discussed the "greenness" of the crew of CVE 21 when first commissioned and how the trials and the missions in the Atlantic had molded them into a cohesive fighting unit. Hughes responded, "Outstanding! It's the adaptability of the American man. All of these stock brokers, bankers, lawyers, farmers are all taken into the Navy and adapt themselves to the Navy routine. They turn out a fighting man within a period of six months or a year. It was marvelous!"[9]

Captain Ramsey, serving now as chief of staff and aide to the commander Fleet

Air at Norfolk, publicly spoke of the lost ship he first brought into reality. To a group of officers he said, "Like the *Hornet* the career of the ship lasted just a little longer than one year, being sunk on May 29, 1944."[10] He gave high praise to the officers on board in getting the men off the vessel in a timely manner. He noted that while six sailors were lost, all of these were killed as a result of the torpedo explosions, and no sailors died after entering the Atlantic waters. In speaking of the evacuation, Ramsey proudly boasted, "Someone should get a medal out of that business."[11] When an officer in the audience asked Ramsey of the composition of the officers on CVE 21, he spoke at length. "One of the most remarkable things on the ships was the large number of reserve officers and how well they performed their duties. When the ship went down I think there were only 3 regular officers on board, the Captain, the Executive Officer and the Air Officer. All the rest were reserve officers. Outside of the regular officers, none of the reserve officers had ever been on a carrier before."[12]

Ramsey continued, describing the trust he had placed in those officers around him. The graduate of the 1919 Academy class told the officers gathered, "The Captain cannot be on the bridge all the time."[13] In recalling one particular incident, he said, "On one occasion, we had a submarine contact, and by the time I had gone up to the Bridge, the officer of the deck, who was a Philadelphia lawyer, had done everything there was to be done on his own initiative, and there was absolutely nothing that I could do to add to what he had done."[14] In speaking of his successor's aggressiveness, Ramsey said Hughes "had continuous operations at one time, air operations, for over 288 hours without ceasing. I don't believe that it has been done before by any carrier in the world."[15] Ramsey also praised the enlisted men of the air squadron and noted that only the implementation of a revolving sleep schedule allowed these continuous operations to take place for almost a fortnight. He also noted that the loss of CVE 21 for one particular FBI enlisted sailor represented his fourth survived sinking. He concluded, "The spirit of the crew was indicated by their response to the general quarters alarm. There were no less than 37 cases of scalp lacerations suffered by various members of the crew, which were due to the men racing to their assigned stations, and bumping in projecting bulkheads, etc."[16] Ramsey recalled a telegraph from the First Lord of the Admiralty in Winston Churchill's cabinet, the Right Honorable A. V. Alexander, addressing the loss of CVE 21. Alexander wrote, "I have followed the career of the *Block Island* from the very beginning, and I wish to express my deep regrets at the loss of such a gallant and splendid ship."[17]

As Hughes and Ramsey attempted to make Navy history, the crew members spread out across America. Gunner's Mate Third Class John Suprey rode a train north to Lowell, Massachusetts. Suprey had joined the Navy at the age of sixteen by forging his father's signature. The Suprey family had paid a heavy price in this war, with one son killed and another held as a POW. His parents read of *Block Island*'s demise in the Lowell paper and received no other information. Their phone rang, and his father heard his son's voice from Norfolk stating he was coming home for thirty days. His father waited at the Lowell station. Suprey's father told him to put his bags in the car; then the father and his seventeen-year-old son walked into a nearby Irish bar. Crossing the street his father said, "Now you are a man, you can have a drink." While in Lowell on leave, Suprey, like other crew members, received orders to report to Bremerton, Washington.[18] Here, the shipbuilders of Todd Pacific continued assembling a new Commencement Bay–class escort carrier. This classification, constructed from the keel up as a war vessel, would include a USS *Block Island*, CVE 106. The story of the Fighting *Block Island* would continue with a new mission, on a new ocean, and a with new enemy.

❁

While the news of the sinking spread in the small towns and neighborhoods of *Block Island* sailors, the Allied invasion of Normandy just nine days later grabbed America's attention. On June 6, 1944, the cover of the *New York Times* informed a nation of the long-awaited cross-channel invasion of France. The first pages of the newspaper contained a collage of photographs, graphics, and maps on the event collectively known today as D-Day. Located on page 8 was a small article on the USN, publicly confirming the loss of CVE 21. The article "Escort Carrier Sunk in Atlantic: Casualties Light on the *Block Island*, Victim of Enemy" noted that the loss of the American carrier was the first in the Atlantic and the sixth of the entire war.[19] The piece opened, "The escort carrier *Block Island* was sunk in the Atlantic during May, the Navy announced tonight."[20] While no official cause was listed other than enemy action, the article accurately surmised it was the result of a U-boat attack. The only specific individual mentioned was the skipper, Capt. Francis Massie Hughes, and the Navy spokesman confirmed that Hughes had survived the sinking. However, for the families of those of CVE 21, it was excruciating to read only short articles on the sinking. While wartime newspaper articles lacked specifics in order to keep the enemy in the dark on intelligence, families were left asking more questions after reading such abridged columns. Terminology such as "casualties light" applied to a thousand-man crew generated innumerable questions, some with hopeful, others with unthinkable, answers.

Sailor Bill Tokarz's mother read about the sinking in the newspaper and, more frighteningly, her son's name in stark black and white listing him as "missing in action" (MIA). His mother read every different newspaper available in the Boston region, but wartime coverage included nothing more on the loss of her son's carrier. The sinking of one small ship in a very big war earned no more mentions, but across the country parents and family members still combed daily papers for any word on the fate of their sons, brothers, and uncles. Tokarz, after safely being transported to Casablanca on the DE *Ahrens*, was never given the opportunity to telegraph home. Weeks later, after passage across the Atlantic, Tokarz received his leave upon arrival in Norfolk. Here he picked up a phone and called home. Upon hearing their son's voice, his parents were relieved, as being listed MIA in a naval engagement was a near death sentence. He joked fifty years later, "They were not quite done writing the obituary."[21]

Crew member Rex Coen arrived in Norfolk and received his survivor's leave and $35. He wired a message home. He recalled, "My mom had heard the *Block Island* had been sunk but that was all. One minute she had me 'Missing in Action,' the next, she got a wire begging for $100 so I could come home."[22] Psychologically, American families dealt with husbands and sons listed as MIA. For many this meant the odds of seeing their loved one again were slim, and if they did, it would be after the conclusion of the war. Across the nation, this status also confounded friends and acquaintances alike when someone they knew of was officially listed as MIA. Whether this information moved through a community by local newspapers or word of mouth, those who knew the listed servicemen were left wondering what to say to the affected family members. Once back in Texas, Coen experienced a strange feeling while walking around town. He stated, "People thought I was MIA and seeing me was like seeing a ghost for a lot of them."[23]

For the crew members of *Block Island*, the America they returned home to in the summer of 1944 contrasted sharply with the one they had left. They witnessed this transformation firsthand, with absent male friends and relations off fighting in the war. Sailors noticed the rationing of foodstuffs while dining with their families. They saw their sisters and female friends leaving their homes dressed in factory uniforms going off to jobs that had been dominated by men before the war. Many took advantage during this new lease on life and quickly married girlfriends. Engagements were short, as the thirty days went by quickly. Arlie "Buster" Lapeyrolerie returned to what is known as the "Golden Triangle," the very southeasternmost portion of Texas, heavily influenced by French colonists known as Cajuns. Buster married his longtime girlfriend, Audrey, in a simple ceremony before the survivor's leave came to a close.[24] All too quickly, across the nation, telegrams arrived from the USN with new orders for these veterans of the lost CVE 21.

Crew members along the eastern seaboard were first ordered to Norfolk. Then they boarded a westbound train to join the crew of the second *Block Island*. This included three Massachusetts sailors, Walter Cyr from Walpole, John Suprey of Lowell, and Bill "Slick" Connolly of Natick. Connolly had visions of riding across the country in a lavish Pullman train car and eating meals in the dining car as America flashed by. The train that awaited them pulled converted cattle cars stuffed with bunks for sleeping. It was mid-July, and with doors open for ventilation, the sailors and their gear were soon saturated with two forms of dust, one from the Great Plains they traversed and the other from the coal-burning engine pulling them westward. The seven-day journey included a southern route to Seattle via Texas, only adding to the heat and duration of the experience.[25] War still waged on and the crew members, some collectively and others by themselves, made their way west to a new ship.

The *Tacoma News Tribune* reported on November 17, 1944, that the local Todd Pacific Shipyards had produced a second escort carrier USS *Block Island*. The article titled "Crew of Lost *Block Island* to Man Giant New Carrier of Same Name" noted the accomplishments of the first USS *Block Island*, CVE 21. While vague on numbers of U-boats engaged and sunk, due to wartime censorship, the article noted the crew's adopting the name FBI—Fighting *Block Island*. The subtitle and first paragraph read:

> Navy Precedent Broken in Commissioning Tacoma Built Ship;
> Her Predecessor, Also Built Here, Made Great Record
>
> When the second USS *Block Island*, giant new type aircraft carrier puts to sea from Tacoma's Todd shipyards she will shatter all precedents. For, while it has long been a custom of the U.S. navy to pass the names of veteran ships lost in action on to their successors, these namesake ships hitherto have carried different crews. Survivors of lost ships through the exigencies of war, have been scattered throughout the fleet to new commands. But proudly manning every station on the new Tacoma built *Block Island* will be the same ship's company that fought on the old *Block Island* on her last cruise before she went down last May.[26]

The paper reported that after the sinking of the vessel, Captain Hughes had stated to his officers and men, "We'll get another ship and stay together! This is too fine a crew to be broken up!"[27] The article concluded, "It was not a simple matter, for nothing like it had ever been done before in our navy—and the old Block's crew is intact today, save for the honored few who gave their lives in her passing, and a new and greater ship of the same name is being readied at Todd's for this gallant crew. The Fighting *Block Island* will make plenty more history before the last gun in this war is fired!"[28] Sparks still flew at the Todd Pacific dockyards as the men and women who molded metal into CVE 106 labored on.

Hughes's efforts to keep the ship's company intact were relentless and went all the way up to Admiral King. One FBI officer later wrote, "He succeeded: Fleet Admiral Ernest J. King himself took action and for the first time in the United States Navy a surviving crew from one lost ship was ordered directly to a new ship of the

Figure 15. As the last series of escort carriers, the Commencement Bay class incorporated many of the lessons learned in the evolution of the CVEs. As the second Commencement Bay class to be commissioned, USS *Block Island*, CVE 106, would serve in World War II till the close of the conflict and into the postwar era. Courtesy of the USS Block Island Association.

same name."[29] The *Fort Lauderdale Daily News* proudly reported his feat. "Captain Hughes, whose sons Eynon, 11, and Massie, Jr., 8, live with his sister, Mrs. Anna Haas, 801 NE Third St., was skipper of the Naval Air Station at Sanford for a year ending in November, 1943."[30] The article continued, "Transfer of Captain Hughes and his crew intact to a new vessel bearing the same name as the one on which they had previously fought was an arrangement unique in Naval history. It was accomplished by order of Fleet Adm. Ernest J. King, Commander in Chief of the Fleet."[31] With the rapid production time of escort carriers, a number of these were already in various stages of completion when Hughes began lobbying in Norfolk. At the Todd Pacific Shipyards back in Tacoma, where the first *Block Island* was put together, a new Commencement Bay–class escort carrier awaited a new crew. CVE 106, originally named *Sunset Bay*, was rechristened USS *Block Island*. The launching ceremony included Mrs. E. J. Hallenbeck, the mother of the famed Marine fighter ace Major Gregory "Pappy" Boyington.

The Navy investigation into the sinking of CVE 21 cleared Hughes of any misconduct. In fact, the admiral in charge of the inquiry personally congratulated Hughes on successfully abandoning such a large ship in a timely fashion. Hughes, a near-constant source of profanities, responded, "Well, thank'ee Admiral, but that's a hell of a thing to have to be good at!"[32] At the new vessel's commissioning on December 30, 1944, Captain Hughes, reading his orders out loud, took over command of the new CVE 106, and the commission pennant went up at 1521. This ceremony also included the presentation of medals by Rear Admiral J. J. Ballentine, commander Fleet Air in Seattle. He awarded the Legion of Merit to Captain Hughes for his success in leading hunter-killer missions on CVE 21. Ballentine opened his award speech with, "As Commanding Officer of the USS *Block Island* and Commander of the Atlantic Fleet anti-submarine task force, Capt. Francis M. Hughes achieved outstanding success in combined air and surface operations against enemy submarines."[33] The Legion of Merit was also awarded to the executive officer, Cdr. Delos Edwin Wait. Chief carpenter, Clarence Meyers Bailey, was called up front and issued the Navy and Marine Corps medal. Twelve sailors were issued the Bronze Star Medal and Commendation Ribbon for their services during the sinking of CVE 21. Lastly, an unveiling took place by the Todd workers of a bronze plaque memorializing the lost CVE 21, mounted on the hangar deck. A newspaper account of this gift wrote, "For it will be the second time that a fighting vessel of the same name has been commissioned during the present war—at the same shipyard—built by most of the same men and women who saw their labor go into completion of the original escort carrier bearing the now-famous name. Workers at the local yard of Todd Pacific Shipbuilders, Inc., have a special place in their hearts for the words, '*Block Island*.'"[34] It bore the inscription, "THE FIGHTING BLOCK ISLAND," and below and inscribed in bronze, "Indicative of the good will existing between those that build the ships and those who sail them."[35]

The news of the commissioning event caused the town council of Block Island, Rhode Island, the vessel's namesake, to send a message via telegram. It concluded, "We pray for the safety of you, your crew and the new *Block Island*. That you may carry on to greater achievements is our most sincere wish and hope. Bon voyage and sock 'em often."[36]

❋

The USN's very first escort carrier experiment began with the conversion of USS *Long Island*, CVE 1. Evolution in engineering resulted in differing classes of escort carriers, which affected construction practices and physical aspects of the vessels. The Navy's view of the usefulness of these vessels' roles during the war also evolved, as seen in the different naval classifications for *Long Island*. The Navy first designated *Long Island*, AVG 1, as an auxiliary aircraft carrier. In July 1943 the Navy issued a final reclassification designating it a war vessel. Thus, *Long Island* became CVE 1, for "escort carrier" signifying a warship fully engaging the enemy.[37] As one scholar wrote of these designations, "each change mark[ed] a step up the ladder of respectability."[38]

As the final classification for the escort carriers, the Commencement Bay class embodied the entire evolutionary process of CVEs, which included the Long Island, Avenger, Sangamon, Bogue, and Casablanca classifications.[39] Not morphed from a prefabricated merchant hull, the second *Block Island* represented one of nine Commencement Bay vessels constructed from the keel up as a war vessel. A valuable lesson was learned in the construction of the four Sangamon class of escort carriers. These carriers were unique in that these were converted not on merchant hulls but on tanker hulls. The USN found the Sangamon classification, constructed from the T3 hull of a tanker, better suited for carrier operations in comparison with the C3 merchant hull. The tanker hull shape allowed for the placement of not only a longer flight deck but also a longer hangar deck. Additionally, the tanker hull allowed for a much greater displacement in comparison with the Bogue and Casablanca classifications. Where the standard displacement of the Sangamon class was 10,500 tons, a full load displacement could be 23,875 tons.[40] Thus, the USN found that the Sangamon-class CVEs, converted from a tanker hull rather than a merchant hull, experienced expanded range and could transport fuel oil for refueling other vessels. However, as the T3 hulls were in great demand for the construction of oilers, only four were ever constructed. For the USN the lesson found in the Sangamon class and her tanker hull was applied to the Commencement Bay class, resulting in a longer flight deck and greater displacement.

The kamikaze also greatly impacted the design of the final classification of CVE. Over the course of the Pacific war, three CVEs were sunk as a result of kamikaze strikes.[41] As a result, the designers of the Commencement Bay class used her perimeter to vastly increase antiaircraft defenses in comparison to previous CVE classifications. In total these upgraded defenses included thirty-six 40 mm guns and twenty 20 mm Oerlikons cannons.[42] While the blueprints of escort carriers changed over time, so did the required human energy breathing life into steel in molding together a fifty-story skyscraper that floated. Whereas rivets were used in piecing together the larger Navy vessels, such as carriers, cruisers, and battleships, the last classification of CVE utilized welding. The persistent trait of accelerated construction time persisted with the CVEs. Using welding, the Commencement Bay class decreased construction time and made USS *Block Island*, CVE 106, one of the largest all-welded vessels of the conflict.[43] Shipfitter James Cole and his four daughters aided in the fabrication. His eighteen-year-old daughter Florabelle also worked in fabrication, while Fannie, age twenty-three, labored as an electrician's helper. His other two daughters Mary, age twenty-two, and Ruby, age twenty-nine, handled explosive gases, which when combined and ignited molded the vessel together. All these five members of the Cole family labored in what the Todd workers classified as another "big one."[44] While Todd Pacific Shipyards could physically replace the stricken CVE 21, the psychological damage to the crew surviving the sinking was not so easily identified and repaired.

As the men reported to Bremerton in July 1944, the effects of their saltwater baptism were not far from their minds. Sailor Irv Biron recalled the psychological damage inflicted on a close friend, which manifested itself in uncontrolled shaking even after the month of leave. He stated, "He was so shook up he got a medical. He could not hold a glass of water in his hand."[45] Walter Cyr recalled that Navy psychologists interviewed members of the crew, seeking to identify those suffering from lasting mental effects of losing one's ship at sea. Navy slang termed these doctors as "squirrel robbers."[46] Questions posed to Cyr by today's standards seem near medieval, with many of them focusing on his sexuality. Among those questions fielded by Cyr in investigating the lasting impact of the sinking on his psyche were, "Do you like girls?" and "Would you go out with your sister?'[47] These inquiries highlight the deficient understanding at the time of the manifestations of psychological problems resulting from wartime trauma.

The lack of military preparation for mental illness is evident in the fact that the entire Army Medical Corps at the time the US entered the war employed a total of only thirty-five doctors practicing psychiatry. The rapid need for doctors by 1943 witnessed the establishment of twenty-two hospitals just for the most seriously mentally ill. The horrific conditions faced by servicemen, including that of sinking were the primary reason for mental strain. One brigadier general of the Medical Corps wrote of the new weapons used in this war, "Bombing, more powerful artillery, tanks, flame-throwers, rockets, suicidal attacks, and other devices intensified the strains of war a hundred fold. . . . All these increased the psychological stress."[48] For those surviving a sinking on the high seas, the mental strain could result from a number of factors they experienced, including hearing the exploding torpedoes abandoning ship, feeling underwater explosions while in the water, and nighttime conditions when rescue finally arrived.

Nevertheless, the demise of CVE 21 conversely provided some good news for other CVE crews. One British sailor wrote in his memoir, "Later that morning I was looking through the most recent Naval Report and read an article which noted that the very successful USS *Block Island*, a sister ship of the *Nabob*, had been sunk after being hit by three torpedoes off the Canary Island in late May. What was notable, the article stated, was that out of all the CVEs like *Nabob* that had been torpedoed, she was the first one that hadn't blown up and the first in which more than ten of her crew survived."[49]

20
St. Valentine's Day Massacre

One *Block Island* sailor, in comparing these differing escort carriers with the same name, described them "as two different worlds."[1] CVE 21 of the early Bogue classification inherited improvements learned from the very first experiment in converting a merchant hull into a carrier with CVE 1. Bogue improvements included a power plant of twin turbines, rather than the originally designed diesel-powered engines and the addition of two elevators to expedite flight operations. However, these minor modifications paled in comparison to the technological jump the FBI sailors experienced when coming aboard USS *Block Island*, CVE 106. First, the Commencement Bay classification was constructed from the keel up as an aircraft carrier. In comparison to the oiler hull conversions, this class offered protection from enemy torpedoes. Tanks sixteen feet in width located along the waterline containing seawater were designed to absorb explosive detonations against the hull. The lengthened flight deck held two catapults, one standard H-2 catapult and one heavier H-4 catapult. This configuration of this dual installation allowed the carrier later in the war to launch thirty-two aircraft, of four different classes, in under twenty minutes.[2] Steam propulsion powered two screws, not just one. Built for waging war in the Pacific where Japanese aircraft inflicted heavy casualties on surface vessels, 40 mm antiaircraft mounts ringed nearly the entire vessel. The single most advanced technological leap, however, was the modern radar and other electronics on board, further demonstrating how far the escort carrier design had evolved. The construction time alone spoke volumes as to the improvements and energy poured into these vessels. While the first CVE, *Long Island*, was converted from a merchant hull in just under ninety days, the Commencement Bay vessels, even with a fully mobilized American economy geared for victory, took fifteen months to complete.[3]

Present at the commissioning were 660 men and fifty-two officers from the first *Block Island*. The second ship displaced 12,000 tons, had a length of 557 feet, a flight deck with thirteen arresting wires, and a top speed of over eighteen knots.[4] The complement of aircraft included up to thirty-four planes and 1,066 men. Fully loaded, the vessel doubled in weight, up to 24,275 tons. On January 10 she set sail into Puget Sound.[5]

For the FBI crew, the trials of the Battle of the Atlantic, including battling seas, hunting U-boats, and surviving the sinking, forged a core experience. Due to the compartmentalized nature of war vessels, and especially so for the relatively larger ones above ten thousand tons, most of the crew did not know the intimate details of each other's backgrounds, such as their individual boyhood upbringings, family backgrounds, and hopes and fears of the future. However, the experience of losing CVE 21, and subsequently floating together before rescue, cemented a bond that transcended metal bulkheads and divisional layout that physically divided a crew while on board ship. This bond easily molded to a new vessel. As the crewmen explored and became familiar with their new environs of CVE 106, the spirit of the FBI was back in business.

Nonetheless, these seasoned sailors and new escort carrier were entering a different world in terms of naval engagements. Leaving behind the hunter-killer missions where the captain had a great deal of freedom of operation, CVE 106 entered the logistical maze of competing strategies between the US Army and Navy in defeating Japan. Rather than independently leading a task force of five or six Allied vessels surrounded by the vastness of the Atlantic, CVE 106 would enter the island-hopping campaigns of the Pacific as one of thousands of other vessels. While an average day in the Atlantic consisted of combing thousands of square miles seeking the elusive enemy, their Pacific role would mostly consist of cruising in circular patterns, near small islands, launching aircraft in support of Allied invasions. Another change was that a Marine air squadron would be operating from the ship's flight deck. Lastly, the thoughts of potential danger drifted from the enemy torpedo to the kamikaze.[6] Of this new tactic, one noted historian wrote, "American sailors regarded the Kamikazes with a mixture of disbelief, dread, and disdain. A frequent observation was that this Japanese innovation was outside all normal human experience."[7] While changes abounded with this upcoming mission, the fighting spirit of the FBI remained.

There is more than one way to gather a sense of a vessel's size besides dry facts about cold steel. A more human measurement is found in the duty of Machinist's Mate First Class Cleveland T. Martin. Raised in Jackson County, Kansas, Martin survived the sinking, and his primary duties on board included close contact with the cooks in maintaining the refrigerators and freezers that preserved food for up to months at a time.[8] The consumption of human energy provides a window into the scale of the operation. In the weeks before the vessel departed into the Pacific, the galley staff loaded on board fresh products from the area. Local products included 2,250 dozen eggs, forty gallons of oysters, 350 pounds of salmon, and 250 pounds of sole, which cooks quickly used once at sea for thousands of meals. Another shipment received included $250,000 from the Tacoma branch of the Bank of California, to serve as payroll for the men. Liquid power pumped on board included 218,000 gallons of "navy special fuel oil."[9]

As CVE 106 sailed south, zigzagging along the Pacific coast, her crew's experience contrasted sharply with the first time cruising out of Puget Sound. Men quickly ran to their new battle stations as klaxons screamed, announcing drills, including that of abandoning ship. The men stationed on the flight deck in these GQ drills witnessed another indicator of war: a USN blimp escorted the ship.[10] As the vessel cruised down the California coast, she turned eastward toward San Francisco. Pulling into the harbor, USS *Block Island*, CVE 106, sailed under the Golden Gate Bridge at nine in the morning en route to the Alameda Naval Air Station. At Alameda, hoisted on board the new FBI's empty flight and hangar decks were seven damaged planes and five picket boats, each weighing thirteen tons. Also pumped on board were 100,000 gallons of aviation fuel and 8,000 gallons of aviation lube. While these operations took place, the men were given shore leave to visit the Bay Area.[11] One of the sailors that disembarked the ship was Patrick Chan, whose Chinese descent made him stand out as an FBI sailor. While Japanese Americans were banned from serving in the USN, it did accept the enlistment of Chinese Americans. Chan with the rest of his old crew would soon head into the Pacific. Walking the streets of Oakland in his Navy uniform, he decided to get a haircut. Chan's experience in the barbershop made a lasting impression: he was refused a haircut because of his ethnicity.[12]

As with the testing of weaponry and detection gear conducted from the deck of CVE 21, the USN selected CVE 106 to serve as the first USN escort carrier to house an all-Marine fighter wing. In San Diego both the Marine Fighting Squadron VMF 511 and Marine Torpedo Bombing Squadron VMTB 233, along with thirteen officers and 216 enlisted men, joined *Block Island*. Up to this point in the war, almost all Marine squadrons operated from forward-operating airfields. Thus, these marines were not accustomed to fueling, arming, and launching planes from the confines of a carrier. Learning these skills took time, and once leaving San Diego the vessel cruised west to train off the California coast.[13] These marine aviators in the preceding weeks had practiced "simulated carrier landings" on land-based airfields in Southern California.[14] However, simulation on land contrasted sharply with actually landing on an escort carrier. One escort carrier sailor described observing these landings. He wrote, "Watching aircraft landing held a kind of macabre fascination."[15]

One of the first to attempt to land on the new wooden flight deck was the executive officer of VMF-511, Maj. R. Bruce Porter, who had three confirmed air victories against Japanese pilots. Porter flew the Grumman F6F Hellcat and served as night-flight leader. Before attempting the bold feat of landing and taking off from

Figure 16. Marine Corps pilots settling into life on board in the ready room of the USS *Block Island*, CVE 106. In this room pilots were briefed on the missions over the skies of Okinawa. Some pilots and aircrew would not return. Courtesy of the USS Block Island Association.

a carrier deck at night, Porter and his group of night-flight pilots had to secure landings and become carrier qualified with five daytime landings. In his memoir he described his lack of confidence, with only "simulated carrier landings" under his belt. He wrote, "Everyone of us knew well that we had been landing on solid, unmoving earth."[16]

On February 4, 1945, off the coast of Southern California, *Block Island* landed its first aircraft, an F-4U Corsair piloted by squadron leader Lt. Col. John F. Dobbin, a veteran of Guadalcanal. For this particular aircraft to be the first to land on the new CVE is rather ironic for the fact that at the beginning of the war, the USN rejected the Corsair on account of its not being suitable for carrier landings. Visibility and difficulty in maintaining control at slow speeds were the major drawbacks of the F-4U in the eyes of the USN. But the US Marine Corps embraced the gull-winged fighter from the start of the war and used it extensively on Pacific airfields. Minor modifications to the F-4U granted pilots increased visibility and more control at slower speeds and made these craft more suited for carrier operations.[17]

Over the next ten days, *Block Island* docked in San Diego and picked up more marines of the air group and continued practicing its air operations. The transition from the field to the platform-based operations took more than time; it also required help from a core group of *Block Island* veterans. While most of the Navy aircrew personnel had been transferred off, a handful remained behind to ease the transition of Marine ground crew personnel accustomed to working on airfields, not the confines of CVE flight and hangar decks. A carrier's hangar held an incredibly concentrated amount of explosive fuels and weapons. Thus, learning the safe movement and maintenance procedures within these confines required expertise. One such Navy crew member was Yeoman Second Class Jack Greer, who operated what, on the hangar deck, was simply referred to as the "big green board."[18] This large chalkboard contained a visual up-to-the-minute summary of all aircraft. One glance gave the viewer a display of all aircraft aloft, on the flight deck, or undergoing a range of maintenance procedures in the hangar. During this period, Greer tutored these Marines on the inner workings of storing, maneuvering, and maintaining aircraft on board ship.[19]

❋

Bruce Porter controlled his nervousness well. Before lining up the approach for his first landing, he had successfully shot down three Japanese aircraft, but this scared the hell out of him. In writing about his first landing, he recalled his days as an athlete at USC. Before a game he experienced the signs of nerves, such as "anxiety, tightness in the stomach, perspiring hands, dry throat, shortness of breath, pounding heart, momentary lightheadedness."[20] In the spring of 1945, these same feelings returned as he looked out of the cockpit of his fighter aircraft ten thousand feet above the Pacific. Out his window the nearly 600-foot-long vessel looked amazingly small against the vast blue sea. He recalled later that his first thought on seeing CVE 106 "was that the flight deck looked to be about the size of a postage stamp."[21] Nearing the escort carrier on final approach, *Block Island* did increase in size. However, from Porter's perspective she was "never bigger than a mere cork bobbing in a huge swell."[22] Approaching the vessel, Porter's eyes focused on the LSO, who guided the pilot in landing on the deck. If the aircraft's direction and speed were true, the LSO signaled that the engine be cut. Two things surprised Porter upon landing. First, the speed with which his Grumman Hellcat came to a stop. Second, the furious activity surrounding his plane as marines wearing colorful jerseys denoting their responsibilities on the flight deck unhooked the aircraft from the arrester wires and taxied him forward.[23]

Porter, in wanting to know as much as possible about carrier landings, befriended the man whom these pilots trusted with their lives, the LSO. Capt. Marshall "Stork" Tutton was a veteran Corsair pilot, and his 6'4" frame was put to good use visually communicating to the incoming pilots. After Porter completed his first landing on CVE 106, he stood near Stork and his LSO platform on the fantail, as unqualified Corsair and Avenger pilots were slated to land next. Stork pointed to the only method of escape as these rookie pilots circled the carrier's position above. Porter wrote, "A large net hung out over the wake of the ship ten feet below and level of the flight deck. If Stork felt the need to clear out, he could only go into the net, or overboard, depending on his aim."[24] This almost proved needed advice, as a veteran Marine pilot in an Avenger had to be waved off repeatedly by Stork. Both Stork and Porter could see on every pass the ever-anxious face of the radioman pressed against the glass, wishing for the hook to come into contact with one of the arrester wires. As dusk was approaching and the Avenger was the only craft not on board, a written message from Massie Hughes came down from the air officer's perch on the island of CVE 106. It read, "Get that son of a bitch onboard now!"[25] While it was nowhere near perfect, Stork, on the next approach, had the pilot cut the engine just in time for the large craft to catch the last arresting wire. The rightly frightened radioman from the Avenger jumped out before the craft finished taxiing. As Porter recalled, "His legs started wind milling while he was still in midair, and he was going, going, once the instant his feet gained traction on the wooden deck."[26]

With all pilots on board safely after this first day of landings, these veteran marines would soon learn how quickly training could turn deadly. On the morning of Valentine's Day, pilot Bruce Porter took off in his Hellcat, along with all twenty-six other aircraft of the squadron, in the first round of two scheduled mock airstrikes on a small island off of Santa Barbara. Both pilots and aircrew in the assemblage of Corsairs, Avengers, and Hellcats noticed threatening weather in the distance. With bombing runs completed in textbook fashion, the weather soon turned. Visibility deteriorated to the point where all twenty-seven planes formed a lateral line, with each pilot keeping the pilot to his left and right in sight. This was done to increase their chances of seeing the deck of CVE 106 in the ever-gathering masses of storm clouds. Once spotted, Stork expertly guided all aircraft down without any problems. Porter and his fellow pilots had planned to head to the ready room after the completion of the first mission to get intelligence on the next scheduled strike. However, Porter went to his compartment to take off his flight suit. As Porter recalled in his memoir, "I could not imagine flying into the murk again."[27] Then, Porter heard his name over the speaker system on board ship ordering him to the CIC headquarters.

The squadron commander, Lt. Col. Dobbins, asked Porter his thoughts on continuing on with the training mission. He said, "Bruce, I need your opinion. You're the senior night-fighter pilot aboard; can you lead the second strike on instruments? What do you think about the weather?"[28] Porter told him that the mission, if not absolutely necessary, should be cancelled. He wrote, "Weather such as this, in tandem with my former cockiness, had nearly killed me at least three times in less than a year."[29] Dobbins concurred and both men reported to Hughes and gave their assessment. After hearing this, Hughes dismissed both men and stated he would look at an updated weather report. Hughes, ever the aggressive leader, ordered the missions to continue. Over the loudspeakers rang the familiar phrase, "All pilots, man your planes."[30]

The stunned Porter could not believe his ears as he strapped himself into the Hellcat. Firing up his engines, he identified a faulty magneto (small electrical generator), which scrubbed his participation in the mission. He would sit this strike out. The mechanical failure may very well have saved his life. Porter returned to the CIC compartment and, with Dobbins, listened to the progress of the strike. Rapidly the weather deteriorated, and soon after, aircraft became separated from one another. Complicating matters, the storm interfered with CVE 106's radar, and thus accurate fixes to the location of the lost pilots could not be ascertained. Finally, Hughes ordered the mission aborted. Pilots could return to ship or nearby airfields. Porter wrote, "A great hand reached down and squeezed my soul. I knew that we would be losing some friends today."[31]

Only one aircraft was able to successfully land on CVE 106. Others attempted to land on San Nicolas Island, where three aircraft crashed, resulting in the deaths of five. An Avenger, unable to land on the island, attempted to reach the nearest mainland field in Bakersfield; it crashed short of the runway, killing all three crew. The three remaining aircraft successfully ditched their planes near Santa Barbara Island, and the crews were later rescued. In total, the training missions cost the lives of eight marines and hospitalized nine others.[32]

Porter, when awakening the next morning, could not help himself and ran to the flight deck to check the weather. He later wrote, "The next day, the weather was perfect; I was physically ill."[33] The board of inquiry totally absolved Hughes and stated the deaths and injuries resulted from pilot error. Porter, in his memoir, referred to their deaths as the "St. Valentine's Day Massacre."[34] He wrote, "I held the ship's captain responsible for every one of those absolutely needless deaths, while I had been at pains to mask my true feelings, there had been friction between us."[35]

As Porter on the sunny flight deck contemplated the role of fate in grounding him and in the loss of his fellow marines, local newspapers in California informed their readership on the training deaths. Page 1 of the *Madera Tribune* contained war-related information from both the European and Pacific theaters. The Canadian Army was on the banks of the Rhine, American forces were clearing the island of Corregidor, and Nazi forces had just blown up dikes in a desperate effort to stop the Allied advance. At the very bottom of page 1, a small piece marked the marine deaths. It read, "Six marine corps fighter and torpedo planes crashed at various points in southern California early today when they flew into bad weather and ran out of gasoline."[36] These training deaths due to freakish weather shocked the entire crew of

CVE 106. Less than a year before, they had lost CVE 21 to enemy action that cost the lives of six on board and four pilots in the air. Almost within sight of the American coast, and fearful of future operations in the Pacific, many sailors felt stunned by the loss. Yet here they stood at attention for a memorial service on the wooden flight deck of a carrier that had not been in a war zone. In interviews with veterans decades after the war, the loss of these pilots proved emotionally powerful.[37]

❋

Four more weeks of intense training continued as the flight deck catapulted and retrieved aircraft before the vessel headed west and into the Pacific.[38] The last day the crew of *Block Island* had cruised in a war zone was the day their first vessel, CVE 21, received three German torpedoes. Nine months later, as they entered the central Pacific, the Allied forces occupied all of France, and within six weeks Germany would surrender. Much had transpired in the Pacific theater since the day CVE 21 sank. The Pacific island-hopping campaign pushed closer to the home islands of Japan, including landings in retaking the Philippines. The continued war with Japan produced massive casualties for sailors in the USN, including former crew members of the first Fighting *Block Island*.

With the Marine fighter wing assigned to the new CVE 106, about three hundred crew members that survived the sinking of CVE 21 in May 1944 were transferred to other vessels, including the fleet aircraft carrier USS *Franklin*, CV 13.[39] At dawn on March 19, 1945, near the coast of Japan's home islands, an undetected Japanese aircraft came within striking distance of the massive carrier. Two 550-pound bombs hit the flight deck filled with armed and fueled aircraft, heavily damaging the carrier. The massive fire and subsequent explosions cost the lives of 724 sailors. Stories of these losses caused from just two bomb hits on the fleet carrier caused serious anxiety for the sailors on Navy vessels, doubly so for the crew members of *Block Island* who had lost shipmates on board *Franklin*.[40] However, the kamikaze caused the most rumors and discussion. One reason for this tactic was, ironically, the amazingly successful use of antiaircraft guns by USN surface vessels against Japanese aircraft attempting to drop traditional bombs or torpedoes. Thus, this new suicide tactic aimed to cause as much damage as possible to slow the war and possibly save the home islands from Allied invasion. Escort carriers off shore providing close ground support were prime targets of opportunity for the kamikaze.[41]

The first large-scale use of kamikaze pilots was in late October 1944, in the Philippines at the Battle of Leyte Gulf. Japanese pilots took off from airfields in the Philippine islands and naturally looked for the largest target of opportunity. In the first days of the use of kamikazes, the CVEs would pay a heavy price for their role in the war. As the Leyte ground invasion advanced, two kamikazes slammed into nearby CVEs. USS *St. Lo*, CVE 63, sustained a kamikaze hit with such force that it sank the escort carrier, while USS *Santee*, CVE 29, took enough damage to cause her temporary retirement.[42]

As the Philippine campaign continued with the ground invasion of Luzon in early 1945, escort carriers carried on in ground support. With continuous attacks on road junctions and stores of munitions, the CVEs attracted kamikazes. Three days before the initial ground operations on January 6, a single kamikaze inflicted massive damage on USS *Ommaney Bay*, CVE 79. Efforts to save the ship lasted until the crew was forced to abandon ship the next day. The attack cost the USN not only a ship but also over one hundred members of the crew. Over the next ten days of kamikaze attacks, thirty-nine vessels were struck, four of which sank. The attacks killed 738 Navy personnel and wounded over 1,400.[43] These desperate attacks, which seemed unimaginable to Western eyes, added one more source of anxiety for escort carrier sailors aiding in the island-hopping campaign closing in on Japan.

Six days out from San Diego, *Block Island* entered Pearl Harbor, on March 26, 1945. In Pearl, an officer with a unique skill set was brought on board, a man whose training warranted his flying in from Chicago to join CVE 106 on this mission. Second Lt. Joe Zook had first trained as a naval aviator; however, fearful of missing the war, he volunteered as an LSO, as these were in short supply.[44] One observer described the LSO: "His job always seemed to me to resemble that of the conductor of an orchestra."[45] Standing on the aft end of a shifting flight deck and directing approaching aircraft to safely land on the deck of a carrier is harrowing enough; however, Zook performed this task in the dark. Wearing a suit with fluorescent strips, and holding illuminated paddles, Zook officially assisted in landing the aircraft. All pilots were under orders to follow the LSO's commands to cut the engine to land or to power away if not lined up correctly. Even in daylight most propeller-powered aircraft did not grant the field of view to clearly see the flight deck, thus producing the necessity of the LSO. The lack of the pilot's correct perspective on the fast-approaching deck was only exacerbated at night.[46] While Zook directed the night landings, Captain Hughes requested Chaplain MacInnes watch from the bridge to provide spiritual assistance with these dangerous landings.[47]

For three weeks *Block Island* and USS *Shipley Bay*, CVE 85, sailed in the vicinity of the Hawaiian Islands conducting intensive air training operations. Day and night operations took place, which meant the escort carrier flight decks never stopped launching and retrieving aircraft. After extensive training *Block Island* was deemed ready for the Pacific theater. After docking one last time at Pearl Harbor on April 11, she began her first war cruise.[48] The next day President Franklin Roosevelt died in Warm Springs, Georgia. However, the war continued, and *Block Island* cruised west on April 17.[49]

Three days after leaving Pearl, CVE 106 crossed the International Date Line. On the twenty-ninth, *Block Island* anchored off the small island of Mog Mog, a tiny island of the Ulithi Islands, allowing for liberty.[50] While the escort carriers did house a general store, five barbers, and two libraries, once in war operations the sailors rarely left the vessel. Certain comforts existed, including a daily newspaper and nightly movies shown on the hangar deck; however, the monotony combined with the isolation inflicted its toll. Ernie Pyle, writing of carrier crews in the Pacific in comparison to the infantrymen of Africa and Europe, said the sailors had "nothing to look forward to. They never saw anybody but themselves. They sailed and sailed, and never arrived anywhere."[51] The visit to the small island offered time to sit under a palm tree, play baseball, and drink several cans of warm beer.[52]

The segregation of officers and enlisted men in Navy life endured on this tiny island. All offloaded men walked the same trail inland and encountered a sign that read, "Officers Left, Enlisted Personnel Right."[53] The officers relaxed in an impromptu officers' club, outfitted with a swimming pool and a selection of beers and spirits. The enlisted men walked into a fenced-in area to keep them away from the local population.[54] Under nearby palm trees stood cardboard cases of warm beer. Some men did not drink, thus allowing larger portions to be consumed by those that did. After a few hours, the combination of young sailors and beer resulted in fights breaking out. Officers from *Block Island* were assigned to contain the worst of the brawls on Mog Mog. Second Lt. Joe Zook recalled one large altercation of twenty men. Luckily for Zook, most could not stand. Sailors unable to walk were hoisted in cargo nets onto auxiliary craft that carried the crew back to CVE 106.[55] After the sailors experienced a few short hours on solid earth, the vessel weighed anchor and sailed toward an ongoing battle in what would be the largest naval siege in military history.

21
Okinawa

A crescent pattern of 140 volcanic islands stretches from Japan's most southern island of Kyushu toward the southwest pointing to Taiwan (known as Formosa during the war) and mainland China. Combined, these islands constitute a land area just bigger than the state of Rhode Island. The main collection of islands making up Okinawa compose one quarter of the total area of this archipelago. Of particular importance to military strategists were the island's airfields and two bays.[1] Allied military planners estimated the island contained 77,000 Japanese forces, thus requiring an initial invasion force of over 200,000 men of the US Marines and Army, with CV and CVE groups providing air support for these invading ground forces. However, the fleet aircraft carrier groups over this period of operation also carried out attacks on airfields on the home island of Japan. Thus, once the invasion began on April 6, 1945, the CVEs represented the only constant source of ground support for Allied forces.[2]

With the compression of the Japanese empire against its traditional boundaries, the kamikaze attacks increased on a massive scale, which created unprecedented danger for USN vessels off Okinawa. During the course of the battle, over 1,900 kamikaze attacks occurred on surface ships, killing 3,389 sailors, sinking thirty-six vessels, and severely damaging over 350 vessels of the fleet.[3] As CVE 106 cruised ever westward and approached Okinawa, her sailors and marines contemplated not only the forthcoming battle but also this new suicide tactic. For many of the crew, the fear of a sudden explosion was not new after four hunter-killer missions in the Atlantic and the loss of CVE 21 due to German torpedoes. The fear of a lone submarine, this time Japanese, still persisted. However, now a death strike could drop out of the skies above.

On April 28, as *Block Island* cruised west, the crew spotted an unidentified plane approaching the vessel. The previous day the crew had conducted training that consisted of shooting at a drone target pulled in the air by friendly aircraft, using the 40 mm antiaircraft batteries. Now these men on their guns witnessed this unidentified aircraft headed straight toward their vessel. The battle report states: "Order to open fire was given, whereupon the 40 mm quads on the forecastle threw up a heavy barrage which straddled the approaching plane."[4] The aircraft veered away, and shortly thereafter two Hellcats scrambled off the deck to investigate. After a few minutes two aircraft approached CVE 106 from starboard, causing the batteries of 40 mm to open fire. Quickly, the "cease fire" was issued once the planes were identified as friendly.[5] While not kamikaze attacks, these two incidents demonstrate the mental strain these battery crews experienced in their mission of keeping suicide planes from slamming into their home. The USN addressed the kamikaze menace with the designation of radar picket stations, which ringed the Okinawa archipelago over the course of the invasion. Concentrations of over two hundred ships and 36,000 men plotted radar contacts above the Okinawan skies seeking to identify all aircraft, friendly and otherwise.[6]

The weeks of training off the coasts of California and Hawaii in merging a Marine squadron with a CVE were about to be tested. Once activity commenced it would rarely cease on the hangar and flight decks, for each pilot would conduct up to four missions a day. Thirty-four aircraft aboard could fly a daily total of 136 missions, each requiring refueling, rearming, and continuous maintenance in keeping the Marine aviators in the air. These consisted of twelve F-4U gull-winged Corsair fighters, ten F6F Hellcats flying night operations, and twelve TBM Avenger torpedo/bombers. Screaming over the skies of Okinawa, Marine aircraft from CVE 106 would be dropping bombs, launching rockets, and firing machine guns in support of the Allied invasion.[7] The month of May produced particularly foul weather in the area around Okinawa. Rain, winds, and lightning not only yielded difficult weather for flying but also greatly complicated the tasks of radar operators, as the electrical disturbances from lightning interfered with these early radar prototypes.[8]

On May 4, CVE 106 detached to join TU 52.1.3, commanded by Rear Adm. William D. Sample and composed of four escort carriers. *Block Island*'s three sister CVEs were all of the Bogue class. These were USS *Suwannee*, CVE 27; USS *Santee*, CVE 29; and USS *Chenango*, CVE 28. CVE 106 joined this grouping to replace USS *Sangamon*, CVE 26, returning stateside after sustaining massive damage from a kamikaze attack. As *Block Island* neared the task force, her sailors saw firsthand the *Sangamon*'s damage inflicted by the kamikaze. As *Block Island* took her position in the formation, *Sangamon* pulled away to seek repairs. A blackened, charred deck of this sister CVE replaced any vague theory of what a single kamikaze could do. Now, sailors already on edge possessed a visual reference for their fear of the suicide tactic. While these small carriers were tough enough to survive such attacks, the costs were still high. Besides mangling *Sangamon*'s flight deck, the attack killed thirty-six and critically wounded twenty-one more sailors.[9] One historian summed up the unseen kamikaze stress: "Long hours at battle stations and the knowledge that a suicide attack could occur at any time left men in a continuous state of nervous tension which could not be overcome."[10]

It had been eleven months since the crew of CVE 21 had been in combat. On May 10 at 0635, aircraft took off from *Block Island*, CVE 106, for the first time, to perform strikes on Japanese ground targets. The very first attack consisted of four

TBM Avengers, each armed with ten 100 lb. General-Purpose (GP) bombs, eight 5-inch rockets, and machine-gun rounds. These planes made diving attacks on Japanese mortar and trench positions with guidance from the commander Air Support Control Unit. This first attack checked off one of the two missions of CVE 106 in this operation, that of providing ground support for the marines and US Army units engaged in combat on the ground. The afternoon mission addressed the second objective, that of striking and eliminating Japanese airfields. At 1600, fifteen aircraft, including eight F-4U Corsairs, each armed with one 500 lb. GP bomb and eight 5-inch rockets, and seven F-6F Hellcats, each carrying one 500 lb. GP bomb and six 5-inch rockets, went aloft. An additional Hellcat, unarmed except for machine-gun rounds, and classified as F6F-5(P), lifted off last to carry out a photo reconnaissance mission. While the F6F-5(P) missions reduced the offensive punch, the images taken by the Hellcat, later developed and printed on board CVE 106, provided invaluable intelligence about the effectiveness of operations and tactics. This included measuring the potency of the Japanese in repairing bombed runways during the night.[11]

These initial bombings and rocket attacks on May 10 came with a high price, as Japanese antiaircraft fire struck a number of aircraft. A somber message was read over CVE 106's PA system to the crew members, noting that this resulted in the loss of one aircraft. It read, 'It is with deep regret that we must announce that Second Lt. Douglas Herrin, pilot, Staff Sergeant Edward Thomas Gunning, turret gunner, and Sgt. Joseph Lawrence Butehorn, radio gunner, are missing in action."[12] On their second pass in attacking an airfield, their Avenger encountered heavy Japanese antiaircraft fire from which the aircraft did not recover. The attack also wounded the Avenger of Capt. Frank Takacs; however, he was able to nurse his craft out to sea and successfully ditch. USS *Butler*, DD 636, successfully picked up all three crew members and safely transported them back to *Block Island*.[13]

For the average sailor and Marine, the experience on board CVE 106 contrasted sharply with that of the infantrymen fighting on Okinawa. Soldiers battling on land witnessed the immediate horrors of war and experienced firsthand tangible dangers. They heard enemy fire, felt the earth when ducking in foxholes, and smelled the rotting flesh of the dead. Sailors wrestled with unseen dangers. Two of the greatest fears, strikes from a torpedo or a kamikaze, could yield a conflagration instantaneously. Sailors' minds processed the possible dangers, such as swift death from an undetermined blast or being painfully basted by high-pressure steam erupting from ruptured piping. These concealed enemies, lurking either in the skies above or in the waters below, created anxiety that differed from that felt by those battling on the ground. These fears were heightened when the carrier was receiving, or delivering, a range of combustible fuels while at sea. An attack, even an accident, could produce deadly repercussions, nearly all of which centered on a conflagration of massive proportions, such as fuel disposition to other vessels. In an operation that took just under three hours, the carrier secured lines with the oiler USS *Monongahela*, AO 42. Lookouts scanned the Pacific skies for attacking aircraft as pumps moved on board 10,245 gallons of diesel fuel, 324,647 gallons of fuel oil, and just over 68,000 gallons of aviation gasoline. Even with the conclusion of these operations, the duties of refueling were not over, as CVE 106 would secure additional lines to smaller DDs and DEs in topping up their fuel reserves.[14]

Hours and missions merged together as, day after day, escort carriers launched aircraft attacking someplace over the horizon. One sailor summed up this feeling: "islands attacked but never seen."[15] The crew of CVE 106 completed daily tasks trusting in each other, in case another sudden explosion rocked their vessel. Technical malfunctions could kill just as easily as the enemy. Returning aircraft at times landed on the flight deck with misfired rockets still attached to aircraft wings. More than once during aircraft entrapment, these rockets broke away from the wing mount and continued down the wooden flight deck and over the bow. Luckily, these incidents never produced an explosion, which could have proved catastrophic on the flight deck full of armed aircraft. On May 11 a bomb that failed to drop off the wing of an Avenger was vectored out to the nearby Kenena airfield, where the plane safely landed with the loose bomb without incident. Still the flight deck environs proved deadly, as a member of the aircraft squadron was struck by a taxiing aircraft and pushed overboard and down onto the catwalk one deck below. While not killed immediately, this man did die of his wounds and was buried at sea as the task force continued operations to the south of Okinawa.[16]

Tangible signs of the battle raging over Okinawa did materialize in the form of battle-damaged aircraft limping back to the carrier as a result of Japanese antiaircraft fire. On May 15 First Lt. Edward Wallof returned from a mission. While just one of thousands, this particular landing demonstrated a feat stemming from the merging of training, teamwork, and bravery. Wallof's cockpit canopy was shattered after taking a direct hit from a Japanese 20 mm shell. This explosion produced shrapnel, which "slashed his left eye, leaving his eyeball hanging partially out on his cheek."[17] After sustaining this wound, Wallof continued his rocket attack against an enemy position, then a fellow Marine aviator talked Wallof, with blood streaming down his face, the one hundred miles back to *Block Island*, and more amazingly, onto her moving deck. With one good eye, and the steady voice of a fellow Marine aviator who was flying next to him, plus a strong motivation of survival, Wallof safely placed his shattered plane and body back on the deck of *Block Island* just before sunset.[18] A bloodied cockpit and fractured canopy functioned as testaments for the crew members of the dangers these pilots faced on every mission.

While dangers lurked in the skies above Okinawa, working on the flight and hangar decks also proved hazardous in creating nonlethal injuries. In just one week of operations on board, a number of accidents transpired. A plane, during landing, slammed into a parked aircraft, injuring one sailor. During the unfolding of a compressed wing, a crew member was severely wounded in the face. Lastly, on the hangar deck, an aircraft's machine gun accidentally discharged, firing three rounds. Rounds designed to rip aircraft apart while in flight, amazingly, killed no one and injured only one person.[19] These ongoing missions produced stress not only on aircraft but on the men flying the machines and the crews keeping them aloft. GQ was frequently called, particularly when the vessel was most vulnerable, at sunrise and sunset, when the silhouetted aircraft carrier stood in stark contrast against the scarlet Pacific sky. The dangers of enemy submarines proved all too real again for the crew on the evening of May 24, when USS *Hemminger*, DE 746, detected a submarine immediately astern of CVE 106. The carrier immediately took evasive action. Hearing what was reported as "screw noises and a definite metallic echo," *Hemminger* promptly dropped a depth charge attack, which later produced a mile-long oil slick on the surface. No further detection of the enemy submarine was made.[20] However, this encounter again exemplified the vulnerability of large craft to enemy submarines, which most of the FBI crew members had experienced first-hand in the Atlantic just one year earlier.

While this is a microhistory of the crew that served on two CVEs, it must be noted that at any given time, dozens of other escort carriers also participated in this colossal operation. In fact, with the occurrence of sudden weather changes, these CVEs depended on each other to capture their squadron's aircraft if the escort carrier's flight deck was unable to retrieve aircraft due to Pacific rain and winds. Continuous missions depleted bomb magazines of the CVEs; thus, they made way and docked on the Allied-controlled island of Kerama Rhetto. To expedite the re-arming process, CVEs would launch the majority of their aircraft to clear space on both the flight and hangar decks. Over the course of the Okinawa campaign, the *Block Island* needed to rearm three times at Kerama Rhetto. Rearming was a dangerous operation for any escort carrier. USS *Wake Island*, CVE 65, and USS *Sangamon*, CVE 26, were both damaged by suicide attacks during such missions. Moored offshore, landing craft brought out the ammunition. What transpired next was described this way: "With craft alongside, using jury-rigged improvised camels [sawed-off telephone poles] that protected the ship inadequately in rough anchorage, the crew in all-hands evolution swamped the ammunition aboard. Imminence of air attack at any time had pointed to the necessity of getting the ammunition below decks into its magazines as fast as it came aboard; this was accomplished by the splendid performance of the working parties."[21]

As rearming required hours, *Block Island*'s aforementioned pilots landed on nearby CVEs after completing their assigned missions. With CVE 106 fully armed and back at sea, the aircrews and their craft returned to *Block Island*. Working as

Figure 17. One year after the sinking of CVE 21 in the Atlantic, the crew of USS *Block Island*, CVE 106, arm aircraft for strikes on enemy targets in Okinawa. The bomb in this image marks the anniversary. Courtesy of the USS Block Island Association.

members of a larger CVE team, individual carriers also utilized each other's decks in assisting damaged aircraft returning from strikes over Okinawa. On the morning of May 25, an F6F Hellcat from USS *Chenango*, CVE 28, attempted an emergency landing on the deck of *Block Island*. The pilot's engine failed on approach, and he was forced to ditch in the wake of CVE 106. A quick-thinking deckhand tossed a raft off the stern of the escort carrier. The pilot, fortunately having cleared his aircraft, was seen swimming toward the raft. The Action Report sadly noted, "However, when a destroyer arrived on the scene a few minutes later he could not be found. A thorough but unsuccessful search of the entire area was made."[22] The deckhands of the crew experienced how quickly death could strike. An unknown pilot survived a water landing and escaped his sinking plane only to vanish in a matter of moments.

On May 27 the commanding officer of VMF 511, Maj. R. C. Maze, USMC, led four Corsair rocket attacks near Ishigaki, a location of a boat-works and concentration of small enemy watercraft. After he had fired his rockets, Maze's aircraft did not pull up and slammed into the shallow water just offshore. Enemy antiaircraft fire was suspected as the cause of the crash. The work of VMF 511 went on. The executive officer of the squadron, Capt. James Secrest, an aggressive leader and a veteran pilot, took over command for the lost Maze. Eerily, later reconnaissance photographs taken of the area showed Maze's submerged Corsair in the shallow waters off the coast.[23] While the loss of Maze was a shock, the missions continued, and on May 27 the squadron lost another pilot. Flight Surgeon Cdr. J. L. Custer completed two MIA reports for this costly day. Second Lt. Robert A. Goldberg, USMCR, was last seen making a dive on enemy installations and shipping on Ishigaki Jima, Sakishima Gunto. The three other Corsair pilots reported him missing upon returning to the carrier. Custer noted, "After an attempt at radio contact brought no answer a thorough search of the area was made by the pilots, who could not find any trace of his plane."[24]

The Fighting *Block Island* fought in the last forty-three days of the eighty-three-day naval siege of Okinawa. However, one particular date, May 29, 1945, held a special meaning, as it marked the one-year anniversary of the sinking of CVE 21. The crew recognized the date by taking the war to the enemy in a unique way. While the bakers in the vessel's galley produced a memorial cake honoring CVE 21, as the ship's history described, "what was more important and made that day a special day in the air operations, all bombs and rockets were marked as memorials."[25] Bomb surfaces served as canvases for messages inscribed with chalk to the Axis and those commemorating both lost ship and shipmates. On this day, *Block Island* fighters fired ten thousand rounds of ammunition and 161 five-inch "Holy Moses" rockets. Pilots also dropped nineteen thousand pounds of bombs, all covered with illustrated messages of remembrance. Nonetheless, those CVE 21 veterans on this twenty-ninth of May experienced loss once again.[26]

A TBM Avenger flown by 2nd Lt. Jack Marconi, USMC, in the afternoon attacked Ishigaki airbase. On the second pass over the target, his port wing sustained antiaircraft fire and ripped off. Other Marine aviators reported that Marconi's Avenger crashed and immediately exploded. Flight Surgeon Cdr. J. L. Custer once again filled out the required form, noting not only the death of Marconi but also those of two other marines in the Avenger, SSgt. Joe Survoy and SSgt. Ben Cannan Jr. In Custer's report all three names were followed by, "Killed in Action, body not recovered."[27] This sentence summed up the difficulty of processing these deaths for the sailors back on CVE 106. Just a handful actually witnessed the deaths of their comrades in arms, and none saw their dead bodies. While fellow aviators viewed a plane falling out of the sky, the vast majority of the crew were left to digest that one plane did not return. Somewhere on board, three footlockers enclosed the personal effects of the dead men. One Navy aviator summed up the emotion of losing a fellow aviator over the skies of Okinawa. He wrote, "There was no body, no grave, and no funeral, no one, it seemed, to mourn for."[28]

The first day of June ushered in another first for the crew of USS *Block Island.* An alert lookout spotted an untethered mine, and the carrier went into emergency maneuvers to avoid it. The turn successfully dodged the rust-colored mine. Deck crew gazed down from the starboard side, watching the floating projectile pass by. The destroyer USS *Landowne*, DD 486, fired upon the horned-type Japanese mine, and a large explosion followed.[29] For those on the flight deck witnessing the explosion, the thought of this violent chemical reaction taking place against their escort carrier hull could not be far from their imaginations. It seemed that chance, or rather providence, placed this untethered piece of flotsam of this vast war in their path during the daylight hours to be avoided, rather than to randomly strike CVE 106 like a bolt of lightning in the darkened night. Mother Nature also caused natural dangers in June in the Pacific. Flight operations were cancelled on the afternoon of June 4 and all of June 5 as the task force passed to the east of a massive typhoon.[30] On June 6 the operations over the skies of Okinawa continued and lasted for another eleven days. The last day of these operations on June 16 proposed that a portion of the squadron attack a new position. Kyushu, the southernmost of the four main islands, was chalked on to the board in CVE 106's ready room as the next target.

At 0510 six Corsairs and nine Hellcats lifted off to strike Japan. En route the aircraft landed on the island of Kadena for refueling, loading of fragmentation bombs, and a briefing on the mission, which consisted of seventy carrier-based planes and sixty shore-based fighters. Fourteen *Block Island* aircraft flew north in a formation composed of 130 total planes. Encountering a number of strong weather fronts off the southern coast of Japan, at 1015 the mission headed for the secondary target, a group of islands collectively known as Amami Gunto. Installations attacked included a Koniya seaplane base. Heavy antiaircraft fire resulted in the loss of one aircraft of the squadron when 2nd Lt. Albert E. Jones, USMC, crashed into the ocean in his first pass over the target. Listed as "killed in action," Jones represented the final death for the squadron, following forty-three days of operations off Okinawa. Returning aircraft, which needed to refuel once again at Kadena on the return leg of the trip, landed on the deck of CVE 106 at 1855.[31]

Less than an hour after all aircraft returned, *Block Island*, along with three other escort carriers and four destroyers, detached from task unit 32.1.3 and headed south for anchorage at Leyte Gulf.[32] During operations off Okinawa, *Block Island* had launched 1,202 sorties. From May 4 to June 16, over 400,000 pounds of bombs tumbled down and away from her aircraft. In addition, her craft fired over 2,600 five-inch rockets and expended nearly 300,000 rounds of ammunition. Ground targets, besides enemy troop installations, included radar, cable, and radio stations. On the island of Ishigaki, her craft also targeted enemy ships and barracks. The average operating area of the vessel was eighty miles off the southwest coast of Okinawa, an area 320 miles from Formosa and 920 from Tokyo.[33] The ship's history stated, "The shortest line from the *Block Island* to New York City, we knew, was by the way of Tokyo."[34]

22
The Last D-Day

Completing the last attacks on Okinawa on the morning of June 16, *Block Island* set a course for the Philippines. Entering Leyte Gulf three days later, she anchored with other Allied ships in the largest concentration of vessels in the history of man. Away from the battle zone, liberty parties on the island of Samar allowed men to drink two cans of beer each and participate in baseball games and swimming. The brief hiatus for enlisted men from ship-based life took place behind a wire-enclosed area to limit the sailors' and marines' interactions with the native Filipinos. The wire did little to deter trading with the Filipinos for local goods and trinkets. While the men enjoyed their brief time off ship, sealed orders arrived on board for new operations farther to the south.[1]

On June 29, CVE 106 cruised for the Straits of Makassar. Entering these straits symbolized the collapsing Japanese empire, as the FBI was among the first large USN vessels in these waters since early 1942. Observing the magnificent indigo hue, one sailor described the waters of the strait as "blue Jello."[2] Leaving the Straits of Makassar and entering the Celebes Sea marked a rite of passage of a naval tradition centuries older than the USN, for the men earned the distinction of crossing the equator. Naval heritage called for a hazing ritual. In a hostile area of operations, however, the fraternal activities that normally followed this event were postponed for the recrossing back into the Northern Hemisphere.

By July 1, *Block Island* gathered as part of task force 78.4, sixty miles off of Balikpapan, Borneo. TF 78.4, under the overall command of Gen. Douglas MacArthur on USS *Phoenix*, CL 46, had orders to participate in what would be the last major amphibious landing of World War II. Alongside CVE 106 were two other escort carriers, USS *Gilbert Islands*, CVE 107, and USS *Suwannee*, CVE 27, and an assemblage of cruisers, destroyers, and destroyer escorts. As a mostly Australian force poured onto the beaches, planes from *Block Island* provided air support day and night over the skies of Balikpapan. On the morning of July 2, four *Block Island* F-4U Corsairs led by Capt. J. L. Secrest, USMC, loitered over the landing beaches. Ground support aircraft (GSA) located an enemy motor convoy just three and a half miles from the Corsairs' operating area. Attacking singly, these Marines dove from three thousand feet to just one hundred feet in their nine runs on the convoy. Attacking in a north-to-south direction, these four gull-winged Corsairs screamed over the jungle and utilized all rockets and bombs. In the attack they destroyed four enemy vehicles and damaged twelve others. Enemy troops exiting these vehicles ran for the slit trenches along the highway, which the Corsairs strafed with machine-gun fire. Individual casualties on the ground went unseen. Just twenty minutes after this attack, the Allied Seventh Division landed at 0900 at Balikpapan. The deck of CVE 106 worked around-the-clock in these days, keeping support aircraft aloft twenty-four hours a day.[3]

In three days of operations, the Marines from the deck of CVE 106 dropped forty 100 lb. and thirty-seven 500 lb. bombs. Ninety-two 5-inch HVA rockets were fired, along with over ten thousand rounds of .50-caliber machine-gun rounds.[4] Many of these weapons were deployed on July 3, when twenty-two CVE 106 aircraft attacked Japanese troop facilities four miles inland from the invasion beaches. Pilots ran 170 passes over the targets, fired over eighty rockets and dropped eleven tons of bombs. Capt. Richard W. Johnson fired four of these rockets into a warehouse adjacent to a road cut through thick jungle. When his rockets struck, a massive explosion erupted, dwarfing all the chaos occurring below. The Aircraft Action Report for the overall attack stated that Johnson's four rockets struck an enemy ammunition dump.[5] While Johnson's rockets were singled out as the most important contribution of CVE 106 in these landings, a true anomaly in the history of the *Block Islands* took place in the early morning hours of the third of July.

At 0330, a Grumman F6F Hellcat, piloted by 1st Lt. B. J. Reuter, USMCR, took off from *Block Island* on a combat air patrol. At 0540, Reuter was directed toward a bogey (unknown radar contact) picked up fifty miles in distance from Balikpapan with a bearing of 180 degrees. Guided by CIC within four miles of the bogey, Reuter then tracked the aircraft on his radar screen. In the black of night, Reuter used the radar to close the distance with the bogey. This placed him slightly below and directly behind what he identified as a Japanese Aichi E13A long-range reconnaissance seaplane used by the Imperial Japanese Navy, which was commonly known to the Allies as a "Jake." The Action Report stated that Reuter "then pulled up behind the JAKE and slightly to the port quarter, squeezed the trigger, and saw his tracers rake the engine cowling, cockpit and fuselage. The JAKE burst into flames almost immediately and spun down to the sea where it crashed."[6] This victory could be squarely pointed to the advanced stage of Allied radar capacity, as the enemy pilot made no evasive action and was completely taken by surprise in the darkened Pacific sky. In the history of both USS *Block Islands*, this represented the first and only time a fighter from her deck successfully engaged and destroyed an enemy aircraft while in the air.

Even for the non-aircrew veterans on *Block Island*, this operation was unique. While they had earned two battle stars in the Atlantic and participated in the campaigns above Okinawa, all these operations for the most part consisted of launched

Figure 18. The ever-feisty Capt. Massie Hughes (on the right) seen here walking on the flight deck of CVE 106 during the operations near Okinawa. Courtesy of the USS Block Island Association.

planes that attacked somewhere over the horizon. For the crew on board, in their countless hours laboring, they saw very little tangible evidence of their vessel's offensive punch. On this operation, however, sailors could see the island of Borneo in the distance. This ground support mission contrasted sharply from past missions, as large guns firing from Allied vessels against Japanese ground positions lightened the dark Pacific night. One sailor recollected, "The biggest red balls I ever saw in my life went out from those battleships."[7] After just three days of operations, their mission was over, and *Block Island* cruised north and recrossed the equator, entering the realm of Neptunus Rex.

Crossing the equator for the first time was a milestone in any seafarer's career as one entered the realm of Neptunus Rex, who faithfully paid a ceremonial visit to any vessel entering his domain. The event temporarily erased the USN hierarchy. As one scholar wrote, "Apart from usual divisions of rating and rank, men aboard warships fall into two classifications: so-called 'shellbacks,' who have crossed the equator before, and 'pollywogs,' who have not."[8] While *Block Island*'s core group of sailors' seafaring résumé included battling North Atlantic storms, taking on German U-boats, and even surviving a sinking, the majority held pollywog status, as the first USS *Block Island*, CVE 21, never crossed the equator. This meant a large pollywog contingent needed to pass muster with Neptunus Rex's Royal Court. On this fourth of July, this centuries-old tradition took place on the deck of CVE 106.

The Action Report for this date simply noted, "0830–1130—Shellback initiation of all 'pollywogs' aboard."[9]

The royal visit changed not only the hierarchy but the vessel as a whole, as the American flag was removed, and the skull and cross bones of the Jolly Roger flew above the bridge. On the flight deck, veteran sailors, dressed as Neptunus Rex and his Royal Court, including his Queen, barber, and undertaker, prepared for inspection of the pollywogs. Shellbacks of the crew of the Fighting *Block Island* dressed as pirates and carried paddles. The overweight chief cook, dressed as the Royal Baby, had his big belly exposed and covered in grease. The class of pollywogs stood on the flight deck in shorts and socks and awaited their meeting with the Royal Court. They crawled on all fours toward Neptunus Rex as shellbacks prodded them with paddles.[10] Once in front of Rex, the worthiness of the pollywog was rendered. Punishment included a visit to the Royal Barber or kissing the greased belly of the Royal Baby. However, no matter the punishment individually handed out, all pollywogs ran the gauntlet. This consisted of crawling through a mixture of grease and other undisclosed debris, after which they were baptized by shellbacks in the swimming pool placed on the forward elevator. After the event, King Neptunus Rex informed Captain Hughes of his approval of the crew of *Block Island*, and he welcomed them back to his realm on a future visit. One sailor recalled, "It was something different than the war you know."[11] As the day's activities returned to normal with the Royal Court's departure, the entire crew of shellbacks on board returned to the Pacific war.

Block Island anchored once again in Leyte Gulf and awaited orders. On July 23, along with the destroyer USS *Peiffer*, DE 588, she traveled east to Apra Harbor off Guam. While at anchor on August 1, Captain Hughes was relieved of command by Capt. Wallace M. Beakley. Born in 1903, Beakley had graduated from the Academy in 1924. He first served on the battleship USS *Utah*, BB 31. He earned his wings at Pensacola in late 1926, after which he served as a naval aviator on board the light cruisers USS *Trenton*, CL 11, and USS *Marblehead*, CL 12. For three years, between 1932 and 1935, Beakley studied aeronautical engineering and earned a master's degree from the California Institute of Technology. Two years later he served as a naval aviator on board USS *Lexington*, CV 2. Like many of the crew of *Block Island*, he was also "baptized" by surviving a sinking. At the beginning of the conflict, he was assigned as commanding officer of Fighting Squadron Five, and later the air group commander on the on USS *Wasp*, CV 7, which was sunk by a Japanese torpedo at the Battle of Guadalcanal. Beakley, soon rescued by a destroyer, continued flying from CVs in strikes on Marcus and Tarawa Islands.[12] When Beakley took over command in the first week in August, CVE 106 was undergoing modifications to the landing equipment on and under the flight deck. Meanwhile, the group of men on the communication watch in the early morning hours intercepted a message that an amazing new weapon had been dropped on and destroyed an entire Japanese city. This message, received two days after the actual bombing of Hiroshima, manufactured rumors that rippled through the crew. Wilder gossip included Japanese surrender. While fabrication improvised for lack of facts, no official word surfaced. Five days later, on August 13, 1945, Fighting *Block Island*, along with five other vessels, steamed toward war.[13]

World War II is ironic in that modernity allowed civilians at home to know more of the overall conflict than did those battling in it. As the world celebrated the ending of the war, and Alfred Eisenstaedt snapped his iconic photo in Times Square of the sailor kissing a nurse in uniform on August 14, *Block Island* cruised. Hours after the official announcement back in the US, when the morning sun's first rays shed light on New York streets full of residue of celebration and the residents slept off their hangovers, the crew of the FBI got the news. While en route to the Philippines at 1630 on August 15, *Block Island* received the official message announcing the surrender of Japanese forces and a termination of offensive actions. Soon after, the message was read over the loudspeakers on board. An additional message from Captain Beakley ordered all hands to report to the flight deck.[14] Drinking alcohol on a USN vessel was illegal outside of medical purposes. This contrasted with the Royal Navy, which still allowed a daily rum ration. On special celebratory occasions, the Royal Navy allotted more rum than the normal daily ration. The terminology for this over-portion, derived from the Age of Sail, was known as "splicing the main brace."[15] Captain Beakley, in a sense, issued his own "splicing the main brace" order, as he had cases of beer, normally reserved for brief visits to small islands, hauled up to the flight deck. CVE 106, in seven months of operations, had cruised enough to circle the earth one and a half times since commissioning, traveling 37,932 miles.[16] Sailors climbing up ladders from all levels of the ship poured onto the flight deck. Skies above held summer thunderstorms, and soon rain fell heavily on tables heaving with bottles of beer. Men drank beer, hugged one another, and listened as trombones and saxophones wailed in celebration despite the downpour. One sailor said, "We almost drowned from the rain but nobody cared. It was such a good feeling that the war was over."[17] While rain poured on the enlisted men, nothing dampened their spirits. Beer caps flew off in collective celebration of surviving the war. Some had predicted that the war would go on into 1947 or even 1948. Home awaited and loved ones would be embraced again. Free from this war, they would soon be also free from the Navy and each other. A victory cake with white frosting, hastily fashioned by the ship's bakers, showed a red, white, and blue flag next to the two letters "V J." Victory had arrived; however, the men would witness firsthand the true cost of the war, and its unfathomable suffering, in the weeks to come.[18]

While the flight deck contained the celebrations of the enlisted men, a smaller cohort of naval aviators celebrated in the ready room. One pilot called it "our environment, our club, our sanctuary."[19] LSO Joe Zook remembered that a large bowl appeared with a huge block of ice placed inside. Pilots' locker doors opened, and all the illegally owned bottles of booze were poured over the ice block. The men lifted Zook on their shoulders, raising in the air the man who had brought them safely down from the skies.[20] The shooting war was over, but much remained undone in operations taking control of Japanese-occupied areas. In these postwar operations, the men of CVE 106 witnessed human suffering inflicted on a scale difficult to imagine unless seen firsthand.

23
"Yanks Are on Their Way!"

Laying anchor once again in Leyte Gulf in the Philippines on August 17, *Block Island* waited for all the members of task force 77.1 to materialize. The force consisted of two escort carriers and three destroyer escorts whose mission centered on aiding in Allied landings in the Keijo area of Korea. Operational plans called for providing air cover and aiding in the minesweeping operations into Jinsen Harbor to begin Allied occupation of postwar Korea. On the twenty-ninth of August the group sailed north from the Philippines toward the Yellow Sea.[1] While en route, however, an old Japanese ally intervened. Northwest of TF 77.1, the same natural force was materializing that saved the Japanese home islands from invasion in the thirteenth century. As Japan had faced almost certain destruction from the Mongols in 1281, divine assistance in the form of a typhoon decimated the Mongol fleet and secured the home islands, thus bringing about the legend of the "divine wind," or "kamikaze."[2] A typhoon shifting northeast blocked TG 77.1's entrance into the Yellow Sea. From September 1 to 3, the vessels skirted the storm by retreating southeast toward Formosa. Although they avoided the heart of the storm, the men still experienced what one officer described as being "buffeted by monstrous winds and seas."[3]

The storm not only delayed the operations of the Allied landings in Korea but also caused *Block Island* and her task force to receive more pressing orders. On the island of Formosa, more than a thousand Allied prisoners of war held by the Japanese awaited rescue. While the shooting had stopped, the true extent of the Japanese atrocities was yet to surface. With the sudden conclusion of the war, military planners were caught off guard, and none more so than those charged with the logistics of getting the Allied servicemen home. At the top of logistical tasks facing Allied planners rested the recovery of POWs held by the Japanese. In a military operation called Recovery of Allied Military Personnel (RAMP), the escort carriers' spacious hangar decks seemed tailormade for the recovery of these POWs. Two of the first escort carriers assigned to these new missions were USS *Block Island*, CVE 106, and USS *Santee*, CVE 29. Working in concert, these vessels transformed from the traditional role of launching and recovering aircraft to that of serving as a floating haven for the first leg of the POWs' journey home.[4]

At 0615, as dawn broke on the morning of September 5, aircraft from the escort carriers USS *Block Island* and USS *Santee* flew over Taipei in a show of force to the

Japanese and to the relief of the 1273 POWs scattered across camps around the island. These aircraft dropped over the airfield at Taipei written instructions for the Japanese command. Messages floating down on parachutes informed the Japanese command that two US destroyer escorts, USS *Thomas J. Gary*, DE 326, and USS *Kretchmer*, DE 329, were stationed off the port of Keelung to the east. The instructions asked for a pilot boat to escort both vessels safely through the heavily mined harbor. Once docked, thirty-two Marines and members of the *Block Island* medical team disembarked the DEs in preparation for the forthcoming evacuation. While this action secured the needed port for transferring the POWs to the carriers, another phase sought to bring immediate aid to the prisoners located in the three camps near Taipei city.[5]

In the minutes after ten in the morning, Marine aviator Capt. Dick Johnson took off in an Avenger not loaded with weapons but transporting intelligence officer Maj. Peter Folger. Their plane, the first Allied plane to land on Formosa, arrived at the Matsuyama Airport on the northern outskirts of Taipei. Folger, transported by a Japanese officer to a number of the prisoner of war camps, quickly determined how to accomplish the most good in the shortest amount of time. His assessment, radioed to Hellcat fighters hovering over the airport, was then relayed back to CVE 106 off the northern coast of Formosa. Marines, trained to load weapons onto planes, packed food and medical supplies onto aircraft that took off and landed at the Matsuyama airfield.[6] In the afternoon hours, *Block Island* and *Santee* launched nearly ten thousand pounds of supplies. One flight included Pharmacist's Mate First Class Ben Owens, who had orders to provide immediate medical aid for the prisoners. After landing at the airfield, Owens and the other medical staff and supplies were transported by the Japanese in a 1937 Buick to the Maruyama #4 Camp located in the northern part of the city. Pulling into the gate of the camp, Owens and the team were greeted by over three hundred POWs, many of whom were in extremely ill health due to their internment. Owens, used to treating just a handful of sailors on a daily basis, now faced a nearly endless supply of those who needed treatment for a range of major and minor ailments. Owens personally encountered the global nature of this war with POWs hailing from Britain, the United States, Australia, and Holland. With less than twenty-four hours to prepare the men before moving them out to the American vessels, as Owens wrote years later, "I have never worked so hard in my life as we did to prepare these men for transport to the DE's and then to the Carriers."[7] Laboring through the night, the medical team's work was interrupted only by the arrival of more marines and supplies from *Block Island* and *Santee*.[8]

Flight operations on CVE 106 continued throughout the day in the delivery of food and medical supplies. Staples included eighty loaves of bread, 120 pounds of canned carrots, three hundred pounds of powdered milk, and 179 cases of K

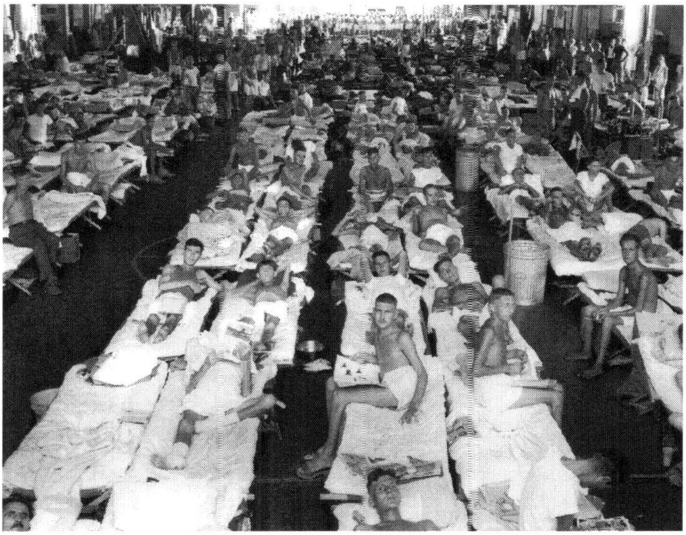

Figure 19. Hangar deck of the Fighting *Block Island* converted to house and transport Allied POWs held by the Japanese on Formosa. Once on board, prisoners showered, received new clothing, and ate their first real meals in years. Courtesy of the Taiwan POW Camps Memorial Society.

rations. Also, luxuries were loaded into the bomb bays of Avengers, including eight hundred pounds of coffee, 1,100 pounds of sugar, 7,500 packs of cigarettes, and 4,608 bars of candy.[9] As one witness wrote, *Block Island* marines "broke out white bread and real butter and watched with tears in their eyes as their Allied comrades dived into the first decent food they had tasted in more than three years."[10] Malnutrition had taken its toll. The men who had worked at the Kinkaseki copper mine camp over the past two years had awoken at dawn each day, then walked over a large hill and descended into a valley to the mine's entrance. They labored in the worst conditions within the copper mine, where local Taiwanese refused to work. Due to the heat, men at times worked naked. If the work quotas of copper ore were not met, beatings soon followed. With a daily diet consisting of little more than small amounts of rice, most weighed less than eighty pounds, and edema swelled up the legs of many prisoners.[11]

Of the British servicemen, many had been captive since early 1942, having fought in the battles raging down the Malayan Peninsula. Eighty-nine men were Americans, including some who had survived the Bataan Death March. Others were Dutch and Chinese prisoners.[12] The prisoners healthy enough for transport went by truck, then train, to the docked destroyer escorts. The sailors of the FBI had experienced two theaters of war from aboard two different escort carriers, but what was about to come on board would stun the toughest sailor. One witness wrote years later that the FBI crew "watched in awe as the redeemed prisoners made their way painfully up the gangplank."[13]

The *Block Island* band gathered on the hangar deck and awaited their new passengers. One sailor recalled, "Those poor guys looked like scarecrows, they were all skin and bones."[14] The former prisoners were welcomed with renditions of "God Save the King" and "Rum and Coca-Cola." Boarding the ship, they disposed of their slave garb, showered, and received new Navy-issue clothing. Those in the weakest state, carried on board on stretchers, received medical treatment. Decades later, veteran Bill Tokarz recalled with emotion a friend of his named Johnny Walsh, from Connecticut, carrying some of the weakest POWs up the short distance from the DE to the CVE. He stated, "He carried them on board, right up the ladder, and put them down, 'cause the guy could not walk."[15] Meals were devoured and divine services took place, during which many POWs continued to vomit as a result of their vacant stomachs adjusting to the large dose of calories.

Machinist Mate First Class Rex Coen mingled with the newly arrived POWs with protruding hip bones and toothpick-thin arms. Talking with these men, he witnessed a range of emotions, from tears of joy at finally being released from their hell of captivity to just plain smiles of thankfulness. Coen heard a range of the ways English is spoken, from the King's English of Britain to the twang of Australia. Among these men he found an American who spent the majority of the war as a prisoner. This man chalked up his survival to his observation of animals. Years later Coen recalled, "He told me that they would watch the animals and eat the grass that they ate. They'd also eat any snakes, lizards, and insects they could get their hands on."[16] The hangar was easily transformed into a floating sanctuary. Replacing Marine Corps Avengers and Corsairs designed to rain death on the enemy were neat rows of cots with freshly washed sheets aligned to bring comfort to those who had suffered so much. The POWs' thin frames reduced by the years of captivity rested in this space. One heard vomiting from starved stomachs attempting to digest their first full meals in years.

One of the men walking on board USS *Block Island* was Maurice A. Rooney whose alien-looking body testified to years of brutality at the Kinkaseki camp Waking in the morning every day as a POW, Rooney and his fellow prisoners entered a mine tunnel and descended a mile underground. Laboring naked in temperatures up to 130 degrees, the prisoners worked in extremely dangerous conditions with inadequate tools. The conditions of their internment deteriorated their British-issued army clothing and erased their last tangible connections to Britain However, while clothing rotted away in captivity, their identity as Britons did not They retained their culture and sense of self by singing. Songs helped keep hope of survival alive. One such song ended with the line "Yanks Are on Their Way!"[17]

After three years and most men losing half their prewar weight, their song's prophecy finally came true.

The night before the POWs disembarked *Block Island* at Manila, the crew put on a variety show, including the "St. Louis Blues." With Commander Gilman playing in the band, all joined in singing "Auld Lang Syne." Its lyrics from a poem written by Scotsman Robert Burns in 1788, the song is most known for being sung on New Year's Eve. Crew members and former prisoners joining arms sang this song in closing their time together. One sailor recalled in a letter to his mother, "It was impressive—our—strong arms interlocking with some that looked like toothpicks. But the faces of those liberated men were those of people who had discovered peace beyond any that we will ever know in this world."[18]

The crew of the Fighting *Block Island* had experienced much in this war, but the rescue of the POWs greatly impacted them. While short in duration, as these men disembarked in Manila, their time with the POWs at the conclusion of the mission provided an intense experience. Irv Biron had survived North Atlantic gales and a sinking; however, in speaking of the POWS, emotion overcame him. He recalled, "Till this day it still hurts . . . what they went through."[19] This rescue, on the most human level, brought the true realities of the war into focus. One sailor later wrote that it provided "a sobering insight to the nature of the harrowing conditions ashore that they had been so energetically seeking to bring to an end."[20]

24
Magic Carpet

After dispatching the rescued POWs to Manila, CVE 106 traveled to Okinawa. In the middle of October, the vessel received orders to return to Formosa.[1] As part of a show of force in support of the Seventieth Chinese Infantry Army Division in retaking the island from the Japanese forces, *Block Island* provided air cover in support of the Nationalist Chinese forces. After her three-day mission there, she traveled to Saipan for a month between October 23 and November 23.[2] She then served in what one scholar termed "history's greatest sealift."[3]

With the war's sudden cessation, millions of American servicemen awaited the return trip home and discharge. The US military faced an unrivaled logistical challenge. *Block Island*, in late November, joined the Herculean effort of transporting US servicemen home, a nightmare of administration with some twelve million men in uniform scattered all over the planet. The closing of the conflict witnessed the rapid demobilization of the US Armed Forces. By the beginning of 1946, the US Army had discharged eight million men, and the USN shrank from over three million sailors in 1945 to under half a million by 1947. As Army general George C. Marshall quipped about this sharp decline, "It was not a demobilization, it was a rout!"[4] Demobilization could proceed only as fast as servicemen arrived stateside, and thus forty-six escort carriers participated in Operation Magic Carpet, including USS *Block Island*.[5]

Many armed forces personnel found themselves hitching a States-bound ride aboard a range of vessels, including the cramped quarters of the USN's smaller vessels, such as destroyers and Liberty ships. The journey crossing the Pacific in a slow-going Liberty ship with incremental stops at Pacific islands could take upward of a month. The CVEs and larger aircraft carriers provided ideal platforms in the transportation of men home, with hangar decks providing space for sleeping and recreation. Also, in comparison to the confines of smaller vessels, these carriers offered near luxury, with the showing of films, well-stocked ship's stores for purchasing cigarettes, galleys producing three hot meals a day, and more ice cream than could be eaten. For those ground forces used to walking in mud and residing in tents, carriers equaled first class accommodations on their homebound journey.[6] *Block Island*'s role in Magic Carpet commenced at Guam on November 24, 1945, where armed forces personnel walked on board. Leaving the same day, CVE 106 headed east toward Pearl Harbor. Docking at Pearl eight days later, on December 2, she rested there three days before pushing off on the final leg of the journey, arriving at the Naval Station in San Diego on December 11.[7] For those original FBI sailors who had served on USS *Block Island*, CVE 21, these last six days of cruising the Pacific between Pearl Harbor and the California coast represented the final miles sailed in their naval careers. Possessing high numbers in the discharge point system due to their length of service, almost all FBI sailors packed their bags and disembarked *Block Island*. With one final signature, sailors received their discharge orders and commenced their postwar lives.

As on all ships in the Navy, rotation was a part of life on both *Block Islands*. Air groups were assigned for a mission and taken off, commanding officers served for periods of time, and enlisted crew members came and went. No matter the length of service, bonds were formed One sailor wrote, "You live for many months with the same faces and the same voices. They become part of your life."[8] However, for the survivors of the sinking of CVE 21, this bond was forged by far more than just proximity over time. These men, "baptized by salt water," shared a bond that transcended the aspects of mere friendship, such as knowing one another's nicknames and hometowns. Due to the compartmentalized nature of the vessel, with assigned compartments coinciding with assigned duties, sailors were also compartmentalized in their relationships. However, surviving the sinking transcended the metal bulkheads that hampered a formal friendship. Men who did not formally know one another were brothers as a result of the sinking.

An escort carrier sailor from the Royal Navy, writing in a memoir, noted the experience of leaving his vessel. Of boarding a small launch to depart, he wrote, "A space of oily water widens between the drifter and the grey-blue camouflaged shape you know so well."[9] Seeing his shipmates waving, he concluded, "In a few minutes they will have gone forever out of your life in to the gulf of memory and time."[10] While this last sentiment proved true for the majority of US naval personnel as well, the bonds of the Fighting *Block Island* years later bridged this "gulf of memory and time." Their bond proved stronger than those on other vessels and did not end with the issuing of discharge papers.

Receiving their discharges, the men of *Block Island*, such as Machinist's Mate First Class Cleveland Martin, disembarked and headed home for the holidays. Martin's time over the past year had included working on refrigeration units within the vessel in the mostly tropical climates of the South Pacific. Packing away his Navy uniform and heading home to Kansas, Martin wore civilian clothes on the train. Seating priority was given to servicemen in uniform, so Martin had to stand near the doorway in the train car as they left San Diego. As the train moved closer to his native Kansas, the temperature outside dropped rapidly, and discomfort increased for the sailor used to the environs of the South Pacific. Finally, in

Oklahoma City, enough passengers departed for Martin to secure a seat for the rest of the journey to Topeka, where his parents waited for him in the -6°F weather. On Christmas Eve 1945, the three Martins, two parents and the newly made veteran rode in the family's pickup truck to their Jackson County farm.[11]

The rapid conclusion of the war did not mean that the deaths suddenly stopped in the Pacific. In October, Irv Biron, still assigned to CVE 106, received notification that his brother serving as a navigator on a C-47 had died in a plane crash. As a result, Biron was given a priority one order to report home, meaning in theory he could fly home weeks ahead of *Block Island.* Exiting CVE 106 in Saipan, Biron soon learned that swift orders in the hands of an enlisted man meant very little. A quick flight home would never materialize with a never-ending line of officers from all the services having priority over enlisted personnel. After a few frustrating days at the airfield, Biron decided to hop the first vessel eastbound for the United States, which turned out to be a decrepit merchant marine tanker headed for Eniwetok Atoll. There he then boarded a tiny landing craft infantry (LCI) crawling its way to San Diego. Forty-four days after he had left *Block Island* in Saipan, Biron's LCI entered San Diego Bay. Gazing at the American coast, Biron heard over the speakers the captain calling him to the bridge. Of course, the thought entered his mind, "What did I do wrong?" The captain, with his arm pointed to Navy Base San Diego, asked, "Biron, didn't you sail on the *Block Island*?" Biron looked and docked half a mile away was the escort carrier with "106" painted on the side. She had beaten Biron by three days.[12]

Researching a naval vessel mirrors writing the history of a college campus, with many ebbs and flows, as witnessed in transitioning crews, tactics, weapons, and leaders. Arriving in San Diego in December of 1945, *Block Island* said goodbye to those hundreds of sailors whose connection went back to the original CVE 21. Echoing the graduation of a large class of seniors, the vessel moved forward in a number of adaptive uses into the postwar era. This transition started with cruising to Norfolk, Virginia. Traveling through the Panama Canal, CVE 106 arrived in Norfolk on January 20, 1946. In the months of March and April, she anchored in the York River off Camp Perry, Virginia, and served as a recruit-training vessel.

In May of 1946, she was removed from the roll of active vessels and given the status of "In Service, In Reserve."[13] On June 7, 1946, *Block Island* was taken to the Naval Academy to serve as a base of training for naval cadets as "a floating schoolship."[14] As she rested in the bed of the Severn River opposite the grounds of the Academy, midshipmen for three years trained on her as a floating classroom. After the outbreak of the Korean War, she was refloated from the riverbed to undergo an overhaul. Recommissioned on April 28, 1951, she returned to active duty in the Atlantic fleet with new engines and flight deck.[15] Under the command of Capt. Arthur S. Hill, she participated in a number of training missions off the Virginia coast.[16] Her new mission in the Cold War focused on anti-submarine warfare (ASW), defined as "to deprive the enemy of the effective use of his submarines."[17] These operations mirrored missions carried out by CVE 21 at the height of World War II, with four such missions taking place in the Caribbean Sea and one in European waters.[18] However, the technology in both detection and weapons had also transformed.

During these missions in the Atlantic, CVE 106 housed two ASW squadrons, including VS-22 and VS-30. The workhorse in tracking enemy submarines was the Grumman AF Guardian, with a wingspan of over sixty feet. As the largest-ever single-engine carrier-based plane powered by piston, this aircraft could carry a 4,000-pound bomb load and wing-mounted rockets. The squadron also included a twin tandem-rotored Piasecki HUP helicopter. With a range of over three hundred miles and able to carry up to six people, the craft proved very effective in the rescue of pilots and crew from the ocean.[19] Her aircraft combed the depths of the Atlantic in the beginning stages of the Cold War. However, she was decommissioned once again and placed in the mothball fleet.[20] She entered the USN's bureaucratic limbo. The ever-changing technological circumstances of the Cold War produced transforming notions of the Navy's role, which can be seen in the treatment of the remaining CVEs. This shuffle resulted in the demise of CVE 106 in the summer of 1960.

No escort carrier officially existed after July 1, 1957. The Navy designated most escort carriers at this time, including CVE 106 resting in the mothball fleet, as landing platform helicopter (LPH). However, for CVE 106, this official reclassification did not go beyond the simply bureaucratic readjustment, and she still awaited a future role. When the Nav canceled the LPH classification, the paper classification of CVE 106 became cargo ship and aircraft ferry (AKV). While some AKVs' classification did go forward in the actual conversion of former escort carriers, CVE 106 was once again left untouched. For the CVEs that the Navy selected for the AKV reincarnation, their later lives were diverse, including, in the early 1960s, the transportation of military aircraft to Vietnam.[21] Ironically, one of the last CVEs to exist in some form was the first CVE, USS *Long Island*, CVE 1, which was decommissioned in March 1946. Surviving World War II, she saw conversion into the passenger ship *Nelly* and transported immigrants fleeing war-torn Europe to Canada in the immediate postwar period. In 1953, converted once more, she lived as *Seven Seas*, serving as a floating university transporting students around the world. Worn down, in 1966 she was purchased by the University of Rotterdam and used as dormitories for medical students. Her engines dead, she floated and housed students for over a decade, before being scrapped in Belgium in 1977.[22] Her loss represented one of the final acts of purging of the escort carriers.

The birth of a ship entails an amazing amount of activity. The construction of USS *Block Island*, CVE 106, included fifteen months of round-the-clock labor by hundreds of Todd Pacific workers. Hundreds of dignitaries and other guests gathered on CVE 106 for the commissioning. These bursts of activity in the birth of a vessel contrasted sharply with those vessels moored in the mothball fleet in Philadelphia. Moored indefinitely, CVE 106's compartments were quiet, as no human activity took place on board. Her fate rested in the hands of the military staff devoted to US Cold War policy on the high seas, who sat behind desks at the Pentagon far away from these exiled vessels. As rust accumulated over the years, possible conversions for the escort carriers dwindled, and the fate of USS *Block Island*, CVE 106, was sealed on July 1, 1959, with her removal from the USN, coldly termed as "stricken from the record."[23] Her fate was in no way unique. Rapid advances in naval aviation, such as jet engines and steam catapults, rapidly accelerated in the fifteen years after the conclusion of World War II. The CVEs' military usefulness had ended, and thus destruction awaited.

If any adage about human life would apply to the thousands of vessels scrapped by the USN after the war, it is "We all die alone." In Philadelphia in early 1960, FBI veteran sailor John Suprey drove a tractor-trailer north toward a truck terminal in Elizabeth, New Jersey. Suprey, who had served on both USS *Block Islands*, was finishing a run from Baltimore that day. Looking out his windshield, he spotted an old escort carrier docked, with the number 106 on the side of the bridge. Pulling into his company's truck terminal nearby, he spoke with the dispatch personnel about the fate of his ship. Suprey heard her destiny. After being gutted of any military usefulness, her lifeless hull would be towed way. She had just recently been sold for scrap to a Japanese company.[24]

The FBI intelligence officer Roy Swift wrote his history of both vessels in 1965. Of the transfer of CVE 106, he wrote, "Stricken from the Navy list 1 July 1959, she was sold in New York, 23 February 1960 for $250,078 to Kowa Koeki Col., Ltd., Mitsubishi Naka, of Chiyoda-Ku, Tokyo, Japan."[25] The Philadelphia newspaper the *Evening Bulletin* reported on April 19, 1960, "The once-mighty 12,000 ton escort carrier *Block Island*, powerless and without steering, floated down the Delaware River last week on a 10,000 mile trip to Japan."[26] Two vessels accompanied the escort carrier, the oceangoing Dutch tug *Clyde* and a local river tug. Reaching the waters where the Delaware River merged with the sea, "the river tug tooted good-by and left."[27]

Clyde held a crew of thirty-three and traveled south for the Panama Canal. While the Commencement Bay–class vessel with four large boilers delivering 16,000 hp to her two screws allowed a cruising speed of nineteen knots, *Clyde*

Figure 20. While this image on June 1, 1944, shows sailors smiling on reaching land in Casablanca after surviving the sinking of CVE 21, many wrestled with experiencing the sinking for the rest of their days. Some veterans placed a great deal of meaning on objects that survived the sinking with them, such as a piece of clothing or objects found in their pockets, once the ordeal was over. Courtesy of the USS Block Island Association.

methodically dragged *Block Island* at eight knots. The 10,000-mile, two-month trip was predicted as uneventful by the tug's skipper. The writer concluded his article with, "The sturdy, weather-beaten seaman said he anticipates no difficulty during the trip. It's just an ordinary towing job to him."[28] One aspect of the Fighting *Block Island* narrative of both vessels is unpredictability. North Atlantic storms, hunter-killer missions, typhoons, all pointed to the randomness of naval warfare. As *Clyde* pulled *Block Island*'s lifeless hull across the Pacific and toward the Hawaiian Islands, the largest recorded earthquake in history up until this writing took place. A magnitude 9.5 quake rocked the Chilean coast on May 22, 1960, and killed over 1,600 people.[29] A twenty-foot tsunami struck the town of Ancud, Chile, nearly three hundred miles from the epicenter, sweeping away over a hundred people.[30] Rippling out on the bottom of the high seas, this unseen force attacked vessels all over the Pacific, including what was left of *Block Island*. While this earthquake caused a delay, her fate in Japan was not altered. Arriving in Nagasaki on June 20, 1960, the $33 million vessel completed in 1945 was completely broken up for scrap by the end of August.[31]

25
Remembering

The renowned philosopher and historian Lewis Mumford, in his highly accessible yet complex narratives, produced countless quotable lines on a host of subjects. Exploring the built environment, Mumford originated insightful comparisons on the human use of space, from the skyscrapers of the 1930s to the irrigation projects of ancient Mesopotamia. His short sentences often function as gateways to larger philosophical questions. For example: "The burial of the body tells us more about man's nature than would the tool that dug the grave."[1] While this quote on burials on land may seem diametrically opposed to a narrative dealing with loss on the high seas, embracing a broad definition of "burial" to include the actions of remembering lost shipmates and vessels yields significant revelations.

Actions on the high seas lack a tangible land-based site to function as sacred ground for remembering. For centuries nations and individual naval veterans have invented their own methods for recalling. While the very sites of land battles, such as Hastings and the Normandy beaches, function after the fighting as a site for the burial of the dead, erection of stone markers, and hosting of commemorative events, naval heritage is more convoluted. With the employment of innovative concepts of remembering, the buoyant battlefield of a sinking can be commemorated to honor both sailors and ships lost at sea. Innovation also allows the marking of naval battles thousands of miles away from the actual coordinates of the engagements. A glimpse of this long-standing phenomenon is seen in the methods of remembrance employed by sailors of both *Block Islands*.

Survivors of CVE 21 utilized artifacts in speaking of the experience of sinking. During interviews about the sinking, veterans exhibited objects saved from the lost CVE 21. Perhaps in wrestling with the emotionally charged memory, including the torpedo strikes and their time in the water, shifting of the focus onto an object and away from themselves transferred the violence of the experience. It is much easier to grapple with the randomness of survival for an object found in their pocket after surviving the sinking than processing the role of chance in how they survived it. During interviews, survivors also spoke of objects lost as a result of the sinking. Seated in his Scottsdale home, Hector Vernetti gave a familiar statement about an important photograph lost: "It was in my locker on the bottom of the ocean."[2]

Over the course of my interviews, sailors spoke of losing not only photographs but wallets, lighters, trinkets from Casablanca, and gifts from family members, in addition to, of course, shipmates. All the lost items made those few that survived all the more important; thus, objects from the baptism morphed into artifacts that functioned as testaments to an experience. Part talisman, part testimonial, these salvaged objects denoted their ordeal and simultaneously symbolized redemption, survival, and loss.

The viewing of artifacts saved and preserved from the sinking leads one to reconsider World War II veterans not only as former members of the military but also functioning as their own archivists. In their homes I saw naval relics displayed on walls and coffee tables. Hanging near family portraits were photographs and artifacts giving visual testimony to the veterans' naval service and the lost USS *Block Island*, CVE 21. Plank owner's certificates, signifying being the member of a crew at the time of the USN's commissioning of a war vessel, were framed on walls. Personal exhibitions on home walls included black-and-white images of groupings of sailors, an oil-stained dollar bill retrieved from a pocket after the sinking, and framed photographs of both escort carriers. During interviews the sailors referred to objects in the room. One sailor, mid-interview, stated, "All I got off that ship was me, a dollar bill with oil on it, and my dog-tags."[3]

The importance of these artifacts is seen at the Block Island Historical Society on Block Island, Rhode Island. It was there in the summer of 2003, during the completion of a summer internship, that I uncovered numerous boxes of items seemingly unrelated to the small coastal community of Block Island. A wristwatch frozen at 8:20 as the result of immersion in salt water, white Navy-issue skivvies transformed black that smelled of fuel oil, and handwritten letters of sailors, were all donated and demonstrated the givers' need for the artifacts to survive them. With postmarks from such places as Utah, Missouri, and Washington state, on the surface it seemed that these items had no direct connection to this small pork-chop-shaped New England island. However, when combined, the randomness of this assemblage related to the USN in World War II faded away. With background research into escort carriers, these artifacts coalesced into a powerful sea tale of loss and deliverance. Such objects with symbolic meaning donated in perpetuity demonstrate naval veterans seeking to tether their artifacts against the raging sea of time. Facing their own physical oblivion with the advancing of years, these sailors sought to preserve their personal testaments to their experiences and vessels. In doing so they located a small local museum and the community that shared a name with their vessels.

Model making was an additional phenomenon of retrospection. Hours of patiently piecing together plastic components and the application of paint allowed veterans to construct objects in the exhibition of escort carrier naval heritage. This therapeutic task, taking a matter of weeks or even months, gave the model builder-veteran hours of time to consider his former vessel while his hands remained occupied as he assembled a visual, nonverbal testament to his vessel. And, as many veterans constructed these models after retirement, they understood this testament would outlast them.

But model making yields a deeper meaning for sailors who survived a sinking, for they are constructing a miniaturized plastic version of their lost home. Bill "Slick" Connolly survived the loss of an aircraft carrier in both the Pacific and the Atlantic. While I was speaking with him in his kitchen over a cup of coffee in his home in Natick, Massachusetts, Connolly retrieved two models he had assembled. Both hand built by Connolly, the fact that USS *Lexington*, CV 2, and USS *Block Island*, CVE 21, were both 1/700 scale allowed Slick to give a comparative lecture on these two very different aircraft carriers. Connolly, in speaking of both sinkings, focused on the models, pointing and describing his location during the traumatic events such as abandoning ship.[4]

While attending the reunions of the USS *Block Island* Association, I noted the veterans' bodies exhibited their naval service. Short sleeves revealed faded tattoos acquired in Norfolk, New York, and ports overseas. While I visited, many asked me to speak up, illustrating the loss of hearing that commenced while manning a 40 mm or five-inch guns with little or no ear protection. I had to assist Walter Cyr in getting out of his wheelchair to use the bathroom. Holding his tattooed arm, I could feel his surprising strength, but his lungs did not match this hidden power. He had breathed the deadly glassy microfibers of asbestos insulation not only on *Block Island*, where they lined its piping, but also while serving on board vessels after the war as a merchant marine. With each breath, microscopic slices reduced lung capacity.

In the course of interviews, however, it became apparent that the sinking had a larger psychological impact that few men wished to speak about. Like a disturbance under the surface of a large body of water, while unfelt from the perspective of the viewer floating above, the glassy concentric circles of turmoil echoing out hinted of something deep and powerful below the waves. During interviews I listened more closely. Many times I heard nothing; however, a few times I did get a sense of the impact those three torpedo strikes, swimming in oil, and surviving the ordeal had brought upon these young sailors. One such opening took place in an interview with Jack Greer in his trailer home in north Phoenix. This flash of insight came in as he was speaking about his postwar life.

On the morning of April 29, 1965, Greer was working on the third floor of a multistory limestone government office building in Seattle. It was a pleasant spring afternoon. The large windows were open, inviting in the spring weather.[5] Belying the calm of this spring afternoon, stored-up stress deep within the earth was about to rupture. Under Puget Sound, an earthquake buried the needle on the seismographic device at the University of Washington. For forty-five seconds the quake, later measured at 6.5 on the Richter scale, struck the Pacific Northwest.[6] When the reverberations from within began to shake this government building, they also rattled something embedded deep within Greer's unconscious. Greer is at a loss as to what happened after the vibrations registered in his brain. His next recollection was standing on the green lawn a block away looking at the visibly damaged workplace building. He had absolutely no memory of how he had reached this location. During the interview he said, "And I thought to myself, how in the hell did I get out here?" Finding himself in a group of bewildered coworkers, he asked a trusted friend what happened. Greer heard that after the first sign of the quake, he climbed out of the third-floor window and slid down the side of the building using a rain drain. The coworker said, "The last thing I saw of you was your hair."[7]

Asked about the meaning of this experience in hindsight, Greer opened up. He said that after the quake, "The only thing on my mind were those torpedoes."[8] At the risk of the narrative becoming bogged down in psychoanalysis, it is worth noting Greer's experience during the sinking. Working on the hangar deck, Greer was on a ladder when the first torpedo struck. Around him on the hangar bulkheads hung depth charges and large nets full of life jackets. When the first explosion rocked the ship, Greer fell, and, as he colorfully described decades later, "knocked on my ass, out colder than a cucumber."[9] Unconscious on the hangar deck, in the chaos, Greer went unnoticed by his shipmates. As the escort carrier came to a stop, sailors grabbed life jackets and ran topside when ordered to abandon ship. All the while, Greer lay unconscious and unnoticed. When Greer came to, *Block Island* was listing badly to both port and stern. The net holding the life jackets from the ceiling had been released, and amazingly, on the deck under it was just one life jacket. He quickly grabbed it as he ran to abandon ship.

Perhaps for decades after the war, the persistent thought of lying unconscious on the hangar deck echoed in his psyche. The general quarters order, a third torpedo exploding underneath, an ever-listing ship, were not enough to revive him. This could germinate a number of questions. What if he had not awoken? Or even worse, what if he had regained consciousness only to drown in the process of the ship sinking? Such internal processes could produce both conscious or unconscious fears of the next torpedo strike or sudden life-altering event, such as two decades later when the ground underneath Seattle started to shake uncontrollably.

The sinking invites the historian to fall into the classic myopic mistake of many military histories, that of just one intense, overly focused beam of concentration to reduce an entire battle, campaign, or even war, to just one engagement. While the sinking is central to the history of the crew, individual interviews demonstrated that many other days were just as significant on the individual level. The loss of a pilot, death of a brother in the war, an accident on the flight deck, all produced life-altering implications for the individual sailors even though the vast majority of these incidents would never be noted in any narrative of World War II. Looking into the margins of war stories, where the classic military history ends and real life for the veteran begins, offers fertile ground for discovering how survivors continued on with their lives. This is especially noticeable in interviewing veterans about their reentry into civilian life after the conclusion of the war.

One individual I interviewed had just a few days' connection to the story of the *Block Islands*. As a British POW rescued from Formosa in September 1945, his journey to freedom started with the evacuation from the island. The first and only time I met Cecil Clarke was at a ship's reunion in 2007, held in Rhode Island. He had journeyed from England, and, on the night before his return, Mr. Clarke and I finally spoke in private. It was ironic that our first private conversation was over dinner, since our conversation centered on his years of starvation as a Japanese POW.

Late in 1941, steaming around the Horn of Africa on a troopship, Cecil Clarke and his fellow members of the Royal Army Engineers of the British Eighteenth Division, first received word of the attack on Pearl Harbor. Landing in Singapore a few weeks before the fall of the island outpost, Clarke and his fellow troops marched to take on the enemy that in the past weeks had not only attacked Hawaii but also launched coordinated attacks on numerous locations in Southeast Asia. In February 1942, with Singapore quickly overrun, Clarke's unit was taken prisoner after being ordered to surrender by the British lieutenant general Arthur Percival. Transported to Formosa by ship in such dehumanizing conditions that some soldiers lost one pound of weight a day, he and others labored as slaves in copper mines. For three and a half years, he ate little more than a small amount of rice daily.

Imprisonment meant more than just working as slaves. Brutal conditions took their toll, with Cecil dropping from 160 pounds to under 80 pounds by the end of the war. Other POWs lost their lives, and Clarke remembered seeing many of his fellow POWs lose the will to live, and death visiting them soon after. Cecil and his fellow prisoners dug many shallow graves on a hill near the prison camp for friends. After years of captivity, and losing half his body weight, Cecil was told by a Japanese guard that with the continued successes of the empire, the war was nearly over. Japan was in its final push to victory over the United States. However, as the weeks passed into 1945, in the skies above the camp a sign of hope arrived, that of USN fighter planes. Clarke and his fellow POWs were forced to run for cover due to Allied fighter pilots who, mistaking them for Japanese troops, made strafing runs. While these certainly proved unpleasant, American aircraft above signaled to the prisoners that indeed the tide of the war had shifted in the Allies' favor.[10] Up until this event, with no connection to the outside world, these prisoners from

Britain, Australia, and the Dutch East Indies had no idea of the massive Allied campaign in the Pacific. In the middle of August 1945, the Japanese guards simply disappeared from the camp.

The first tangible proof of their deliverance came from the skies above. A carrier-based Avenger aircraft circled their camp and then landed at a nearby airstrip. The normal load of weapons absent, the craft ferried humanitarian aid. Medical staff from the *Block Island* quickly disembarked the craft, unloaded supplies, and sought out those prisoners in the worst condition. Then the Avenger's radial engine fired back to life and the plane returned to CVE 106 for another load of food and medical supplies. The following day, after getting their first calorie-rich meal in over three years, Cecil and his fellow prisoners were shuttled to the coast in trucks and trains. Upon their arrival at Keelung Harbor, American destroyer escorts transported them to the nearby escort carriers, USS *Block Island*, CVE 106 and USS *Santee*, CVE 29. Over four hundred human skeletons climbed on board each escort carrier.

As I interviewed USS *Block Island* veterans, while many spoke of painful experiences, very few would, or could, talk about seeing Cecil and his fellow POWs. One veteran could tell me only one line, "They were alive, but that was about it."[11] Sailor John Suprey, who as a large fifteen-year-old had had no problem signing up for the Navy underage, was by far the most physically powerful veteran I interviewed. He drove trucks before and after the war and remained a lifelong member of the Teamsters. By the 1960s he left the truck cab and served as a "business representative" for the labor union. As he lived in Dracut, Massachusetts, just outside Boston, his duties included picking up Jimmy Hoffa at Logan Airport. When I interviewed John at his kitchen table, after a number of alcoholic beverages, he spoke of all aspects of the war, including his brother being a POW in Europe, and the sinking of CVE 21. However, when I asked about the Formosa operations and the men like Cecil Clarke walking on board, he stopped talking. He waved both his arms left and right parallel to the table holding our whiskey, indicating the oral history interview was over. Contradicting his crass exterior, for a full minute he could not speak.[12]

I asked Mr. Clarke what he did in his free time on his months long trip home after three years as a POW. His reply was, "Eat."[13] In the four-month journey back to England, he put on nearly a pound a day. After transport to Manila on the carrier, he faced a slow traverse of the Pacific on a troopship to Canada's west coast, then a train ride crossing North America, and one final sea voyage to England. Back on British soil, he was again 160 pounds.[14] However, once home he confronted one last challenge, the massive number of internal migrations in Great Britain during the war years. The British Post Office, from 1939 to 1945, recorded sixty million changes of addresses in a nation of just forty million people.[15] Walking up to his mother's home in England, he knocked on the door. A stranger answered, telling him he had resided in the house for quite some time and had no contact information for his mother. Cecil found a neighbor who informed him that his mother, like many mothers, thought her son dead after hearing nothing for over three years and had moved to a new town. Luckily, he had the address, and Cecil completed the final leg of this four-year trip around the world by knocking on an unknown door for the first time and embracing his mother. He had survived hell and went on to lead a life filled with kids, grandkids, and great-grandkids.[16]

Conclusion

Void of Memory

In interviewing veterans about the sinking, on a few occasions I encountered a situation where, during the course of an interview, it seemed as if the subject should have been able to provide more information in a manner comparable to others who spoke at length. As the sinking had taken place five decades earlier and was emotionally powerful, I encountered a range of reactions to my questions, from veterans who willingly shared written recollections, to those who were extremely tightlipped about one of the most terrifying experiences of their lives. Some deferred my questions by changing the subject to a memory not related to the sinking, while others flat out told me that they were never afraid while abandoning CVE 21. Reflecting on this group, I found myself wondering if the total lack of fear that some sailors reported might be rooted in the conceptions of masculinity that they grew up with in 1930s America: perhaps their sense of manliness could not, or would not, ever allow them to admit experiencing fear, even after fifty years. Alternatively, another possible reason that some sailors reported a lack of fear, I speculated, might result from the fact that the frontal lobe of the teenage brain is not fully developed—maybe some of the younger sailors were simply unable to process the experience of abandoning ship as being dangerous.

But most perplexing to me was a near-total lack of memory about the sinking in the experience of some sailors. I first came across this phenomenon when interviewing CVE 21/106 veteran Arlie "Buster" Lapeyrolerie. He painted a very vivid picture of what occurred on board *Block Island* when the torpedoes struck. Also, he remembered in fine detail DE sailors plucking him from the oily water and specifics of the three-day ride to Casablanca. But when asked about his time in the water, he admitted he could not remember much. He continued that this was not the result of time's passing, but that even immediately after the sinking he could only remember being in the water no more than two to three minutes. Even if Buster was one of the first pulled from the Atlantic, his communal oily and chaotic experience lasted at least ninety minutes.[1]

This poses a rather philosophical question. How can a life-changing event be identified or mean something to someone who doesn't remember it at all? Seeking evidence of a void is a practice most commonly associated with astrophysics. Black holes were long impossible to detect, as nothing, not even light, can escape them; nevertheless, one can still find proof of their existence in their interactions with whatever is nearby. The same is true for historians. My clearest glimpse into this phenomenon resulted from interviewing Joe Zook, who served as the LSO in night landings on CVE 106. In his retirement community in Sun City, Arizona, Mr. Zook spoke of joining the Marine Corps as a pilot and, fearful he would miss the war, signing up for LSO training upon hearing these positions were in high demand in the Pacific. His tales of the more colorful variety included stealing a Honolulu Fire Department's fire truck with fellow marines for a Christmas Eve joy ride.

Sitting in his small residence decades later, Zook spoke of one particularly taxing experience as an LSO. He had successfully guided all but one of the returning night fighters back onto the darkened deck, but one plane remained aloft. After repeated wave-offs, CVE 106 found herself pulling farther and farther away from the neighboring task force, as she needed to cruise into the wind to complete the landing. Zook noted that most captains rarely interfered with his work, due to the pressure and specialization of the task of guiding craft flying at 150 knots onto a moving deck of an escort carrier at night. This time, however, after repeated wave-offs, with the pilot coming either too high or low, Captain Hughes broke protocol. Over the loudspeaker on the deck, the captain's booming voice bellowed for all to hear, "Zook! Get that man down!!"[2] On the next approach, the pilot was still coming in too high. Zook compensated by having the pilot cut his engine early, which did the trick. Slamming the deck hard, a bumpy but successful landing was completed.

Fast-forward twenty-five years. Zook, as a traveling salesman in 1970, was at the Cleveland Hopkins International Airport waiting for a flight to Chicago. While walking to his gate, he encountered this same Marine pilot who had experienced such difficulty landing that night. According to Zook, they reminisced about numerous aspects of the war, including both painful and joyful moments from the Pacific. They talked about their private celebration in the ready room at the end of the war, including the pilots lifting Zook into the air on their shoulders in triumph. The two men also spoke of fellow airmen who perished from their squadron. However, over the course of their coincidental encounter in Cleveland, this pilot never mentioned that specific landing that had been so difficult. I asked him, "Mr. Zook, what do you think that means?" He replied, "I don't think he remembers it."[3] Zook reflected that of the hundreds of landings he had successfully guided over the course of his career as an LSO, this particular landing was the most stressful. However, the pilot did not speak of it when they conversed about their shared war experience. Zook was sure if he had remembered this trying event, he would have brought it up. But he didn't. The pilot's nondisclosure hints at a void in memory—a memory so fearful that the human mind in an act of self-protection, in some ways mirroring a compartmentalized war vessel, places this specific memory in the fathomless subsection of the subconscious mind.

❋

Of all the escort carriers produced during the war, none survived into the 1970s, when the urge to remember World War II transformed just a fraction of the few remaining obsolete USN vessels still in existence into stationary museums. Such platforms of memory, including aircraft carriers, battleships, and destroyers, today function as ambassadors to the past for thousands of visitors. Stationary emissaries to the past, they introduce visitors not only to the individual histories of the specific vessel and sailors but also to the greater heritage of the nation-state for which they served.

This history focuses on just two escort carriers. Whatever remains of CVE 21 is scattered on the Atlantic floor. After torpedoes caused her descent into the blackness, the depth charges strapped within her hangar devoured the hull. As for CVE 106, cut up in the scrapyards in 1960, her metal was devoured by the economic miracle of postwar Japan. Thus, the alloys from thousands of archaic World War II era vessels from a host of nations were refashioned into such products as Nissan automobiles and television components. As one *Block Island* sailor said, "Every time I see a Mitsubishi or another Japanese car, I look for CVE 106 on the side of it."[4] The fate of scrappage awaited all escort carriers that survived the war, as their small size and relatively slow speed negated any career as an aircraft carrier into the 1960s. While conversion into aircraft ferries (AKV) and amphibious assault ships (LPH) added a few years of life to a handful of CVE hulls, none survived to be refitted into a ship museum.

It may seem straightforward to assume that all that remains of the escort carriers are the memories of the few sailors who are still with us. However, history has a way, from time to time, of resuscitating subjects known only to a few. In 1999 a tidal storm on a body of water called the Firth of Clyde washed ashore wooden blocks on a Scottish beach. This discovery by a beach walker was posted to an online blog. The stream of posts that followed connected the wooden blocks to the story of the escort carriers. The flotsam and jetsam produced by the Atlantic swells demonstrated that the story of the CVEs is alive and well for family members of lost sailors. These teak blocks were later confirmed to be from an Avenger-class escort carrier, of which only four were ever constructed. These particular blocks came from one of the three given to the British under Lend-Lease. HMS *Dasher*, BAVG 5, after assisting in the Allied landings in North Africa in November 1942, returned to operations in the North Atlantic. On March 27, 1943, a massive internal explosion sank the vessel in under nine minutes just off the west coast of Scotland, killing 379 out of the 528 crew members. Most of the dead were never recovered. Debate surrounded the event, as the source of the explosion is still unknown, but all evidence points to the accidental ignition of fuel fumes internally, and not the result of enemy action.[5]

For the British families who experienced the sudden loss of a loved one with the demise of *Dasher*, these teak blocks represented a tangible connection to a sixty-year-old tragedy. The sudden termination of these sailors' lives on board their escort carrier created a gaping wound for the many families who never retrieved their loved ones' mortal remains. This discovery made waves when published on the HMS *Dasher* website. This bit of local history resurfaced, and the circumstances of the sinking gained local attention with newspaper articles shedding light on the escort carrier. Additionally, one of the teak blocks from the flight deck of *Dasher* was exhibited in *Flotsam and Jetsam*, an exhibition held at the Millennium Dome in London. This public display showcased the history that continues to wash ashore on the island nation. Teak blocks from a submerged escort carrier publicly conveyed the private loss of over three hundred British families. Such events make one think of a line from William Faulkner's *Requiem for a Nun*: "The past is never dead. It's not even past."[6]

Joseph Amato once wrote, "And we learn over and over again that events surprise us. History eludes order. The explanation follows rather than precedes the happening."[7] In 1961 the FBI officer Sygmund Paradinski wrote a letter to the editor of *All Hands*. He opened with, "Sir: It seems strange that hardly anyone but those individuals directly concerned ever heard much about the sinking of USS *Block Island* (CVE 21) during World War II."[8] Paradinski followed this with a short written history of the accomplishments of the FBI crews on both the Atlantic and Pacific. The majority of the letter was devoted to the loss of CVE 21 on May 29, 1944. He and other officers were enjoying a large cake in the wardroom, marking the one thousandth landing on this mission. Then two torpedo strikes radically altered their fates. He wrote, "There was no doubt as to what that crash was—I often wondered in the quiet hours of a sea-going night what a torpedo would feel like, and now I knew. It was the way I imagined—a shattering impact that seemed to start in the very center of the vessel and shake every frame and plate in the ship until it jarred every bone in my body."[9] Once on the flight deck, he recalled, "(I) could see that our ship was beginning to open up in a sickening way about two thirds of the way down the flight deck."[10] Then, a third torpedo strike.

> I was flipped into the air like a rubber ball but as I came down I grabbed one of the arresting cables, a circumstance that probably prevented me from falling down onto one of the sponsons twenty feet below. The old command, heard so many times in drill practice, but now in deadly seriousness, came by megaphone from the bridge,

> "Prepare to abandon ship, but do not abandon." However, this was followed shortly thereafter with "Abandon ship. Abandon ship." The old warrior was now trailing around in a slow semicircle, utterly helpless and going down by the stern. . . . We all lowered ourselves down life lines into the water. . . . Up to this time we had little time to think about getting scared. But now, as we helplessly drifted around with our various floating aids, the steadily increasing chill of the water, the recurring underwater concussions that pounded our bodies from the exploding bombs and torpedoes of the sinking *Block Island*—plus the gnawing feeling that the enemy submarine or submarines were still lurking in the area and could pick off the destroyers at will—filled us with a foreboding dread. I timed the sinking of *Block Island* on my wrist watch. It took thirty-four minutes as she slowly—very slowly—sank beneath the peaceful surface of the ocean. She seemed reluctant to go and even after she disappeared from sight we heard the angry bursting of explosives whose charges were set off by the pressure of the deep.[11]

Paradinski then went on to tell that the tale of the FBI crew did not end with the sinking. The retired reserve officer wrote "that for the discerning eye the words *Fighting Block Island*, can now be found on the pages of history that delineate the long and bloody campaign of Okinawa, the capture of Borneo and the Celebes, the evacuation of prisoners of war from Formosa, and activities of its all-Marine bomber and fighter groups."[12]

The piece in *All Hands* concluded with a remark from the editor: "Thanks. We wish we could receive more letters like this one. They really add to our knowledge of the Navy."[13]

Notes

Introduction

1. Joe Booi, interview by author, digital recording, San Antonio, Texas, May 30, 2006.

2. CO CVE 21, F. M. Hughes, to COMINCH, E. J. King, *Action Report of Commanding Officer, U.S.S. Block Island concerning the Loss by Enemy Action of That Vessel on 29 May 1944*, 30 June 1944, WW II Action and Operations Reports (A&ORs), Records Relating to Naval Activity during WW II (Box 854), Records of the Office of the CNO (RG 38), National Archives Building, College Park, Maryland (NACP), 2.

3. Booi, interview by author.

4. CO CVE 21, F. M. Hughes, to COMINCH, E. J. King, *Action Report of Commanding Officer, U.S.S. Block Island concerning the Loss by Enemy Action of That Vessel on 29 May 1944*, 30 June 1944, A&ORs WW II (Box 854), RG 38, NACP, 6.

5. Booi, interview by author.

6. Booi, interview by author.

7. Booi, interview by author.

8. Hector Vernetti, interview by author, digital recording, Tempe, Arizona, October 15, 2009.

9. Thomas C. Hone, Norman Friedman, and Mark D. Mandeles, *American and British Aircraft Carrier Development: 1919–1941* (Annapolis: Naval Institute Press, 1999), 131.

10. W. J. R. Gardner, *Decoding History: The Battle of the Atlantic and Ultra* (Annapolis: Naval Institute Press, 1999), 13.

11. USS Block Island Association, "The Story of Two Block Island Escort Carriers," April 3, 2018, http://www.ussblockisland.org.

12. Chester Wentworth, interview by author, digital recording, Natick, Massachusetts, December 4, 2006.

Chapter 1

1. In addition to the *Intrepid*, these four other museums preserve the USS *Midway*, CV 41, USS *Hornet*, CV 12, USS *Yorktown*, CV 10, and USS *Lexington*, CV 16.

2. *Intrepid* Sea, Air & Space Museum Complex, "Exhibits," June 7, 2018, https://www.intrepidmuseum.org.

3. Stephen Pyne, *Voyager: Seeking Newer Worlds in the Third Great Age of Discovery* (New York: Viking Press, 2010), 166.

Chapter 2

1. C. Bradford Mitchell, *Every Kind of Shipwork: A History of Todd Shipyards Corporation, 1916–1981* (New York: Todd Shipyards, 1981), 137–39.

2. Jim Noles, *Twenty-Three Minutes to Eternity: The Final Voyage of the Escort Carrier USS* Liscome Bay (Tuscaloosa: University of Alabama Press, 2004), 4.

3. Noles, *Twenty-Three Minutes to Eternity*, 4.

4. Samuel Eliot Morison, *The Two-Ocean War: A Short History of the United States Navy in the Second World War* (Boston: Little, Brown, 1963), 583.

5. Noles, *Twenty-Three Minutes to Eternity*, 4–5.

6. Mark Stille, *US Navy Escort Carriers, 1942–45* (Oxford: Osprey, 2018), Kindle edition, 682–729.

7. Stille, *US Navy Escort Carriers*, 750.

8. *Dictionary of American Naval Fighting Ships, Vol. I* (Washington, DC: Navy Department, 1959), 131.

9. Alvin Kernan, *Crossing the Line: A Bluejacket's World War II Odyssey* (Annapolis: Naval Institute Press, 1994), 83, 84, 133.

10. Kernan, *Crossing the Line*, 83.

11. Kernan, *Crossing the Line*, 83.

12. F. D. Ommanney, *Flat-Top: The Story of an Escort Carrier* (New York: Longmans, Green, 1945), 7.

13. Ommanney, *Flat-Top: The Story of an Escort Carrier*, 7.

14. Charles Herbert Read Jr., *Memoirs of the Flight Surgeon of HMS Nabob* (Coaldale, Alberta: Lammi, 2018), Kindle edition, 215–16.

15. Walter Cyr, interview by author, digital recording, Natick, Massachusetts, December 3, 2006.

16. William T. Y'Blood, *The Little Giants: U.S. Escort Carriers against Japan* (Annapolis Naval Institute Press, 1987), vii–viii.

17. Y'Blood, *Little Giants*, vii.

18. Noles, *Twenty-Three Minutes to Eternity*, 7.

19. Noles, *Twenty-Three Minutes to Eternity*, 113.

20. Noles, *Twenty-Three Minutes to Eternity*, 116.

Chapter 3

1. Mark Stille, *US Navy Escort Carriers, 1942–45* (Oxford: Osprey, 2018), Kindle edition, 977.

2. Jim Noles, *Twenty-Three Minutes to Eternity: The Final Voyage of the Escort Carrier USS* Liscome Bay (Tuscaloosa: University of Alabama Press, 2004), 58–59.

3. Barrett Tillman, *On Wave and Wing: The 100-Year Quest to Perfect the Aircraft Carrier* (Washington, DC: Regnery History, 2017), Kindle edition, 65.

4. Tillman, *On Wave and Wing*, 65.

5. Denny Moller, interview by author, digital recording, New Orleans, Louisiana, May 28, 2010.

6. R. Bruce Porter, with Eric Hammel, *Ace! A Marine Night-Fighter Pilot in World War II* (New York: Berkley, 1987), 259.

7. Stefan Terzibaschitsch, *Escort Carriers and Aviation Support Ships of the U.S. Navy* (New York: Rutledge Press, 1981), 20.

8. Terzibaschitsch, *Escort Carriers and Aviation Support Ships of the U.S. Navy*, 20.

9. The U.S. Navy first classified these vessels as auxiliary aircraft escort vessels (AVG), which then changed to auxiliary aircraft carrier (ACV). This narrative uses the final designation of escort carrier (CVE) throughout the work for the sake of simplicity.

10. Naval History and Heritage Command, "U.S. Navy Active Ship Force Levels, 1886–present," http://www.history.navy.mil; June 29, 2011.

11. Lewis Mumford, *Technics and Civilization* (Boston: Harcourt, Brace, 1934), 209.

12. Mumford, *Technics and Civilization*, 209.

13. Tillman, *On Wave and Wing*, 65.

14. Roger Chesneau, *Aircraft Carriers of the World, 1914 to the Present* (Annapolis: Naval Institute Press, 1984), 216.

Chapter 4

1. Personal letter from Logan C. Ramsey to Mr. J. Carroll Cone, 16 February 1943, Logan C. Ramsey Papers COLL/307 (LCRP), Box 4, Folder 2 Correspondence: Official and Personal, Building 57, Archives Branch (AB), Naval History and Heritage Command (NHHC), Washington, DC.

2. *Hearings before the Joint Committee on the Investigation of the Pearl Harbor Attack* (Washington, DC: US Government Printing Office, 1946), Part 32, 444.

3. Lieutenant Commander Logan C. Ramsey, "Aerial Attacks on Fleets at Anchor," *Proceedings* 63-8-414 (August 1937): 1127.

4. Ramsey, "Aerial Attacks on Fleets at Anchor," 1127.

5. Ramsey, "Aerial Attacks on Fleets at Anchor," 1128.

6. Ramsey, "Aerial Attacks on Fleets at Anchor," 1128–29.

7. Francis Massie Hughes Jr, interview by author, digital recording, New Orleans, Louisiana, May 27, 2011.

8. Captain James Ogden, "Airborne at Pearl," *Proceedings Magazine*, Summer 1993, series 119–12–1090.

9. *Appendix D: Biographical Sketch of Captain Francis Massie Hughes, U.S.N., U.S. Navy* from *USS Block Island (CVE 106) Unit History from Commissioning, 30 December 1944 to V-J, 2 September 1945*, Aviation Commands 1941–1952, Box 154, Folder 8, Building 200, Archival Branch (AB), Naval History & Heritage Command (NHHC), Washington, DC, 2.

10. Ogden, "Airborne at Pearl," 62.

11. Ogden, "Airborne at Pearl," 62.

12. Ogden, "Airborne at Pearl," 62.

13. Ogden, "Airborne at Pearl," 62.

14. Ogden, "Airborne at Pearl," 62.

15. Mary Anne Ramsey, "Only Yesteryear," *Naval History*, Winter 1991, 26.

16. Geoffrey C. Ward, *The War: An Intimate History, 1941–1945* (New York: Alfred A. Knopf, 2007), 1–5.

17. Jim Noles, *Twenty-Three Minutes to Eternity: The Final Voyage of the Escort Carrier USS* Liscome Bay (Tuscaloosa: University of Alabama Press, 2004), 3.

18. John T. Kuehn, *Agents of Innovation: The General Board and the Design of the Fleet That Defeated the Japanese Navy* (Annapolis: Naval Institute Press, 2008), 60.

19. Roger Chesneau, *Aircraft Carriers of the World, 1914 to the Present* (Annapolis: Naval Institute Press, 1984), 206.

20. Samuel Eliot Morison, *The Two-Ocean War: A Short History of the United States Navy in the Second World War* (Boston: Little, Brown, 1963), 5.

21. Ward, *War: An Intimate History*, 5, 13.

22. CVE 8 was commissioned as USS *Block Island* on January 11, 1943. This vessel was never manned by US Navy personnel, as a result of being transferred to the Royal Navy under Lend-Lease. Here she served as HMS *Hunter* (D 80).

23. Morison, *Two-Ocean War*, 109.

24. Michael Gannon, *Operation Drumbeat: The Dramatic True Story of Germany's First U-Boat Attacks along the American Coast in World War II* (New York: Harper and Row, 1990), 176.

25. Morison, *Two-Ocean War*, 109.

26. William T. Y'Blood, *Hunter-Killer: U.S. Escort Carriers in the Battle of the Atlantic.* (Annapolis: Naval Institute Press, 1983), 5–6.

27. Ward, *War: An Intimate History*, 22.

28. Gannon, *Operation Drumbeat*, 343.

29. Gannon, *Operation Drumbeat*, 389.

Chapter 5

1. Walter Cyr, interview by author, digital recording, Natick, Massachusetts, December 3, 2006.

2. Benjamin Hruska, "A Small Vessel in a Big War," *Block Island Times*, May 24, 2014, 5–6.

3. Samuel Hynes, *Flights of Passage: Reflections of a World War II Aviator* (Annapolis: Naval Institute Press, 1988), 15.

4. Emory J. Jernigan, *Tin Can Man* (Arlington, VA: Vandamere Press, 1993), 19.

5. Jernigan, *Tin Can Man*, 19.

6. Chester Wentworth, interview by author, digital recording, Natick, Massachusetts, December 4, 2006.

7. Ronald H. Spector, *Eagle against the Sun: The American War with Japan* (New York: Vintage Books, 1985), 537.

8. Alvin Kernan, *Crossing the Line: A Bluejacket's World War II Odyssey* (Annapolis: Naval Institute Press, 1994), 11.

9. Joe Booi, interview by author, digital recording, San Antonio, Texas, May 30, 2006.

10. Jernigan, *Tin Can Man*, 19.

11. Floyd Beaver, *Sailor from Oklahoma: One Man's Two-Ocean War* (Annapolis: Naval Institute Press, 2009), 19–20.

12. National Institutes of Health, poster, US National Library of Medicine, Digital Collections, https://collections.nlm.nih.gov/catalog/nlm:nlmuid-101584655X24-img; Beaver, *Sailor from Oklahoma*, 17, 22.

13. Kernan, *Crossing the Line*, 15.

14. Beaver, *Sailor from Oklahoma*, 17, 20–21.

15. Kernan, *Crossing the Line*, xiii.

16. Spector, *At War at Sea: Sailors and Naval Combat in the Twentieth Century* (New York: Penguin Books, 2001), 145.

17. Thomas C. Hone, Norman Friedman, and Mark D. Mandeles, *American and British Aircraft Carrier Development: 1919–1941* (Annapolis: Naval Institute Press, 1999), 24, 25.

18. Hone, Friedman, and Mandeles, *American and British Aircraft Carrier Development*, 62.

19. Scot MacDonald, "Evolution of Aircraft Carriers: Last of the Fleet Problems," *Naval Aviation News*, September 1962, 37.

20. CO Scouting Plane Squadron Ten, USS *Chicago* to CO Western Force, *Operation Order 1–35*, 28 April 1935, Logan C. Ramsey Papers COLL/307 (LCRP), Box 4, Folder 8, Building 57, Archives Branch (AB), Naval History and Heritage Command (NHHC), Washington, DC, 1.

21. Craig C. Felker, *Testing American Sea Power: U.S. Navy Strategic Exercises, 1923–1940* (College Station: Texas A&M Press, 2007), Kindle edition, 62.

22. Personal letter from Capt. E. J. King to Lieut. Logan C. Ramsey, 7 November 1931, Logan C. Ramsey Papers COLL/307 (LCRP), Box 4, Folder 2 Correspondence: Official and Personal, Building 57, Archives Branch (AB), Naval History and Heritage Command (NHHC), Washington, DC.

23. Felker, *Testing American Sea Power*, 74.

24. Felker, *Testing American Sea Power*, 489.

25. Felker, *Testing American Sea Power*, 1722.

26. Lieutenant Commander Logan C. Ramsey, "The Influence of Aircraft on the Exercise of Sea Command," *Proceedings* 64-10-428 (October 1938): 1406.

Chapter 6

1. Mark Harris, *Five Came Back: A Story of Hollywood and the Second World War* (New York: Penguin Books, 2014), Kindle edition, 152.

2. Harris, *Five Came Back*, 152.

3. Harris, *Five Came Back*, 152.

4. Harris, *Five Came Back*, 172–73.

5. *Battle of Midway*, dir. John Ford (1942; Los Angeles, CA: 20th Century Fox, 2002), DVD.

6. *Chips off the Old Block: Block Island Celebrates Anniversary*, Vol. 1, No. 18, March 8, 1944, Logan C. Ramsey Papers COLL/307 (LCRP), Box 4, Building 57, Archives Branch (AB), Naval History & Heritage Command (NHHC), Washington, DC, 1.

7. *Battle of Midway*, dir. John Ford.

8. *Lucky Bag* (Annapolis: United States Naval Academy, 1919), 247.

9. Walter Lord, *Incredible Victory* (New York: Harper and Row, 1967), 52.

10. Naval History and Heritage Command, "Biographical Essay Attached to the Logan C. Ramsey Papers," July 11, 2018, https://www.history.navy.mil.

11. Thomas C. Hone, Norman Friedman, and Mark D. Mandeles, *American and British Aircraft Carrier Development: 1919–1941* (Annapolis: Naval Institute Press, 1999), 196.

12. Lieutenant Logan C. Ramsey, "Hydrographic Surveying with Aircraft," *Proceedings* 53–7–293 (July 1927): 780.

13. Ramsey, "Hydrographic Surveying with Aircraft," *Proceedings*, 780.

14. "The Defensive Value of the Plane," editorial, *New York Herald Tribune*, August 1, 1930, 12.

15. Naval History and Heritage Command, "Biographical Essay Attached to the Logan C. Ramsey Papers."

16. Gordon W. Prange, *Miracle at Midway* (New York: McGraw-Hill, 1982), 117.

17. Naval History and Heritage Command, "Biographical Essay attached to the Logan C. Ramsey Papers."

18. Prange, *Miracle at Midway*, 118.

19. Prange, *Miracle at Midway*, 118.

20. Prange, *Miracle at Midway*, 121.

21. *Lucky Bag*, 145.

22. *Appendix D: Biographical Sketch of Captain Francis Massie Hughes, U.S.N., U.S. Navy* from *USS Block Island (CVE 106) Unit History from Commissioning, 30 December 1944 to V-J, 2 September 1945*, AC, Box 154, AB, NHHC, 1.

23. Naval History and Heritage Command, "Sports in the Navy: 1775 to 1963," January 20, 2019, https://www.history.navy.mil.

24. *Appendix D: Biographical Sketch of Captain Francis Massie Hughes, U.S.N., U.S. Navy* from *USS Block Island (CVE 106) Unit History from Commissioning, 30 December 1944 to V-J, 2 September 1945*, AC, Box 154, AB, NHHC, 1.

25. USS Block Island Association, "CVE 106 Officers & Crew," accessed July 15, 2018, http://www.ussblockisland.org.

26. "What's in a Name? Massie Hughes Drive in Norfolk," *Virginian-Pilot*, July 15, 2018, https://pilotonline.com.

27. "F. Massie Hughes, Rear Admiral, 61," *New York Times*, December 24, 1960, 15.

28. Naval History and Heritage Command [NHHC], "Recollections of Commander John Ford, USNR, Adapted from Commander John Ford USNR interview in box 10 of World War II Interviews," Archives, December 8, 2018, https://www.history.navy.mil.

29. NHHC, "Recollections of Commander John Ford."

30. NHHC, "Recollections of Commander John Ford."

31. Personal letter from Logan C. Ramsey to Mr. J. Carroll Cone, 16 February 1943, LCRP, Box 4, AB, NHHC.

32. Personal letter, Ramsey to Cone, NHHC.

33. Personal letter, Ramsey to Cone, NHHC.

34. Cmdr. Naval Base Air Defense, P. N. L. Bellinger, to Commander-in-Chief, U.S. Pacific Fleet, *Commander Logan C. Ramsey, U.S. Navy—Recommendation for Promotion*

to Captain, 8 June 1944, Logan C. Ramsey Papers COLL/307 (LCRP), Box 4, Folder 5, Building 57, Archives Branch (AB), Naval History and Heritage Command (NHHC), Washington, DC.

Chapter 7

1. Personal letter from Logan C. Ramsey to Capt. T. P. Jeter, U.S. Navy, 16 January 1943, Logan C. Ramsey Papers COLL/307 (LCRP), Box 4, Folder 2 Correspondence: Official and Personal, Building 57, Archives Branch (AB), Naval History & Heritage Command (NHHC), Washington, DC.

2. Roy Swift, *The Fighting Block Island!*, personal memoir Ships History–Decommissioned–Prior to 1 Jan 2001 (SHD), Block Island (CVE 21) Block Island (CVE 106), Box 107, Folder 1, Building 200, Archival Branch (AB), Naval History and Heritage Command (NHHC), Washington, DC, 1, 4.

3. "Stories about Chaplain, Lt. G. A. MacInnes USNR: Who Served on Both the USS *Block Island* Ships," Folder 21, Box 1, USS Block Island Association (USSBIA), San Diego, California.

4. F. D. Ommanney, *Flat-Top: The Story of an Escort Carrier* (New York: Longmans, Green, 1945), 8.

5. Ommanney, *Flat-Top: The Story of an Escort Carrier*, 9.

6. Floyd Beaver, *Sailor from Oklahoma: One Man's Two-Ocean War* (Annapolis: Naval Institute Press, 2009), 122, 160.

7. *Excerpts from Captain Ramsey Talk*, date unknown, Aviation Commands (AC) 1941–1952, Box 107, Folder 4, Archival Branch (AB), Naval History and Heritage Command (NHHC), Washington, DC, 4.

8. *Excerpts from Captain Ramsey Talk*, NHHC, 2–3.

9. Theodore Roscoe, *United States Destroyer Operations in World War II* (Annapolis: United States Naval Institute, 1953), 287.

10. Denny Moller, interview by author, digital recording, New Orleans, Louisiana, May 28, 2010.

11. "Newton's Third Law," National Aeronautics and Space Administration, June 1, 2018https://www.grc.nasa.gov.

12. Ernie Pyle, *Last Chapter* (New York: Henry Holt, 1946), 57.

13. Pyle, *Last Chapter*, 62.

14. Pyle, *Last Chapter*, 63.

15. Andrew Faltum, *The Independence Light Aircraft Carriers* (Charleston, SC: Nautical & Aviation Publishing Company of America, 2002), 117.

16. "Knickerbocker Bean Soup," *Cook Book of the United States Navy*, ed. 1944; February 28, 2011, http://www.ibiblio.org.

17. Barrett Tillman, *Enterprise: America's Fightingest Ship and the Men Who Helped Win World War II* (New York: Simon and Schuster, 2012), 254.

18. Public Data Section, U.S. Navy, *Composite History of USS Block Island (CVE-21) and USS Block Island (CVE-106)* (Navy Department: Office of Public Relations, 1948),

Ships History–Decommissioned–Prior to 1 Jan 2001 (SHD), Block Island (CVE 21) Block Island (106), Box 107, Folder 1, Building 200, Archival Branch (AB), Naval History and Heritage Command (NHHC), Washington, DC, 1.

19. Night Order Book, Capt. Logan Ramsey, Logan C. Ramsey Papers COLL/307 (LCRP), Box 2, Folder 23, Building 57, Archives Branch (AB), Naval History and Heritage Command (NHHC), Washington, DC.

20. Night Order Book, Capt. Logan Ramsey, NHHC.

21. *Chips Off the Old Block*, Vol. 3, 1996, 5. Quarterly newsletter of the USS Block Island Association [hereafter cited as *Chips*], Folder 1996, Box 1, USSBIA.

22. *Chips*, Vol. 3, 2009, 8. Folder 2009, Box 1, USSBIA.

23. Night Order Book, Capt. Logan Ramsey, 3–4 April 1943, LCRP, Box 2, Folder 23 Building 57, AB, NHHC.

24. J. Bryan III, *Aircraft Carrier: What It Was Really Like on the Giant* Yorktown *in the Pacific War* (New York: Ballantine Books, 1954), 32.

25. *Chips*, Vol. 1, 2004, 9. Folder 2004, Box 1, USSBIA.

26. Bryan, *Aircraft Carrier*, 32.

27. Bryan, *Aircraft Carrier*, 32.

28. Swift, *Fighting Block Island!*, SHD, Box 107, AB, NHHC, 6.

29. CO CVE 21, L. C. Ramsey, to Mary Ann Ramsey, personal letter dated 3 May 1943, Logan C. Ramsey Papers COLL/307 (LCRP), Box 2, Folder 12, Building 57, Archives Branch (AB), Naval History and Heritage Command (NHHC), Washington, DC, 1.

30. Capt. Logan Ramsey, to John Ford, personal letter dated 3 May 1943, The John Ford Papers, Correspondence Box 1, Lilly Library Special Collection, Indiana University, Bloomington, Indiana.

31. *USS Block Island, War Diary, May 1943*, Reel A-426, transcribed by J. B. Jennings, 15 June 1944, AC, AB, NHHC, 1.

32. Swift, *Fighting Block Island!*, SHD, Box 107, AB, NHHC, 6.

33. *Chips*, Vol. 1, 2011, 5. Folder 2011, Box 1, USSBIA.

34. Nick Norwood, ed., *Buz Sawyer: The War in the Pacific, Vol.1* (Seattle: Fantagraphic Books, 2011), 23–35.

35. Irv Biron, interview by author, digital recording, San Antonio, Texas, June 3, 2005.

36. Jeb Turner, "Remembering CVE 21," *Chips*, Vol. 1, 2012, 13. Folder 2012, Box 1, USSBIA.

37. *USS Block Island, War Diary, June 1943*, Reel A-426, transcribed by J. B. Jennings, 15 June 1944, AC, AB, NHHC, 1.

38. Samuel Eliot Morison, *History of United States Naval Operations in World War II*, vol. 10 of *The Atlantic Battle Won, May 1943–May 1945* (Boston: Little, Brown, 1956), 80–81.

39. Emory J. Jernigan, *Tin Can Man* (Arlington, VA: Vandamere Press, 1993), 28.

40. Jernigan, *Tin Can Man*, 29.

41. Glenn A. Knoblock, *Black Submariners in the United States Navy, 1940–1975* (Jefferson, NC: McFarland, 2005), 24.

Chapter 8

1. Samuel Eliot Morison, *History of the United States Naval Operations in World War II* vol. 1, *The Battle of the Atlantic, September 1939–1943* (Boston: Little, Brown, 1947), xi.

2. Morison, *History of the United States Naval Operations in World War II,* 1:xi.

3. W. J. R. Gardner, *Decoding History: The Battle of the Atlantic and Ultra* (Annapolis: Naval Institute Press, 1999), ix.

4. Gardner, *Decoding History*, 13, 22, 91.

5. Ronald H. Spector, *Eagle against the Sun: The American War with Japan* (New York: Vintage Books, 1985), 256.

6. Captain Logan C. Ramsey, "The Aero-Amphibious Phase of the Present War," *Proceedings* 69–5–483 (May 1943): 695.

7. Ramsey, "Aero-Amphibious Phase of the Present War," 696.

8. Ramsey, "Aero-Amphibious Phase of the Present War," 696.

9. Ramsey, "Aero-Amphibious Phase of the Present War," 697.

10. Ramsey, "Aero-Amphibious Phase of the Present War," 699.

11. Geoffrey L. Rossano and Thomas Wildenberg, *Striking the Hornets' Nest: Naval Aviation and the Origins of Strategic Bombing in World War I* (Annapolis: Naval Institute Press, 2015), 26.

12. Ramsey, "Aero-Amphibious Phase of the Present War," 699.

13. Morison, *History of the United States Naval Operations in World War II,* 1:xi.

14. Kathleen Broome Williams, *Secret Weapon: U.S. High-Frequency Direction Finding in the Battle of the Atlantic* (Annapolis: Naval Institute Press, 1996), xviii.

15. David Syrett, *The Defeat of the German U-Boats: The Battle of the Atlantic* (Columbia: University of South Carolina Press, 1994), ix–x.

16. Karl Dönitz, *Memoirs: Ten Years and Twenty Days* (Annapolis: Naval Institute Press, 1990), 228.

17. Syrett, *Defeat of the German U-Boats,* ix.

18. *USS Block Island, War Diary, August 1943*, Reel A-426, transcribed by J. B. Jennings, 15 June 1944, AC, AB NHHC, 1.

19. Roy Swift, *The Fighting Block Island!*, personal memoir, Ships History–Decommissioned–Prior to 1 Jan 2001 (SHD), Block Island (CVE 21) Block Island (CVE 106), Box 107, Folder 1, Building 200, Archival Branch (AB), Naval History and Heritage Command (NHHC), Washington, DC, 8.

20. *USS Block Island, War Diary, August 1943*, Reel A-426, transcribed by J. B. Jennings, 15 June 1944, AC, AB, NHHC, 1.

21. The Roosevelt Hotel, "The Story of the Roosevelt Hotel NYC," May 5, 2018, http://www.theroosevelthotel.com.

22. "The History and Words of Auld Land Syne," Scotland Is Now, January 24, 2019, https://www.scotland.org.

23. Swift, *Fighting Block Island!*, SHD, Box 107, AB, NHHC, 7.

24. Emory J. Jernigan, *Tin Can Man* (Arlington, VA: Vandamere Press, 1993), 34.

25. Hector Vernetti, interview by author, digital recording, Tempe, Arizona, October 15, 2009.

26. Vernetti, interview by author.

27. *USS Block Island, War Diary, August 1943*, Reel A-426, transcribed by J. B. Jennings, 15 June 1944, AC, AB, NHHC, 1.

28. William C. Cline, *In the Nick of Time: Motion Picture Sound Serials* (Jefferson, NC: McFarland, 1984), 92.

29. Swift, *Fighting Block Island!*, SHD, Box 107, AB, NHHC, 5.

30. Timothy S. Wolters, *Information at Sea: Shipboard Command and Control in the U.S. Navy from Mobile Bay to Okinawa* (Baltimore: Johns Hopkins University Press, 2013), 183.

31. Samuel Eliot Morison, *The Two-Ocean War: A Short History of the United States Navy in the Second World War* (Boston: Little, Brown, 1963), 37.

32. Morison, *Two-Ocean War*, 241.

33. *USS Block Island, War Diary, August 1943*, Reel A-426, transcribed by J. B. Jennings, 15 June 1944, AC, AB, NHHC, 1.

34. Vernetti, interview by author.

35. Louis Harlan, *All at Sea: Coming of Age in World War II* (Urbana: University of Chicago Press, 1996), 34.

36. Bill Connolly, interview by author, digital recording, Natick, Massachusetts, December 3, 2006.

37. *USS Block Island, War Diary, September 1943*, Reel A-426, transcribed by J. B. Jennings, 15 June 1944, AC, AB, NHHC, 1.

Chapter 9

1. Norman Polmar, *Aircraft Carriers: A Graphic History of Carrier Aviation and Its Influence on World Events* (New York: Doubleday, 1969), 136–40.

2. John Norris, "Aircraft Carrier Is Navy's New Queen of the Seas," *Washington Post*, May 24, 1942, B1.

3. Norris, "Aircraft Carrier Is Navy's New Queen of the Seas," B1.

4. Norris, "Aircraft Carrier Is Navy's New Queen of the Seas," B1.

5. Norris, "Aircraft Carrier Is Navy's New Queen of the Seas," B1.

6. Norris, "Aircraft Carrier Is Navy's New Queen of the Seas," B1.

7. John G. Norris, "U.S. Navy Bombards Kiska Forts Again," *Washington Post*, July 11, 1943, M8.

8. Norris, "U.S. Navy Bombards Kiska Forts Again," *Washington Post*, M8.

9. Samuel Eliot Morison, *The Two-Ocean War: A Short History of the United States Navy in the Second World War* (Boston: Little, Brown, 1963), 586.

10. Ronald H. Spector, *Eagle against the Sun: The American War with Japan* (New York: Vintage Books, 1985), 100.

11. "Stories about Chaplain, Lt. G. A. MacInnes USNR: Who Served on Both the USS *Block Island* Ships," Folder 21, Box 1, USSBIA.

12.Irv Biron, interview by author, digital recording, San Antonio, Texas, June 3, 2006.

13. Morison, *Two-Ocean War*, 240.

14. *USS Block Island, War Diary, October 1943*, Reel A-426, transcribed by J. B. Jennings, 15 June 1944, AC, AB, NHHC, 3.

15. Theodore Roscoe, *United States Destroyer Operations in World War II* (Annapolis: United States Naval Institute, 1953), 287.

16. Roscoe, *United States Destroyer Operations in World War II*, 287.

17. Morison, *Two-Ocean War*, 366.

18. *Excerpts from Captain Ramsey Talk*, date unknown, AC, Box 107, Folder 4, AB, NHHC, 2.

19. CO VC-1, R. A. Beveridge, to CO CVE 21, L. C. Ramsey, *Comments and Observations of VC-1 While Embarked in U.S.S. Block Island, 14 October–25 November 1943*, 23 November 1943, Logan C. Ramsey Papers COLL/307 (LCRP), Box 4, Folder 3, Building 57, Archives Branch (AB), Naval History and Heritage Command (NHHC), Washington, DC, 2.

20. Alvin Kernan, *Crossing the Line: A Bluejacket's World War II Odyssey* (Annapolis: Naval Institute Press, 1994), 24.

21. Samuel Hynes, *Flights of Passage: Reflections of a World War II Aviator* (Annapolis: Naval Institute Press, 1988), 113.

22. Floyd Beaver, *Sailor from Oklahoma: One Man's Two-Ocean War* (Annapolis: Naval Institute Press, 2009), 31–32.

23. CO VC-1, R. A. Beveridge, to CO CVE 21, L. C. Ramsey, *Comments and Observations of VC-1 While Embarked in U.S.S. Block Island, 14 October–25 November 1943*, 23 November 1943, LCRP, AB, NHHC, 2.

24. J. Bryan III, *Aircraft Carrier: What It Was Really Like on the Giant* Yorktown *in the Pacific War* (New York: Ballantine Books, 1954), 7.

25. Roy Swift, *The Fighting Block Island!*, personal memoir, Ships History–Decommissioned–Prior to 1 Jan 2001 (SHD), Block Island (CVE 21) Block Island (CVE 106), Box 107, Folder 1, Building 200, Archival Branch (AB), Naval History and Heritage Command (NHHC), Washington, DC, 8–9.

26. Hector Vernetti, interview by author, digital recording, Tempe, Arizona, October 15, 2009.

27. Vice Chief of Naval Operations, F. J. Horne to Secretary of the Navy, William Franklin Knox, *Board of Investigation—Collision between the U.S.S. BLACK (DD666) and the U.S.S. BLOCK ISLAND (CVE21): Convened by COTCLANT, 2 Oct. 1943*, 25 March 1944, Logan C. Ramsey Papers COLL/307 (LCRP), Box 5, Folder 1, Building 57, Archives Branch (AB), Naval History and Heritage Command (NHHC), Washington, DC, 1–2.

28. Melville Bell Grosvenor, "Cruise on an Escort Carrier," *National Geographic Magazine*, November 1943, 513.

29. Grosvenor, "Cruise on an Escort Carrier," 513.

30. William T. Y'Blood, *Hunter-Killer: U.S. Escort Carriers in the Battle of the Atlantic* (Annapolis: Naval Institute Press, 1983), 82.

31. Y'Blood, *Hunter-Killer*, 82.

32. Kathleen Broome Williams, *Secret Weapon: U.S. High-Frequency Direction Finding in the Battle of the Atlantic* (Annapolis: Naval Institute Press, 1996), 51.

CHAPTER 10

1. Keith A. Lewis, "The Old Man" (unpublished memoir in the author's possession), 10.

2. John R. Lewis, "Captain Lewis Remembers . . .," *Block Island Times*, June 19, 1993, 20–21.

3. Lewis, "Captain Lewis Remembers . . .," 20–21.

4. Lewis, "Captain Lewis Remembers . . .," 20–21.

5. Michael Gannon, *Operation Drumbeat: The Dramatic True Story of Germany's First U-boat Attacks along the American Coast in World War II* (New York: Harper & Row, 1990), 348.

6. Gannon, *Operation Drumbeat*, 348.

7. Commander Logan C. Ramsey, "Air Power Is Sea Power," *Proceedings* 67-7-461 (July 1941): 925.

8. *Annex A—Analysis of Night Action, October 25* from CO CVE 21 L. Ramsey to The Commander-in-Chief, United States Atlantic Fleet, *Report on Anti-Submarine and Convoy Escort Operations by Task Group 21.16—October 15 to November 25, 1943*, Logan C. Ramsey Papers COLL/307 (LCRP), Box 3, Folder 18, Building 57, Archives Branch (AB) Naval History and Heritage Command (NHHC), Washington, DC, 1–3.

9. *Annex A—Analysis of Night Action, October 25* from CO CVE 21 L. Ramsey to The Commander-in-Chief, LCRP, 3.

10. Appendix One to Task Group 21/16 Communication Plan, no date provided, Logan C. Ramsey Papers COLL/307 (LCRP), Box 3, Folder 6, Building 57, Archives Branch (AB), Naval History & Heritage Command (NHHC), Washington, DC, 1–3.

11. Appendix One to Task Group 21/16 Communication Plan, LCRP, 1–3.

12. *Annex A—Analysis of Night Action*, October 25 from CO CVE 21 L. Ramsey to The Commander-in-Chief, United States Atlantic Fleet, LCRP, 2.

13. John F. White, *The Milk Cows: The U-Boat Tankers at War, 1941–1945* (Barnsley, UK: Pen and Sword Books, 2009), 197.

14. Joe Booi, interview by author, digital recording, San Antonio, Texas, May 30, 2006.

15. Clifford Shaw, his experience in World War II, as told in his own words, interviewed by Brad Hoopes, digital recording, Northern Veterans History Project, Colorado State University Libraries, 2018–01–11T15:43:12Z.

16. Shaw, his experience in World War II, as told in his own words, interviewed by Brad Hoopes.

17. Shaw, his experience in World War II, as told in his own words, interviewed by Brad Hoopes.

18. *Annex C—Search Plans Used* from CO CVE 21 L. Ramsey to The Commander-in-Chief, United States Atlantic Fleet, *Report on Anti-Submarine and Convoy Escort Operations by Task Group 21.16—October 15 to November 25, 1943*, Logan C. Ramsey Papers COLL/307 (LCRP), Box 3, Folder 18, Building 57, Archives Branch (AB), Naval History and Heritage Command (NHHC), Washington, DC, 2.

19. CO CVE 21 L. Ramsey to The Commander-in-Chief, United States Atlantic Fleet, *Report on Anti-Submarine and Convoy Escort Operations by Task Group 21.16—October 15 to November 25, 1943*, Logan C. Ramsey Papers COLL/307 (LCRP), Box 3, Folder 18, Building 57, Archives Branch (AB), Naval History and Heritage Command (NHHC), Washington, DC, 4.

20. Roy Swift, *The Fighting Block Island!*, personal memoir, Ships History–Decommissioned–Prior to 1 Jan 2001 (SHD), Block Island (CVE 21) Block Island (CVE 106), Box 107, Folder 1, Building 200, Archival Branch (AB), Naval History and Heritage Command (NHHC), Washington, DC, 11.

21. *USS Block Island, War Diary, October 1943*, Reel A-692, transcribed by J. B. Jennings, 15 June 1944, Aviation Commands 1941–1952, Box 107, Archival Branch, Naval History and Heritage Command (NHHC) Washington, DC, 5.

22. White, *Milk Cows*, 197.

23. *Chips*, Vol. 1, 2004, 11. Folder 2004, Box 1, USSBIA.

24. *Chips*, Vol. 3, 2008, 7. Folder 2008, Box 1, USSBIA.

25. William T. Y'Blood, *Hunter-Killer: U.S. Escort Carriers in the Battle of the Atlantic* (Annapolis: Naval Institute Press, 1983), 110.

26. *Annex B—Notes on Enemy Intelligence* from CO CVE 21 L. Ramsey to The Commander-in-Chief, United States Atlantic Fleet, *Report on Anti-Submarine and Convoy Escort Operations by Task Group 21.16—October 15 to November 25, 1943*, Logan C. Ramsey Papers COLL/307 (LCRP), Box 3, Folder 18, Building 57, Archives Branch (AB), Naval History and Heritage Command (NHHC), Washington, DC, 1–3.

Chapter 11

1. *USS Block Island, War Diary, November 1943*, Reel A-726, transcribed by J. B. Jennings, 15 June 1944, Aviation Commands 1941–1952, Box 107, Archival Branch, Naval History and Heritage Command (NHHC), Washington, DC, 1–2.

2. John Suprey, interview by author, digital recording, Dracut, Massachusetts, December 4, 2006.

3. Emory J. Jernigan, *Tin Can Man* (Arlington, VA: Vandamere Press, 1993), 30.

4. Richard Brown, "My War Memories," *Chips*, Vol. 4, 1999, 9. Folder 1999, Box 1, USSBIA.

5. James Delhomme, "My Father Remembered," *Chips*, Vol. 2, 2001, 9. Folder 2001, Box 1, USSBIA.

6. Samuel Hynes, *Flights of Passage: Reflections of a World War II Aviator* (Annapolis: Naval Institute Press, 1988), 189.

7. William T. Y'Blood, *Hunter-Killer: U.S. Escort Carriers in the Battle of the Atlantic* (Annapolis: Naval Institute Press, 1983), 111.

8. Hector Vernetti, interview by author, digital recording, Tempe, Arizona, December 12, 2010.

9. Diary of Louis Delhomme Jr., property of his son David L. Delhomme, emailed to the author on September 15, 2009.

10. Diary of Louis Delhomme Jr.

11. Diary of Louis Delhomme Jr.

12. Michael Bess, *Choices under Fire: Moral Dimensions of World War II* (New York: Alfred A. Knopf Press, 2006), 342.

13. *Chips*, Vol. 4, 2006, 5. Folder 2006, Box 1, USSBIA.

14. J. Bryan III, *Aircraft Carrier: What It Was Really Like on the Giant* Yorktown *in the Pacific War* (New York: Ballantine Books, 1954), 7.

15. Roy Swift, *The Fighting Block Island!*, personal memoir, Ships History–Decommissioned–Prior to 1 Jan 2001 (SHD), Block Island (CVE 21) Block Island (CVE 106), Box 107, Folder 1, Building 200, Archival Branch (AB), Naval History and Heritage Command (NHHC), Washington, DC, 13.

16. Swift, *Fighting Block Island!*, SHD, Box 107, AB, NHHC, 13.

17. Kenneth G. Wynn, *U-Boat Operations of the Second World War* (Annapolis: Naval Institute Press, 1989), 150.

18. *USS Block Island, War Diary, December 1943*, Reel A-813, transcribed by J. B. Jennings, 15 June 1944, Aviation Commands 1941–1952, Box 107, Archival Branch, Naval History and Heritage Command (NHHC), Washington, DC, 2–3.

19. Swift, *Fighting Block Island!*, SHD, Box 107, AB, NHHC, 14.

20. Jack Major, interview by author, digital recording, San Antonio, Texas, June 3, 2006.

21. CO CVE 21, L. C. Ramsey, Annex *Resume of Crashes*, attached to CO CVE 21, L. C. Ramsey to COMINCH, E. J. King, *Report of Operations, Task Group 21.16—December 15, 1943 to February 1, 1944*, 13 February 1944, Logan C. Ramsey Papers COLL/307 (LCRP), Box 3, Folder 6, Building 57, Archives Branch (AB), Naval History and Heritage Command (NHHC), Washington, DC, F2.

22. CO CVE 21, L. C. Ramsey, Annex *Resume of Crashes*, LCRP, F2.

23. CO CVE 21, L. C. Ramsey, Annex *Resume of Crashes*, LCRP, B1.

24. CO CVE 21, L. C. Ramsey, Annex *Resume of Crashes*, LCRP, C3.

25. CO CVE 21, L. C. Ramsey to COMINCH, E. J. King, *Report of Operations, Task Group 21.16—December 15, 1943 to February 1, 1944*, 13 February 1944, LCRP, AB, NHHC, 1–2.

26. CO CVE 21, L. C. Ramsey to COMINCH, E. J. King, *Report of Operations*, LCRP, 2–3.

27. CO CVE 21, L. C. Ramsey to COMINCH, E. J. King, *Report of Operations*, LCRP, 2–3.

28. CO CVE 21, L. C. Ramsey to COMINCH, E. J. King, *Report of Operations*, LCRP, 2–3.

29. *Flight Operations—USS Block Island*, 15 December 1943 to 31 January 1944, Logan C. Ramsey Papers COLL/307 (LCRP), Box 3, Folder 20, Building 57, Archives Branch (AB), Naval History and Heritage Command (NHHC), Washington, DC, A-13.

30. Swift, *Fighting Block Island!*, SHD, Box 107, AB, NHHC, 15.

31. *Annex "A"—Day and Night Action Task Group 21.16 and Enemy Submarines December 29, 1943* from CO CVE 21, L. C. Ramsey to COMINCH, E. J. King, *Report of Operations, Task Group 21.16—December 15, 1943 to February 1, 1944*, 13 February 1944, Logan C.

Ramsey Papers COLL/307 (LCRP), Box 3, Folder 6, Building 57, Archives Branch (AB), Naval History & Heritage Command (NHHC), Washington, DC, 1.

32. Swift, *Fighting Block Island!*, SHD, Box 107, AB, NHHC, 17.

33. Swift, *Fighting Block Island!*, SHD, Box 107, AB, NHHC, 17.

34. Spector, *At War at Sea: Sailors and Naval Combat in the Twentieth Century* (New York: Penguin Books, 2001), 143.

35. *Annex "A"—Day and Night Action Task Group 21.16 and Enemy Submarines December 29, 1943* from CO CVE 21, L. C. Ramsey to COMINCH, E. J. King, *Report of Operations, Task Group 21.16—December 15, 1943 to February 1, 1944*, 13 February 1944, LCRP, AB, NHHC, 3.

36. Swift, *Fighting Block Island!*, SHD, Box 107, AB, NHHC, 19.

37. Daniel Morgan and Bruce Taylor, *U-Boat Attack Logs: A Complete Record of Warship Sinkings from Original Sources* (Barnsley, UK: Seaforth, 2011), 339, 348.

38. Swift, *Fighting Block Island!*, SHD, Box 107, AB, NHHC, 19–20.

39. *Annex "C"—Night Tactics, CVE Task Groups* from CO CVE 21, L. C. Ramsey to COMINCH, E. J. King, *Report of Operations, Task Group 21.16—December 15, 1943 to February 1, 1944*, 13 February 1944, Logan C. Ramsey Papers COLL/307 (LCRP), Box 3, Folder 6, Building 57, Archives Branch (AB), Naval History and Heritage Command (NHHC), Washington, DC, 1.

40. CO CVE 21, L. C. Ramsey to COMINCH, E. J. King, *Report of Operations, Task Group 21.16—December 15, 1943 to February 1, 1944*, 13 February 1944, LCRP, AB, NHHC, 1–8.

41. *USS Block Island, War Diary, December 1943*, Reel A-813, transcribed by J. B. Jennings, 15 June 1944, AC AB, NHHC, 6.

42. Vernetti, interview by author, digital recording, Tempe, Arizona, October 15, 2009.

43. Vernetti, interview by author, October 15, 2009.

Chapter 12

1. Roy Swift, *The Fighting Block Island!*, personal memoir, Ships History–Decommissioned–Prior to 1 Jan 2001 (SHD), Block Island (CVE 21) Block Island (CVE 106), Box 107, Folder 1, Building 200, Archival Branch (AB), Naval History and Heritage Command (NHHC), Washington, DC, 18.

2. CO CVE 21, L. C. Ramsey to COMINCH, E. J. King, *Report of Operations, Task Group 21.16—December 15, 1943 to February 1, 1944*, 13 February 1944, Logan C. Ramsey Papers COLL/307 LCRP, AB, NHHC, 8.

3. *USS Block Island, War Diary, January 1944*, Reel A-813, transcribed by J. B. Jennings, 15 June 1944, Aviation Commands 1941–1952, Box 107, Archival Branch, Naval History and Heritage Command (NHHC) Washington, DC, 7.

4. "TBF Pilots Describe Fireworks in First Rocket Attack on U-Boat," *All Hands*, July 1944, 18.

5. "TBF Pilots Describe Fireworks in First Rocket Attack on U-Boat," 18.

6. "TBF Pilots Describe Fireworks in First Rocket Attack on U-Boat," 18.

7. CO CVE 21, L. C. Ramsey to COMINCH, E. J. King, *Report of Operations, Task*

Group 21.16—December 15, 1943 to February 1, 1944, 13 February 1944, LCRP, AB, NHHC, 1–2.

8. "TBF Pilots Describe Fireworks in First Rocket Attack on U-Boat," 18.

9. "TBF Pilots Describe Fireworks in First Rocket Attack on U-Boat," 18.

10. Spector, *At War at Sea: Sailors and Naval Combat in the Twentieth Century* (New York: Penguin Books, 2001), 100.

11. James D. Hornfischer, *The Last Stand of the Tin Can Sailors: The Extraordinary World War II Story of the U.S. Navy's Finest Hour* (New York: Random House, 2004), 306.

12. Hornfischer, *Last Stand of the Tin Can Sailors*, 306.

13. Michael Gannon, *Operation Drumbeat: The Dramatic True Story of Germany's First U-Boat Attacks along the American Coast in World War II* (New York: Harper & Row, 1990), 112.

14. Heinz Schaeffer, *U-Boat 977* (London: William Kimber, 1952), 76.

15. Montgomery C. Meigs, *Slide Rules and Submarines: American Scientists and Subsurface Warfare in World War II* (Honolulu: University Press of the Pacific, 2002), 107.

16. CO CVE 21, L. C. Ramsey to COMINCH, E. J. King, *Report of Operations, Task Group 21.16—December 15, 1943 to February 1, 1944*, 13 February 1944, LCRP, AB, NHHC, 4.

17. Meigs, *Slide Rules and Submarines*, 100.

18. W. J. R. Gardner, *Decoding History: The Battle of the Atlantic and Ultra* (Annapolis: Naval Institute Press, 1999), 103–4.

19. Kathleen Broome Williams, *Secret Weapon: U.S. High-Frequency Direction Finding in the Battle of the Atlantic* (Annapolis: Naval Institute Press, 1996), xv, 5, 9.

20. Williams, *Secret Weapon*, 11.

21. Morison, *Battle of the Atlantic*, xx.

22. Williams, *Secret Weapon*, 11, 224.

23. CO Destroyer Division Fifty-Eight, R. B. Ellis, to CINCLANT, Annex H attached to CO CVE 21, L. C. Ramsey to COMINCH, E. J. King, *Report of Operations, Task Group 21.16—December 15, 1943 to February 1*, 13 February 1944, Logan C. Ramsey Papers COLL/307 (LCRP), Box 3, Folder 6, Building 57, Archives Branch (AB), Naval History and Heritage Command (NHHC), Washington, DC, H3.

24. Night Order Book, Capt. Logan Ramsey, 13–14 January 1944, LCRP, Box 2, Folder 23, Building 57, AB, NHHC.

25. CO CVE 21, L. C. Ramsey to COMINCH, E. J. King, *Report of Operations, Task Group 21.16—December 15, 1943 to February 1, 1944*, 13 February 1944, Logan C. Ramsey Papers COLL/307 LCRP, AB, NHHC, 5.

26. Louis Harlan, *All at Sea: Coming of Age in World War II* (Urbana: University of Chicago Press, 1996), 122.

27. Harlan, *All at Sea*, 122.

28. Swift, *Fighting Block Island!*, SHD, Box 107, AB, NHHC, 12–13.

29. Hector Vernetti, interview by author, digital recording, Tempe, Arizona, October 15, 2009.

30. Irv Biron, interview by author, digital recording, San Antonio, Texas, June 3, 2006.

31. *USS Block Island, War Diary, January 1944*, Reel A-813, transcribed by J. B. Jennings, 15 June 1944, AC AB, NHHC, 9

32. Top Secret Report on German Prisoners Taken Aboard the USS *Block Island*, CVE-21, January 14, 1944, from U-231, Ships History–Decommissioned–Prior to 1 Jan 2001, USS Block Island Box 107, Folder 3, Building 200, Archival Branch (AB), Naval History and Heritage Command (NHHC). Washington, DC, 1–6.

33. Top Secret Report on German Prisoners Taken Aboard the USS *Block Island*, CVE-21, January 14, 1944, from U-231, NHHC, 6.

34. Vernetti, interview by author, December 12, 2010.

35. Navy Department, Office of Public Relations, Aviation Section, Interview of Captain F. Massie Hughes, U.S.N. by Lieutenant A. Wright, June 17, 1944, Aviation Commands (AC) 1941–1952, USS Block Island, Box 154, Building 200, Archival Branch (AB), Naval History and Heritage Command (NHHC), Washington, DC, 13.

36. "Tries Suicide on Capture: U-Boat Skipper 'Loses' to RAF, Is Caught by U.S. Navy," *New York Times*, April 19, 1944, 3.

37. *Chips*, Vol. 3, 2008, 7. Folder 2008, Box 1, USSBIA.

Chapter 13

1. Kenneth Rose, *Myth and the Greatest Generation: A Social History of Americans in World War II* (New York: Routledge, 2008), 178.

2. "Presidential Poker," History Net, January 26, 2019, https://www.historynet.com.

3. "Presidential Poker."

4. Hector Vernetti, interview by author, digital recording, Tempe, Arizona, October 15, 2009.

5. Brad Bradley, interview by author, digital recording, New Orleans, Louisiana, May 30, 2010.

6. J. Bryan III, *Aircraft Carrier: What It Was Really Like on the Giant* Yorktown *in the Pacific War* (New York: Ballantine Books, 1954), 194.

7. Alvin Kernan, *Crossing the Line: A Bluejacket's World War II Odyssey* (Annapolis: Naval Institute Press, 1994), 23.

8. Vernetti, interview by author, October 15, 2009.

9. Theodore Roscoe, *United States Destroyer Operations in World War II* (Annapolis: United States Naval Institute, 1953), 287.

10. Barrett Tillman, *On Wave and Wing: The 100-Year Quest to Perfect the Aircraft Carrier* (Washington, DC: Regnery History, 2017), Kindle edition, 78.

11. Roscoe, *United States Destroyer Operations in World War II*, 287.

12. Roscoe, *United States Destroyer Operations in World War II*, 287.

13. *U.S.S. Block Island CVE 21 and CVE 106, United States Navy: "The Story of Two Escort Carriers Who Carried the War to the Enemy during Three Years of Conflict"* (Annapolis: U.S. Navy, 1945), LCRP, COLL/307, Box 6, AB, NHHC, 12–14.

14. CO CVE 21, L. C. Ramsey to COMINCH, E. J. King, *Report of Operations, Task Group 21.16—December 15, 1943 to February 1, 1944*, 13 February 1944, LCRP, AB, NHHC, 6.

15. *Annex "E"—Logistics* from CO CVE 21, L. C. Ramsey to COMINCH, E. J. King, *Report of Operations, Task Group 21.16—December 15, 1943 to February 1, 1944*, 13 February 1944, Logan C. Ramsey Papers COLL/307 (LCRP), Box 3, Folder 6, Building 57, Archives Branch (AB), Naval History and Heritage Command (NHHC), Washington, DC, 1.

16. CO CVE 21, L. C. Ramsey to COMINCH, E. J. King, *Report of Operations, Task Group 21.16—December 15, 1943 to February 1, 1944*, 13 February 1944, LCRP, AB, NHHC, 6.

17. Night Order Book, Capt. Logan Ramsey, 26–27 January 1944, LCRP, Box 2, Folder 23, Building 57, AB, NHHC.

18. CO Destroyer Division Fifty-Eight, R. B. Ellis, to CINCLANT, Annex H attached to CO CVE 21, L. C. Ramsey to COMINCH, E. J. King, *Report of Operations, Task Group 21.16—December 15, 1943 to February 1*, 13 February 1944, LCRP, AB, NHHC, H2.

19. Timothy S. Wolters, *Information at Sea: Shipboard Command and Control in the U.S. Navy from Mobile Bay to Okinawa* (Baltimore: Johns Hopkins University Press, 2013), 175.

20. Wolters, *Information at Sea*, 3.

21. Wolters, *Information at Sea*, 5.

22. Wolters, *Information at Sea*, 225.

23. Night Order Book, Capt. Logan Ramsey, 13–14 January 1944, LCRP, Box 2, Folder 23, Building 57, AB, NHHC.

24. *Chips*, Vol. 4, 2004, 11. Folder 2004, Box 1, USSBIA.

25. Ernie Pyle, "Destroyer Escorts," *Chips*, Vol. 3, 2009, 4. Folder 2009, Box 1, USSBIA.

26. Pyle, "Destroyer Escorts."

27. Michael Gannon, *Operation Drumbeat: The Dramatic True Story of Germany's First U-Boat Attacks along the American Coast in World War II* (New York: Harper & Row, 1990), 392.

28. *Chips*, Vol. 1, 2005, 3. Folder 2005, Box1, USSBIA.

29. W. J. R. Gardner, *Decoding History: The Battle of the Atlantic and Ultra* (Annapolis: Naval Institute Press, 1999), 109.

30. Bryant Bradley, email to the author, October 5, 2012.

Chapter 14

1. Samuel Eliot Morison, *The Two-Ocean War: A Short History of the United States Navy in the Second World War* (Boston: Little, Brown, 1963), 126.

2. Montgomery C. Meigs, *Slide Rules and Submarines: American Scientists and Subsurface Warfare in World War II* (Honolulu: University Press of the Pacific, 2002), 109.

3. *Chips*, Vol. 1, 2005, 3. Folder 2005, Box1, USSBIA.

4. W. J. R. Gardner, *Decoding History: The Battle of the Atlantic and Ultra* (Annapolis: Naval Institute Press, 1999), 104.

5. "Remembering Paul Dimock," *Chips*, Vol. 2, 1999, 2. Folder 1999, Box 1, USSBIA.

6. Russell V. Lewis, *A Civilian at War: A Unique WWII Experience* (Self-published, 2001), iii.

7. Lewis, *Civilian at War*, 138, 180.

8. Meigs, *Slide Rules and Submarines*, 99.

9. Lewis, *Civilian at War*, 78.

10. Lewis, *Civilian at War*, 44, 90.

11. Meigs, *Slide Rules and Submarines*, 106.

12. Morison, *Two-Ocean War*, 124.

13. Lewis, *Civilian at War*, 87.

14. Meigs, *Slide Rules and Submarines*, 122.

15. Lewis, *Civilian at War*, 74.

16. Lewis, *Civilian at War*, 77.

17. Lewis, *Civilian at War*, 79.

18. Lewis, *Civilian at War*, 84.

19. Lewis, *Civilian at War*, 84.

20. Night Order Book, Capt. Logan Ramsey, 1–2 March 1944, LCRP, Box 2, Folder 23, Building 57, AB, NHHC.

21. CO CVE 21, Logan C. Ramsey, *Night Action 29 February–1 March 1944*, unknown date, Logan C. Ramsey Papers COLL/307 (LCRP), Box 3, Folder 18, Building 57, Archives Branch (AB), Naval History and Heritage Command (NHHC), Washington, DC, 1.

22. Lewis, *Civilian at War*, 85.

23. Lewis, *Civilian at War*, 85.

24. Ramsey, *Night Action 29 February–1 March 1944*, LCRP, 1–6.

25. Ramsey, *Night Action 29 February–1 March 1944*, LCRP, 6.

26. Ramsey, *Night Action 29 February–1 March 1944*, LCRP, 7.

27. Roy Swift, *The Fighting Block Island!*, personal memoir, Ships History–Decommissioned–Prior to 1 Jan 2001 (SHD), Block Island (CVE 21) Block Island (CVE 106), Box 107, Folder 1, Building 200, Archival Branch (AB), Naval History and Heritage Command (NHHC), Washington, DC, 85.

28. Ramsey, *Night Action 29 February–1 March 1944*. LCRP, 1–7.

29. Uboat.net, "Preussen," accessed on January 26, 2019, https://uboat.net/ops/wolfpacks/181.html.

30. Lewis, *Civilian at War*, 85.

31. Lewis, *Civilian at War*, 85.

32. Lewis, *Civilian at War*, 85.

33. Lewis, *Civilian at War*, 85.

34. Lewis, *Civilian at War*, 85.

35. Lewis, *Civilian at War*, 88.

36. Lewis, *Civilian at War*, 88.

37. Lewis, *Civilian at War*, 88.

38. Lewis, *Civilian at War*, 88.

39. Lewis, *Civilian at War*, 90.

40. Lewis, *Civilian at War*, 90.

41. Lewis, *Civilian at War*, 90.

42. Lewis, *Civilian at War*, 90.

43. Lewis, *Civilian at War*, 91.

44. Meigs, *Slide Rules and Submarines*, 219–20.

45. Lewis, *Civilian at War*, 91.

Chapter 15

1. Russell V. Lewis, *A Civilian at War: A Unique WWII Experience* (Self-published, 2001), 93.

2. Logan C. Ramsey, Last Address to Crew of CVE 21 on March 10, 1944, Logan C. Ramsey Papers COLL/307 (LCRP), Box 4, Folder 2 Correspondence: Official and Personal, Building 57, Archives Branch (AB), Naval History and Heritage Command (NHHC), Washington, DC.

3. *Lucky Bag* (Annapolis: United States Naval Academy, 1919), 247; *Lucky Bag Annapolis: United States Naval Academy* (1923), 145.

4. John Carr, "Memories from the Flight Deck," *Chips*, Vol. 2, 2010, 3. Folder 2010, Box 1, USSBIA.

5. Carr, "Memories from the Flight Deck."

6. Carr, "Memories from the Flight Deck."

7. Carr, "Memories from the Flight Deck."

8. Ronald H. Spector, *Eagle against the Sun: The American War with Japan* (New York: Vintage Books, 1985), 386.

9. Barrett Tillman, *Enterprise: America's Fightingest Ship and the Men Who Helped Win World War II* (New York: Simon and Schuster, 2012), 251.

10. J. Bryan III, *Aircraft Carrier: What It Was Really Like on the Giant* Yorktown *in the Pacific War* (New York: Ballantine Books, 1954), 18.

11. Bryan, *Aircraft Carrier*, 18.

12. "Music on the Block," *Chips*, Vol. 2, 2003, 3. Folder 2003, Box 1, USSBIA.

13. Samuel Hynes, *Flights of Passage: Reflections of a World War II Aviator* (Annapolis: Naval Institute Press, 1988), 182.

14. Hector Vernetti, interview by author, digital recording, Tempe, Arizona, October 15, 2009.

15. Floyd Beaver, *Sailor from Oklahoma: One Man's Two-Ocean War* (Annapolis: Naval Institute Press, 2009), 149.

16. USS Block Island Association, "CVE 21 History," May 20, 2018, http://www.ussblockisland.us.

17. Norman Taylor Dowty, *Down Memory Lane—Letters from Airmen to His Father*, contributed by his daughter, Mrs. Amy Dowty Lore. Folder 17, Box 1, USSBIA.

18. Kathleen Broome Williams, *Secret Weapon: U.S. High-Frequency Direction Finding in the Battle of the Atlantic* (Annapolis: Naval Institute Press, 1996), xvii.

19. Navy Department, Office of Public Relations, Aviation Section, Interview of Captain F. Massie Hughes, U.S.N. by Lieutenant A. Wright, June 17, 1944, AC, AB, NHHC, 6.

20. Lewis, *Civilian at War*, 99.

21. Lewis, *Civilian at War*, 99.

22. "Remembering the Avenger," *Chips*, Vol. 2, 2005, 8–9. Folder 2005, Box 1, USSBIA.

23. Interview of Captain F. Massie Hughes, U.S.N. by Lieutenant A. Wright, June 17, 1944, AC, AB, NHHC, 14.

24. Vernetti, interview by author, October 15, 2009.

25. "To the Atlantic," *Chips*, Vol. 4, 2007, 18. Folder 2007, Box 1, USSBIA.

26. Interview of Captain F. Massie Hughes, U.S.N. by Lieutenant A. Wright, June 17, 1944, AC, AB, NHHC.

27. Commander Logan Ramsey to Secretary of the Navy. *Commander Fleet Air, Norfolk Recommends That the Congressional Medal of Honor Be Granted Posthumously to Lieutenant Junior Grade Norman T. Dowty, U.S. Naval Reserve, with the Proposed Citation*, 25 May 1944, Logan C. Ramsey Papers COLL/307 (LCRP), Box 4, Folder 2 Correspondence: Official and Personal, Building 57, Archives Branch (AB), Naval History and Heritage Command (NHHC), Washington, DC.

28. "Norman T Dowty, LTJG—Military Timeline," Together We Served.com, accessed on January 22, 2019, https://navy.togetherweserved.com/usn/servlet/tws.webapp.WebApp?cmd=SBVTimeLine&type=Person&ID=452722.

29. Lewis, *Civilian at War*, 101.

30. Lewis, *Civilian at War*, 102.

31. Roy Swift, *The Fighting Block Island!*, personal memoir, Ships History–Decommissioned–Prior to 1 Jan 2001 (SHD), Block Island (CVE 21) Block Island (CVE 106), Box 107, Folder 1, Building 200, Archival Branch (AB), Naval History and Heritage Command (NHHC), Washington, DC, 35–36.

32. Lewis, *Civilian at War*, 102.

33. Swift, *Fighting Block Island!*, SHD, Box 107, AB, NHHC, 35–36.

34. Swift, *Fighting Block Island!*, SHD, Box 107, AB, NHHC, 35–36.

Chapter 16

1. Roy Swift, *The Fighting Block Island!*, personal memoir, Ships History–Decommissioned–Prior to 1 Jan 2001 (SHD), Block Island (CVE 21) Block Island (CVE 106), Box 107, Folder 1, Building 200, Archival Branch (AB), Naval History and Heritage Command (NHHC), Washington, DC, 35–36.

2. Swift, *Fighting Block Island!*, SHD, Box 107, AB, NHHC, 110.

3. Joe Booi, interview by author, digital recording, San Antonio, Texas, May 30, 2006.

4. Bill Connolly, interview by author, digital recording, Natick, Massachusetts, December 3, 2006.

5. Connolly, interview by author.

6. Uboat.net, "List of All German U-Boat Commanders," accessed March 1, 2015, http://uboat.net/men/commanders/.

7. Wolf Loch letter to Roy Swift, 26 May 1948, Folder 1, Box 66, USSBIA, San Diego.

8. Loch letter to Swift.

9. Uboat.net, "List of All German U-boat Commanders."

10. Swift, *Fighting Block Island!*, SHD, Box 107, AB, NHHC, 36.

11. Swift, *Fighting Block Island!*, SHD, Box 107, AB, NHHC, 37.

12. Navy Department, Office of Public Relations, Aviation Section, Interview of Captain F. Massie Hughes, U.S.N. by Lieutenant A. Wright, June 17, 1944, AC, AB, NHHC, 2.

13. Swift, *Fighting Block Island!*, SHD, Box 107, AB, NHHC, 36.

14. Lewis, *Civilian at War*, 112.

15. Navy Department, Office of Public Relations, Aviation Section, Interview of Captain F. Massie Hughes, U.S.N. by Lieutenant A. Wright, June 17, 1944, AC, AB, NHHC, 5.

16. F. M. Hughes, *Surviving Prisoners from U-66*, Report on May 18, 1944, Ships History Decommissioned—Prior to 1 Jan 2001 (SHD) USS Block Island, Box 107, Folder, 2, Building 200, Archival Branch (AB), Naval History and Heritage Command (NHHC), Washington, DC, 2.

17. Hughes, *Surviving Prisoners from U-66*, SHD, AB, NHHC, 2–5.

18. "Attack on U 66," *Chips*, Vol. 2, 2004, 6. Folder 2004, Box 1, USSBIA.

19. Interview of Captain F. Massie Hughes, U.S.N. by Lieutenant A. Wright, June 17, 1944, AC, AB, NHHC, 2–5.

20. Hughes, *Surviving Prisoners from U-66*, SHD, AB, NHHC, 3.

21. Swift, *Fighting Block Island!*, SHD, Box 107, AB, NHHC, 40.

22. Interview of Captain F. Massie Hughes, U.S.N. by Lieutenant A. Wright, June 17, 1944, AC, AB, NHHC, 3, 4.

23. Interview of Captain F. Massie Hughes, U.S.N. by Lieutenant A. Wright, June 17, 1944, AC, AB, NHHC, 9.

24. Hughes, *Surviving Prisoners from U-66*, SHD, AB, NHHC, 5.

25. Hughes, *Surviving Prisoners from U-66*, SHD, AB, NHHC, 8.

26. Swift, *Fighting Block Island!*, SHD, Box 107, AB, NHHC, 41.

27. Interview of Captain F. Massie Hughes, U.S.N. by Lieutenant A. Wright, June 17, 1944, AC, AB, NHHC, 31.

28. Denny Moller, interview by author, digital recording, New Orleans, Louisiana. May 28, 2010.

29. Interview of Captain F. Massie Hughes, U.S.N. by Lieutenant A. Wright, AC, AB, NHHC, 8.

30. Interview of Captain F. Massie Hughes, U.S.N. by Lieutenant A. Wright, AC, AB NHHC, 15.

31. Interview of Captain F. Massie Hughes, U.S.N. by Lieutenant A. Wright, AC, AB NHHC, 15.

32. Interview of Captain F. Massie Hughes, U.S.N. by Lieutenant A. Wright, AC, AB NHHC, 32.

Chapter 17

1. Personal correspondence CO CVE 21, Captain "Massie" Hughes, to Captain Logan C.

Ramsey, Chief of Staff, Fleet Air, Norfolk Naval Air Station, dated May 22, 1944, Logan C. Ramsey Papers COLL/307 (LCRP), Box 3, Folder 2, Archival Branch (AB), Naval History and Heritage Command (NHHC), Washington, DC.

2. Roy Swift, *The Fighting Block Island!*, personal memoir, Ships History–Decommissioned–Prior to 1 Jan 2001 (SHD), Block Island (CVE 21) Block Island (CVE 106), Box 107, Folder 1, Building 200, Archival Branch (AB), Naval History and Heritage Command (NHHC), Washington, DC. 43.

3. Swift, *Fighting Block Island!*, SHD, Box 107, AB, NHHC, 42–44.

4. Harry Jones, interview by author, digital recording, Wellesley, Massachusetts, December 4, 2006.

5. Samuel Eliot Morison, *The Two-Ocean War: A Short History of the United States Navy in the Second World War* (Boston: Little, Brown, 1963), 375–76.

6. Jones, interview by author.

7. Jones, interview by author.

8. Bill Connolly, interview by author, digital recording, Natick, Massachusetts, December 3, 2006.

9. CO CVE 21, F. M. Hughes, to COMINCH, E. J. King, *Action Report of Commanding Officer, U.S.S. Block Island concerning the Loss by Enemy Action of That Vessel on 29 May 1944*, 30 June 1944, WW II Action and Operations Reports (A&ORs), Records Relating to Naval Activity during WW II (Box 854), Records of the Office of the CNO (RG 38), National Archives Building, College Park, Maryland (NACP), 6.

10. Irv Biron, interview by author, digital recording, San Antonio, Texas, June 3, 2006.

11. *U.S.S. Block Island (CVE 21), War Damage Report No. 49*. U.S. Hydrographic Office, November 20, 1944, Ships History Decommissioned—Prior to 1 Jan 2001 (SHD), USS Block Island, Box 107, Folder 3, Building 200, Archival Branch (AB), Naval History and Heritage Command (NHHC), Washington, DC, 6–8.

12. CO CVE 21, F. M. Hughes, to COMINCH, E. J. King, *Action Report of Commanding Officer, U.S.S. Block Island concerning the Loss by Enemy Action of That Vessel on 29 May 1944*, A&ORs WW II (Box 854), RG 38, NACP, 6.

13. CO CVE 21, F. M. Hughes, to COMINCH, E.J. King, *Action Report of Commanding Officer, U.S.S. Block Island concerning the Loss by Enemy Action of That Vessel on 29 May 1944*, A&ORs WW II (Box 854), RG 38, NACP, 6.

14. Hector Vernetti, interview by author, digital recording, Tempe, Arizona, October 15, 2009.

15. Helen E. Grenga, *Movies on the Fantail: A Sailor's Diary and Memories from Other Men of the USS* Barr *DE 576/APD 39* (Newman, GA: Yeoman Press, 2001), 11.

16. Grenga, *Movies on the Fantail*, 12.

17. Grenga, *Movies on the Fantail*, 12.

18. "Memories of Rex Coen," *Chips*, Vol. 2, 1998, 7. Folder 1998, Box 1, USSBIA.

19. "Memories of Rex Coen."

20. "Memories of Rex Coen."

21. "Memories of Rex Coen."

22. *U.S.S. Block Island (CVE 21), War Damage Report No. 49*. U.S. Hydrographic Office, November 20, 1944, SHD, AB, NHHC, 4.

23. Irv Biron, interview by author, digital recording, San Antonio, Texas, June 3, 2006.

24. CO CVE 21, F. M. Hughes, to COMINCH, E. J. King, *Action Report of Commanding Officer, U.S.S. Block Island concerning the Loss by Enemy Action of That Vessel on 29 May 1944*, A&ORs WW II (Box 854), RG 38, NACP, 13.

25. CO CVE 21, F. M. Hughes, to COMINCH, E. J. King, *Action Report of Commanding Officer, U.S.S. Block Island concerning the Loss by Enemy Action of That Vessel on 29 May 1944*, A&ORs WW II (Box 854), RG 38, NACP, 4.

26. Joe Browne, "Experience of the Sinking of the USS Block Island," 4. Folder 5.29.44, Box 1, USSBIA.

27. CO CVE 21, F. M. Hughes, to COMINCH, E. J. King, *Action Report of Commanding Officer, U.S.S. Block Island concerning the Loss by Enemy Action of That Vessel on 29 May 1944*, A&ORs WW II (Box 854), RG 38, NACP, 6–7.

28. Connolly, interview by author.

29. John Suprey, interview by author, digital recording, Dracut, Massachusetts, December 4, 2006.

30. *U.S.S. Block Island (CVE 21), War Damage Report No. 49*, SHD, AB, NHHC, 7.

31. Walter Cyr, interview by author, digital recording, Natick, Massachusetts, December 3, 2006.

32. Mike Dunham, "A Sailor's Story," *Anchorage Daily News*, May 25, 1997, 8.

33. Vernetti, interview by author, 2009.

34. Vernetti, interview by author, 2009.

35. "Portuguese Man-of-Wars," National Geographic, accessed February 28, 2011, http://animals.nationalgeographic.com/animals/invertebrates/portuguese-man-of-war.html.

36. Joe Browne, "Experience of the Sinking of the USS Block Island," 4. Folder 5.29.44, Box 1, USSBIA.

37. Joe Browne, "Experience of the Sinking of the USS Block Island," 4. Folder 5.29.44, Box 1, USSBIA.

38. Bill Tokarz, interview by author, digital recording, Taunton, Massachusetts, December 2, 2006.

39. Tokarz, interview by author.

40. Theodore Roscoe, *United States Destroyer Operations in World War II* (Annapolis: United States Naval Institute, 1953), 308.

41. Jones, interview by author.

42. USS Block Island Association, "U-Boat Battles," February 28, 2011, http://www.ussblockisland.org.

43. Navy Department, Office of Public Relations, Aviation Section, Interview of Captain F. Massie Hughes, U.S.N. by Lieutenant A. Wright, June 17, 1944, AC, AB, NHHC, 23.

44. CO CVE 21, F. M. Hughes, to COMINCH, E. J. King, *Action Report of Commanding Officer, U.S.S. Block Island concerning the Loss by Enemy Action of That Vessel on 29 May 1944*, 30 June 1944, A&ORs WW II (Box 854), RG 38, NACP, 9–10.

45. Jones, interview by author, 2009.

46. Jones, interview by author, 2009.

47. Benjamin Hruska, "A Small Vessel in a Big War," *Block Island Times*, May 24, 2014, 5–6.

48. James D. Hornfischer, *The Last Stand of the Tin Can Sailors: The Extraordinary World War II Story of the U.S. Navy's Finest Hour* (New York: Random House, 2004), 359.

49. Joe Browne, "Experience of the Sinking of the USS *Block Island*," 4. Folder 5.29.44, Box 1, USSBIA.

50. Interview of Captain F. Massie Hughes, U.S.N. by Lieutenant A. Wright, June 17, 1944, AC, AB, NHHC, 22.

51. Interview of Captain F. Massie Hughes, U.S.N. by Lieutenant A. Wright, June 17, 1944, AC, AB, NHHC, 22.

52. Vernetti, interview by author, 2009.

53. Vernetti, interview by author, 2009.

Chapter 18

1. Joe Browne, "Experience of the Sinking of the USS *Block Island*," 4. Folder 5.29.44, Box 1, USSBIA.

2. Browne, "Experience of the Sinking of the USS *Block Island*," 4. Folder 5.29.44, Box 1, USSBIA.

3. Walter Cyr, interview by author, digital recording, Natick, Massachusetts, December 3, 2006.

4. Denny Moller, interview by author, digital recording, New Orleans, Louisiana, May 28, 2010.

5. Navy Department, Office of Public Relations, Aviation Section, Interview of Captain F. Massie Hughes, U.S.N. by Lieutenant A. Wright, June 17, 1944, AC, AB, NHHC, 27.

6. Hector Vernetti, interview by author, digital recording, Tempe, Arizona, October 15, 2009.

7. Vernetti, interview by author, October 15, 2009.

8. Vernetti, interview by author, October 15, 2009.

9. Browne, "Experience of the Sinking of the USS *Block Island*," 5. Folder 5.29.44, Box 1, USSBIA.

10. James D. Hornfischer, *The Last Stand of the Tin Can Sailors: The Extraordinary World War II Story of the U.S. Navy's Finest Hour* (New York: Random House, 2004), 359.

11. Harry Jones, interview by author, digital recording, Wellesley, Massachusetts, December 4, 2006.

12. Jones, interview by author.

13. Joe Browne, "Experience of the Sinking of the USS Block Island," 4. Folder 5.29.44, Box 1, USSBIA.

14. Lewis, *Civilian at War*, 124, 125.

15. Chester Wentworth, interview by author, digital recording, Natick, Massachusetts, December 4, 2006.

16. Joe Browne, "Experience of the Sinking of the USS *Block Island*," 4. Folder 5.29.44, Box 1, USSBIA.

17. Lewis, *Civilian at War*, 125.

18. Lewis, *Civilian at War*, 125.

19. Lewis, *Civilian at War*, 126.

20. Jones, interview by author.

21. Roy Swift, *The Fighting Block Island!*, personal memoir, Ships History–Decommissioned–Prior to 1 Jan 2001 (SHD), Block Island (CVE 21) Block Island (CVE 106), Box 107, Folder 1, Building 200, Archival Branch (AB), Naval History and Heritage Command (NHHC), Washington, DC, 52.

22. "Eternal Father—The Navy Hymn," America's Navy, January 28, 2019, https://www.navy.mil.

23. Lewis, *Civilian at War*, 126.

24. "Memories of Rex Coen," *Chips*, Vol. 2, 1998, 7. Folder 1998, Box 1, USSBIA.

25. Swift, *Fighting Block Island!*, SHD, Box 107, AB, NHHC, 29.

26. Cyr, interview by author.

27. Joe Browne, "Experience of the Sinking of the USS *Block Island*," 4. Folder 5.29.44 Box 1, USSBIA.

28. "Sinking of CVE 21," *Chips*, Vol. 2, 2004, 2. Folder 2004, Box 1, USSBIA.

29. "Sinking of CVE 21," *Chips*, Vol. 2, 2004, 2. Folder 2004, Box 1, USSBIA.

30. "Sinking of CVE 21," *Chips*, Vol. 2, 2004, 2. Folder 2004, Box 1, USSBIA.

31. "Sinking of CVE 21," *Chips*, Vol. 2, 2004, 2. Folder 2004, Box 1, USSBIA.

32. Lewis, *Civilian at War*, 129–30.

Chapter 19

1. Joe Booi, "Remembering the Sinking of the Block Island CVE 21," Folder 24, Box 2, USSBIA.

2. Booi, "Remembering the Sinking of the Block Island CVE 21," Folder 24, Box 2, USSBIA.

3. Booi, "Remembering the Sinking of the Block Island CVE 21," Folder 24, Box 2, USSBIA.

4. Irv Biron, interview by author, digital recording, San Antonio, Texas, June 3, 2006.

5. Bill Connolly, interview by author, digital recording, Natick, Massachusetts, December 3, 2006.

6. F. D. Ommanney, *Flat-Top: The Story of an Escort Carrier* (New York: Longmans, Green, 1945), 62.

7. William T. Y'Blood, *The Little Giants: U.S. Escort Carriers against Japan* (Annapolis: Naval Institute Press, 1987), 180.

8. Roy Swift, *The Fighting Block Island!*, personal memoir, Ships History–Decommissioned–Prior to 1 Jan 2001 (SHD), Block Island (CVE 21) Block Island (CVE 106), Box 107, Folder 1, Building 200, Archival Branch (AB), Naval History and Heritage Command (NHHC), Washington, DC, 29.

9. Navy Department, Office of Public Relations, Aviation Section, Interview of Captain F. Massie Hughes, U.S.N. by Lieutenant A. Wright, June 17, 1944, AC, AB, NHHC, 29.

10. *Excerpts from Captain Ramsey Talk*, Date unknown, AC, AB, NHHC, 1.

11. *Excerpts from Captain Ramsey Talk*, Date unknown, AC, AB, NHHC, 1.

12. *Excerpts from Captain Ramsey Talk*, Date unknown, AC, AB, NHHC, 2.

13. *Excerpts from Captain Ramsey Talk*, Date unknown, AC, AB, NHHC, 3.

14. *Excerpts from Captain Ramsey Talk*, Date unknown, AC, AB, NHHC, 3.

15. *Excerpts from Captain Ramsey Talk*, Date unknown, AC, AB, NHHC, 4.

16. *Excerpts from Captain Ramsey Talk*, Date unknown, AC, AB, NHHC, 4.

17. *Excerpts from Captain Ramsey Talk*, Date unknown, AC, AB, NHHC, 2.

18. John Suprey, interview by author, digital recording, Dracut, Massachusetts, December 4, 2006.

19. "Escort Carrier Sunk in Atlantic," *New York Times*, June 6, 1944, 8.

20. "Escort Carrier Sunk in Atlantic," 8.

21. Bill Tokarz, interview by author, digital recording, Taunton, Massachusetts, December 2, 2006.

22. "Memories of Rex Coen," *Chips*, Vol. 2, 1998, 6. Folder 1998, Box 1, USSBIA.

23. "Memories of Rex Coen," *Chips*, Vol. 2, 1998, 6. Folder 1998, Box 1, USSBIA.

24. Arlie "Buster" Lapeyrolerie, interview by author, digital recoding, New Orleans, Louisiana, May 28, 2010.

25. John Suprey, Walter Cyr, and Bill Connolly, interview by author, digital recording, Natick and Dracut, Massachusetts, December 4, 2006.

26. "Crew of Lost *Block Island* to Man Giant New Carrier of Same Name," *Tacoma News Tribune*, November 17, 1944, 5.

27. "Crew of Lost *Block Island* to Man Giant New Carrier of Same Name," 5.

28. "Crew of Lost *Block Island* to Man Giant New Carrier of Same Name," 5.

29. Swift, *Fighting Block Island!*, SHD, Box 107, AB, NHHC, 54.

30. "Capt. Hughes, Crew Assigned to New Craft," *Fort Lauderdale Daily News*, May 29, 1945, 3.

31. "Capt. Hughes, Crew Assigned to New Craft," 3.

32. Swift, *Fighting Block Island!*, SHD, Box 107, AB, NHHC, 55.

33. "Capt. Hughes, Crew Assigned to New Craft," 3.

34. "To Commission *Block Island*," *Tacoma Times*, December 29, 2944, 16.

35. "Commissioning of CVE 106," *Chips*, Vol. 2, 1999, 4. Folder 1999, Box 1, USSBIA.

36. Robert M. Downie, "Block Island's Pair of Aircraft Carriers," *Block Island Times*, May 29, 1993, 8.

37. Scot MacDonald, "Evolution of Aircraft Carriers: Emergence of the Escort Carrier," *Naval Aviation News*, December 1962, 51.

38. Henry M. Dater, "Development of the Escort Carrier," *Military Affairs* 12 (1948): 81.

39. "U.S. Escort Carrier Notes," World War II in the Pacific, October 5, 2011, http://www.ww2pacific.com.

40. Roger Chesneau, *Aircraft Carriers of the World, 1914 to the Present* (Annapolis: Naval Institute Press, 1984), 214–15.

41. USS *St. Lo*, CVE 63, sank on October 25, 1944; USS *Ommaney Bay*, CVE 79, was struck by a kamikaze on January 4, 1945, and later scuttled by the destroyer USS *Burns*,

DD 588; and USS *Bismarck Sea*, CVE 95, sank on February 21, 1945, after taking two kamikaze hits.

42. Chesneau, *Aircraft Carriers of the World*, 248.

43. "Constructing Escort Carriers," *Chips*, Vol. 2, 2000, 4. Folder 2000, Box 1, USSBIA.

44. "Constructing Escort Carriers," *Chips*, Vol. 2, 2000, 4. Folder 2000, Box 1, USSBIA.

45. Biron, interview by author.

46. Floyd Beaver, *Sailor from Oklahoma: One Man's Two-Ocean War* (Annapolis: Naval Institute Press, 2009), 284.

47. Cyr, interview by author.

48. Brig. Gen. William C. Menninger, "Psychiatry and the War," *Atlantic Monthly*, November 1945, 108–9.

49. Charles Herbert Read Jr., *Memoirs of the Flight Surgeon of HMS* Nabob (Coaldale, Alberta: Lammi, 2018), Kindle edition, 626–27.

Chapter 20

1. Jack Greer, interview by author, digital recording, Phoenix, Arizona, March 30, 2007.

2. *U.S. Navy* from *USS Block Island (CVE 106) Unit History from Commissioning, 30 December 1944 to V-J, 2 September 1945*, Aviation Commands (AC) 1941–1952, Box 154, Folder 9, Building 200, Archival Branch (AB), Naval History and Heritage Command (NHHC), Washington, DC, 6.

3. Stefan Terzibaschitsch, *Escort Carriers and Aviation Support Ships of the U.S. Navy* (New York: Rutledge Press, 1981), 36, 128.

4. Public Data Section, *Composite History*, SHD, Box 107, AB, NHHC, 6, 11.

5. Roy L. Swift and Robert J. Cressman, "The Tale of Two Block Islands," *CVE "Piper,"* May/June 1996, 16, Box Piper, USSBIA.

6. Greer, interview by author.

7. Ronald Spector, *At War at Sea: Sailors and Naval Combat in the Twentieth Century* (New York: Penguin Books, 2001), 307.

8. "Cleveland T. Martin Jr. U.S. Navy service, WWII, U.S.S. Block Island," Washburn University Alumni, Washburn University, October 29, 2015, http://www.washburn.edu.

9. Deck Log, Records of the Bureau of Naval Personnel, 1798–2007, Entry A1–118: Logbooks of U.S. Navy Ships and Stations, 1941–1983, Record Group 24 (RG 24), National Archives College Park, Maryland (NACP), *USS Block Island*, CVE-106, January 9–10, 1945.

10. Deck Log, Records of the Bureau of Naval Personnel, 1798–2007, Entry A1–118: Logbooks of U.S. Navy Ships and Stations, 1941–1983, RG24, NACP, *USS Block Island*, CVE-106, January 20, 1945.

11. Deck Log, Records of the Bureau of Naval Personnel, 1798–2007, Entry A1–118: Logbooks of U.S. Navy Ships and Stations, 1941–1983, RG24, NACP, *USS Block Island*, CVE 106, January 22, 1945.

12. "Stories about Chaplain, Lt. G. A. MacInnes USNR: Who Served on Both the USS *Block Island* Ships," Folder 21, Box 1, USSBIA.

13. Roy Swift, *The Fighting Block Island!*, personal memoir, Ships History–Decommis-

sioned–Prior to 1 Jan 2001 (SHD), Block Island (CVE 21) Block Island (CVE 106), Box 107, Folder 1, Building 200, Archival Branch (AB), Naval History and Heritage Command (NHHC), Washington, DC, 30–31.

14. R. Bruce Porter, with Eric Hammel, *Ace! A Marine Night-Fighter Pilot in World War II* (New York: Berkley, 1987), 217.

15. F. D. Ommanney, *Flat-Top: The Story of an Escort Carrier* (New York: Longmans, Green, 1945), 41.

16. Porter, *Ace!*, 218.

17. Robin L. Rielly, *Kamikazes, Corsairs, and Picket Ships: Okinawa, 1945* (Havertown, PA: Casemate, 2008), Kindle edition, 1236.

18. Greer, interview by author.

19. Porter, *Ace!*, 218.

20. Porter, *Ace!*, 220.

21. Porter, *Ace!*, 219.

22. Porter, *Ace!*, 219.

23. Porter, *Ace!*, 222.

24. Porter, *Ace!*, 240.

25. Porter, *Ace!*, 242.

26. Porter, *Ace!*, 242.

27. Porter, *Ace!*, 243.

28. Porter, *Ace!*, 244.

29. Porter, *Ace!*, 244.

30. Porter, *Ace!*, 244.

31. Porter, *Ace!*, 245.

32. Swift, *Fighting Block Island!*, SHD, Box 107, AB, NHHC, 31.

33. Porter, *Ace!*, 259.

34. Porter, *Ace!*, 259.

35. Porter, *Ace!*, 259.

36. "Marine Planes Crash in South," *Madera Tribune*, February 15, 1945, 1.

37. Irv Biron, interview by author, digital recording, San Antonio, Texas, June 3, 2006.

38. *U.S.S. Block Island CVE 21 and CVE 106, United States Navy: "The Story of Two Escort Carriers Who Carried the War to the Enemy during Three Years of Conflict"* (Annapolis: U.S. Navy, 1945), LCRP, COLL/307, Box 6, AB, NHHC, 24.

39. John Suprey, interview by author, digital recording, Dracut, Massachusetts, December 4, 2006.

40. Patrick Degan, *Flattop Fighting in World War II: The Battles between American and Japanese Aircraft Carriers* (Jefferson, NC: McFarland, 2003), 221.

41. Degan, *Flattop Fighting in World War II*, 222.

42. Spector, *At War at Sea*, 300.

43. Degan, *Flattop Fighting in World War II*, 223.

44. Joe Zook, interview by author, digital recording, Sun City, Arizona, April 18, 2010.

45. Ommanney, *Flat-Top: The Story of an Escort Carrier*, 47.

46. Zook, interview by author.

47. "Stories about Chaplain, Lt. G. A. MacInnes USNR," Folder 21, Box 1, USSBIA.

48. Porter, *Ace!*, 239–40.

49. Public Data Section, *Composite History*, SHD, Box 107, AB, NHHC, 6.

50. "Log of USS Block Island CVE-106," Smiley Burnette Collection, Box 1, Block Island Historical Society, Block Island, RI [hereafter cited as BIHS].

51. Ernie Pyle, *Last Chapter* (New York: Henry Holt, 1946), 59, 67.

52. Pyle, *Last Chapter*, 67.

53. Alvin Kernan, *Crossing the Line: A Bluejacket's World War II Odyssey* (Annapolis: Naval Institute Press, 1994), 142.

54. Kernan, *Crossing the Line*, 143.

55. Zook, interview by author.

Chapter 21

1. Samuel Eliot Morison, *History of the United States Naval Operations in World War II*, vol. 14, *Victory in the Pacific* (Boston: Little, Brown, 1960), 79–80.

2. Morison, *History of the United States Naval Operations in World War II*, 14: 90–92.

3. Michael Bess, *Choices under Fire: Moral Dimensions of World War II* (New York: Alfred A. Knopf Press, 2006), 195.

4. *War Diary from the U.S.S Block Island (CVE 106)*, Walter "Smiley" Burnette—U.S.S. Block Island Collection, BIHS.

5. *War Diary from the U.S.S Block Island (CVE 106)*, Walter "Smiley" Burnette—U.S.S. Block Island Collection, BIHS.

6. Robin L. Rielly, *Kamikazes, Corsairs, and Picket Ships: Okinawa, 1945* (Havertown, PA: Casemate, 2008), Kindle edition, loc. 205.

7. Robert Sherrod, *History of Marine Corps Aviation in World War II* (Baltimore: Nautical & Aviation Publishing Company of America, 1987), 395.

8. Rielly, *Kamikazes, Corsairs, and Picket Ships*, loc. 4373.

9. CO CVE 106, F. M. Hughes, to The Commander-in-Chief, U.S. Fleet, *Action Report for Operations in Support of Occupation of Okinawa and in the Neutralization of Sakashima Gunto*, Serial: 065, WW II Action and Operations Reports, Records relating to naval activity during WW II, Records of the Office of the CNO (RG 38), National Archives Building, College Park, Maryland, 5–6.

10. Rielly, *Kamikazes, Corsairs, and Picket Ships*, loc. 5970.

11. Rielly, *Kamikazes, Corsairs, and Picket Ships*, loc. 5970.

12. Sherrod, *History of Marine Corps Aviation in World War II*, 62.

13. CO CVE 106, F. M. Hughes, to The Commander-in-Chief, U.S. Fleet, *Action Report for Operations in Support of Occupation of Okinawa and in the Neutralization of Sakashima Gunto*, Serial: 065, A&OR, WW II, RG 38, NACP, 14.

14. CO CVE 106, F. M. Hughes, to The Commander-in-Chief, U.S. Fleet, *Action Report for Operations in Support of Occupation of Okinawa and in the Neutralization of Sakashima Gunto*, Serial: 065, A&OR, WW II, RG 38, NACP, 17.

15. Alvin Kernan, *Crossing the Line: A Bluejacket's World War II Odyssey* (Annapolis: Naval Institute Press, 1994), 35–36.

16. CO CVE 106, F. M. Hughes, to The Commander-in-Chief, U.S. Fleet, *Action Report for Operations in Support of Occupation of Okinawa and in the Neutralization of Sakashima Gunto*, Serial: 065, A&OR, WW II, RG 38, NACP, 14–19.

17. Roy Swift, *The Fighting Block Island!*, personal memoir, Ships History–Decommissioned–Prior to 1 Jan 2001 (SHD), Block Island (CVE 21) Block Island (CVE 106), Box 107, Folder 1, Building 200, Archival Branch (AB), Naval History and Heritage Command (NHHC), Washington, DC.

18. CO CVE 106, F. M. Hughes, to The Commander-in-Chief, U.S. Fleet, *Action Report for Operations in Support of Occupation of Okinawa and in the Neutralization of Sakashima Gunto*, Serial: 065, A&OR, WW II, RG 38, NACP, 16.

19. Deck Log, Records of the Bureau of Naval Personnel, 1798–2007, Entry A1–118: Logbooks of U.S. Navy Ships and Stations, 1941–1983, RG24, NACP, *USS Block Island*, CVE 106, May 24–28, 1945.

20. CO CVE 106, F. M. Hughes, to The Commander-in-Chief, U.S. Fleet, *Action Report for Operations in Support of Occupation of Okinawa and in the Neutralization of Sakashima Gunto*, Serial: 065, A&OR, WW II, RG 38, NACP, 21.

21. *U.S. Navy* from *USS Block Island (CVE 106) Unit History from Commissioning, 30 December 1944 to V-J, 2 September 1945*, AC, AB, NHHC, 19.

22. *U.S. Navy* from *USS Block Island (CVE 106) Unit History from Commissioning, 30 December 1944 to V-J, 2 September 1945*, AC, AB, NHHC, 25.

23. *U.S. Navy* from *USS Block Island (CVE 106) Unit History from Commissioning, 30 December 1944 to V-J, 2 September 1945*, AC, AB, NHHC, 22.

24. The Senior Medical Officer CVE 106, J. L. Custer, to The Chief of the Bureau of Medicine and Surgery, *Report of Casualties*, 1 June 1945, Page 4 of Annex 5 of CO CVE 106, F. M. Hughes, to The Commander-in-Chief, U.S. Fleet, *Action Report, with Annexes, of the Block Island (CVE 106) for the Operation in Support of the Amphibious Landing at Balikpapan, Borneo, Covering the Period 26 June through 6 July 1945*, WW II Action and Operations Reports, Records relating to naval activity during WW II, Records of the Office of the CNO (RG 38), National Archives Building, College Park, Maryland, 9.

25. *U.S.S. Block Island CVE 21 and CVE 106, United States Navy: "The Story of Two Escort Carriers Who Carried the War to the Enemy during Three Years of Conflict"* (Annapolis: U.S. Navy, 1945), LCRP, COLL/307, Box 6, AB, NHHC, 26.

26. *U.S.S. Block Island CVE 21 and CVE 106, United States Navy: "The Story of Two Escort Carriers Who Carried the War to the Enemy during Three Years of Conflict"* (Annapolis: U.S. Navy, 1945), LCRP, COLL/307, Box 6, AB, NHHC, 26, 31.

27. The Senior Medical Officer CVE 106, J. L. Custer, to The Chief of the Bureau of Medicine and Surgery, *Report of Casualties*, 1 June 1945, Page 3 of Annex 5 of CO CVE 106, F. M. Hughes, to The Commander-in-Chief, U.S. Fleet, *Action Report, with Annexes, of the Block Island (CVE 106) for the Operation in Support of the Amphibious Landing at Balikpapan, Borneo, Covering the Period 26 June through 6 July 1945*, A&OR, WW II, RG 38, NACP, 9.

28. Samuel Hynes, *Flights of Passage: Reflections of a World War II Aviator* (Annapolis: Naval Institute Press, 1988), 206.

29. CO CVE 106, F. M. Hughes, to The Commander-in-Chief, U.S. Fleet, *Action Report, with Annexes, of the Block Island (CVE 106) for the Operation in Support of the Amphibious Landing at Balikpapan, Borneo, Covering the Period 26 June through 6 July 1945*, WW II Action and Operations Reports, Records relating to naval activity during WW II, Records of the Office of the CNO (RG 38), National Archives Building, College Park, Md., 24.

30. CO CVE 106, F. M. Hughes, to The Commander-in-Chief, U.S. Fleet, *Action Report, With Annexes, of the Block Island (CVE 106) For the Operation in Support of the Amphibious Landing at Balikpapan, Borneo*, RG 38, College Park, 26.

31. CO CVE 106, F. M. Hughes, to The Commander-in-Chief, U.S. Fleet, *Action Report, With Annexes, of the Block Island (CVE 106) For the Operation in Support of the Amphibious Landing at Balikpapan, Borneo*, RG 38, College Park, 28–30.

32. CO CVE 106, F. M. Hughes, to The Commander-in-Chief, U.S. Fleet, *Action Report, With Annexes, of the Block Island (CVE 106) for the Operation in Support of the Amphibious Landing at Balikpapan, Borneo*, RG 38, College Park, 31.

33. CO CVE 106, F. M. Hughes, to The Commander-in-Chief, U.S. Fleet, *Action Report, With Annexes, of the Block Island (CVE 106) for the Operation in Support of the Amphibious Landing at Balikpapan, Borneo*, RG 38, College Park, 35.

34. *U.S.S. Block Island CVE 21 and CVE 106, United States Navy: "The Story of Two Escort Carriers Who Carried the War to the Enemy during Three Years of Conflict"* (Annapolis: U.S. Navy, 1945), LCRP, COLL/307, Box 6, AB, NHHC, 26, 27.

Chapter 22

1. Roy Swift, *The Fighting Block Island!*, personal memoir, Ships History–Decommissioned–Prior to 1 Jan 2001 (SHD), Block Island (CVE 21) Block Island (CVE 106), Box 107, Folder 1, Building 200, Archival Branch (AB), Naval History and Heritage Command (NHHC), Washington, DC, 36.

2. *U.S.S. Block Island CVE 21 and CVE 106, United States Navy: "The Story of Two Escort Carriers Who Carried the War to the Enemy during Three Years of Conflict"* (Annapolis: U.S. Navy, 1945), LCRP, COLL/307, Box 6, AB, NHHC, 12–14, 36.

3. CO CVE 106, F. M. Hughes, to The Commander-in-Chief, U.S. Fleet, *Action Report, with Annexes, of the Block Island (CVE 106) for the Operation in Support of the Amphibious Landing at Balikpapan, Borneo*, National Archives Building, RG 38, College Park, Maryland, 9.

4. CO CVE 106, F. M. Hughes, *Action Report, with Annexes, of the Block Island (CVE 106) for the Operation in Support of the Amphibious Landing at Balikpapan, Borneo*, RG 38, 13.

5. CO CVE 106, F. M. Hughes, to Commander Task Force Seventy-Eight, *Aircraft Action Reports, Aca-1, for MCAG-1-Forwarding of: Covers Strike on Amami Gunto on 2 July 1945 in Support of Balikpapan Operation, in Task Unit 32.1.3*, WW II Action and Operations Reports, Records relating to naval activity during WW II, Records of the Office of the CNO (RG 38), National Archives Building, College Park, Maryland, 4.

6. CO CVE 106, F. M. Hughes, to Commander Task Force Seventy-Eight, *Aircraft Action Reports, Aca-1*, RG 38, 20.

7. Irv Biron, interview by author, digital recording, San Antonio, Texas, June 3, 2006.

8. Public Data Section, *Composite History*, SHD, Box 107, AB, NHHC, 8.

9. CO CVE 106, F. M. Hughes, to The Commander-in-Chief, U.S. Fleet, *Action Report, with Annexes, of the Block Island (CVE 106) for the Operation in Support of the Amphibious Landing at Balikpapan, Borneo, Covering the Period 26 June through 6 July 1945*, A&OR, WW II, RG 38, NACP, 6.

10. James D. Hornfischer, *The Last Stand of the Tin Can Sailors: The Extraordinary World War II Story of the U.S. Navy's Finest Hour* (New York: Random House, 2004), 38.

11. Bill Tokarz, interview by author, digital recording, Taunton, Massachusetts, December 2, 2006.

12. *Appendix E: History of Captain Wallace Morris Beakley, U.S. Navy* from *USS Block Island (CVE 106) Unit History from Commissioning, 30 December 1944 to V-J, 2 September 1945*, AC, AB, NHHC, 1.

13. *U.S.S. Block Island CVE 21 and CVE 106, United States Navy: "The Story of Two Escort Carriers Who Carried the War to the Enemy during Three Years of Conflict"* (Annapolis: U.S. Navy, 1945), LCRP, COLL/307, Box 6, AB, NHHC, 38–40.

14. Swift, *Fighting Block Island!*, SHD, Box 107, AB, NHHC, 37.

15. Floyd Beaver, *Sailor from Oklahoma: One Man's Two-Ocean War* (Annapolis: Naval Institute Press, 2009), 206.

16. *U.S. Navy* from *USS Block Island (CVE 106) Unit History from Commissioning, 30 December 1944 to V-J, 2 September 1945*, AC, AB, NHHC, 22.

17. Bill Connolly, interview by author, digital recording, Natick, Massachusetts, December 3, 2006.

18. Ben Owen, "World War II, Lest We Forget," memoir essay. Folder 5.29.44, Box 1, USSBIA.

19. Samuel Hynes, *Flights of Passage: Reflections of a World War II Aviator* (Annapolis: Naval Institute Press, 1988), 131.

20. Joe Zook, interview by author, digital recording, Sun City, Arizona, April 18, 2010.

Chapter 23

1. Roy Swift, *The Fighting Block Island!*, personal memoir, Ships History–Decommissioned–Prior to 1 Jan 2001 (SHD), Block Island (CVE 21) Block Island (CVE 106), Box 107, Folder 1, Building 200, Archival Branch (AB), Naval History and Heritage Command (NHHC), Washington, DC, 38.

2. Patrick Degan, *Flattop Fighting in World War II: The Battles between American and Japanese Aircraft Carriers* (Jefferson, NC: McFarland, 2003), 220.

3. Swift, *Fighting Block Island!*, SHD, Box 107, AB, NHHC, 38.

4. William T. Y'Blood, *The Little Giants: U.S. Escort Carriers against Japan* (Annapolis: Naval Institute Press, 1987), 413–14.

5. CO CVE 106, Wallace W. Beakley, to Commander-in-Chief, United States Fleet, *Action Report—Evacuation of Prisoners of War from Formosa, 29 August through 9 September 1945*. 9 September, WWII Action and Operational Reports, Records Relating to Naval Activity during World War II, Records of the Office of the CNO (RG 38), National Archives Building, College Park, Maryland, 5.

6. "Hellcat in Action," *Chips*, Vol. 3, 2009, 2–3. Folder 2009, Box 1, USSBIA.

7. Ben Owen, "World War II, Lest We Forget," Memoir essay. Folder 5.29.44, Box 1, USSBIA.

8. Ben Owen, "World War II, Lest We Forget," Memoir essay. Folder 5.29.44, Box 1, USSBIA.

9. CO CVE 106, Wallace W. Beakley, to Commander-in-Chief, United States Fleet, *Action Report-Evacuation of Prisoners of War from Formosa, 29 August through 9 September 1945*. 9 September, A&ORs, WW II, RG 38, NACP, 8.

10. Swift, *Fighting Block Island!*, SHD, Box 107, AB, NHHC, 39.

11. Cecil Clarke, interview by author, digital recording, Boston, Massachusetts, June 3, 2007.

12. Public Data Section, *Composite History*, SHD, Box 107, AB, NHHC, 9.

13. Swift, *Fighting Block Island!*, SHD, Box 107, AB, NHHC, 40.

14. Bill Connolly, interview by author, digital recording, Natick, Massachusetts, December 3, 2006.

15. Bill Tokarz, interview by author, digital recording, Taunton, Massachusetts, December 2, 2006.

16. "Memoirs of Rex Coen," *Chips*, Vol. 2, 1998, 8. Folder 1998, Box 1, USSBIA.

17. Maurice A. Rooney, self-interviewed, unknown date, Box 3, USSBIA.

18. "Letters *Not* to the Editors," *Saturday Evening Post*, January 12, 1946, 54.

19. Irv Biron, interview by author, digital recording, San Antonio, Texas, June 3, 2006.

20. Swift, *Fighting Block Island!*, SHD, Box 107, AB, NHHC, 41.

Chapter 24

1. *CVE "Piper,"* July/August 1996, 19. Box Piper, USSBIA.

2. Public Data Section, *Composite History*, SHD, Box 107, AB, NHHC, 10.

3. Owen Gault, "Operation Magic Carpet," *Sea Classics*, September 2005, 22.

4. Gault, "Operation Magic Carpet," 22.

5. William T. Y'Blood, *The Little Giants: U.S. Escort Carriers against Japan* (Annapolis: Naval Institute Press, 1987), 413.

6. Gault, "Operation Magic Carpet," 22.

7. Public Data Section, *Composite History*, SHD, Box 107, AB, NHHC, 10.

8. F. D. Ommanney, *Flat-Top: The Story of an Escort Carrier* (New York: Longmans, Green, 1945), 62.

9. Ommanney, *Flat-Top: The Story of an Escort Carrier*, 63.

10. Ommanney, *Flat-Top: The Story of an Escort Carrier*, 63.

11. "Cleveland T. Martin Jr. U.S. Navy Service, WWII, U.S.S. *Block Island*," Washburn University Alumni, Washburn University, October 29, 2015, http://www.washburn.edu.

12. Biron, interview by author.

13. Roy Swift, *The Fighting Block Island!*, personal memoir, Ships History–Decommissioned–Prior to 1 Jan 2001 (SHD), Block Island (CVE 21) Block Island (CVE 106), Box 107, Folder 1, Building 200, Archival Branch (AB), Naval History and Heritage Command (NHHC), Washington, DC, 41.

14. Roger Chesneau, *Aircraft Carriers of the World, 1914 to the Present* (Annapolis: Naval Institute Press, 1984), 249.

15. Swift, *Fighting Block Island!*, SHD, Box 107, AB, NHHC, 41–42.

16. *CVE "Piper,"* July/August 1996, 19. Box Piper, USSBIA.

17. *Welcome Aboard: This Is a Hunter-Killer Group 81.2* (Norfolk: U.S. Navy Fifth Naval District Publications and Printing Office), Walter "Smiley" Burnette U.S.S. *Block Island* Collection, BIHS, 13.

18. *Dictionary of American Naval Fighting Ships, Vol. 1* (Washington, DC: Naval Historical Division, Navy Department, 1959), 132.

19. USS Block Island Association, "Aircraft," October 29, 2015, http://www.ussblockisland.org; USS Block Island Association.

20. *Dictionary of American Naval Fighting Ships*, 1:132.

21. Norman Polmar, *Aircraft Carriers: A Graphic History of Carrier Aviation and Its Influence on World Events* (New York: Doubleday, 1969), 740–41.

22. *Dictionary of American Naval Fighting Ships, Vol. IV* (Washington, DC: Naval Historical Division, Navy Department, 1969), 139.

23. "Log of the USS *Block Island* CVE 106," Box 1, Walter "Smiley" Burnette, U.S.S. *Block Island* Collection, BIHS.

24. John Suprey, interview by author, digital recording, Dracut, Massachusetts, December 4, 2006.

25. Swift, *Fighting Block Island!*, SHD, Box 107, AB, NHHC, 42.

26. William A. Forsythe, "Carrier *Block Island* Starts Long Trip to Japan—In Tow," *Evening Bulletin*, April 19, 1960, 12.

27. Forsythe, "Carrier *Block Island* Starts Long Trip to Japan," 12.

28. Forsythe, "Carrier *Block Island* Starts Long Trip to Japan," 12.

29. "Earthquake Hazards Program," USGS: Science for a Changing World, accessed on October 29, 2015, http://earthquake.usgs.gov/learn/facts.php.

30. "Tidal Wave Sweeps Away 130 as New Quakes Raise Chile Toll," *New York Times*, May 23, 1960, 1.

31. Swift, *Fighting Block Island!*, SHD, Box 107, AB, NHHC, 28, 42.

Chapter 25

1. Lewis Mumford, *Myth of the Machine: Technics and Human Development* (New York: Harcourt Brace Jovanovich, 1967), 25.

2. Hector Vernetti, interview by author, digital recording, Tempe, Arizona, October 15, 2009.

3. Irv Biron, interview by author, digital recording, San Antonio, Texas, June 3, 2006.

4. Bill Connolly, interview by author, digital recording, Natick, Massachusetts, December 3, 2006.

5. Jack Greer, interview by author, digital recording, Phoenix, Arizona, March 30, 2007.

6. "Quake Kills 2 in Seattle, Rocks Pacific Northwest," *New York Times*, April 29, 1965, 1.

7. Greer, interview by author.

8. Greer, interview by author.

9. Greer, interview by author.

10. Cecil Clarke, interview by author, digital recording, Boston, Massachusetts, June 3, 2007.

11. Jack Major, interview by author, digital recording, San Antonio, Texas, June 3, 2006.

12. John Suprey, interview by author, digital recording, Dracut, Massachusetts, December 4, 2006.

13. Clarke, interview by author.

14. Clarke, interview by author.

15. R. A. C. Parker, *The Second World War: A Short History* (Oxford: University of Oxford Press, 1989), 293–94.

16. Clarke, interview by author.

Conclusion

1. Arlie "Buster" Lapeyrolerie, interview by author, digital recoding, New Orleans, Louisiana, May 28, 2010.

2. Joe Zook, interview by author, digital recording, Sun City, Arizona, April 18, 2010.

3. Zook, interview by author.

4. John Suprey, interview by author, digital recording, Dracut, Massachusetts, December 4, 2006.

5. "Family Requests," HMS *Dasher*, http://www.hmsdasher.co.uk; March 15, 2016.

6. William Faulkner, *Requiem for a Nun* (New York: Garland, 1987), 286.

7. Joseph A. Amato, *Surfaces: A History* (Berkeley: University of California Press, 2013), 238.

8. "*Block Island*'s Battle in the Atlantic," *All Hands*, March 1961, 26

9. "*Block Island*'s Battle in the Atlantic," 26.

10. "*Block Island*'s Battle in the Atlantic," 27.

11. "*Block Island*'s Battle in the Atlantic," 27.

12. "*Block Island*'s Battle in the Atlantic," 27.

13. "*Block Island*'s Battle in the Atlantic," 27.

Bibliography

KEY

A&ORs: WW II Actions and Operations Reports

AB: Archives Branch at Naval History and Heritage Command, Washington Navy Yard, Washington, DC

BIHS: Block Island Historical Society, Block Island, Rhode Island

LCRP: Logan C. Ramsey Papers (Coll/307) at Naval History and Heritage Command, Washington Navy Yard, Washington, DC

NACP: National Archives and Records Administration at College Park, Maryland

NHHC: Naval History and Heritage Command, Washington Navy Yard, Washington, DC

SHD: Ships History Decommissioned

USSBIA: USS Block Island Association Archives, home of longtime editors of the Association Bill and Judy MacInnes, San Diego, California.

OFFICIAL DOCUMENTS

Annex A—Analysis of Night Action, October 25 from CO CVE 21 L. Ramsey to The Commander-in-Chief, United States Atlantic Fleet, *Report on Anti-Submarine and Convoy Escort Operations by Task Group 21.16—October 15 to November 25, 1943*. LCRP, Box 3, Folder 18, Building 57, AB, NHHC.

Annex "A"—Day and Night Action Task Group 21.16 and Enemy Submarines December 29, 1943 from CO CVE 21, L. C. Ramsey to COMINCH, E. J. King, *Report of Operations, Task Group 21.16—December 15, 1943 to February 1, 1944*. 13 February 1944. LCRP, Box 3, Folder 6, Building 57, AB, NHHC.

Annex B—Notes on Enemy Intelligence from CO CVE 21 L. Ramsey to The Commander-in-Chief, United States Atlantic Fleet, *Report on Anti-Submarine and Convoy Escort Operations by Task Group 21.16—October 15 to November 25, 1943*. LCRP, Box 3, Folder 18, Building 57, AB, NHHC.

Annex C—Search Plans Used from CO CVE 21 L. Ramsey to The Commander-in-Chief, United States Atlantic Fleet, *Report on Anti-Submarine and Convoy Escort Operations by Task Group 21.16—October 15 to November 25, 1943*. LCRP Box 3, Folder 18, Building 57, AB, NHHC.

Annex "C"—Night Tactics, CVE Task Groups from CO CVE 21, L. C. Ramsey to COMINCH, E. J. King, *Report of Operations, Task Group 21.16—December 15, 1943 to February 1, 1944*. 13 February 1944. LCRP, Box 3, Folder 6, Building 57, AB, NHHC.

Annex "E"—Logistics from CO CVE 21, L. C. Ramsey to COMINCH, E. J. King, *Report of Operations, Task Group 21.16—December 15, 1943 to February 1, 1944*. 13 February 1944. LCRP, Box 3, Folder 6, Building 57, AB, NHHC.

Appendix D: Biographical Sketch of Captain Francis Massie Hughes, U.S.N., U.S. Navy from *USS Block Island (CVE 106) Unit History from Commissioning, 30 December 1944 to V-J, 2 September 1945*. AC, Box 154, Folder 8, Building 200, AB, NHHC.

Appendix One to Task Group 21/16 Communication Plan. No date provided. LCRP, Box 3, Folder 6, Building 57, AB, NHHC.

Capt. Logan Ramsey, Night Order Book. LCRP, Box 2, Folders 23–24, Building 57, AB, NHHC.

Chips off the Old Block. "Block Island Celebrates Anniversary." Vol. 1, No. 18, March 8, 1944. LCRP, Box 4, Building 57, AB, NHHC.

Comdr. Naval Base Air Defense, P.N.L. Bellinger, to Commander-in-Chief, U.S. Pacific Fleet, *Commander Logan C. Ramsey, U.S. Navy-Recommendation for Promotion to Captain*. 8 June 1944. LCRP, Box 4, Folder 5, Building 57, AB, NHHC.

CO CVE 21, F. M. Hughes, to COMINCH, E. J. King, *Action Report of Commanding Officer U.S.S. Block Island concerning the Loss by Enemy Action of That Vessel on 29 May 1944*. 30 June 1944. A&ORs, WW II, RG 38, NACP.

CO CVE 21 L. C. Ramsey, Annex *Resume of Crashes*, attached to CO CVE 21, L. C. Ramsey to COMINCH, E. J. King, *Report of Operations, Task Group 21.16–December 15, 1943 to February 1, 1944*. 13 February 1944. LCRP, Box 3, Folder 6, Building 57, AB, NHHC.

CO CVE 21, L. C. Ramsey to COMINCH, E. J. King, *Report of Operations, Task Group 21.16–December 15, 1943 to February 1, 1944*. 13 February 1944. LCRP, Box 3, Folder 6, Building 57, AB, NHHC.

CO CVE 21, L. C. Ramsey, to Mary Ann Ramsey. Personal letter dated 3 May 1943. LCRP, Box 2, Folder 12, Building 57, AB, NHHC.

CO CVE 21 L. Ramsey to The Commander-in-Chief, United States Atlantic Fleet, *Report on Anti-Submarine and Convoy Escort Operations by Task Group 21.16–October 15 to November 25, 1943*. LCRP, Box 3, Folder 18, Building 57, AB, NHHC.

CO CVE 21 Logan C. Ramsey, *Night Action 29 February–1 March 1944*. Unknown date. LCRP, Box 3, Folder 18, Building 57, AB, NHHC.

CO CVE 106, F. M. Hughes, to Commander Task Force Seventy-Eight, *Aircraft Action Reports, Aca-1, For MCAG-1-Forwarding Of: Covers Strike on Amami Gunto On 2 July 1945 in Support of Balikpapan Operation, in Task Unit 32.1.3*. A&ORs, WW II, RG 38, NACP.

CO CVE 106, F. M. Hughes, to The Commander-in-Chief, U.S. Fleet, *Action Report for Operations in Support of Occupation of Okinawa and in the Neutralization of Sakashima Gunto*, Serial: 065. A&ORs, WW II, RG 38, NACP.

CO CVE 106, F. M. Hughes, to The Commander-in-Chief, U.S. Fleet, *Action Report, with Annexes, of the Block Island (CVE 106) for the Operation in Support of the Amphibious Landing at Balikpapan, Borneo, Covering the Period 26 June through 6 July 1945*. A&ORs, WW II, RG 38, NACP.

CO CVE 106, Wallace W. Beakley, to Commander-in-Chief, United States Fleet, *Action Report-Evacuation of Prisoners of War from Formosa, 29 August through 9 September 1945*. 9 September. A&ORs, WW II, RG 38, NACP.

CO Scouting Plane Squadron Ten, USS *Chicago* to CO Western Force, *Operation Order 1–35*. 28 April 1935. LCRP, Box 4, Folder 8, Building 57, AB, NHHC.

CO VC-1, R. A. Beveridge, to CO CVE 21, L. C. Ramsey, *Comments and Observations of VC-1 While Embarked in U.S.S. Block Island, 14 October–25 November 1943.* 23 November 1943. LCRP, Box 4, Folder 3, Building 57, AB, NHHC.

Commander Logan Ramsey to Secretary of the Navy, *Commander Fleet Air, Norfolk Recommends That the Congressional Medal of Honor Be Granted Posthumously to Lieutenant Junior Grade Norman T. Dowty, U.S. Naval Reserve, with the Proposed Citation.* 25 May 1944. LCRP, Box 4, Folder 2 Correspondence: Official and Personal, Building 57, AB, NHHC.

Deck Log, *USS Block Island,* CVE-106, January 9–10, 1945. Records of the Bureau of Naval Personnel, 1798–2007. Entry A1–118: Logbooks of U.S. Navy Ships and Stations, 1941–1983, RG 24, NACP.

Excerpts from Captain Ramsey Talk. Date unknown. AC, Box 107, Folder 4, AB, NHHC.

F. M. Hughes, *Surviving Prisoners from U-66.* Report on May 18, 1944. SHD, Box, 107, Folder, 2, Building 200, AB, NHHC.

Flight Operations—USS Block Island, 15 December 1943 to 31 January 1944. LCRP, Box 3, Folder 20, Building 57, AB, NHHC.

Hearings before the Joint Committee on the Investigation of the Pearl Harbor Attack. Washington, DC: U.S. Government Printing Office, 1946

Logan C. Ramsey, Last Address to Crew of CVE 21 on March 10, 1944. LCRP, Folder 2, Box 3, Building 57, AB, NHHC.

Navy Department, Office of Public Relations, Aviation Section, Interview of Captain F. Massie Hughes, U.S.N. by Lieutenant A. Wright, June 17, 1944, AC, AB, NHHC, 6.

Personal letter from Capt. E. J. King to Lieut. Logan C. Ramsey. 7 November 1931. LCRP, Box 4, Folder 2 Correspondence: Official and Personal, Building 57, AB, NHHC.

Personal letter from Logan C. Ramsey to Capt. T. P. Jeter, U S. Navy. 16 January 1943. LCRP, Box 4, Folder 2 Correspondence: Official and Personal, Building 57, AB, NHHC.

Personal letter from Logan C. Ramsey to Mr. J. Carroll Cone. 16 February 1943. LCRP, Box 4, Folder 2 Correspondence: Official and Personal, Building 57, AB, NHHC.

Public Data Section. U.S. Navy, *Composite History of USS Block Island (CVE-21) and USS Block Island (CVE-106).* Navy Department: Office of Public Relations, 1948. SHD, Box 107, Folder 1, Building 200, AB, NHHC.

Roy Swift, *The Fighting Block Island!* Personal Memoir. SHD, Block Island (CVE 21) Block Island (CVE 106), Box 107, Folder 1, Building 200, AB, NHHC.

The Senior Medical Officer CVE 106, J. L. Custer, to The Chief of the Bureau of Medicine and Surgery, *Report of Casualties,* 1 June 1945, Page 4 of Annex 5 of CO CVE 106, F. M. Hughes, to The Commander-in-Chief, U.S. Fleet, *Action Report, with Annexes, of the Block Island (CVE 106) for the Operation in Support of the Amphibious Landing at Balikpapan, Borneo, Covering the Period 26 June through 6 July 1945.* A&ORs, WW II, RG 38, NACP.

United States, Pacific Fleet and Pacific Ocean Areas Press Release No. 56. June 16, 1942. Station KGMB. LCRP, Box 3, Building 57, AB, NHHC.

U.S. Navy from *USS Block Island (CVE 106) Unit History from Commissioning, 30 December 1944 to V-J, 2 September 1945.* AC, Box 154, Folder 9, Building 200, AB, NHHC.

U.S.S. Block Island (CVE 21), War Damage Report No. 49. U.S. Hydrographic Office. November 20, 1944. SHD, Box, 107, Folder 3, Building 200, AB, NHHC.

USS Block Island, War Diary, May 1943, Reel A-426. Transcribed by J. B. Jennings. 15 June 1944. AC, Box 107, AB, NHHC.

USS Block Island, War Diary, October 1943, Reel A-692. Transcribed by J. B. Jennings. 15 June 1944. AC, Box 107, AB, NHHC.

USS Block Island, War Diary, November 1943, Reel A-726. Transcribed by J. B. Jennings. 15 June 1944. AC, Box 107, AB, NHHC.

USS Block Island, War Diary, December 1943, Reel A-813. Transcribed by J. B. Jennings. 15 June 1944, AC, Box 107, AB, NHHC.

Vice Chief of Naval Operations, F. J. Horne to Secretary of the Navy, William Franklin Knox, *Board of Investigation—Collision between the U.S.S. BLACK (DD666) and the U.S.S. BLOCK ISLAND (CVE21): Convened by COTCLant, 2 Oct. 1943*. 25 March 1944. LCRP, Box 5, Folder 1, Building 57, AB, NHHC.

INTERVIEWS

Biron, Irv. Interviewed June 3, 2006, digitally recorded by author in San Antonio, Texas.

Booi, Joe. Interviewed May 30, 2006, digitally recorded by author in San Antonio, Texas.

Bradley, Brad. Interviewed May 30, 2010, digitally recorded by author in New Orleans, Louisiana.

Clarke, Cecil. Interviewed June 3, 2007, digitally recorded by author in Boston, Massachusetts.

Connolly, Bill. Interviewed December 3, 2006, digitally recorded by author in Natick, Massachusetts.

Cyr, Walter. Interviewed December 3, 2006, digitally recorded by author in Natick, Massachusetts.

Greer, Jack. Interviewed March 30, 2007, digitally recorded by author in Phoenix, Arizona.

Hughes, Francis Massie Jr. Interviewed May 27, 2011, digitally recorded by the author in New Orleans, Louisiana.

Jones, Harry. Interviewed December 4, 2006, digitally recorded by author in Wellesley, Massachusetts.

Lapeyrolerie, Arlie "Buster." Interviewed May 28, 2010, digitally recoded by author in New Orleans, Louisiana.

Major, Jack. Interviewed June 3, 2006, digitally recorded by author in San Antonio, Texas.

Moller, Denny. Interviewed May 28, 2010, digitally recorded by author in New Orleans, Louisiana.

Rooney, Maurice A. Self-interviewed on unknown date, audio recording on tape, Box 3, USS-BIA, San Diego, California.

Shaw, Clifford. Interviewed January 11, 2018, digitally recorded by Brad Hoopes in Fort Collins, Colorado. Northern Veterans History Project, Colorado State University Libraries, 2018–01–11T15:43:12Z.

Suprey, John. Interviewed December 4, 2006, digitally recorded by the author in Dracut, Massachusetts.

Tokarz, Bill. Interviewed December 2, 2006, digitally recorded by author in Taunton, Massachusetts.

Vernetti, Hector. Interviewed October 15, 2009, and December 12, 2010, digitally recorded by author in Tempe, Arizona.

Wentworth, Chester. Interviewed December 4, 2006, digitally recorded by author in Natick, Massachusetts.

Zook, Joe. Interviewed April 18, 2010, digitally recorded by author in Sun City, Arizona.

PRIMARY RESOURCES

Battle of Midway, directed by John Ford (1942; Los Angeles, CA: 20th Century Fox, 2002), DVD.

"Block Island's Battle in the Atlantic." *All Hands*. March 1961.

"Capt. Hughes, Crew Assigned to New Craft." *Fort Lauderdale Daily News*. May 29, 1945.

Capt. Logan Ramsey to John Ford. Personal letter dated 3 May 1943. The John Ford Papers, Correspondence Box 1, Lilly Library Special Collection, Indiana University, Bloomington, Indiana.

"Crew of Lost *Block Island* to Man Giant New Carrier of Same Name." *Tacoma News Tribune*. November 17, 1944.

Dater, Henry M. "Development of the Escort Carrier." *Military Affairs* 12 (1948): 81.

"The Defensive Value of the Plane." Editorial. *New York Herald Tribune*, August 1, 1930.

"Escort Carrier Sunk in Atlantic." *New York Times*, June 6, 1944.

"F. Massie Hughes, Rear Admiral, 61." *New York Times*, December 24, 1960.

Forsythe, William A. "Carrier *Block Island* Starts Long Trip to Japan—in Tow." *Evening Bulletin*, April 19, 1960.

Gilbert, Price, ed. *The Escort Carriers in Action: The Story, in Pictures, of the Escort Carrier Force U.S. Pacific Fleet—1945*. Atlanta: Ruralist Press, 1945.

Grosvenor, Melville Bell. "Cruise on an Escort Carrier." *National Geographic Magazine*, November 1943.

"Letters *Not* to the Editors." *Saturday Evening Post*, January 12, 1946.

Lucky Bag. Annapolis: United States Naval Academy, 1919.

Lucky Bag. Annapolis: United States Naval Academy, 1923.

"Marine Planes Crash in South." *Madera Tribune*, February 15, 1945.

Menninger, Brig. Gen. William C. "Psychiatry and the War." *Atlantic Monthly* (November 1945): 108–9.

Norris, John. "Aircraft Carrier Is Navy's New Queen of the Seas." *Washington Post*, May 24, 1942.

———. "U.S. Navy Bombards Kiska Forts Again." *Washington Post*, July 11, 1943.

Owen, Ben. "World War II, Lest We Forget." Memoir essay. Folder 5.29.44, Box 1, USSBIA.

"Quake Kills 2 in Seattle, Rocks Pacific Northwest." *New York Times*, April 29, 1965.

Ramsey, Lt. Logan C. "Aerial Attacks on Fleets at Anchor." *Proceedings* 63–8–414, August 1937: 1127.

———. "The Aero-Amphibious Phase of the Present War." *Proceedings* 69–5–483 May 1943: 695.

———. "Hydrographic Surveying with Aircraft." *Proceedings* 53–7–293 (July 1927): 780.

———. "The Influence of Aircraft on the Exercise of Sea Command." *Proceedings* 64–10–428, October 1938: 1406.

———. *Navigation of Aircraft*. New York: Ronald Press, 1929.

———. "A Neglected Phase of Naval Aviation." *Proceedings* 57–8–342 (August 1931): 780.

"750,000 See Parade in Riverside Drive." *New York Times*, May 31, 1944.

"TBF Pilots Describe Fireworks in First Rocket Attack on U-Boat." *All Hands*, July 1944.

"Tidal Wave Sweeps Away 130 as New Quakes Raise Chile Toll." *New York Times*, May 23, 1960.

"To Commission *Block Island*." *Tacoma Times*, December 29, 1944.

"Tries Suicide on Capture: U-Boat Skipper 'Loses' to RAF, Is Caught by U.S. Navy." *New York Times*, April 19, 1944.

Wolf Loch to Roy Swift. Personal letter. Folder 1, Box 66, USSBIA.

VETERANS NEWSLETTERS

"Attack on U 66." *Chips Off the Old Block*, Vol. 2, 2004. Folder 2004, Box 1, USSBIA.

Brown, Richard. "My War Memories." *Chips Off the Old Block*, Vol. 4, 1999. Folder 1999, Box 1, USSBIA.

Carr, John. "Memories from the Flight Deck." *Chips Off the Old Block*, Vol. 2, 2010, 3. Folder 2010, Box 1, USSBIA.

Chips Off the Old Block, Vol. 3, 1996. Quarterly newsletter. Folder 1996, Box 1, USSBIA.

Chips Off the Old Block, Vol. 1, 2004. Folder 2004, Box 1, USSBIA.

Chips Off the Old Block, Vol. 4, 2004. Folder 2004, Box 1, USSBIA.

Chips Off the Old Block, Vol. 1, 2005. Folder 2005, Boxl, USSBIA.

Chips Off the Old Block, Vol. 4, 2006. Folder 2006, Box 1, USSBIA.

Chips Off the Old Block, Vol. 3, 2008. Folder 2008, Box 1, USSBIA.

Chips Off the Old Block, Vol. 3, 2009. Folder 2009, Box 1, USSBIA.

Chips Off the Old Block, Vol. 1, 2011. Folder 2011, Box 1, USSBIA.

"Commissioning of CVE 106." *Chips Off the Old Block*, Vol. 2, 1999. Folder 1999, Box 1, USSBIA.

"Constructing Escort Carriers." *Chips Off the Old Block*, Vol. 2, 2000. Folder 2000, Box 1, USSBIA.

"Hellcat in Action." *Chips Off the Old Block*, Vol. 3, 2009. Folder 2009, Box 1, USSBIA.

"Memories of Rex Coen." *Chips Off the Old Block*, Vol. 2, 1998. Folder 1998, Box 1, USSBIA.

"Music on the Block." *Chips Off the Old Block*, Vol. 2, 2003. Folder 2003, Box 1, USSBIA.

"Remembering Paul Dimock." *Chips Off the Old Block*, Vol. 2, 1999. Folder 1999, Box 1, USSBIA.

"Remembering the Avenger." *Chips Off the Old Block*, Vol. 2, 2005. Folder 2005, Box 1, USSBIA.

"Sinking of CVE 21." *Chips Off the Old Block*, Vol. 2, 2004. Folder 2004, Box 1, USSBIA.

Swift, Roy L., and Robert J. Cressman. "The Tale of Two Block Islands." *CVE "Piper."* May/June 1996. Box Piper, USSBIA.

"To the Atlantic." *Chips Off the Old Block*, Vol. 4, 2007. Folder 2007, Box 1, USSBIA.

Turner, Jeb. "Remembering CVE 21." *Chips Off the Old Block*, Vol. 1, 2012. Folder 2012, Box 1, USSBIA.

PERSONAL PAPERS

Burnette, Smiley Collection, BIHS, Boxes 1–3.
Ramsey, Logan C. Collection, NHHC, Boxes 1–5.

UNPUBLISHED AND PRIVATELY PUBLISHED EYEWITNESS ACCOUNTS

Booi, Joe. "Remembering the Sinking of the Block Island CVE 21." Folder 24, Box 2, USSBIA.
Browne, Joe. "Experience of the Sinking of the USS *Block Island*." Folder 5.29.44, Box 1, USSBIA.
Delhomme, Louis. Personal diary. Property of his son David L. Delhomme, emailed to the author September 15, 2009.
Dowty, Norman Taylor. *Down Memory Lane—Letters from Airmen to His Father*. Contributed by his daughter, Mrs. Amy Dowty Lore. Folder 17, Box 1, USSBIA.
Lewis, Keith A. *The Old Man*. Unpublished memoir about his father, Capt. John Lewis, in the author's possession.
Lewis, Russell V. *A Civilian at War: A Unique WWII Experience*. Self-published, 2001.
Loch, Wolf. Letter to Roy Swift. 26 May 1948. Folder 1, Box 66, USSBIA, San Diego.
Owen, Ben. "World War II, Lest We Forget." Memoir essay. Folder 5.29.44, Box 1, USSBIA.

BOOKS AND ARTICLES

Amato, Joseph A. "Commemoration and Memorials." Unpublished paper emailed to the author, January 15, 2014.
———. *Jacob's Well: A Case for Rethinking Family History*. St. Paul: Minnesota Historical Society Press, 2008.
———. "On the Agency of Dreams." *Fides et Historia* 45, no. 2 (Summer/Fall 2013): 92–96.
———. *Surfaces: A History*. Berkeley: University of California Press, 2013.
Beaver, Floyd. *Sailor from Oklahoma: One Man's Two-Ocean War*. Annapolis: Naval Institute Press, 2009.
Bess, Michael. *Choices under Fire: Moral Dimensions of World War II*. New York: Alfred A. Knopf, 2006.
Bryan, J. III. *Aircraft Carrier: What It Was Really Like on the Giant* Yorktown *in the Pacific War*. New York: Ballantine Books, 1954.
Buchheim, Lothar-Gunther. *U-Boat War*. New York: Alfred A. Knopf, 1978.
Chernow, Ron. *Alexander Hamilton*. New York: Penguin Press, 2004.
Chesneau, Roger. *Aircraft Carriers of the World, 1914 to the Present*. Annapolis: Naval Institute Press, 1984.
Cline, William C. *In the Nick of Time: Motion Picture Sound Serials*. Jefferson, NC: McFarland, 1984.
Davidson, Joel R. *The Unsinkable Fleet: The Politics of U.S. Navy Expansion in World War II*. Annapolis: Naval Institute Press, 1996.

Degan, Patrick. *Flattop Fighting in World War II: The Battles between American and Japanese Aircraft Carriers*. Jefferson, NC: McFarland, 2003.

Dönitz, Karl. *Memoirs: Ten Years and Twenty Days*. Annapolis: Naval Institute Press, 1990.

Downie, Robert M. "Block Island's Pair of Aircraft Carriers." *Block Island Times*, May 29, 1993.

Dunham, Mike. "A Sailor's Story." *Anchorage Daily News*, May 25, 1997.

Eller, E. M., ed. *Dictionary of American Naval Fighting Ships*, Vol. I. Washington, DC: Navy Department, 1959.

Faltum, Andrew. *The Independence Light Aircraft Carriers*. Charleston, SC: Nautical and Aviation Publishing Company of America, 2002.

Faulkner, William. *Requiem for a Nun*. New York: Garland, 1987.

Felker, Craig C. *Testing American Sea Power: U.S. Navy Strategic Exercises, 1923–1940*. College Station: Texas A&M Press, 2007. Kindle edition.

Gannon, Michael. *Operation Drumbeat: The Dramatic True Story of Germany's First U-Boat Attacks along the American Coast in World War II*. New York: Harper and Row, 1990.

Gardner, W. J. R. *Decoding History: The Battle of the Atlantic and Ultra*. Annapolis: Naval Institute Press, 1999.

Gault, Owen. "Operation Magic Carpet." *Sea Classics*, September 2005.

Grenga, Helen E. *Movies on the Fantail: A Sailor's Diary and Memories from Other Men of the USS Barr DE 576/APD 39*. Newman, GA: Yeoman Press, 2001.

Grossnick, Roy A. *United States Naval Aviation, 1910–1955*. Washington, DC: Naval Historical Center, Department of the Navy, 1996.

Harlan, Louis. *All at Sea: Coming of Age in World War II*. Urbana: University of Illinois Press, 1996.

Harris, Mark. *Five Came Back: A Story of Hollywood and the Second World War*. New York: Penguin Books, 2014. Kindle edition.

Hone, Thomas C., Norman Friedman, and Mark D. Mandeles. *American and British Aircraft Carrier Development: 1919–1941*. Annapolis: Naval Institute Press, 1999.

Hornfischer, James D. *The Last Stand of the Tin Can Sailors: The Extraordinary World War II Story of the U.S. Navy's Finest Hour*. New York: Random House, 2004.

Hoyt, Edwin P. *The Men of the* Gambier Bay. Middlebury, VT: Paul S. Eriksson, 1979.

Hynes, Samuel. *Flights of Passage: Reflections of a World War II Aviator*. Annapolis: Naval Institute Press, 1988.

Jernigan, Emory J. *Tin Can Man*. Arlington, VA: Vandamere Press, 1993.

Joyner, Charles W. *Shared Traditions: Southern History and Folk Culture*. Champaign: University of Illinois Press, 1999.

Kernan, Alvin. *Crossing the Line: A Bluejacket's World War II Odyssey*. Annapolis: Naval Institute Press, 1994.

Knoblock, Glenn A. *Black Submariners in the United States Navy, 1940–1975*. Jefferson, NC: McFarland, 2005.

Kuehn, John T. *Agents of Innovation: The General Board and the Design of the Fleet That Defeated the Japanese Navy*. Annapolis: Naval Institute Press, 2008.

Lewis, John R. "Captain Lewis Remembers . . .." *Block Island Times*, June 19, 1993.

Lord, Walter. *Incredible Victory*. New York: Harper & Row, 1967.

MacDonald, Scot. "Evolution of Aircraft Carriers: Emergence of the Escort Carrier." *Naval Aviation News*, December 1962.

———. "Evolution of Aircraft Carriers: Last of the Fleet Problems." *Naval Aviation News*, September 1962.

Marling, Karal Ann, and John Wetenhall. *Iwo Jima: Monuments, Memories, and the American Hero*. Cambridge: Harvard University Press, 1991.

Meigs, Montgomery C. *Slide Rules and Submarines: American Scientists and Subsurface Warfare in World War II*. Honolulu: University Press of the Pacific, 2002.

Mitchell, C. Bradford. *Every Kind of Shipwork: A History of Todd Shipyards Corporation: 1916–1981*. New York: Todd Shipyards, 1981.

Morgan, Daniel, and Bruce Taylor. *U-Boat Attack Logs: A Complete Record of Warship Sinkings from Original Sources*. Barnsley, UK: Seaforth, 2011.

Morison, Samuel Eliot. *History of United States Naval Operations in World War II*. Vol. 1, *The Battle of the Atlantic, September 1939–1943*. Boston: Little, Brown, 1947.

———. *History of United States Naval Operations in World War II*, Vol. 10, *The Atlantic Battle Won, May 1943–May 1945*. Boston: Little, Brown, 1956.

———. *History of United States Naval Operations in World War II*, Vol. 14, *Victory in the Pacific*. Boston: Little, Brown, 1960.

———. *The Two-Ocean War: A Short History of the United States Navy in the Second World War*. Boston: Little, Brown, 1963.

Mumford, Lewis. *Myth of the Machine: Technics and Human Development*. New York: Harcourt Brace Jovanovich, 1967.

———. *Technics and Civilization*. Boston: Harcourt, Brace, 1934.

Noles, Jim. *Twenty-Three Minutes to Eternity: The Final Voyage of the Escort Carrier USS* Liscome Bay. Tuscaloosa: University of Alabama Press, 2004.

Nora, Pierre. "Between Memory and History: Les Lieux de Mémoire," *Representations* 26 (Spring 1989): 7–24.

Norwood, Nick, ed. *Buz Sawyer*, Vol. 1, *The War in the Pacific*. Seattle: Fantagraphic Books, 2011.

Ogden, Captain James. "Airborne at Pearl." *Proceedings*, Summer 1993.

Ommanney, F. D. *Flat-Top: The Story of an Escort Carrier*. New York: Longmans, Green, 1945.

Parker, R. A. C. *The Second World War: A Short History*. Oxford: University of Oxford Press, 1989.

Polmar, Norman. *Aircraft Carriers: A Graphic History of Carrier Aviation and Its Influence on World Events*. New York: Doubleday, 1969.

Porter, R. Bruce, and Eric Hammel. *Ace! A Marine Night-Fighter Pilot in World War II*. New York: Berkley, 1987.

Prange, Gordon W. *Miracle at Midway*. New York: McGraw-Hill, 1982.

Pyle, Ernie. *Last Chapter*. New York: Henry Holt, 1946.

Pyne, Stephen. *Voyager: Seeking Newer Worlds in the Third Great Age of Discovery*. New York: Viking Press, 2010.

Ramsey, Mary Anne. "Only Yesteryear." *Naval History*, Winter 1991.

Read, Charles Herbert Jr. *Memoirs of the Flight Surgeon of HMS* Nabob. Coaldale, Alberta: Lammi, 2018. Kindle edition.

Rielly, Robin L. *Kamikazes, Corsairs, and Picket Ships: Okinawa, 1945*. Havertown, PA: Casemate, 2008. Kindle edition.

Roscoe, Theodore. *United States Destroyer Operations in World War II*. Annapolis: United States Naval Institute, 1953.

Rose, Kenneth. *Myth and the Greatest Generation: A Social History of Americans in World War II*. New York: Routledge, 2008.

Rossano, Geoffrey L., and Thomas Wildenberg. *Striking the Hornets' Nest: Naval Aviation and the Origins of Strategic Bombing in World War I*. Annapolis: Naval Institute Press, 2015.

Schaeffer, Heinz. *U-Boat 977*. London: William Kimber, 1952.

Sherrod, Robert. *History of Marine Corps Aviation in World War II*. Baltimore: Nautical & Aviation Publishing Company of America, 1987.

Spector, Ronald H. *At War at Sea: Sailors and Naval Combat in the Twentieth Century*. New York: Penguin Books, 2001.

———. *Eagle against the Sun: The American War with Japan*. New York: Vintage Books, 1985.

"Stories about Chaplain, Lt. G. A. MacInnes USNR: Who Served on Both the USS *Block Island* Ships." Folder 21, Box 1, USSBIA.

Syrett, David. *The Defeat of the German U-boats: The Battle of the Atlantic*. Columbia: University of South Carolina Press, 1994.

Terzibaschitsch, Stefan. *Escort Carriers and Aviation Support Ships of the US Navy*. New York: Rutledge Press, 1981.

Tillman, Barrett. *Enterprise: America's Fightingest Ship and the Men Who Helped Win World War II*. New York: Simon and Schuster, 2012.

———. *On Wave and Wing: The 100-Year Quest to Perfect the Aircraft Carrier*. Washington, DC: Regnery History, 2017. Kindle edition

Ward, Geoffrey C. *The War: An Intimate History, 1941–1945*. New York: Alfred A. Knopf, 2007.

White, John F. *The Milk Cows: The U-Boat Tankers at War, 1941–1945*. Barnsley, UK: Pen and Sword Books, 2009.

Williams, Kathleen Broome. *Secret Weapon: U.S. High-Frequency Direction Finding in the Battle of the Atlantic*. Annapolis: Naval Institute Press, 1996.

Wolters, Timothy S. *Information at Sea: Shipboard Command and Control in the U.S. Navy from Mobile Bay to Okinawa*. Baltimore: Johns Hopkins University Press, 2013.

World Atlas of the Oceans. Hamburg, Germany: RM Buch, 2001.

Wynn, Kenneth G. *U-Boat Operations of the Second World War*. Annapolis: Naval Institute Press, 1989.

Y'Blood, William T. *Hunter-Killer: U.S. Escort Carriers in the Battle of the Atlantic*. Annapolis: Naval Institute Press, 1983.

———. *The Little Giants: U.S. Escort Carriers against Japan*. Annapolis: Naval Institute Press, 1987.

INTERNET RESOURCES

"Cleveland T. Martin Jr. U.S. Navy Service, WWII, U.S.S. Block Island." Washburn University Alumni, Washburn University. October 29, 2015. http://www.washburn.edu.

"Earthquake Hazards Program." USGS: Science for a Changing World. October 29, 2015. http://earthquake.usgs.gov.

"Eternal Father—The Navy Hymn." America's Navy. January 28, 2019. https://www.navy.mil.
"Family Requests." March 15, 2016. HMS *Dasher*. http://www.hmsdasher.co.uk.
"Harding Becomes First President to Be Heard on the Radio." History Channel. January 10, 2019. https://www.history.com.
"The History and Words of 'Auld Land Syne.'" Scotland Is Now. January 24, 2019. https://www.scotland.org.
Intrepid Sea, Air & Space Museum Complex. "Exhibits." June 7, 2018. https://www.intrepidmuseum.org.
"Knickerbocker Bean Soup." *Cook Book of the United States Navy*, ed. 1944. February 28, 2011. http://www.ibiblio.org.
National Institutes of Health, poster, US National Library of Medicine, Digital Collections, https://collections.nlm.nih.gov/catalog/nlm:nlmuid-101584655X24-img
"Newton's Third Law." National Aeronautics and Space Administration. June 1, 2018. https://www.grc.nasa.gov.
Naval History and Heritage Command. "Biographical Essay Attached to the Logan C. Ramsey Papers." July 11, 2018. https://www.history.navy.mil.
———. "Recollections of Commander John Ford, USNR, Adapted from Commander John Ford USNR interview in box 10 of World War II Interviews, Archives, Naval History and Heritage Command." December 8, 2018. https://www.history.navy.mil.
———. "Sports in the Navy: 1775 to 1963." January 20, 2019. https://www.history.navy.mil.
———. "U.S. Navy Active Ship Force Levels, 1886–present." June 29, 2011. http://www.history.navy.mil.
"Norman T Dowty, LTJG—Military Timeline." January 22, 2019. Together We Served.com. https://navy.togetherweserved.com.
"Portuguese Man-of-Wars." National Geographic. February 28, 2011. http://animals.nationalgeographic.com.
"Presidential Poker." January 26, 2019. History Net. https://www.historynet.com.
Roosevelt Hotel. "The Story of the Roosevelt Hotel NYC." May 5, 2018. http://www.theroosevelthotel.com.
Uboat.net. "List of all German U-boat Commanders." March 1, 2015. http://uboat.net.
———. "Preussen." January 26, 2019. https://uboat.net.
———. "U-709." January 26, 2019. https://uboat.net.
"U.S. Escort Carrier Notes." October 5, 2011. World War II in the Pacific. http://www.ww2pacific.com.
USS Block Island Association. "Aircraft." October 29, 2015. http://www.ussblockisland.org.
———. "CVE 21 History." May 20, 2018. http://www.ussblockisland.org.
———. "CVE 106 Officers & Crew." July 15, 2018. http://www.ussblockisland.org.
———. "The Story of Two Block Island Escort Carriers." April 3, 2018. http://www.ussblockisland.org.
———. "U-Boat Battles." February 28, 2011. http://www.ussblockisland.org.
"What's in a Name? Massie Hughes Drive in Norfolk." *Virginian-Pilot*, July 15, 2018. https://pilotonline.com.

INDEX

Page numbers in italics refer to figures.